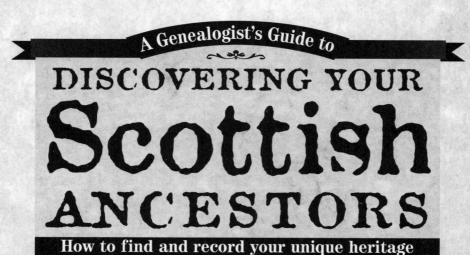

A Genealogist's Guide to

DISCOVERING YOUR
Scottish
ANCESTORS

How to find and record your unique heritage

Linda Jonas & Paul Milner

BETTERWAY BOOKS
CINCINNATI, OHIO

www.familytreemagazine.com

Permissions

Some material in this publication is reprinted by permission of The Church of Jesus Christ of Latter-day Saints. In granting permission for this use of copyrighted material, The Church does not imply or express either endorsement or authorization of this publication.

The Web pages from Scots Origins are reproduced with the kind permission of the Registrar General for Scotland and Origins.net.

The civil registration certificates, index entries, old parish register entries, and census records are reproduced with the kind permission of the Registrar General for Scotland.

The illustrations for records and finding aids for kirk sessions, testaments, Services of Heirs, and Sasines are reproduced with the kind permission of the National Archives of Scotland.

The testament index for the Commissariot of Dunkeld (Figure 10-1) is reproduced courtesy of the Scottish Record Society.

The Crieff parish entry (Figure 9-1) from Key to the Parochial Registers of Scotland is used with permission of V. Ben Bloxham, author.

A Genealogist's Guide to Discovering Your Scottish Ancestors. © 2002 by Linda Jonas and Paul Milner. Manufactured in the United States of America. All rights reserved. No part of this book may be reproduced in any form or by any electronic or mechanical means including information storage and retrieval systems without permission in writing from the publisher, except by a reviewer, who may quote brief passages in a review. Published by Betterway Books, an imprint of F&W Publications, Inc., 4700 East Galbraith Road, Cincinnati, Ohio 45236. (800) 289-0963. First edition.

Other fine Betterway books are available from your local bookstore or on our Web site at www.familytreemagazine.com. To subscribe to Family Tree Magazine Update, a free e-mail newsletter with helpful tips and resources for genealogists, go to http://newsletters.fwpublications.com.

06 05 04 03 02   5 4 3 2 1

Library of Congress Cataloging-in-Publication Data

Jonas, Linda
     A genealogist's guide to discovering your Scottish ancestors / Linda Jonas and Paul Milner.
          p.   cm.
     Includes bibliographical references and index.
     ISBN 1-55870-599-6 (alk. paper)
          1. Scotland—Genealogy—Handbooks, manuals, etc. 2. Scottish Americans—Genealogy—Handbooks, manuals, etc. I. Milner, Paul. II. Title.
     CS462 .J66   2002
     929'.1'0899163—dc21   2002022625
                                                                          CIP

Editor: Sharon DeBartolo Carmack, CG
Production editor: Brad Crawford
Production coordinator: John Peavler
Interior designer: Sandy Conopeotis Kent
Icon designer: Cindy Beckmeyer

DEDICATION

To Frederick A. Hill and David G. Cameron
without whom this book would never have been written

To Norma Milner, Paul's mother,
his first and most important ancestor

To our ancestors, whose lives continue to inspire us
to find out more about our pasts

Acknowledgments

Because we live thousands of miles apart and have different backgrounds, experiences, viewpoints, and access to resources, we have been excited by the process of learning from one another as we have written this book. We find our collaboration to be a perfect combination, especially because finding our Scottish ancestors is a subject about which we are both passionate.

Of course, none of this could have been done without the assistance of many others. We first wish to thank the many students, clients, workshop participants, and library patrons who over the years have asked questions that forced us to learn and to become better teachers.

We gratefully acknowledge the following researchers who read our book and gave us valuable input: Sharon DeBartolo Carmack CG, FUGA; John and Glenys Dyer; Diane C. Loosle, AG; George F. Sanborn Jr.; Paul F. Smart, M.A., FSG, AG, CGRS; Jacqueline B. Torrance; and Judith Eccles Wight, AG, CGRS. Our foreign reviewers were especially insightful: Dr. David Dobson (Scotland), Michael Gandy (England), Tony McCarthy (Ireland), and David Thomson, AG (Australia). We are also grateful to our editor Brad Crawford, who patiently understood our desire for perfection.

We thank the staff and volunteers of the Family History Library of The Church of Jesus Christ of Latter-day Saints for their continuing efforts to make accessible the original records and tools needed by family historians all over the world. Family history would not be as popular today as it is without their ongoing efforts.

We now thank some people who have helped us individually.

Linda Jonas

A great number of people helped me write this book. I have spent thousands of hours with some of the best family historians in the world: reading their books and articles, listening to their lectures, listening to their personal advice, and bouncing ideas off of them. The following people offered to help me in any way they could, and I appreciate them more than they will ever know: Nancy Ellen Carlberg from the Los Angeles Family History Center; Judith Eccles Wight, Paul F. Smart, Darris G. Williams, and Dean Hunter from the Family History Library; David Thomson from Australia; Peter Wilson Coldham from England; David Dobson from St. Andrews, Scotland; and Kathleen B. Cory from Edinburgh, Scotland.

Two family historians went above and beyond the call of duty. Nancy Lee Bier (Los Angeles), and Michael Gandy (London), toured cities with me, showed me relatively unknown sources in American and foreign repositories, and spent numerous hours discussing their vast knowledge of British and Irish family history with me.

Two professors of British history, David A. Cressy (The Ohio State University) and Donna L. Boutelle (California State University at Long Beach), took a special interest in me. David taught me how to research; Donna taught me how to think. Both of them inspired me with their love for British history and have encouraged me to do much more than just read about it. I will be forever grateful for their time, personal dedication, and interest.

Of course, good family history research takes more than just knowledge. It takes money, access to resources, and the patience, understanding, and encouragement of friends and family. I gratefully acknowledge the staff of the Los Angeles Family History Center, especially Director Ross Birdsall and his wife, Barbara, for supporting the tremendous British collection there. A deep debt of gratitude goes to the Board of Directors and membership of the British Isles Family History Society-U.S.A., and especially Sid Maddocks, for their personal support and for their interest in bringing great family history resources and talent to the United States. I also wish to thank the staff of the McLean Family History Center and the McLean, Virginia, Stake of The Church of Jesus Christ of Latter-day Saints, especially John and Glenys Dyer and Richard and Jackie Thomas, for their support of family history in the area and for helping to build the British collection there.

My family members are the most important people in my life, and without their support I could do nothing. I want to thank my husband, Bill Jonas, and my children John, Kimberly, Stephen, Robert, Katie, Annie, Betsie, and Julie Jonas for pitching in (and sometimes taking over) while I was writing. They are the best family anyone could hope for.

Paul Milner, my friend and colleague, aside from coauthoring the book, has been an enormous personal help. We work well together. We have gone through every emotion while writing this book, but mostly we have spent a lot of time laughing and getting excited over new ways to present the material. I thank him for his support, patience, understanding, dedication, and humor.

I dedicate this book to two men who are directly responsible for its writing. David G. Cameron at his death wanted his family history to be preserved. The family in this book is his. My friend Frederick A. Hill has for many years supported me in my obsession to bring British family history resources to the United States and to make them more accessible. He was the one who urged me to write this book, but his subsequent stroke prevented him from reading it. I hope that both David and Fred will somehow be able to read this book and be pleased with what they started.

Paul Milner

In preparation to write this book, we have spent a lifetime reading almost everything in print dealing with how to do Scottish genealogical research. This has been, and continues to be, a wonderful journey to learn from the experience of others and become knowledgeable about a topic we love—family history.

On that journey I have encountered many individuals who have taught, supported, and encouraged me and struggled with me to solve problems. Some of my contacts, particularly at the Family History Library in Salt Lake City, overlap Linda's. Over the years Dean J. Hunter, John M. Kitzmiller II, Diane C. Loosle, Bert J. Rawlins, David E. Rencher, Paul F. Smart, Judith Eccles Wight, and Darris G. Williams have guided me in my work there. I have watched each one of them light up with excitement as we all learned something new after being asked questions that were a little out of the ordinary. These people have become friends as we have worked together in Salt Lake City, at national and regional conferences, and on the Board of the Federation of Genealogical Societies.

I have lectured for many societies, highland games, and Scottish cultural events across the United States and Canada. I especially want to thank Duncan Dunbar Chaplin III and his wife, Ann Theopold Chaplin, for their repeated invitations and hospitality at the New Hampshire Highland Games. Also, thanks to Wayne Rethford and Jacqueline B. Torrance of the Illinois Saint Andrew Society for having me as the professional adviser to their genealogical society.

Many individuals have stood out over the years for their teaching and leadership. Thank you to George F. Sanborn of the New England Historic Genealogical Society for emphasizing understanding the Gaelic language and naming patterns in Scottish research and for sharing his knowledge of the Scots in the maritime provinces of Canada. Thanks to Craig Roberts Scott of Willow Bend Books for publishing short-run Scottish resource books. Thanks also for the guidance, friendship, and ongoing support of Sandra Hargreaves Luebking, who helped me break onto the national genealogical lecturing circuit and who as the editor of the Federation of Genealogical Societies *Forum* continues to make me look good in print.

Linda Jonas is and always will remain a good friend with whom I shared the excitement of the research chase. Whenever we found a gem, one of us would say "look" and usually no further explanation was needed. We were both excited by the find. The desire to provide you with the book we wish had been available when we were beginners pushed us to find you the answers. We grew together in the profession as friends and colleagues.

Special thanks to my wife, Carol Becker, who as a writer herself gently encouraged me to improve my writing skills and who put up with the many days and nights when I simply disappeared into my office to work on the book. Thanks also to my children Heather and Eric who gave up much of their time with me during the past two years so I could complete this project.

Finally, I dedicate this book to my mother, Norma Milner, my most important ancestor, who lives in England close to the border with Scotland. Searching for our ancestors set me on the journey to learn how to do Scottish research. Thanks, Mother, for everything.

About the Authors

Linda Jonas and Paul Milner are the authors of *A Genealogist's Guide to Discovering Your English Ancestors*, published in 2000 by Betterway Books. This book is a continuation of that collaborative effort to provide good research tools for fellow family historians.

LINDA JONAS, a U.S. native, is the immediate past president of the British Isles Family History Society-U.S.A. Linda has been a full-time family historian for more than twenty years and has focused on helping Americans find their British Isles ancestry. She has been supervisor, staff trainer, and instructor at the Los Angeles Family History Center, which holds the largest British Isles resource collection outside of Salt Lake City. She is a popular lecturer and writer on all aspects of U.S. and British Isles research. Linda is now the Director of the McLean [Virginia] Family History Center, which specializes in Scottish research.

PAUL MILNER is a native of northern England. He is a professional genealogical researcher who has specialized in British Isles research for more than twenty years. He is a past president of the British Interest Group of Wisconsin and Illinois (BIG-WILL). Since 1992, he has written and edited the society newsletter. He writes book reviews for *Forum*, the Federation of Genealogical Societies' quarterly journal. Paul is a nationally known and popular speaker at genealogical conferences and seminars and typically draws audiences of several hundred genealogists for his lectures.

Table of Contents At a Glance

Table of Contents

NOTE FOR READERS: The following chapters deal with individual record types. We will trace one family through the records to show how we accumulate more information with each document. For each major record group, we provide background on what the record is and when and why it was created. We explain the actual recording process. We give step-by-step guidelines and illustrations for searching the records without going to Scotland. We highlight available tools to make the process easier, tell you what to do if you can't find your ancestor in the records, provide bibliographies for further research, and suggest the next steps.

Icons Used in This Book

Case Study
Examples of this book's advice at work

CD Source
Databases and other information available on CD-ROM

Citing Sources
Reminders and methods for documenting information

\di'fin\ vb
Definitions
Terminology and jargon explained

For More Info
Where to turn for more in-depth coverage

Hidden Treasures
Family papers and home sources

Idea Generator
Techniques and prods for further thinking

Important
Information and tips you can't overlook

Internet Source
Where on the Web to find what you need

Library/Archive Source
Repositories that might have the information you need

Microfilm Source
Information available on microfilm

Money Saver
Getting the most out of research dollars

Notes
Thoughts, ideas and related insights

Printed Source
Directories, books, pamphlets, and other paper archives

Quotes
Useful words direct from the experts

Reminder
"Don't-Forget" items to keep in mind

Research Tip
Ways to make research more efficient

See Also
Where in this book to find related information

Sources
Where to go for information, supplies, etc.

Step By Step
Walkthroughs of important procedures

Supplies
Advice on day-to-day office tools

Technique
How to conduct research, solve problems, and get answers

Timesaver
Shaving minutes and hours off the clock

Tip
Ways to make research more efficient

Warning
Stop before you make a mistake

Introduction

This book was designed for people who want to find out more about their family but do not have decades to devote to learning about Scottish research. You shouldn't have to give up playing with your grandchildren in order to record your family history for them, and you shouldn't have to neglect your math homework in order to find enough about your ancestors in time to write your history research paper. We understand. Paul does his family history while working a full-time job, and Linda does it while raising seven children. We found that Scottish research is an absolute pleasure, but we had to get obsessive to learn enough to do it effectively. We spent years taking classes and reading every book on Scottish genealogy. We don't want you to have to do that. Therefore, we wrote the book we always wished we could find.

A Genealogist's Guide to Discovering Your Scottish Ancestors is unlike any other book on Scottish research. Most books on Scottish research give an overview of many types of records. These books usually mention where you can find the records in Scotland, and a few of them even tell you that you can find the same records at the Family History Library. However, they don't give you the call numbers, show you how to use the record, or tell you what to do after you've found it. Our book is entirely different.

We will discuss the essential things you need to know to begin Scottish research. We will then focus on the major records. We will tell you what each record is, why it was created, and why it is important to us now. More interestingly, we will describe the people behind the documents. You will learn where your ancestor was when the record was created and what your ancestor and the person recording the document actually did. Their personal knowledge, motivations, and desires may have combined to create a record that served a purpose quite different from the one that was originally intended. We will tell you who originally kept the record, who holds the original or a copy now, and how you can see it yourself. Because you have other things to do, we won't make you figure out how to find it; we will give you the exact procedure including any call numbers, Web site addresses, or other identifying information. Then we'll show you how to use it! We will take you from start to finish in the least time and with as little expense as possible.

This book is a personal conversation between you and us. Together, we will research a real family. We will look for background information about the area where they lived. Then we will search for this family in civil registration records, census records, parish registers, and probate and land records to see what we can find out about the family members. We'll look at each document in detail and discuss how to weave the bare facts into a story about our ancestors. Together we will get onto the Internet, walk into a Family History Center, see how to find the sources you need, and talk about how to read and interpret them. You'll discover why the documents may not be telling what you expect. You'll learn which record to search next. As we search for "our" family, you will see how you can find the same kind of information for your own ancestors. Best of all, if you don't find your ancestor in a record, we'll give you the probable reasons and tell you what to do about it.

While this book is perfect for beginners, it is also essential for experienced researchers who do not live in Scotland. Some of the records you will read about will truly be accessible to all Scottish researchers for the first time. For example, unless you are in the National Archives of Scotland, finding Scottish testaments has, until the publication of this book, been a frustrating experience for several reasons. Most importantly, you must determine the commissariot in which your ancestor lived, and there are numerous errors in many of the standard sources for finding the appropriate commissariot. Using Scottish Services of Heirs has been even more difficult. The Services of Heirs can be an absolute gold mine to genealogists, but they can be difficult to use for even the most advanced researchers. Books on Scottish genealogy rarely go beyond mentioning that the records were recorded in Latin. They do not show you how to read them, so most researchers are too intimidated by the Latin to use the Services of Heirs. However, they were recorded in a standard format. We will provide the standard Latin format alongside an English translation so that the Services of Heirs will finally be accessible to the average researcher.

When we wrote *A Genealogist's Guide to Discovering Your English Ancestors*, we wanted it to be a book that you actually use, not one that sits on your shelf. We have been very pleased to see people carrying it around with them and referring to it as they search for documents about their English ancestors. The need for a step-by-step book for Scottish research is even more critical. We hope you like it.

ONE

Getting Started

W hether you are new to genealogy or have been researching for years, you are now ready to trace your Scottish ancestors. You are in for a real treat. No matter who you are or where you live, you can find your Scottish ancestors! *A Genealogist's Guide to Discovering Your Scottish Ancestors* will give you step-by-step instructions for tracing your Scottish ancestry without traveling to Scotland. You will learn about the most important records for Scottish research and see the latest techniques for using them anywhere in the world.

WHO ARE YOU?

1. You were born in Scotland or are a child of a recent immigrant. You are new to genealogy. You live outside of Scotland and want to know how to find your Scottish ancestors.
2. Your ancestors left Scotland many generations ago. You are probably an experienced researcher and have traced your ancestors in the country where you are now living. You know that your immigrant ancestors came from Scotland, and you want to know how to start your Scottish research.
3. You've done some Scottish research but now need more ideas.

No matter what your circumstances, we can help you. Linda Jonas specializes in tracing immigrant ancestry. All of her ancestors came to America before the Revolutionary War. Paul Milner is an immigrant. All of his ancestors were born in the British Isles, but Paul's research has been done since he moved to the United States. Both of us have more than twenty years of experience doing Scottish research outside of Scotland. We can assure you that a trip to Scotland is not a necessity for doing Scottish research. If you are looking for a reason to go to Scotland, though, don't worry; it won't be to spend your time in libraries. You will spend it out in the countryside doing really effective research!

If you are new to genealogy, you will soon find that tracing your family is challenging and exciting. Most genealogists believe that once you start looking for your family, you will be hooked for life. It can be one of the most interesting and enjoyable things you've ever done. If you are an experienced researcher, you already know the joys of finding your family. But you are in for an even bigger thrill now! As exciting as tracing your American ancestors can be, not much can compare to finding the origins of your immigrant ancestors.

WHO ARE YOUR IMMIGRANT ANCESTORS?

Some people begin their genealogy looking for famous ancestors or hoping to find royal lines. A few people are even disappointed when they think that their immigrant ancestor was just an average person. Be assured that your immigrant was not average. Your immigrant ancestors never led "normal" lives. These people did something extraordinary; they left their homes, possessions, families, friends, and homeland forever to try to find a better life.

Most immigrants left Scotland for economic reasons. A few of your ancestors left for religious reasons, such as in the 1680s when Scottish Quakers left to avoid persecution. These Quakers came to east New Jersey and the Delaware Valley. At the same time, a group of Scottish Presbyterians tried to establish a Presbyterian colony in South Carolina. Sometimes the immigrants had both religious and economic motives. Furthermore, some of your immigrants did not come by choice. For example, many Scots came as prisoners under Oliver Cromwell or as a result of the Jacobite Rebellions in 1715 and 1745. Sometimes Scottish prisons were cleared and convicts shipped to the American colonies. Some women and children were even kidnapped from the countryside or from the streets of cities such as Aberdeen and Leith to provide needed colonial laborers. Many Scots serving in the British Army saw the opportunity to own land and chose to stay in the Mohawk Valley area rather than return to Scotland when their regiments were disbanded following the French and Indian Wars. They later brought their families from Scotland. Whatever their reasons for leaving Scotland, all immigrants left the only lives they had known and came to their new country with hope for a brighter future.

When your ancestors arrived in the new land, they may have been disappointed. Your ancestors did not find the American streets to be paved with gold. No matter when or where they arrived, whether they came to the wilderness or to a large city already settled with people they knew from their homeland, your immigrants were pioneers. They all have incredible stories.

WHAT DO YOU KNOW ABOUT YOUR SCOTTISH ANCESTORS?

How did your ancestors live in Scotland? Of what social class were they? What religion did they practice? How did social class and religion influence their lives? What were your ancestors' occupations, and how did they practice them? What kind of work did the women do? Did your ancestors stay in one place, or did they move around? Did your ancestors receive poor relief (welfare)? Where did your ancestors meet, fall in love, and get married? Where did the women have their

Notes

babies? How many children did they have? Did all of the children survive to adulthood? Did your ancestors go to school? Did any of them attend universities?

You are not expected to know the answers to these questions yet, but you will soon learn how to find out about your ancestors' lives in Scotland.

Why did your immigrant ancestor leave Scotland? What was happening in Scotland at that time? Where did he live, and how was his life there? What were the circumstances when he left? Whom did he leave behind? Did your ancestor travel alone? How difficult was the farewell? Did he have property to sell? Did he distribute goods to family or friends? What did he decide to take with him? How much money did he have? Were there people he loved that were left behind and never seen again? Did he find a better life? Was it worth it?

You are not expected to know the answers to these questions either. Throughout the book, we will examine various sources that will help you discover why your immigrant ancestor left Scotland.

FINDING MORE ABOUT YOUR SCOTTISH ANCESTORS

Finding more about your Scottish ancestors is the focus of this book, so just follow the examples. If you follow the step-by-step procedures, you will often find your ancestors in the records. You'll learn how to evaluate the information you find and learn which record to check next. If you don't find your ancestor in a particular record, we will suggest why you have not found him and what you can do about it.

It is often easier to trace your ancestors from outside of Scotland than it is to trace them by going to Scotland! That may be hard to believe, but it's true. Because records are stored in many repositories in Scotland, you could travel to many libraries and archives to find your ancestors. However, you can get great results without ever leaving your hometown. Your ability to conduct effective research in your local area is far greater today than it ever has been—even a few months ago—and it keeps getting better and better!

Important

Because of the microfilming efforts of the Genealogical Society of Utah, almost all of the original records you need to begin your research are available from the Family History Library in Salt Lake City and through its Family History Centers worldwide. That means that you can do the majority of your research in one building. Furthermore, because of the indexing efforts of family history societies throughout the world, there are many new indexes to make your research easier. Several indexes are available on compact disc and on the Internet. These indexes contain vast amounts of information never before available. In fact, the Scottish indexes are among the best in the world. Many background materials are available over the Internet or by loan through a public library. This book gives specific instructions for accessing and using the information available from the Internet, libraries, and especially Family History Centers.

You can start your research in the comfort of your own home, then use the services of libraries and Family History Centers in your area. Therefore, **this book uses three basic search procedures involving**

Technique

- the Internet
- local public, private, and university libraries
- Family History Centers

We examine each of these approaches in the next chapter.

When you've found your family on the Internet, at a library, and at a Family History Center, you may want to celebrate by taking a trip to Scotland to find your ancestral home. That will be the most fun of all.

FIND OUT HOW YOUR ANCESTORS LIVED

Your ancestors had more than three events (birth, marriage, and death) in their lives. The fascinating stories of how they lived do not fit on pedigree charts and family group sheets, the standard genealogical forms. Discovering the stories of your ancestors will bring real meaning to your research. There are clues to your ancestors' lives in Scotland in public documents. This book points you to Scottish documents that allow you to retrace your ancestors' footsteps and reconstruct their stories. But it is up to you to go beyond compiling the names, dates, and places on a pedigree chart and begin to find out how your ancestors really lived. Once you have discovered the stories about your family members, you will understand more about them, your country, their country, and yourself. Your Scottish ancestors have beautiful and often heart-wrenching stories to tell. It is up to you to tell them.

So, let's go find our Scottish ancestors!

TWO

Research Process Guidelines

WHERE SHOULD I START?

If you are completely new to genealogy, you will want to learn how to collect the information that is available among your own family members and to organize your collection so you know what you have and what you need. Start with a trip to your local library or bookstore to find general books on family history research. You can also borrow books for beginners from your friends who are doing family research. Many books for beginners have been published over the years, but recent books are more likely to give current information on the latest tools available and research standards you should aim to follow.

Good Books to Get You Started

Allen, Desmond Walls. *First Steps in Genealogy: A Beginner's Guide to Researching Your Family History.* Cincinnati, Ohio: Betterway Books, 1998.

Carmack, Sharon DeBartolo. *Organizing Your Family History Search: Efficient & Effective Ways to Gather and Protect Your Genealogical Research.* Cincinnati, Ohio: Betterway Books, 1999.

Crawford-Oppenheimer, Christine. *Long-Distance Genealogy: Researching Your Family History From Home.* Cincinnati, Ohio: Betterway Books, 2000.

Croom, Emily Anne. *Unpuzzling Your Past: The Best-Selling Basic Guide to Genealogy,* 4th ed. Cincinnati, Ohio: Betterway Books, 2001.

Greenwood, Val D. *The Researcher's Guide to American Genealogy,* 3d ed. Baltimore, Md.: Genealogical Publishing Company, Inc. 2000.

Printed Source

A brief introduction to family history research called *Discovering Your Family Tree* is one of the guides from the Family History Library. You can read it online at <www.familysearch.org>, where you can also view and print the basic forms that are necessary in genealogy: pedigree chart, family group record, and research log. For a more comprehensive online introduction, you can look at some of the online genealogy courses for beginners. For example, Brigham Young University Continuing Education, in its Ancestors series, offers courses that can be useful. The "Introduction to Family History Research" course is free and can be found at <www.kbyu.org/ancestors/courses>.

IDENTIFYING YOUR IMMIGRANT ANCESTOR

Research Tip

Before you begin research in Scottish records, find out as much as you can about your Scottish immigrant ancestor. Many genealogists have made the mistake of finding a Scottish surname, finding someone by the same name in Scotland, and assuming that they have found their ancestor. Even worse, they may assume that because their ancestor had a surname associated with a particular clan he was a member of that clan. In the excitement of discovering the possibility of Scottish ancestry, you, too, may be tempted to make assumptions about your ancestor's surname or even to go to Scottish records to begin research. Don't! Your ancestor may not even have emigrated from Scotland. **Find out as much as you can about your ancestor in the records of the area in which he settled.** For example, if your ancestor settled in Virginia, find as much as you can about him in the records of Virginia before trying any Scottish ones. Was your ancestor Scots-Irish? Was he a Highland Scot? These people came from different places, had different attitudes, and settled in different areas of America. What was the history of your ancestor's place of settlement? Who else settled in the area? What do you know about your ancestor, his family, and his associates? Did your ancestor emigrate from Scotland or from Ireland? What language did he speak? What was his religion? If your ancestor really emigrated from Scotland, it is essential that you gather enough information about him to distinguish him from the many others of the same name in that country. It is helpful to know such information as your ancestor's full name; precise place of origin; dates of birth, marriage, and death; spouse's name; children's names; parents' names; date of immigration; occupation; religion; names of cousins, friends, and associates. Of course, you don't have to know all of that before commencing Scottish research, but the more information you have, the easier it will be to identify your ancestor in Scottish records.

Showing you how to find records in North America is beyond the scope of this book, but the following suggestions provide a brief checklist.

Start by looking for information that may be in your home or in the homes of other family members. Some of your ancestors may have left diaries or verbally passed down their stories to their children. Search for diaries, letters, photos, and family Bibles, as well as personal items such as tools, clothing, and sewing implements. The more you can find, the more you will know about your ancestors' lives. Do not give up after asking your immediate family. Contact aunts, cousins, and even family friends.

Once you have examined sources at home, look for documents in the area where your ancestor settled. As with any ancestor, it is always best to start researching your immigrant's life at the end. Genealogy is done working backward through time. Therefore, begin to reconstruct your immigrant's story by searching for books and documents that were generated after his death. Look for local histories that may contain details about your ancestor's community and maybe even your ancestor himself. Look for family histories or genealogies that have been written about your immigrant ancestor or his descendants. Search the Internet to see if someone else has information on your family. A distant relative may have already done much of the work for you. This secondhand data must be verified, but it can give you a head start in your research.

After searching the Internet, looking through books, and contacting relatives, you are ready to look at original records. Often the most revealing records are those written after your ancestor's death. Start first with your ancestor's probate records (his will, the inventory of his estate, etc.), then look for his obituaries. There is often more than one obituary, and these can be found in church, ethnic, society, and town newspapers. An immigrant ancestor's entire family needs to be traced, and often his friends and associates as well. When looking for documents for your ancestor, look for the same documents for each of his children, brothers, sisters, spouses, etc. Search for passenger lists and naturalization records of all family members. Look through land records, court records, baptism and marriage records, military records, death records, etc. Each of these records will tell you more about your ancestor, and one may tell you his hometown. Each document will lead you to others until you have enough information to compile your ancestor's life story.

Many published immigrant indexes are available to help you find your ancestor's origins. The best for North American researchers is

> *Passenger and Immigration Lists Index: A Guide to Published Arrival Records of About 500,000 Passengers Who Came to the United States and Canada in the Seventeenth, Eighteenth, and Nineteenth Centuries* edited by P. William Filby with Mary K. Meyer. 3 vols. Detroit, Mich.: Gale Research Co., 1981. (Annual supplements have increased passenger numbers and expanded time periods.)

Warning

The title of the above book is misleading. This book is not just an index to passenger lists; it is an index to all records that allude to immigrant status. These can include census records, land records, naturalization records, and many others. You will find the name of the immigrant, a date at which he appeared in the records, the place where the record was found, and the book or article from which the index was taken. Note that the date is not necessarily the date that your ancestor immigrated. It is a date when your ancestor was in that place. The series originally contained three volumes, and it has annual supplements. The title changes with each volume as the number of indexed passengers increases. You must check every volume of Filby's indexes if you use them in print. However, you can search all volumes at once on compact disc: Family Tree Maker's CD #354, *Passenger and Immigration Lists Index, 1500s–1950s,* 2001 update. If you do not find your immigrant indexed in the above source, then check this reference for a list of additional sources:

> Filby, P. William, ed. *Passenger and Immigration Lists Bibliography, 1538–1900: Being a Guide to Published Lists of Arrivals in the United States and Canada.* 2d ed. Detroit, Mich.: Gale Research Co., 1988.

After you have read a basic genealogical guidebook and assembled clues to the origins of your immigrant ancestor, you will be ready to begin your Scottish research. That is when the fun really starts!

THE MODERN RESEARCH PROCESS FOR FINDING YOUR SCOTTISH ANCESTORS

Step By Step

Technology is changing the research process. **So let's outline a modern four-step research process**, with more details in later chapters:

1. Internet search
2. library search
3. Family History Centers
4. trip to Scotland

1. Internet Search

An Internet search should be your first step. If you do not have access to the Internet at home, you can use it at many public or university libraries. Let's divide the Internet search into a two-stage process.

The first stage is a surname search to identify what research has been done on a name. Some people have created entire Web sites devoted to a particular family. Others post queries about families they are researching. Contact the individuals who put the information onto the Internet and find out what documentation they will share with you. This way you can avoid the struggle of searching for solutions to problems that have already been solved. Do get the documentation you need. **Be skeptical of all research you find on the Internet (or in print) until you personally verify the material and obtain copies of the original records.**

Warning

The second stage is to use the Internet to find out about your ancestor's environment. Look for information about the area in which your ancestor lived, his occupation, or his military service. Many family history societies now have online information about the individual parishes within their counties. This may include photographs or histories of a church or village, information about the records that have survived for a community, and even lists of people. You can go to other sites to find out about specific occupations. Check out what resources, guides, or indexes have been published. You may be able to purchase many from the county family history society. Many society members will also look up information for you in specific resources they own or can access.

See chapter four, "Accessing the Internet Resources," for specific Internet sites to search.

2. Library Search

This step complements and expands upon what you find on the Internet.

Visit your local public library, and ask if any libraries in the area have genealogy collections. You can also borrow books from distant libraries through interlibrary loan. Don't forget the university libraries in your area. Even though some might claim that they do not have genealogy books, many universities have wonderful collections on Scottish law, history, and geography. These materials are great genealogical sources! There may even be in your area a private library with a good collection. Many privately owned libraries are open to the public. In each library, see if anyone is researching your surname, and check for materials about how your ancestors lived.

Suggestions appear in chapter six, "Library and Family History Center Resources."

3. Family History Centers: Sources for Original Records and Indexes

After you have searched the Internet and local libraries, your next step is to search the original records. This is the most exciting part of genealogy. For anyone outside of Scotland, the place to start looking for copies of original records is the Family History Library (FHL) and its network of Family History Centers (FHCs). Most of the indexes and records that we discuss are available through your nearest Family History Center. Read about the Family History Library in chapter six.

Technique

4. The Final Step in the Research Process: A Trip to Scotland

Of course, you want an excuse to go to Scotland, don't you? Well, the purpose is not to do research, at least not on the first trip. Yes, you may need to go to a District Archive or to the National Archives of Scotland to get a document that was not available on microfilm, but do not spend a lot of time in record offices. You can usually hire someone to get a copy for you.

Go to Scotland to sightsee and to visit the villages and towns where your ancestors lived. You can easily find out what life was like for your ancestors. Go see the churches, the village hall, the market square, the factories, the farms, and the local pubs. You may be able to walk streets that your ancestor once walked or stand in front of the font where your ancestor was baptized. Talk to the local people, listen to how they speak, and learn what is important to people in that part of the country. Some of the people may know stories of those who emigrated long ago. You may even find that you have relatives living there. Get a sense of the culture of the area. The area where your ancestor lived may be radically different from other parts of Scotland.

Visiting Scotland may be a once-in-a-lifetime trip. Don't waste it by spending all your time in record offices. Experience life in Scotland, and explore your ancestral roots.

VERIFY ALL EVIDENCE

No matter where you obtain your information, **verify it—all of it—by examining the original records.** It is tempting, for example, to accept the word of relatives living in Scotland because "they should know." Never take anybody's word for anything! Memories fade, and people make mistakes. Furthermore, just because something is in print doesn't make it true. Indexes, books, and online databases are no substitutes for the original source. An original record may give information that is not recorded in an index and often contains further clues.

Important

EVALUATE THE EVIDENCE

Even original records contain errors. You cannot copy information from any record onto your family group sheet and automatically assume that the information is correct. Look at all information on the record and determine what it is really telling you. Who was the informant? How good was his knowledge of the facts? Did anyone have reason to lie about the facts?

As we examine each type of Scottish record, we will discuss how to decide the accuracy of information. We'll go through the contents of the records and point out what to look for. We'll see many examples of errors and omissions in the original records. You will see what to do when you don't find what you expect.

DETERMINE THE NEXT PROJECT

After you have examined any record in detail and recorded the information, always ask, "Where do I go from here?" What did this record tell you? Did it give you more information about the life of your ancestor? Did you notice differences from previous records? Use any new information to lead you to other records that will tell you more about this ancestor and others.

First, how can you find out more about this particular ancestor? If you find out your ancestor was a coal miner, a fishmonger, or a parlor maid, how did he or she practice the occupation in that time period? Under no circumstances assume that a person doing a job today is doing the same work as someone who had the same occupation in the past. Find out more about the occupation. If you find that your ancestor lived in a small rural cottage, was a domestic servant, or was one among many in a tenement house in the city, try to learn how he lived his daily life. You may be able to find some firsthand accounts written by a person in a similar situation.

Second, does this record provide clues that will allow you to find out more about other people in the family? Where is this information leading you? For example, a street address can lead you to the census returns of the entire family. A mother's maiden name helps you start looking for the marriage of the parents. A daughter's married name allows you to start locating her descendants.

Notes

Make a list of all clues and how you want to follow up on them. Be creative. One document may provide you with a number of leads.

After creating the list, prioritize your options. For example, in one record you may find your ancestor's occupation and a street address. Where you go first will depend upon what records are easily accessible or what you most want to know. If your ancestor was a soldier in the British military and you want to find out more about what he did you may head to the nearest library. On the other hand, if you already have a particular census return at your local Family History Center, you may want to use the address to find his family in the census. No rules dictate what to do first. That's one thing that makes family history research so much fun. You get to decide what you want to do by asking yourself, "What will get me excited? What interests me?"

Every time you find a new ancestor or another place where your ancestors lived, remember to go back through the first three steps of the research process. Look for people who are currently researching the new ancestor's surname, look for what has already been written about this name, and look for original records. Revisit the Internet, your local library, and a Family History Center. Do the same to find out about the place where your ancestor lived: Check sources on the Internet, look for history and geography books in the library, and find original records in a Family History Center.

WHERE DO I GO FROM HERE?

Before you start your Scottish research, find out more about what makes Scottish research different from research in other countries. (See chapter three.) The rest of the book will take you through the research process by examining the tools you will use to trace your ancestor in Scotland. Enjoy the journey.

THREE

Uniqueness of Scottish Research

S cottish research is not the same as U.S. research, and that's what makes it so interesting. These differences, however, can cause roadblocks to those who are unfamiliar with Scotland, its history, and its customs. This chapter outlines some of the major differences between Scottish and American research and explains some terms.

THE COUNTRY

Scotland, of course, is a country of its own. But it can also be described as part of Great Britain, the United Kingdom, and the British Isles. For many North Americans, these names can be confusing. Let's define them.

In 1536, King Henry VIII united England and Wales under one system of laws and government. In 1707, Great Britain was formed when the parliaments of the Kingdom of England and Wales and the Kingdom of Scotland passed the Act of Union. In 1801, Ireland was united politically with Great Britain to form the United Kingdom of Great Britain and Ireland. In 1921, most of Ireland separated from the United Kingdom. Since that time, the full name of the United Kingdom is the United Kingdom of Great Britain and Northern Ireland. It is also known as the U.K. The term *British Isles* has traditionally described the two major islands of Great Britain (England, Scotland, and Wales) and Ireland (Republic of Ireland and Northern Ireland) plus the Channel Islands, the Isle of Man, and all the other islands surrounding the coast.

To summarize:

- **Great Britain** includes Scotland, England, and Wales.
- **The United Kingdom** has different meanings depending on the time period. From 1801 to 1920 it included Scotland, England, Ireland, and Wales. Since 1921 it includes Scotland, England, Wales, and Northern Ireland.
- **British Isles** includes Scotland, England, Ireland, Wales, the Channel Islands, and the Isle of Man.

Population Figures for Scotland, for England and Wales, and for the United States			
Year	Scotland	England and Wales	United States*
1601	800,000	4,109,000	
1707	1,000,000	5,057,000	250,900
1755	1,265,380	5,772,000	1,170,800
1801	1,608,420	8,893,000	5,308,000
1851	2,888,742	17,928,000	23,191,876
1901	4,472,103	35,528,000	76,212,168
1951	5,096,433	43,758,000	151,325,798
1991	4,962,152	48,968,000	248,709,873

*The United States did not exist until the American Revolution. Figures quoted for the United States are based on the previous year's census figures. Population figures prior to 1801 are estimates.

Geographic Area of Scotland			
Country/State	Land Area	Population (1996)	Population Density
Scotland	30,418 sq. mi.	5,120,200	168 per sq. mile
U.S.	3,679,192 sq. mi	263,814,032	72 per sq. mi.
Maine	30,865 sq. mi.		
South Carolina	30,111 sq. mi.		
Indiana	35,870 sq. mi.		

Until recently, all countries of the United Kingdom were controlled by a single parliament based in London. In July 1999, after almost three hundred years, Queen Elizabeth II opened the new Scottish parliament. The Scottish parliament now has legislative power over domestic issues; the government in London retains control over defense, foreign affairs, and macro economic policy.

The Isle of Man and the Channel Islands are dependencies of the British Crown, but they have their own parliaments.

Size

Comparing the geographic area of Scotland to that of the United States, you can see that Scotland, which is only a part of the United Kingdom, is a relatively small area.

THE IMPORTANCE OF PLACE

As in all genealogical research, it is important to locate the places where events occurred in the life of your ancestor. However, for Scotland, it is not enough to know the name of the county where your ancestor lived. The parish is the fundamental administrative and record-keeping organization, so you need to know the name of your ancestor's parish. You should also know (1) where it is in relation to other parishes, (2) who had responsibility for its records, and (3) a little about the surrounding land formations. You will, therefore, need to become very familiar with maps and gazetteers.

Begin by locating the county. In Scotland the county structure changed in 1975

Important

and again in 1996. This means that there are three sets of maps you may need in your research. The map you will need the most as genealogists shows the pre-1975 counties where your ancestors lived, in Figure 3-1 on page 15. In 1975 the counties were replaced by nine regions and three island areas, available at <www .familysearch.org> by looking under Search/Research Helps/Scotland/Scotland Map (Boundaries after 1974). You will probably need this map only where you are searching for modern relatives or using resource guides produced between 1975 and 1996. In 1996, Scotland reorganized into twenty-nine unitary districts and three island areas. You will need this map when you go beyond the basic resources and need to know where records are now stored. For a map of the new areas, see <www.bbc.co.uk/politics97/devolution/scotland/people/intro.shtml>. For a map overlaying the modern areas onto the older administrative areas, see <www.trp.dun dee.ac.uk/data/councils/newregions.html>.

Chapman County Codes for Scotland

ABD	Aberdeenshire	ELN	East Lothian	PEE	Peeblesshire
ANS	Angus	FIF	Fifeshire	PER	Perthshire
ARL	Argyllshire	INV	Inverness-shire	RFW	Renfrewshire
AYR	Ayrshire	KCD	Kincardineshire	ROC	Ross & Cromarty
BAN	Banffshire	KRS	Kinross-shire	ROX	Roxburghshire
BEW	Berwickshire	KKD	Kirkcudbrightshire	SEL	Selkirkshire
BUT	Buteshire	LKS	Lanarkshire	STI	Stirlingshire
CAI	Caithness-shire	MLN	Midlothian	SUT	Sutherland
CLK	Clackmannanshire	MOR	Morayshire	WLN	West Lothian
DFS	Dumfriesshire	NAI	Nairnshire	WIG	Wigtownshire
DNB	Dunbartonshire	OKI	Orkney	SHI	Zetland (Shetland)

For family historians, all pre-1975 counties have been given standardized three-letter codes known as the Chapman County Codes. The Chapman County Codes are not universally used, but the three letters are convenient for recording county names on forms and in computer files. See the list of codes above.

Next, see where your ancestor's parish is located in the county. Good outline maps showing the relationship between parishes during the nineteenth century are found in Cecil Humphrey-Smith's *The Phillimore Atlas and Index of Parish Registers*. Some of the parishes no longer have the boundaries shown on these maps. For example, some parishes in *The Phillimore Atlas* are split into multiple segments, occasionally with segments in different counties. In 1889 the Boundary Commission made adjustments in parish boundaries to eliminate these separated segments within a parish. A source containing modern parish maps is *The Parishes, Registers and Registrars of Scotland*. On either map you can see the proximity of your ancestor's parish to surrounding parishes.

When you have located the parish in the correct county, you then need to identify its parish number. Each parish in Scotland is provided with a unique number. The numbering begins in the north and moves south and from east to west. The parish number is determined by arranging the parishes within a county in alphabetical order and then numbering them consecutively. In 1854 the Registration Act created some new districts, and these were provided with a new sequence of numbers. The

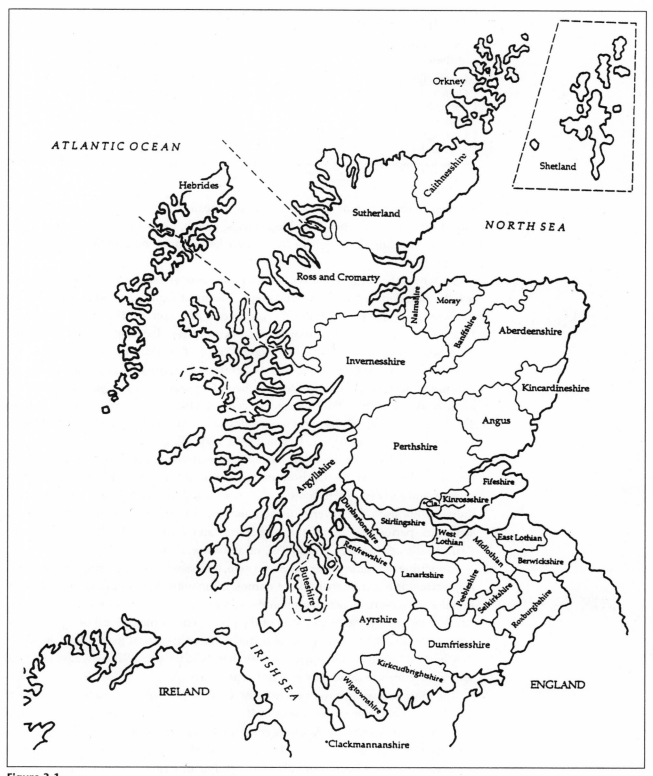

Figure 3-1
Map of Scotland showing pre-1975 county boundaries. *Reprinted by permission. © 1997 by Intellectual Reserve, Inc.*

County Name Changes		
Six Scottish counties were previously known by other names, and you need to be aware of these.		
Edinburghshire	is now	Midlothian
Elginshire	is now	Morayshire
Forfarshire	is now	Angus
Haddingtonshire	is now	East Lothian
Linlithgowshire	is now	West Lothian
Shetland	is now	Zetland

number of the parish or district is used as a means of reference in source citations and is often needed when searching census, parish, and civil registration records. Tools for locating the numbers for all parishes' numbering are discussed later, in chapter nine.

Sources

See where the various towns and other local features are located. **The best maps are the detailed Ordnance Survey maps**. The most readily available maps are the modern Landranger [1:50,000 = 1¼ inches to 1 mile (2cm to 1km)] and Pathfinder [1:25,000 = 2½ inches to 1 mile (4cm to 1km)]. Every location on the Landranger Map Series is identified in *The Ordnance Survey Gazetteer of Great Britain*. You can also search *The Ordnance Survey Gazetteer* at <www.ordsvy.gov.uk/products/landranger/lrmsearch.cfm>. However, the online version of the gazetteer does not identify all locations. Older nineteenth-century Ordnance Survey maps (1 inch to 1 mile [1.6cm to 1km]) have been reproduced by David & Charles (Brunel House, Forde Close, Newton Abbot, Devon TQ12 2DW, England).

When you look for ancestors in major urban areas, the best maps to use are popularly known as the Godfrey maps. The maps are generally late nineteenth century and early twentieth century and are detailed enough to allow you to identify individual houses. The reverse of each map often lists local city directories for the same time period. Contact the publisher at Alan Godfrey Maps, Prospect Business Park, Leadgate, Consett, DH8 7PW, or at <www.alangodfreymaps.co.uk/>.

In addition to locating your place on a map, it is essential that you consult gazetteers. **A gazetteer is a dictionary of place names, often with descriptions providing additional information.** Depending upon the gazetteer, this information may include the name of the parish, the relationship of the place to other major localities, population figures, topographical and historical features, the ecclesiastical jurisdictions in which they lie, and details about nonconformist chapels in the area. Whenever possible use several gazetteers because they give different information.

\di'fin\ *vb*

Definitions

The most accessible gazetteers in print are *A Topographical Dictionary of Scotland* by Samuel Lewis (published in 1846 but reprinted many times) or the abridged *Genealogical Gazetteer of Scotland* compiled by Frank Smith. See the sample entry for Crieff in the sidebar on page 18 for the wealth of detail to be found in Lewis's gazetteer. (You will learn more about the people of Crieff later in the book.)

Another good gazetteer is the *Ordnance Gazetteer of Scotland: A Survey of Scottish Topography, Statistical, Biographical, and Historical* edited by Francis H. Groome. This six-volume set is available through your local Family History Center on microfiche (FHL fiche numbers 6020391–6020411). Other sources worth examining include *Cassell's Gazetteer of Great Britain and Ireland, Being a Complete Topographical Dictionary of the United Kingdom, With Numerous Illustrations and Sixty Maps*, published in six volumes and available through your local FHC on three rolls of microfilm (numbers 599360, 924936, and 599361). All six volumes are also available on CD-ROM from Quintin Publications, at 22 Delta Drive, Pawtucket, Rhode Island 02860-4555 or at <www.quintinpublications.com>.

Or try Wilson's *Gazetteer of Scotland*, published in 1882. This is available as CD52 from Quintin Publications and was reprinted in 1996 by Willow Bend Books, 65 E. Main Street, Westminster, Maryland 21157-5036. It is also available through your local Family History Center on FHL microfiche number 6026374.

Printed versions of these important gazetteers should be available in large public or university libraries.

FAMILY HISTORY SOCIETIES

When you have identified the place where your ancestor originated, **join the family history society for that area.** Local societies open many doors for further research.

Tip

The services vary with each society, but you can expect many things:

1. Most societies produce a high-quality quarterly journal with articles that illustrate family history in that area. The journal includes articles describing local records, information about local indexes, historical articles about life in the area, and information on what is new.

2. You gain access to books and indexes made available through the society. Many are of a very local nature and may be available only through the society.

3. Many societies provide research services to their members. You can receive expert assistance with your personal research. The locals know the records and what is available.

4. You can contact others with similar interests. Most societies publish queries that you can use to find others who are researching your surname. You may even discover a cousin. Even over a distance, many friendships develop as members cooperate on research projects and share their love of tracing families in a given locality in Scotland.

County and regional family history societies in Scotland are members of the Scottish Association of Family History Societies (SAFHS). This organization is the coordinating body for all such societies. To find out how to join a local society, visit the SAFHS Web site at <www.safhs.org.uk>. This site has a list of SAFHS member societies with contact information including a society mailing address and possibly a Web site.

You can also write to the SAFHS and request a current listing of societies and their addresses. You can specify which parts of the country you are interested in. If you are unclear as to which society covers your area of Scotland, explain where you are looking and ask them to advise you. Send with your request two International Reply Coupons, available from your post office, to cover the cost of return postage.

A HIGHLY ABBREVIATED ENTRY FROM SAMUEL LEWIS 1846 *TOPOGRAPHICAL DICTIONARY OF SCOTLAND* FOR THE COMMUNITY OF CRIEFF

CRIEFF, a parish, in the county of PERTH; containing 4333 inhabitants, of whom 3584 are in the town of Crieff, 17 miles (W. By S.) Of Perth and 56 (N.W.) From Edinburgh . . . from an early date regarded as the chief town of Strathearn . . . The town was occupied by the army of Montrose during some of the disturbances of the great civil war; it was burnt by the Highlanders for its loyalty in 1715, and in the rebellion of 1745 was saved from destruction only by the interposition of the Duke of Perth. On the 10th September, 1842, the town was visited by Her Majesty, in the course of her tour in Scotland. . . .

The principal trade carried on is the weaving of cotton for the manufacturers of Glasgow, in which nearly 500 persons are employed at their own homes, in producing checks and handkerchiefs. . . . There are three tanneries . . . Five malting establishments . . . An oil-mill . . . corn, flour and barley mills . . . mail and stage coaches pass through the town daily. . . . The market, held on Thursday, is well attended by the farmers. . . .

The parish is separated into two divisions by the intervening lands of the parish of Monzie. The Highland division comprises the larger portion of the district of Glenalmond. . . . The Lowland division, which may properly be regarded as the parish is about four miles in length, and three in breadth. . . .

For Ecclesiastical purposes the parish is within the bounds of the presbytery of Auchterarder and synod of Perth and Sterling; patron, Lady Willoughby de Eresby . . . Crieff church, built in 1786, and thoroughly repaired in 1827 affords accommodation for 966 persons. An additional church was erected in 1837. . . . There are places of worship for members of the Free Church, the United Presbyterian Synod, Episcopalians, and Roman Catholics. The parochial school affords a useful education. . . .

[The actual entry is five columns of fine print with lots of fascinating details about the history, setting, industry, agriculture, government, and trade within the community.]

You can contact the Scottish Association of Family History Societies by writing to Honorable Secretary Alan J.L. MacLeod, 51/3 Mortonhall Road, Edinburgh, EH9 2HN, Scotland.

MONEY

You will find references to money as you research. For example, a parish history may tell you the average daily wages of a farm laborer.

Types and Values of Scots Coins at the Time of Their Elimination in 1707

Scots Coin	English Equivalent
1 penny	¹⁄₁₂ penny
1 boddle = 2 pence	⅙ penny
1 plack = 2 boddles	⅓ penny
1 bawbee = 3 boddles	1 halfpenny
1 shilling = 2 bawbees	1 penny
1 merck = 13 shillings 4 pence	1 shilling and 1½ pence
1 pound = 20 shillings	1 shilling and 8 pence

British Coins in Use During the Nineteenth Century

1 farthing	=	¼ penny
1 ha'penny	=	½ penny
1 penny	=	1 penny
1 threppence	=	3 pence
1 groat	=	4 pence
1 sixpence	=	6 pence
1 shilling	=	12 pence
1 florin	=	2 shillings
1 half-crown	=	2 shillings and sixpence
1 double-florin	=	4 shillings
1 dollar	=	5 shillings
1 crown	=	5 shillings
1 quarter-guinea	=	5 shillings and threppence
1 third-guinea	=	7 shillings
1 half-sovereign	=	10 shillings
1 sovereign	=	1 pound
	=	20 shillings
	=	240 pence
1 guinea	=	21 shillings
1 double-sovereign	=	2 pounds
1 five-pounds	=	5 pounds

Scots money was equivalent in value to English money until the late fourteenth century. After this it began to depreciate in value until it was completely eliminated under the terms of the Act of Union in 1707. The definitions and values of the Scottish coins as of 1707 appear in the sidebar.

Prior to 1974, Scotland used a monetary system of pounds, shillings, and pence. (The plural of *penny* is *pence* or *pennies*.) A more complete list of coins in use during the nineteenth century appears in the sidebar. There were twelve pence in a shilling, and twenty shillings in a pound. Therefore, 1 pound = 20 shillings = 240 pence. Monetary amounts were written using abbreviations based on the Latin forms of the words, so pounds are represented by *L* or *£*, shillings by *s*, and pence by *d*. For example, you may find a fee recorded as "2s. 6d." (two shillings and sixpence). After 1974, Scotland changed to a decimal currency with one hundred pennies to a pound. For more information, see Colin Chapman's *Weights, Money and Other Measures Used by Our Ancestors*.

SCOTTISH CLANS AND TARTANS

Warning

For many of Scottish heritage, the desire to learn of "their" clan and tartan sparks an interest in tracing their ancestors.

First, let's begin with a warning: **Much of what is written in the popular press about Scottish clans and tartans is pure romantic fantasy with almost no basis in history or fact.** The popular romantic image of the Scottish Highlander was primarily created in the early nineteenth century by the writings of Sir Walter Scott and other romantic writers and businessmen aimed to profit from the sale of supposed clan tartans and kilts.

The clan system and tartans are a fascinating aspect of Scottish history. Lots more details about both subjects can be found in George Way's *Collins Scottish Clan & Family Encyclopedia* and other books listed at the end of this section.

In modern times the clan societies have developed into strong organizations scattered across the world, but they are especially strong in North America. These organizations foster pride in Scottish heritage. They may even be able to help you with your genealogical research. Most of the clan societies have one or more genealogists in their organization. In many ways clan societies have become one-name study groups. They research the main clan name and all allied names associated with that clan name. Contacting the clan genealogist may provide you with clues for you to follow to document your ancestral tree. Document each step on the family tree as you go along. Do not suddenly accept three hundred years' data on a family tree as fact without obtaining proof. First you have to prove that this *is* your family line, then you must prove that the information is correct. Yes, this sounds like a lot of work, but it is not as much work as redoing it after later research disproves something. If the information is true, then it should be easy to find the documentation to prove it. If there is a weak link in the information provided, that should become obvious relatively quickly.

For More Info

For North Americans the most complete directory of clan society contact information is published annually in April's special directory issue in *The Highlander* magazine.

To research the history and development of the clans further, try the following recommended books, which should be obtainable through your local library:

Adam, Frank and Sir Thomas Innes of Learney. *The Clans, Septs, and Regiments of the Scottish Highlands.* Edinburgh, Scotland: W & A.K. Johnson Ltd. 8th ed. 1970. Reprint, Baltimore, Md.: Clearfield Publishing Company, 1999.

Moncreiffe of that Ilk, Sir Iain. *The Highland Clans.* New York: Bramhall House, 1967.

Munro, R.W. *Highland Clans and Tartans.* London: Octopus Books, 1977.

Way, George, of Plean and Romilly Squire. *Collins Scottish Clan & Family Encyclopedia.* Glasgow, Scotland: HarperCollins Publishers, 1994.

THE IMPORTANCE OF RELIGION

Scotland has no separation of church and state. In history the two are intimately intertwined. Understanding this connection will help you understand the context of your ancestors.

The Church in Scotland became Protestant in 1560, with the banning of anything Roman Catholic. For the next 130 years, the leadership of the church varied between Presbyterian [ministers ordained by elders (presbyters)] and Episcopalian (ministers appointed by bishops). In 1690 the Presbyterian Church became the Established Church of Scotland. However, not everything went smoothly after this. Initially a number of schisms (breakaways) occurred, followed later by mergers. Your ancestor may have been Presbyterian, but you may not find him in the major Scottish church record indexes because of this history. Your ancestor may have belonged to one of the other religious groups in Scotland, even though they were much smaller in numbers of congregations or followers. We say more about the history of the churches and religion in chapter nine, "Church Records."

SCOTTISH RECORD KEEPING

Scottish records are different from North American records in the types of records created, where they were created, and who created them. In most U.S. states, the county courthouse is the primary place to locate records. What is recorded often depends upon local laws. In Scotland, almost no records used early in family history research were created by the county government. The first records we discuss were created by the national government. Many earlier records were created by the Church of Scotland in its parishes.

Records Created by the National Government

In the United States, vital statistics are recorded by the various states, and many of the states had no compulsory registration of births and deaths until the twentieth century. In Scotland, the national government has registered all births, marriages, deaths in the country since 1855. This is known as civil registration. The government also compiles nationwide indexes to births, marriages, deaths. See chapter seven on civil registration to find out what these records contain and how to use them.

Since 1801, the British government has taken a national census. Federal censuses have been taken in the United States since 1790. The British census is more difficult to search than the U.S. census because of a lack of indexes, but the results are well worth the effort. See chapter eight on census records for more details.

A centralized probate system covers all of Scotland from the year 1876. There are even nationwide indexes. But even before 1876, the Scottish indexes are so good that you may be able to quickly find your ancestor's records. This is a major difference from North American research. Can you imagine checking a nationwide index for any probate record that occurred in the United States in the year 1876? That would be a dream come true, and you can do that in Scottish research! See chapter ten for more details.

The majority of nationally produced records are stored at the National Archives of Scotland (NAS). The National Archives of Scotland was formerly known as the Scottish Record Office (SRO), so you will find that name in most reference books.

Sources

Warning

Records Created by the Church of Scotland

In the United States, church records can be difficult to find and may even be nonexistent. In Canada, church records are used more in family research. **But in Scotland, church records are your most important resources.** You can use baptism, marriage, and burial records created by the Church of Scotland. See chapter nine on church records for further details.

SPECIAL PROBLEMS WITH SCOTTISH RECORDS
Christian Names

Your ability to recognize your ancestor's name can be a major stumbling block in Scottish research. Your ancestor's Christian name (also known as his first name or given name) and sometimes his surname (last name) can change from record to record. **You may encounter several problems with Christian names in Scotland because Scotland has name variations that are unfamiliar to most foreigners.**

You have seen nicknames throughout your life, but you may be surprised at some of the Scottish ones. For example, you know that two of the nicknames for Alexander are Alec and Alex. But in Scotland, an Alexander may be called Sandy. Therefore, some nicknames and name variations can lead to confusion about whether a child was a boy or a girl. You recognize Christian as a male name, but it is also an alternative for Christina. The name Christopher has an old Scottish version: Christal. Its nicknames were Christie and Kit.

Some names are interchangeable—such as Elizabeth and Isobel—and Scotland has some very common ones that may seem odd. Peter and Patrick, for example, are used interchangeably. So are Daniel and Donald. Agnes, Ann, and Nancy are all variations of the same name. Your ancestor Jane could have been called Jean, Janet, or Jessie.

You may find your ancestor's name in either Gaelic or English, especially in the Highland areas. Some Gaelic names bear no resemblance to their English equivalents. For example, the Gaelic name Eachann is the English name Hector. Gilleaspuig is Gaelic for Archibald, and Tearlach is Gaelic for Charles. The Gaelic form of the female name Grace is Giorsal, and you may find this spelled Grisel or Grizzel. Further, you will find first names recorded in Latin, especially in probate and land records. Therefore, you could find your ancestor's name as James in one record, its Gaelic form Hamish (or Seamus) in another, and its Latin form Jacobus in still another record.

How do you sort out all of these names? The best reference book is Dunkling's *Scottish Christian Names: An A-Z of First Names.* Another good name book is Withycombe's *Oxford Dictionary of English Christian Names.* Both are currently out of print, but you can order them through interlibrary loan. You can also purchase Bardsley's *First Name Variants.* This book is inexpensive and small enough to carry around with you. Volume 3 of Gardner and Smith's *Genealogical Research in England and Wales* includes an excellent listing of Latin forms of English names. Even though the book is about England and Wales, the list includes ancient and unusual names found in records of Scotland. Also, try a good book of baby names showing name variations; any bookstore should have one. You can consult a concise explanation of given names for family historians under the category "Christian Names" in FitzHugh's *Dictionary of Genealogy*.

Naming Patterns

In Scotland many families used a standard naming pattern whereby the first son was given the name of his paternal grandfather and the second son was named for his maternal grandfather. To illustrate, let's assume that a man named John Stewart followed the traditional naming pattern and had four sons named Duncan, Andrew, John, and Archibald. Duncan was the name of John's father, and Andrew was the name of John's wife's father. John gave the third son his own name, and the fourth son, Archibald, was named after one of John's brothers. When the four sons had children, they may have all named the first son John. If so, you could find four John Stewarts in the same generation in the same community. In addition, our John Stewart had at least one brother who would have used many of the same family names, and his children would have used them too. Another Stewart family also could have been in the area. You can see how numerous people with the same Christian name and surname may have lived in one generation in the same location. Knowing the naming pattern may help you find and identify individuals. However, the naming pattern is only a guide. Some families modified it, and others didn't use it at all.

Standard Scottish Naming Pattern	
This naming pattern is a potential guide but not a hard-and-fast rule.	
Child	*Given the name of*
1st son	father's father
2nd son	mother's father
3rd son	father
4th son	father's brother
1st daughter	mother's mother
2nd daughter	father's mother
3rd daughter	mother
4th daughter	mother's sister

Surnames and Patronymics

One of the more interesting problems in Scottish research is that both given names and surnames can vary greatly. For example, some Scottish surnames have Gaelic and English equivalents. The name MacIver is a form of the Gaelic MacIomhair (son of Ivar). In English the name is Iverson. Variants of the name include Makiver, MacKeever, Ivers, Ewers, and many others. Again, some of the Gaelic spellings bear no resemblance to the English spellings. For example, MacDhunnshleibhe is the Gaelic spelling for MacAnlevy. As your surname was recorded through several generations, its form and spelling could have changed many times. This is especially true if your ancestor moved from one part of the country to another, and even more so if he moved from Scotland to another part of the world.

Be careful about occupational surnames or names derived from a description, such as Black or White. If your ancestor had such a surname, look for a Scots, English, Latin, or Gaelic equivalent of the name. For example, the surname Gow is an occupational name from the Gaelic word *gobha*. It means "smith" and may have been translated into English in any record. If you look at a probate or land record written in Latin, you may find the name translated into its Latin form, Faber. The occupation shoemaker is *souter* in Scots and *greusaich* (Grassick) in Gaelic. The surname Grassick could have been translated as Souter; Shoemaker; or the Latin form, Sutor.

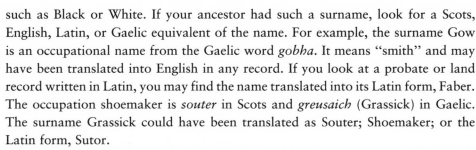

\di'fin\ *vb*

Definitions

Patronymics is the system of deriving a surname from the Christian name of the father. For example, Alexander Donaldson is the son of Donald Johnson who is the son of John Robertson. The surname within a family is not constant; it changes with each generation. Therefore, if you search for the father of Alexander Donaldson in an area where the patronymic system was used, you do not look for someone with the surname Donaldson; you look for a man with the first name Donald. While the surname changes, its form can also change. Donaldson is the English form of MacDonald (*Mac* means "son of") *Mac* can also be spelled as *Mc* or *M'*. The *Mac* can also be dropped entirely. Written in Gaelic, the above Alexander Donaldson would be recorded as Alisdair MacDhomhnuill mhic Iain (Alexander son of Donald son of John). *Mhic* can be written as *Vc* or *V'*, as in Alexander MacDonald VcIain. A woman could have been known as M'Neill, but more likely she was known as N'Neill (daughter of Neill). When families began to adopt permanent surnames, they could have chosen almost any form of the name or a new name altogether. The use of patronymics persisted in the Scottish Highlands until the late eighteenth century and in the Shetland Islands until the mid-nineteenth century.

Another problem with surnames is the ways they can be spelled in Scotland. For example, the letters *qu* are interchangeable with the letters *w* and *wh*. The letter *z* is interchangeable with the letter *y*. These spelling conventions can lead to interesting surname variations: A few spellings for MacQueen are MacQuhyne, Maquhon, M'Kquyne, Mackqueyne, Macwhan, and Macwhin. You also need to consider English forms of Scottish names. For example, Paul Smart from the Family History Library in Salt Lake City was researching the name MacQuilkin. If he didn't know anything about Scottish surnames and spelling variations, he could have looked forever and found no relevant data. But he knew that *Qu* was the Scottish spelling of the letter *W*, and *Mac* means "son of," so the English equivalent of MacQuilkin is Wilkinson. He found the family under both variations.

Perhaps the best book on surname variations and patronymics is George Black's *Surnames of Scotland: Their Origin, Meaning, and History*. This is one book you shouldn't ignore.

A further challenge occurs with clan names. **A family could have adopted the surname of the clan chief.** In one fascinating example, the death record of a woman indicated that her maiden name was Agnes McLeod. The marriage record of her daughter gave the woman's name as Ann McLeod. The woman's own marriage record said that her maiden name was Nancy MacCuaig. At first glance, this appears to be the wrong marriage record, but we had to investigate further. Could Nancy MacCuaig and Ann or Agnes McLeod have been the same person? We know that Ann, Agnes, and Nancy are all variations of the same given name. But what about MacCuaig and

Notes

McLeod? We had to do some searching in original records and published books to resolve that one. In an index to cemetery inscriptions of the area where she lived, we found the notation "The MacCuaigs have changed their name to McLeod." That was quite a find, but why did they do it? We consulted a surname book and found no explanation, but in a book about clans we found that MacCuaig is a sept of MacLeod. Therefore, the family had changed their surname to the clan name. Nancy MacCuaig and Agnes McLeod were indeed the same woman.

In small towns and villages where there were often only a few surnames and frequent duplication of Christian names, some other means was needed to differentiate between individuals. This gave rise to "other names," also called "to-names" or "tee-names." The use of other names is very common in the fishing communities of the northeast, along the border with England, and in the Western Highlands. In *The Surnames of Scotland*, Black gives the example of Findochty, with 182 fisherman householders and only four surnames between them: twenty-four Campbells, thirty-five Smiths, thirty-nine Sutherlands and eighty-four Fletts. Within the community other names may have been added to help distinguish one Sutherland from another. For example, a man might have been known with his surname and a descriptive name such as redhead. A married man might have added the name of his wife. Nicknames may have been added to distinguish between people; examples include: Buckie, Beauty, Biggelugs, Carrot, Doodle, Helldom, the King, the Provost, Snipe, Toothie.

Name variations are probably the most difficult part of Scottish research. But if you remember to always check Dunkling's *Scottish Christian Names* and Black's *Surnames of Scotland*, you will be able to find ancestors when nobody else can.

Handwriting

Several styles of handwriting have been used in the past. By the eighteenth century the secretary style of the prior two centuries had been replaced by the italic style which is very similar to our own handwriting. These two handwriting styles appear in the vast majority of documents that family historians will encounter.

At first glance, they may seem impossible to read, but you can do it! A little practice will produce results. Several handwriting books show how the letters were to be formed. If you practice writing the alphabet yourself, you will become adept at reading the original records.

When you first meet a document with either italic or secretary style, try to transcribe it in full—word for word. Leave a gap for any word or part of a word that you cannot transcribe. By the time you reach the end of the document, you should be able to go back and fill in some of the gaps. Words you need to omit in one part of a document may be easier to read in a different context. When transcribing, remember that any given word may be spelled differently from how it is today, and may even be spelled differently elsewhere in the document.

Although reading a document that's new to you may at first seem formidable, you can accomplish it with practice and patience. Try it, you'll like it!

The best handwriting guide we have found is Grant Simpson's *Scottish Handwriting, 1150–1650: An Introduction to the Reading of Documents*. For an inexpensive basic guide to reading old handwriting, see Eve McLaughlin's *Reading Old Handwriting*.

Technique

English, Scots, Gaelic, and Latin Languages

In Scotland, depending upon the location and time, you may run into the use of languages other than English. There are four major languages to consider. English is the language commonly used in modern Scotland. In the Scottish Highlands, however, Gaelic would have been the spoken language of the people. Outside of the Highlands you could easily encounter Scots language in one or more of its dialect variations. For example, if you want to read the poetry of Robert Burns, you need to understand the Scots language.

You will almost certainly find Scots words in documents. One of the most common is the word *umquile* (which sometimes looks like *Wm quile*, and you may wonder who all of these men named William were). If this word describes your ancestor, it is very important. It means "former" and is usually used instead of the word *deceased*. You will see all kinds of funny words like *compearit* which means "appeared." Do not skip over these words; look them up. You will not find them in an English dictionary. For assistance with the Scots language see Robinson's *Concise Scots Dictionary*; it is available in paperback. For more difficult problems, you may need to consult Craigie's *Dictionary of the Older Scottish Tongue: From the Twelfth Century to the End of the Seventeenth* or Grant's *Scottish National Dictionary: Designed Partly on Regional Lines and Partly on Historical Principles, and Containing All the Scottish Words Known to Be in Use or to Have Been in Use Since c. 1700.*

One of the most common problems in researching Gaelic-speaking ancestors is recognizing names and places. For example, if your immigrant ancestor said his name to an English-speaking person, did he provide his Gaelic name or its English equivalent? Further, your ancestor had a Gaelic accent, so the English-speaking listener probably had difficulty understanding your ancestor's name or place of origin. He probably recorded what he thought your ancestor said and spelled it the way it sounded. This may bear little or no resemblance to what was actually said. You may have to consult a book of given names, a book of surnames, and a book of place names. Several books of place names tell what the place names mean and how they were pronounced. The pronunciation of even well-known Scottish place names can blow your mind. For example, the county Kirkcudbright is pronounced "Kirkcoobree." You can imagine what can be done with the spelling of a small Gaelic place. The word *innis* is a Gaelic word meaning "island." It appears in several place names and is pronounced "insch." A long word containing *innis* could be spelled beyond recognition. See the bibliography at the end of this chapter for name books. You can also try MacLennan's *Pronouncing and Etymological Dictionary of the Gaelic Language: Gaelic-English, English-Gaelic* for other Gaelic words.

You will also find Latin in Scottish documents. The Scottish Services of Heirs up to 1847 (except for 1652–1659) are in Latin, and even the indexes up to 1700 are in Latin. Latin was the language used in these and many other legal documents. Latin terms and abbreviations sometimes appear in documents normally written in English, especially if the writer wanted to highlight a part of the document as being special or different. Latin terms are also on some tombstones.

You can do a lot of Scottish research without ever worrying about Latin. In fact, the majority of records we discuss are all written in English. When you do need

Warning

Latin, we provide the standard Latin format and its English translation. However, a basic familiarity with Latin is useful. For most genealogists, the following resources cover the subject quite well:

1. Family History Library's *Latin Genealogical Word List*. This contains the most common words found in genealogical documents. The *Latin Genealogical Word List* is available as an inexpensive printed booklet which you can order from the Salt Lake Distribution Center (see chapter six for address). It may also be available for purchase at your nearest Family History Center. You can consult this word list, and even download it at no charge, on the FamilySearch Web site (see chapter four).

2. Denis Stuart's *Latin for Local and Family Historians*. You can learn from this book to read most of the Latin you will ever need. It takes you step-by-step through the language and gives you lots of practice.

3. Peter Gouldesbrough's *Formulary of Old Scots Legal Documents*. This source shows the standard format of Scottish legal documents. For each type of record, the book contains a complete sample document. An English translation appears for all records written in Latin.

4. Charles Trice Martin's *The Record Interpreter: A Collection of Abbreviations, Latin Words and Names Used in English Historical Manuscripts and Records*. This is the standard reference work. The book is divided into sections that include Latin abbreviations, French abbreviations, a glossary of Latin words, Latin names of places, Latin forms of English surnames, and Latin Christian names.

Spelling

When you do genealogical research, **it is important to remember that words had no standardized spelling until the mid-nineteenth century**. Even today, people can spell their first names any way they choose. For example, a woman whose name we might spell Rebecca can spell her name Rebeka, Becky, Bekki, Beckie, or any other way. The same was true in the past for surnames and for all words in general. Therefore, do not get stuck on the idea that your ancestor spelled his name any particular way. For one thing, he was not usually spelling it; a clerk chose the spelling of the name. In fact, some clerks seemed to like to show off with how many ways they could spell the same name in the same document.

Scotland has some spelling conventions that are not found anywhere else. We mentioned before that the letters *z* and *y* are interchangeable. The name Monzie is pronounced Monyee or Monee. The parish of Monzievaird has been spelled several ways, including Monivaird and Moneyvaird. *Qu* (and sometimes just the letter *q*) is substituted for the letters *w* or *wh*, so you will find *quat* for *what*, and some odd Scots words such as *whilk* (it means "which") spelled as *qwilke*, *qhiche*, and *quich*. You will run into the Scots word *qua* or *wha*, which means "who." In some parts of Northern Scotland, the letter *j* is pronounced as *ch*, so you may find words and names spelled with a *ch* that you expect to find with a *j*.

Calendar

Dates in old Scottish documents were recorded differently than in modern Scottish ones. Many dates were unique to the country. You need to be aware of

Reminder

- Julian and Gregorian calendars
- ecclesiastical dates
- regnal dates

1. **Julian (Old Style) Calendar:** Prior to 1600, Scotland used the Julian calendar, which was introduced in Rome in 46 B.C. The year ran from 25 March to 24 March. The Church had declared 25 March (Lady Day) to be New Year's Day because it was believed to be the day that Christ was conceived.

Gregorian (New Style) Calendar: The Julian calendar year of 365¼ days was eleven minutes and fourteen seconds longer than the solar year. By 1580, the difference had accumulated to ten days. Pope Gregory XIII commissioned the more accurate Gregorian calendar to correct this. In addition, New Year's Day was moved from 25 March to 1 January. January, February, and March became the first three months of the year instead of the last three months of the year. The Gregorian calendar was adopted at various times throughout the world. Scotland adopted the Gregorian calendar in the year 1600. The American colonies, under English law, adopted this calendar in 1752.

The calendar change from Julian to Gregorian can present research difficulties if you are not careful. The biggest problem is that before 1752, stated years in Scottish documents can be different from those in British documents. Your ancestor can be found in both. The months September, October, November, and December used to be the seventh through tenth months of the year. *Septem* is Latin for "seven," *octo* for "eight," etc. They were abbreviated 7ber, 8ber, 9ber, and 10ber (or Xber), and the abbreviations continued to be used after the calendar change. These month abbreviations should not be confused with July through October, which are now the seventh through tenth months. When finding the parents' marriage date of 14 April 1595 and a child's birth date of 4 March 1595, you could make an incorrect conclusion if you forget the calendar change. This child was born almost ten months after his parents were married. The proper method for transcribing dates in England and America prior to 1752 is to document both Old Style and New Style dates for any date occurring between 1 January and 24 March. That way, you'll have the correct year for all of the British Isles and for America. Thus, a British document dated 15 February 1705 should be transcribed with the date 15 February 1705/6. It is also important to remember the change when calculating birth dates using monumental inscriptions for a person born before 1600 who died after that year.

2. **Ecclesiastical Dates:** Many pre-nineteenth-century documents that you will use were recorded by church officials. Some dates were recorded by a holiday name such as Candlemas (2 February), Lammas (1 August), Michaelmas (29 September), or Martinmas (11 November). Dates may have been recorded in terms of their relationship to a moveable feast or fast in the church calendar, for example, the third Sunday in Trinity. Good sources to help convert these date references are *Dates and Calendars for the Genealogist* by Clifford Webb and *A Handbook of Dates* edited by C.R. Cheney.

3. **Regnal Dates:** Up to the nineteenth century, many official documents were dated using regnal years, which are dates based upon when a monarch came to the

throne. For example, King George I came to the throne 1 August 1714. The first year of his reign is written as 1 George I, and it ran from 1 August 1714 to 31 July 1715. The regnal year 17 George III corresponds with 1776–77. You rarely encounter regnal years in documents used for basic genealogy, but you need to be aware of them and what they mean. The use of regnal years decreased with time, and they are now rarely used. Remember also that Scotland and England had different monarchs before 1603.

THE UNIQUENESS OF SCOTTISH RESEARCH

Records in Scotland are different from those in North America. Some, such as census records, have similarities, but the specifics vary. Scottish geography is different; customs are different; names are different; and even when the English language is used, the words have different meanings! The more in-depth research you do in Scottish records, the more you will realize that you are traveling through a whole new world. That's what makes Scottish family history so interesting. Throughout the rest of this book, we give all kinds of examples of the uniqueness of Scottish research. Watch for them, and enjoy them. You may begin to understand those mysterious ancestors, their funny sayings, and their very different lifestyles. It will be quite an adventure.

WHERE CAN I FIND MORE INFORMATION?

For More Info

Bardsley, Alan. *First Name Variants*. 2d edition. Birmingham, England: Federation of Family History Societies, 1996.

Black, George F. *The Surnames of Scotland: Their Origin, Meaning, and History*. New York: New York Public Library, 1946. 11th reprinting, 1996.

Chapman, Colin. *Weights, Money and Other Measures Used by Our Ancestors*. Baltimore, Md.: Genealogical Publishing Co., Inc., 1996.

Cheney, C.R., ed. (Revision by Michael Jones). *A Handbook of Dates*. New ed. Royal Historical Society Guides and Handbooks 4. Cambridge, England: Cambridge University Press, 2000.

Craigie, Sir William A. *A Dictionary of the Older Scottish Tongue: From the Twelfth Century to the End of the Seventeenth*. Chicago, Ill.: University of Chicago Press, 1937.

Dobson, David. *Scottish Emigration to Colonial America, 1607–1785*. Athens, Ga.: University of Georgia Press, 1994.

Dunkling, Leslie Alan. *Scottish Christian Names: An A-Z of First Names*. London: Cassell Ltd., 1978.

FitzHugh, Terrick V.H. *The Dictionary of Genealogy*. 5th ed. London: A & C Black, 1998.

Gardiner, Juliet and Neil Wenborn, ed. *The History Today Companion to British History*. London: Collins & Brown, Ltd., 1995.

Gardner, David E. and Frank Smith. *Genealogical Research in England and Wales*. 3 vols. Salt Lake City, Utah: Bookcraft, 1964.

Gouldesbrough, Peter, comp. *Formulary of Old Scots Legal Documents.* Edinburgh, Scotland: The Stair Society, 1995.

Grant, William. *The Scottish National Dictionary: Designed Partly on Regional Lines and Partly on Historical Principles, and Containing All the Scottish Words Known to Be in Use or to Have Been in Use Since c. 1700.* Edinburgh, Scotland: Scottish National Dictionary Association, 1931.

Humphery-Smith, Cecil R. *The Phillimore Atlas and Index of Parish Registers.* 2d ed. Chichester, England: Phillimore & Co., Ltd., 1996.

Lewis, Samuel. *A Topographical Dictionary of Scotland.* 2 vols. Originally published 1846. Reprint, Baltimore, Md.: Genealogical Publishing Co., Inc., 1989.

MacLennan, Malcolm. *A Pronouncing and Etymological Dictionary of the Gaelic Language: Gaelic-English, English-Gaelic.* Aberdeen, Scotland: Aberdeen University Library, 1985.

Martin, Charles Trice. *The Record Interpreter: A Collection of Abbreviations, Latin Words and Names Used in English Historical Manuscripts and Records.* Chichester, England: Phillimore & Co., Ltd., 1994.

McLaughlin, Eve. *Reading Old Handwriting.* 2d ed. Birmingham, England: Federation of Family History Societies, 1987.

The Ordnance Survey Gazetteer of Great Britain. Southampton, England: Ordnance Survey. 3d ed. 1992. Reprint, 1995.

The Parishes, Registers and Registrars of Scotland. Edinburgh, Scotland: Scottish Association of Family History Societies, 1993. Reprint, 1995.

Richardson, John. *The Local Historian's Encyclopedia.* New Barnet, England: Historical Publications Ltd., 1974, numerous reprints.

Robinson, Mairi, ed. *The Concise Scots Dictionary.* Aberdeen, Scotland: Aberdeen University Press, 1985. Republished, Edinburgh, Scotland: Polygon, 1999.

Simpson, Grant G. *Scottish Handwriting, 1150–1650: An Introduction to the Reading of Documents.* Aberdeen, Scotland: Aberdeen University Press, 1973. Reprinted with corrections, 1986.

Smith, Frank, comp. *A Genealogical Gazetteer of Scotland.* Logan, Utah: Everton Publishers, 1971.

Stuart, Denis. *Latin for Local and Family Historians.* Chichester, England: Phillimore & Co., Ltd., 1995.

Webb, Clifford. *Dates and Calendars for the Genealogist.* London: Society of Genealogists, 1994.

Wilson, John. *The Gazetteer of Scotland.* 1882. Lovettsville, Va.: Willow Bend Books. Reprint 1996 [CD-ROM Pawtucket, R.I.: Quintin Publications].

Withycombe, E.G., comp. *The Oxford Dictionary of English Christian Names.* London: Oxford University Press, 1947.

WHERE DO I GO FROM HERE?

You're ready to find your family! Step one of the research process is an Internet search. See chapter four.

FOUR

Accessing the Internet Resources

ou can start your Scottish research from the comfort of your home by using the Internet. First look for information that has already been found about your family, then find out about the places where your ancestors lived.

You don't need to know all about the Internet to use it effectively. In this chapter, **we examine three important sites for finding information about your Scottish ancestors.** These are

- FamilySearch, the Web site of the Family History Library
- GENUKI, historical and genealogical information provided by the Federation of Family History Societies and its members
- Cyndi's List, the ideal place to find out what online genealogical resources exist

In the next chapter we examine in more detail the Scots Origins database, an important Web site for Scottish research.

Please note that the Internet changes rapidly. The exercises suggested in this chapter may not work if information on a Web site changes. However, these three sites are here to stay, so you should be able to find them and do your own surveys. Have a great time!

Internet Source

FAMILYSEARCH <www.familysearch.org>

The Web site of the Family History Library is a great place to begin family history research. It includes many of the FHL's computerized research programs and guides. The site made international news when it was introduced in 1999, and it has never stopped evolving and growing. Here you can find out about your family surnames, more about the places where your ancestors lived, and about family history in general. You can even download a free computer program to use to record your genealogy. Become familiar with all aspects of this site.

The International Genealogical Index, Ancestral File, Pedigree Resource File, Vital Records Index, and the Family History Library Catalog are all accessible from the FamilySearch Web site. These programs are described in chapter six.

Start by connecting to the FamilySearch home page at <www.familysearch.org>. After you view the opening screen, click on "Search for Ancestors." Here you can enter your ancestor's name to conduct a search for information. Across the top is what looks like a tabbed card index. This tab alone has five options: "Search for Ancestors," "Research Guidance," "Research Helps," "Web Sites," and "Family History Library Catalog."

The "Search for Ancestors" option is highlighted, and the left side of the screen shows the indexes you can search individually or all at once. These include Ancestral File, the International Genealogical Index (IGI), Pedigree Resource File, U.S. Social Security Death Index, Vital Records Index, and Search Family History Web Sites. Most, but not all, are applicable for Scottish research, but searching all resources can be a good strategy. You never know who might turn up.

Using the International Genealogical Index at FamilySearch

Instead of searching all the databases at once, it can be to your advantage to search each database one at a time so that you better understand the benefits and limitations of the results you obtain.

Step By Step

Let's search the IGI from home for information about the Kay family that we research throughout this book. We begin our research with information we obtained from records our family had and by interviewing family members. Our family records contain the names of several children of the Kay family, including Margaret (born in 1855), Christina (born in 1857), and Lawrence (born in 1874). All we know is that they were born in the County of Perth; we don't know the parish yet. We can search the IGI for individuals, couples, or entire families.

Searching for an ancestor

1. Log onto <www.familysearch.org>. Click on "Search for Ancestors" from the opening screen.
2. You now have the opportunity to search several files at once. We want to search only the International Genealogical Index for this example, so click on "International Genealogical Index" at the left side of your screen.
3. To search for a birth, enter the first and last names of the person in the "First Name" and "Last Name" fields, which are set in bold lettering. Type "Margaret" in the "First Name" field, and "Kay" in the "Last Name" field. In the "Event" field drop-down menu, select "Birth/Christening." In the "Year" field, enter "1855." In the "Region" field, click on "British Isles" in the drop-down menu. We won't use the other options now; we will compare these first results to the ones we obtain using those options later. Click on "Search" at the bottom of the screen.
4. When the search results appear, you will see several Margaret Kays, but only one born in Perth. Click on her name to see the names of her parents as well as the source information. (We'll see what to do with the source information in chapter seven.) Print this page, or transcribe the information.

Searching for other children

5. We can search for other children in the family by going directly to a parent search from this screen. Instead, let's return to the search screen to do this search so you know how to do it anytime. Click on "Search for Ancestors" in the blue bar near the top of the screen, then select "International Genealogical Index" again.

6. This time leave the "First Name" and "Last Name" fields blank. To conduct a parent search, enter only the names of the parents. Type "James" in the "Father" field and "Kay" in the father's "Last Name" field. Type "Isobel" in the "Mother" field and "Brough" in the mother's "Last Name" field. In the "Region" field drop-down menu, select "British Isles." Do not enter any other information. Click the "Search" button at the bottom of the screen.

7. A list of ten children appears, including Margaret, Christina, and Lawrence. The names, dates, and birthplaces of the children verify and expand upon the information we have in our records. We can print this page, but it does not contain source information. You need to click on each name individually to see sources. We can download details, including source information, for all of the children by clicking the boxes to the left of their names. If this were your own family, you might choose to download. In that case, click on "Prepare selected records for download" at the top or bottom of the screen. This gives you a file that you can import into your genealogical program.

Searching for marriages

8. A marriage search is easier on the Internet than it is in the DOS version at Family History Centers because in an Internet search we can enter the names of both parties. To find the marriage of James Kay and Isobel (Isabella) Brough, click on "Search for Ancestors" then "International Genealogical Index."

9. Enter "James" in the "First Name" field and "Kay" in the "Last Name" field. Enter "Isobel" in the "Spouse" field and "Brough" in the spouse's "Last Name" field. Select "British Isles" from the "Region" field drop-down menu. Click on "Search" at the bottom of the screen.

10. Because we searched on the names of both parties, we did not have to filter our search. Our result appears immediately.

Let's try the search as if we had forgotten the name of one of the spouses.

11. Enter "James" and "Kay" in the "First Name" and "Last Name" fields. Select "Marriage" from the "Event" field drop-down menu. We can select a range of years to include in the results. Select "+ or − 10 years" from the "Year Range" field drop-down menu. Enter "1850" in the "Year" field. Filter the search to include only marriages from the county of Perth by selecting "British Isles" from the "Region" field drop-down menu and "Scotland" from the "Country" field drop-down menu. A "County" field then appears. Select "Perth" from the "County" field drop-down menu. Click on "Search" at the bottom of the screen.

12. The results include several James Kays, and we must click on the name to see the spouse and source information details.

Other resources on this site

From the bar at the top of the page, you can click on "Research Helps." The left of the screen shows that you can organize the Research Helps by place, title, subject, or document type. The default setting is by place. Looking for Scotland research helps, click on "S" at the bar with the letters of the alphabet, and then scroll down the screen until you see "Scotland." Here we find all sorts of assistance. All the helps can be read on-screen, and for quality printed copies, some can be downloaded as Adobe Acrobat PDF files or ordered as hard copies. The helps for Scotland include

- 1881 British Census Indexes
- Old Parochial Registers (OPR) Index for Scotland
- Scotland Historical Background
- Scotland Map (Boundaries after 1974)
- Scotland Map (Boundaries before 1974)
- Scotland Research Outline (a must-read)
- Scotland, How to Find a Map
- Scotland, How to Find a Place Name
- Scotland, How to Find Compiled Sources
- Scotland, How to Find Information About the Place Where Your Ancestor Lived
- Sources for Previous Research in the British Isles

Sources

Click on "Scotland Research Outline." **The guide describes all of the major record sources for Scottish research, tells you where to find a record, and describes how to find it in the Family History Library Catalog if it is available there.** A printed version is also available for purchase, but the online Research Outline is far superior. For example, for some particular records described in the online version of the *Scotland Research Outline*, you can click on the title of the record and bring up a list of the associated Family History Library microfilm numbers. This is one of the finest resources in genealogy, and it is available free on the Internet!

"Research Helps" has many other resources that you should investigate. For example, you can look at the *Latin Genealogical Word List* if you encounter any Latin words in Scottish documents. You can purchase many of these guides at your nearest Family History Center.

If you select the "Library" tab at the top, the selections change to "Family History Library," "Family History Centers," "Family History Library Catalog," and "Education." Select "Family History Centers" to search for an FHC near you. Fill in the blanks and click "Search" below them to find out the addresses, telephone numbers, and operating hours (call to check before going) of the Family History Centers in your area.

The FamilySearch Web site is regularly updated and expanded. This is a site you should spend some time exploring. Once you see how much easier it can make your research, you will wonder how anyone ever did family history research without it.

GENUKI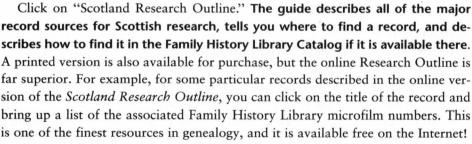

After you have searched the FamilySearch Web site, the GENUKI Web site can help you learn more about the places your ancestors lived. The historical and genealogical information on GENUKI is provided with the cooperation of the Federation of Family History Societies, its member societies, and a large group of volunteers. The site's stated aim is to serve as a "virtual reference library" of genealogical information.

The GENUKI Web site is organized with the same structure as the Family History Library Catalog. Places are organized into four levels: British Isles, country, county, and parish or town. Therefore, you should look for materials that relate to the British Isles as a whole, then for materials relating to all of Scotland. After you have found these general sources, find out more about the county where your ancestor lived, then the individual parish or town. The information for each place is organized with the same subject categories used by the Family History Library Catalog. These subject categories are listed in chapter six.

Let's navigate through the GENUKI site to find information about the British Isles, Scotland, and the County of Perth. Start at the GENUKI home page at <www .genuki.org.uk>. The home page discusses the site in general and leads you to further information about how the site is organized. Read this the first time you use the site. The information for the British Isles is contained in the section called "United Kingdom and Ireland." Click on this link. When "The United Kingdom and Ireland" page appears, add it to your list of bookmarks or favorites. You will return to it again and again. From here you can learn about the major archives and libraries, study some occupations, and more. Explore the various categories at your leisure.

Step By Step

Now click on the map under "Regions." Scotland is the country colored blue. You can now find out about Scotland gazetteers, schools, and many other subjects. Look through the categories, then go to the section that contains a list of counties. Click on "Perthshire" for a general description of the county and its location, information about Perthshire archives and libraries, societies, history, and much more. From there you can go even further and find information about individual parishes or districts within the county.

The GENUKI Web site is continually growing and being updated. This is one of your most important resources for information about places in Scotland.

CYNDI'S LIST <www.cyndislist.com>

FamilySearch and GENUKI give you access to lots of material. After exploring these two sites you may wonder, "What other genealogical resources are out there?" You can answer this question by visiting Cyndi's List. Cyndi Howells has compiled links to genealogy sites of all kinds and organized them by country and by category. The full title of the site is Cyndi's List of Genealogy Sites on the Internet, but everyone calls it Cyndi's List. This site is incredible.

Connect to <www.cyndislist.com>. The home page shows general information about the site first, followed by "Cyndi's List Main Category Index." Scroll down the list to see how much is available for Internet genealogy. Well down the alphabetical list is the link "Scotland." Click on that link to get to a page that contains only links relating to Scotland <www.cyndislist.com/scotland.htm>. Add this page to your list of bookmarks or favorites. Look through the various categories; they

Step By Step

include "General Resource Sites" and "History & Culture." Each subject category contains links to Web sites. Some of the links contain brief descriptions. You should find many things that interest you.

To sample what is available, click on the category "Queries, Message Boards & Surname Lists." You can search the RootsWeb Surname List by typing a surname into the box labeled "Type in your surname from Scotland." One of the names we are looking for is Brough, so type it into the box and click on the button "Search the RSL." This results in nine entries (at the time of this writing). One person is seeking a Brough from Crieff in the period 1895 to 1960. The chances of a connection here are high. Most of the others on the list are in Perthshire where we are looking, so contacting these submitters might be worthwhile. They are all reachable via e-mail, so contact is easy.

Also in the section "Queries, Message Boards & Surname Lists" is "Surname Lists Index from GENUKI." Unfortunately, at the time of writing Perthshire is one of the few counties for which there is no list. This means that you need to check back at a later date, or if you have a strong interest in the county, find out how to start such a list yourself.

You can spend countless hours looking at links from Cyndi's List, but try to come up for air every once in a while so you can finish reading this book! You should also let people know about your research by creating your own Web sites and queries. You can find many opportunities to do this as you explore Cyndi's List links. Genealogical research has never been this easy or this much fun.

WHERE DO I GO FROM HERE?

You should now know something about your Scottish ancestors. Perhaps you know the name of the place where your immigrant ancestor originated. Maybe you know an ancestor's religion or occupation. You should get background information about how your ancestors lived. Armed with that information, you can begin to search original records that contain your ancestors' names. Step two of the research process is to go to public and university libraries in your area. In step three, continue your research at your nearest Family History Center. See chapter six to get started on both.

FIVE

The Scots Origins Database

T he Scots Origins database, available at <www.scotsorigins.com>, provides a significant advance in Scottish research. However, you should also understand what research can be done only through this site versus what you can do through your local Family History Center. This pay-per-view service does not alert researchers to the fact that many of its indexes are also accessible for free elsewhere. This chapter shows what the Scots Origins database provides and how to use it. We show when to use this database and when to use alternative sources.

Please note that at the time of this writing, the Scots Origins Web site is in the second stage of a major change in format. Access may differ from the procedure we describe.

A table comparing what is available through a Family History Center, online through FamilySearch, and at Scots Origins is online at <www.rootsweb.com/~bifh susa/sct-comparisons.html>.

WHAT IS SCOTS ORIGINS, AND HOW DOES IT WORK?

The Scots Origins Web site came online on 6 April 1998. The site allows you to search indexes to Scottish births/baptisms and marriages/banns from 1553 to 1900 and deaths from 1553 to 1925. Each year an additional year of indexes is added. You can also search the 1881, 1891, and 1901 censuses. When using the index, you can search by surname, forename, sex, event type, year of registration (or range of years), age (deaths and census only), parish or registration district, and county (1553–1854 index).

Before you decide to use the service, click on "Read About Scots Origins First." You may also wish to read the "help" and "what's new" sections of the site so that you have an idea of how the site works. You can learn how to plan your search and find out if anything has changed since this chapter was written.

To actually search the indexes and see the results, you must pay six pounds (about eight dollars) by credit card for up to thirty "page credits" in one twenty-four-hour time period. Each page credit contains a minimum of one and a maximum of fifteen entries. Once you have used your thirty page credits, you must pay another six pounds for the next thirty page credits. When you have found the entry you are looking for, you can order online an extract of the entry for an additional fee of ten pounds (about $14.50). You can use additional page credits to view online the actual images of the 1891 and 1901 censuses. Because of the costs of these options, you need to prepare in advance so that you know what you are looking for. Ideally, you should have a list of searches to make so that you do not waste your money if your primary search is accomplished quickly or does not work at all.

THE ONLINE SEARCH PROCESS

Let's work through a couple of examples: searching for a death extract using localities and searching the 1891 census, neither of which we can do easily at a local Family History Center.

On the Scots Origins home page, select "access database." If you are not already registered, you will choose a user name and password that you will use for all subsequent access to the database and enter your contact information (name, address, telephone number, and e-mail address). You will then proceed to the credit/debit card payment screen. After your credit card is processed, you can proceed to the search screen.

Death and Locality Search

How you fill in this screen depends on what you are looking for. We are looking for the death of Hector Cameron, who is thought to have died in Glasgow in the late 1880s or early 1890s. He should have been in his thirties. A completed search screen is shown in Figure 5-1. We are selecting a broad range of dates since we do not know the exact year of death. For a common name, this broad date range might produce too many results, so the year range would need to be narrowed or other criteria specified. Then click on "Search."

This search produced ten Hector Camerons who died between 1886 and 1894 (see Figure 5-2). We eliminated five of the individuals immediately because they died in infancy (see "Age" column). One of the people died in Glasgow, which is where we are looking, but he was of the wrong age. **(The older the person was, the more likely that the age reported is incorrect, but in this example the person was only twenty-five years old.)** Who is left? In our search the most likely candidate is the Hector Cameron who died at age thirty-six in Blythswood. Remember that civil registration events are recorded by registration district and not necessarily by the name of the locality where we expect to find an ancestor.

But where is Blythswood? If we don't know or are unsure, we return to the site's home page. One of the free options is "Place Names." Select this option and you can search the list of places alphabetically or by county. In this case search alphabetically for Blythswood. The list shows that Blythswood was a registration district in Glasgow from 1855 through 1906. This means the thirty-six-year-old Hector Cameron is a very likely candidate. Return to the search entries; if you repeat the

Warning

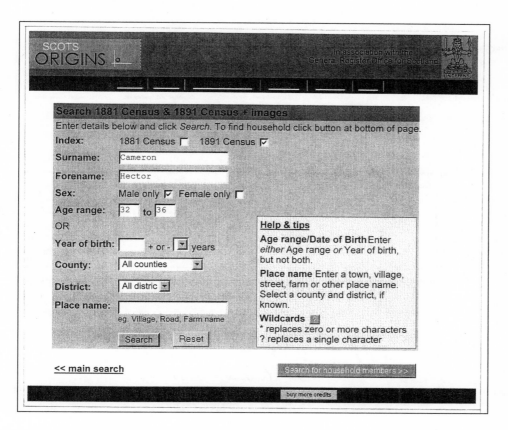

Figure 5-1
Scots Origins search screen showing completed fields for 1891 census search for Hector Cameron. Note assumed age range of four years to allow for errors in reporting of ages.

SCOTS ORIGINS — SRI Death records

Set printer paper orientation to 'Landscape'

Search criteria: Surname:*Cameron*, Forename:*Hector*, Year range:*1886 to 1894*, Sex:*M,,*

ID	SEX	AGE	YEAR	SURNAME	FORENAME	MM	DISTRICT	COUNTY	1	2	3
723550	M	16	1886	CAMERON	HECTOR		Tyree	Argyll	551	1	0039
723572	M	30	1886	CAMERON	HECTOR		Morvern	Argyll	528		0004
723676	M	0	1887	CAMERON	HECTOR MCNEILL		Campbeltown	Argyll	507		0088
724086	M	4	1889	CAMERON	HECTOR		Lochbroom	Ross & Cromarty	075	1	0002
724104	M	25	1889	CAMERON	HECTOR		Kelvin	Lanark	644	9	0335
724220	M	0	1890	CAMERON	HECTOR		Gairloch (Southern)	Ross & Cromarty	066	2	0028
724221	M	0	1890	CAMERON	HECTOR		Falkirk (Burgh)	Stirling	479	1	0163
724431	M	0	1891	CAMERON	HECTOR		Greenock (East)	Renfrew	564	1	0208
724959	M	36	1893	CAMERON	HECTOR		Blythswood	Lanark	644	7	0031
725182	M	54	1894	CAMERON	HECTOR		Urray	Ross & Cromarty	085		0004

KEY

MM: Mother maiden name
1: GRO code 1 - Registration District
2: GRO code 2 - Registration District Suffix
3: GRO code 3 - Registration District Entry

Figure 5-2
Display of results on Scots Origins for the ten Hector Camerons who died between 1886 and 1894. The search assumed a death in 1890 plus or minus five years.

same search within twenty-four hours, you do not get charged again for that search.

To get a copy of the extraction (certificate) for Hector Cameron, click on the extract order button next to the relevant index entry. Provide your credit card information again to pay the ten pound fee for the extract. A copy of the death extract for Hector Cameron will arive within a few days by airmail. See Figure 5-3 for a copy of Hector Cameron's death extract.

1861–1965
Extract of an entry in a REGISTER of DEATHS
Registration of Births, Deaths and Marriages (Scotland) Act 1965

53127

No.	1 Name and surname Rank or profession and whether single, married or widowed	2 When and where died	3 Sex	4 Age	5 Name, surname and rank or profession of father Name and maiden surname of mother	6 Cause of death, duration of disease and medical attendant by whom certified	7 Signature and qualification of informant and residence, if out of the house in which the death occurred	8 When and where registered and signature of registrar
81	Hector Cameron Club Master Married to Christina Hay	1893. January Tenth. oh 55m. P.M. III Douglas Street Glasgow	M	36 Years	Alexander Cameron, Gamekeeper (deceased) Margaret Cameron M. S. Kennedy (deceased)	Alcoholism 3 days As cert. by John Evan Brodie M.D. F.P.S.G.	John Cameron Cousin 28 Crownston St Robert Laing Assistant	1893. January 11th Glasgow. Robert Laing Assistant (Registrar)

The above particulars are extracted from a Register of Deaths for the **District** of **Blythswood**
in the **Burgh** of **Glasgow**
Given under the Seal of the General Register Office, New Register House, Edinburgh, on **22nd November 2000**

The above particulars incorporate any subsequent corrections or amendments to the original entry made with the authority of the Registrar General.

This extract is valid only if it has been authenticated by the seal of the General Register Office. If the particulars in the relevant entry in the statutory register have been reproduced by photography, xerography or some other similar process the seal must have been impressed after the reproduction has been made. The General Register Office will authenticate only those reproductions which have been produced by that office.

Warning
It is an offence under section 53(3) of the Registration of Births, Deaths and Marriages (Scotland) Act 1965 for any person to pass as genuine any copy or reproduction of this extract which has not been made by the General Register Office and authenticated by the seal of that office.

Any person who falsifies or forges any of the particulars on this extract or knowingly uses, gives or sends as genuine any false or forged extract is liable to prosecution under section 53(1) of the said Act.

RXD4(C)
493

Figure 5-3
Copy of Hector Cameron's death extract. Notice the death registered in Blythswood where we find him in the 1891 census. We will learn more about the value of the information on death certificates in chapter seven.

Census Search

You can search the 1881, 1891, and 1901 censuses at the same time, or you can use the check boxes at the top of the search form to search only selected censuses. Let's look for Hector Cameron in only the 1891 census. He was about age thirty-five in that year. Then click on the "Search" button.

This search produces two positive results: a thirty-six-year-old year old Hector in Tyree Argyll and a thirty-four-year-old Hector in Blythswood (see Figure 5-4). In this case it's an easy choice as we think our Hector lived in Blythswood. Print the results so you have a record for your files.

Let's assume that we were not so sure or we had more options. What could we do? This is where knowing other members in the household is valuable. In our case we know Hector's wife was Christina and that she was thirty-three in that year. We can substitute Christina's name for this search. This time it produces only one hit (see Figure 5-5). If there had been no hits or matches, we would have repeated the search using Christina's name shortened and followed by a wild card (*) because Christina could have easily used a variant spelling. If the person was in the same household, the GROS (General Register Office for Scotland) codes will match.

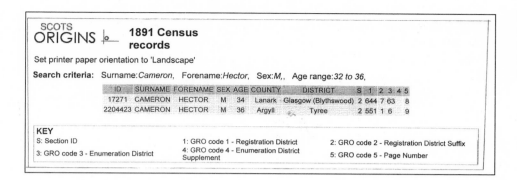

Figure 5-4
Display of two results of search on Scots Origins for thirty-five-year-old Hector Cameron in the 1891 census.

Figure 5-5
Display of results on Scots Origins for thirty-three-year-old Christina Cameron in 1891 census. Compare the Registration District and GROS codes to those of Hector Cameron in Figure 5-4. Because the codes match, Christina and Hector were on the same page of the census.

However, just because the codes match doesn't mean the two people were living in the same household. It just means that they were located on the same page of the census. If there are many people in the area with the same surname, the two names could be from different families. In our searches the numbers match. We are fairly confident that these people are husband and wife, so we order the scanned image of the census record. In this example the household was split across two pages of the census, with a couple of the servants listed on the second page. The split could just as easily have occurred among the members of the family. See Figure 5-6 to view the 1891 census extract for Hector and Christina Cameron.

For each census image you view, five page credits are deducted. Instead of using the 1891 census index and then using your page credits to view the images on the Scots Origins database, you can record the GROS codes from the 1891 census index for your ancestor and use that information to order the microfilm of the census at a Family History Center. You can then use your remaining page credits to search for other family information on the Scots Origins Web site. When you order the census from a Family History Center, you receive an entire microfilm of the census returns for the area and can view the records of your ancestor and his neighbors. You can also search at no additional charge for other potential family members who lived in the area. You will learn how to order census records on microfilm in chapter eight.

Other Searches

Other searches are available on the Scots Origins site. We have demonstrated two searches that can be done easily only at this Web site—a search for a death certificate and an index search of the 1891 census. You may also want to use Scots Origins

Figure 5-6
The 1891 census extract for Hector and Christina Cameron.

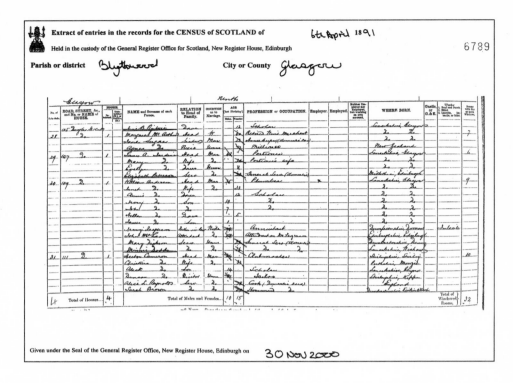

to access the 1901 census. Most of the other searches can be performed using the resources of the Family History Library and often at a much lower cost. Many of the FHL indexes are free, and when you have to order microfilm, the cost of short-term film rental is $3.25 to $4. This cost varies between Family History Centers because they may charge a notification fee. Remember, however, that some of these registers may already be in the permanent collection of your nearest Family History Center. In that case, your only cost will be for photocopying. You can find cost comparison tables at <www.rootsweb.com/~bifhsusa/sct-costs.html>. Regardless of cost, however, the Scots Origins Web site is better when searching for 1891 and 1901 census returns because the censuses are indexed on the Web site. It is also better if you are in a hurry (unless the films are already in the permanent collection of your nearest Family History Center) or when you are searching from home and do not have access to a Family History Center.

WHERE DO I GO FROM HERE?

Before you use the Scots Origins Web site, read the chapters in this book on civil registration, census, and church records so that you will know what you can access elsewhere. These chapters will also help you to understand what you see on the Scots Origins Web site and enable you to better interpret the results.

SIX

Library and Family History Center Resources

LIBRARIES

Public, private, and university libraries house many resources that can help you find more about your Scottish ancestors. In this chapter we suggest several resources that will greatly enhance your understanding of your ancestor and his environment.

Although you have probably been using school and public libraries all of your life, you may still need assistance. Each library in your area may catalog its materials differently, and some of the computerized catalog systems can be difficult to use. Ask if your local library has a genealogy collection, and if not, ask if another library in the area has one. If the library participates in the interlibrary loan program, find out how to order materials from other libraries and how much it costs to do so.

Most libraries have trained staff to assist you with your questions. The library may even have a librarian or research assistant who specializes in genealogy. Printed library guides also are available to help you find resources.

After you orient yourself to the general layout of the library, the first thing you should do is find a pamphlet or other guide that describes the library's cataloging system. Use the catalog to locate the books recommended on page 44. Many libraries now have their catalogs on the Internet, and they usually have help screens to assist you with finding materials. If your local library's catalog is online, you can use the catalog at home.

You should find answers to the following two questions:
1. Has someone else researched your family?
2. What happened where your ancestors lived?

Important

Has Someone Else Researched Your Family?

To find out if anyone has written a book, article, or biographical sketch about your family, begin with the sources listed below. Do not limit yourself to sources that deal specifically with Scottish families. Many Scottish pedigrees are in British and general family history books but not in the Scottish books.

Scottish family histories

Stuart, Margaret. *Scottish Family History: A Guide to Works of Reference on the History and Genealogy of Scottish Families.* 1930. Reprint, Baltimore, Md.: Genealogical Publishing Co., Inc., 1994. This has a good but dated description of how to research and write a family history in Scotland, by Sir James Balfour Paul. The bibliography is arranged by surname then locality identifier to differentiate many works of the same name.

Ferguson, Joan P.S. *Scottish Family Histories Held in Scottish Libraries.* Edinburgh, Scotland: Scottish Central Library. 1986. Contains more than two thousand printed and manuscript Scottish family histories held in seventy-six libraries and compiled from lists sent to the Scottish Central Library.

British family histories

Marshall, George W. *The Genealogist's Guide.* 1903. Reprint, Baltimore, Md.: Genealogical Publishing Co., Inc., 1998. This book indexes pedigrees that include at least three generations in the male line. All were published before 1903. Marshall's work was continued by John B. Whitmore.

Whitmore, John B. *A Genealogical Guide: An Index to British Pedigrees in Continuation of Marshall's Genealogist's Guide, 1903.* London: Society of Genealogists, 1953. Also published by Harleian Society as volumes 99, 101, 102, 104. Whitmore continued the work of Marshall. This book covers pedigrees published between 1900 and 1950. The work was continued by Geoffrey Barrow.

Barrow, Geoffrey B. *The Genealogist's Guide: An Index to Printed British Pedigrees and Family Histories, 1950–1975.* London: Research Publishing Co., 1977. Continuing the work of Marshall and Whitmore, Barrow's book indexes pedigrees published between 1950 and 1975.

Thomson, Theodore R. *A Catalogue of British Family Histories.* 3d ed. with addenda, London: Society of Genealogists, 1980. This book indexes British family histories published before 1980.

Worldwide family histories

You should also consult sources that list family histories in general. The following is one of the best:

Kaminkow, M.J., ed. *Genealogies in the Library of Congress: A Bibliography.* These volumes were reprinted by the Genealogical Publishing Co. in 2001. This source indexes several thousand genealogies, and not just British ones. It contains two volumes and two supplements. *A Complement to Genealogies in the Library of Congress: A Bibliography* provides an additional twenty thousand citations of sources not in the Library of Congress from forty-five libraries. Check all five of these volumes. If you find a book that interests you, you can usually obtain it by interlibrary loan. Many of these are not in the online catalog of the Library of Congress.

Idea Generator

Periodicals

Did someone write an article about your family? If so, he or she could have published it in a periodical anywhere in the world. Of course, individually searching all of the world's journals and magazines is impossible, but you can still find the articles you need.

The most important index to genealogical periodicals, including many Scottish ones, is Periodical Source Index, or PERSI. This index is produced by the Allen County Public Library in Fort Wayne, Indiana. This library holds the largest English-language genealogy and local history periodical collection in the world, with more than 3,200 current subscriptions and more than 4,100 titles. Individual articles are indexed in the *Periodical Source Index*. PERSI indexes surnames or places that appear in the titles of periodical articles; it is not an every-name index. PERSI tells in which periodical an article appeared. The *Periodical Source Index* is available in many libraries as a multivolume print collection or on CD-ROM. It is also available at Family History Centers (see the Family History Library section on page 48). You can purchase a copy on CD-ROM from Ancestry Publishing Company, or you can purchase a membership to Ancestry.com and search PERSI online at <www.ancestry .com>. If your library doesn't have the periodical you want, you can order a photocopy of the article from the Allen County Public Library. Obtain ordering information from <www.acpl.lib.in.us/database/graphics/order_form.html>.

After you've searched PERSI, find a periodical that covers the area where your ancestor lived. Family History Societies in Scotland often publish articles about the families who lived in the area. Most Scottish family history societies are members of the Scottish Association of Family History Societies (SAFHS). See the SAFHS Web site at <www.safhs.org.uk> and click on "Membership Lists" to see a listing of family history societies. Contact the society that covers your ancestor's area. You probably should join it. Ask about any periodicals they publish, and see if you can find back issues through your library.

Biographical sketches

Biographical sketches are written most often about more prominent ancestors. If your ancestor was famous, did anything noteworthy, or held a major office, search the following:

Anderson, William. *The Scottish Nation, or, The Surnames, Families, Literature, Honours, and Biographical History of the People of Scotland.* 1863. This three-volume set contains biographical sketches of prominent Scots. Some of the sketches are very detailed. Reprint, Bowie, Md.: Heritage Books, 1995 [7 vols.].

This source is a British series that describes many Scots:

Dictionary of National Biography. Oxford, England: Oxford University Press, 1995. This was originally published in sixty-three volumes and later updated with supplements. It is now available on CD-ROM (Oxford, England: Oxford University Press, 1995), which allows you to search for any name or place. It is very good for finding those involved in politics, government, law, church, army, and navy, but it also includes coverage of scholarship, literature, art, architecture, music, science, medicine, education, and philanthropy.

If your ancestor was of the nobility, check this source:

Paul, Sir James Balfour, ed. *The Scots Peerage*. 9 vols. Edinburgh, Scotland: David Douglas, 1904–14. This essential and authoritative work deals with the Peers of the Realm, and it also includes historical and genealogical information on the antecedents of the first peer, plus many collateral lines.

Reminder

Remember from chapter three that just because you have an easily identified Scottish name, a clan name, or a Peerage family, **do not under any circumstances assume that you are related to those with the same name.** You have to trace your Scottish line and identify each individual along the way. This book is designed to help you do that. Most family traditions of having a noble ancestor are not true since most noblemen did not emigrate. Contrary to popular belief, few nobles were disowned by family members for unacceptable behavior.

Current research

Once you have searched for published materials about your family, look for people who are currently researching your surname. Consult the following:

The British Isles Genealogical Register. England: Federation of Family History Societies, 1994. 2d ed., 1997. 3d ed., 2000. 1994, 1997 on microfiche. 2000 on CD-ROM. People throughout the world have submitted the names of their British Isles families to this register, known as the BIG R. They may have submitted their research interests to one or more of the editions. These three separate editions are not revisions of one another.

Johnson, Keith A. and Malcolm R. Sainty. *Genealogical Research Directory*. North Sydney, Australia: Genealogical Research Directory [published annually since 1980]. This is a worldwide directory of names that people are researching; it certainly has a strong emphasis on, but is not limited to, ancestors from the British Isles. Researchers may have submitted their ancestral names to any edition. Look through every volume.

What else should I look for?

When you locate any of the above sources, see how it is cataloged, then search that category for other materials. If you can't find a book in the library, ask the librarian if it is available by interlibrary loan. Even more sources are included in the Family History Library section of this chapter.

What Happened Where Your Ancestor Lived?

Once you have found information about your family, look for information about the places where your family lived. You should learn something about the general history of Scotland as well as the specific area where your ancestor lived.

University libraries should have several books about Scottish history. Small public libraries usually do not have large Scottish history collections, but a librarian can help you order materials through interlibrary loan. For a good general overview, see Tom Steel's *Scotland's Story: A New Perspective* (London: Collins, 1984).

Two good social history books are T.C. Smout's *A History of the Scottish People*,

Library/Archive Source

1560–1830 (London: Collins, 1969) and *A Century of the Scottish People, 1830–1950* (London: Collins, 1986).

Once you know some general Scottish history, try to find out what happened in your ancestor's local area. For example, later in this chapter we research a family who lived in Crieff. More than one history has been written on this parish. A particularly good history of the parish is Alexander Porteous's *The History of Crieff From the Earliest Times to the Dawn of the Twentieth Century*. It contains accounts of Crieff not found anywhere else. Look for a book about your ancestor's town or parish. If you can't find one, see if you can find a history of the county.

Three wonderful collections of Scotland parish histories (The Statistical Accounts of Scotland) are available. See the sidebar for details on these works. The first two sets, written in the 1790s and 1840s, are the most valuable for researchers. The parish entries were written usually by the local minister and can give highly detailed pictures of the local communities. The accounts are sometimes very biased; compare the two accounts to learn lots of valuable information about your community. The Statistical Accounts may be available in book form at a large library. If you don't find them in a library near you, that is no problem. These remarkable resources are available on the Internet at <http://edina.ac.uk/cgi/StatAcc/StatAcc.cgi>. Some of the Statistical Accounts are available for circulation from the Family History Library, as discussed later in this chapter.

Again, don't forget Scottish periodicals. Go back to PERSI and search for the place where your ancestor lived. After you have searched PERSI, look for any periodical that covers the locality, and search through all the issues you can find. If

Reminder

STATISTICAL ACCOUNTS OF SCOTLAND

Sinclair, John, ed. *The Statistical Account of Scotland, 1791–1799*. 21 vols. Reprint, edited by Donald J. Withrington and Ian R. Grant, Wakefield, England: EP Publishing Ltd., 1979. Available at the FHL on 322 fiche beginning with number 6026527, but it no longer circulates to Family History Centers. In this reprint all the parish accounts for individual counties are printed together for the first time, with a new introduction and index in each volume.

The New Statistical Account of Scotland. Edinburgh, Scotland: William Blackwood and Sons, 1845. Available through the FHL; see the table in the section "Using the Family History Library Catalog."

The Third Statistical Account of Scotland is a series edited by Alexander Mather and published by Collins of Glasgow in 1987. Currently twenty-six volumes, this twentieth-century series is not complete for all counties. It is available at the Family History Library.

Scanned images of pages from *The Statistical Account of Scotland* and *The New Statistical Account of Scotland* are available online at <http://edina.ac.uk/cgi/StatAcc/StatAcc.cgi>.

your library doesn't have a periodical for the area where your ancestor lived, check the listing of family history societies on the Scottish Association of Family History Societies Web site at <www.safhs.org.uk>.

In addition to using the catalog of your local library, you may want to browse the library shelves in a few important areas. If your library uses the Dewey decimal system, look in the 929 Genealogy section and the 941 Scottish History section of the library. If the library uses the Library of Congress system, genealogy is in the CS section and Scottish history materials are in the DA area. Do not, however, restrict yourself to history and genealogy! Use the catalog to look for travel and tourism books for Scotland. Search for books about your ancestor's occupation. Look for biographies and diaries of other people so that you can find out more about what life was like in Scotland when your ancestors were there. See what magazines and journals are available. If you want a general overview of a subject, you might try materials in the children's or young adults' department. Books written for young people can be valuable for beginning research on old occupations because the books usually give a good overview and have illustrations of tools and of people practicing their trades. Walk through the entire library. Be creative!

If you have more than one library in your area, visit as many of them as possible. You will become adept at finding materials you need. When you complete your library searches, move on to resources of the Family History Library.

ACCESSING THE RESOURCES OF THE FAMILY HISTORY LIBRARY

Can you imagine a giant library devoted entirely to helping you trace your family history? The Family History Library is this dream come true.

What Is the Family History Library?

The Genealogical Society of Utah (GSU) was founded in 1894 to gather genealogical records, and it started a library to house these records. The collection eventually became so large that a new building was needed. The library is called the Family History Library (FHL) and is located directly west of Temple Square in downtown Salt Lake City at 35 North West Temple Street, Salt Lake City, Utah 84150 [telephone (801) 240-2331].

The Family History Library is the largest genealogical library in the world. **It is a private library operated by The Church of Jesus Christ of Latter-day Saints, but it is open free of charge to the general public,** and visitors are not proselytized.

Money Saver

What Does the Family History Library Have?

In 1938 the Genealogical Society of Utah began microfilming records all over the world. These microfilms form the bulk of the collection of the Family History Library. The FHL now has more than 2,500,000 rolls of film. It also has a massive collection of books, periodicals, microfiche, compact discs, maps, resource guides, and many other materials to help you find your ancestors.

The FHL has two types of records:

- Previous research: family history research already done by others

- Original documents: records created at the time of an event in your ancestor's life. Most of the records date from 1550 to 1920.

The Family History Library's largest collections are for the United States and the British Isles. The FHL has five floors: The top floor houses administrative offices, and the other four floors are public research areas. Two floors are dedicated to U.S. research; one floor, to British Isles research; and one floor, to international research. Even more resources are kept in the nearby Joseph Smith Building. Staff is always available to assist you. Library staff also answer questions by telephone. For help with your Scottish research questions, call (801) 240-2367. Try to keep your request simple; do not give long-winded explanations of your questions.

If you have an opportunity to travel to the Family History Library, by all means do so. The many records there make it hard to tear yourself away.

Do I Have to Travel to Salt Lake City to Use the FHL Resources?

No! In 1964, a system of Family History Centers (FHCs) was established to help people living outside the Salt Lake City area. There are currently almost four thousand Family History Centers. They are usually in local church buildings of The Church of Jesus Christ of Latter-day Saints. The FHCs are open to all researchers, regardless of religious affiliation.

Many of the resources of the Family History Library are available through the Family History Centers. Some Family History Centers also have limited access to the Internet, and all of them are expected to be connected in the near future. The most important reason for visiting a Family History Center is to access the microfilmed copies of original Scottish records, many of which are not available anywhere else. For a small fee, you can borrow almost all of them through your local Family History Center. The FHL does not lend other materials and is not a part of the interlibrary loan system, so if the FHL has a book you want that has not been microfilmed, see if other libraries have copies. Your local librarian can help you locate and borrow the books you need. If you cannot locate the materials elsewhere, you may want to use the photocopying service of the Family History Library. You should be able to obtain a "Request for Photocopies" form at any Family History Center.

A list of Family History Center locations and telephone numbers is available from the Family History Library at the address and phone number listed above. You also can find addresses, telephone numbers, and operating hours of Family History Centers worldwide at <www.familysearch.org/eng/Library/FHC/frameset_fhc.asp>. Contact an individual FHC to verify the hours of operation before you visit. If you have more than one FHC in your area, be sure to visit them all. All Family History Centers have the same access to the resources of the Family History Library, but each FHC has different resources of its own.

All Family History Centers are staffed by volunteers. Some are quite knowledgeable, and some are beginners. However, the Family History Library publishes a large number of useful research guides to help you use its resources. It also produces blank pedigree charts, family group record forms, and research logs for recording

For More Info

VISITING THE FAMILY HISTORY LIBRARY

A trip to the Family History Library in Salt Lake City definitely can speed up your research process. If you have never been there and want lots of practical, current advice to use in planning or on your trip, then read *Your Guide to the Family History Library* by Paula Stuart Warren and James W. Warren, Betterway Books, 2001.

your family information. All forms and research guides are available at minimal cost; many are free. They are listed in the *Family History Publications List* (item 34083). You can get this free publication from the FHL, the FHCs, and the Salt Lake Distribution Center. You can read and download many of the publications at no charge on the FamilySearch Web site in the "Research Helps" section at <www.familysearch.org/Eng/Search/Rg/frameset_rhelps.asp>.

Several free research guides are mentioned in this chapter. You can find them at Family History Centers and on the FamilySearch Web site. All of them can be ordered from the Salt Lake Distribution Center, 1999 West 1700 South, Salt Lake City, Utah 84104 [telephone (801) 240-3800].

The Salt Lake Distribution Center is also the place to purchase the Family History Library Catalog, Vital Records Index—British Isles, Pedigree Resource File, and many other valuable resources.

GETTING STARTED AT A FAMILY HISTORY CENTER

When you walk into any Family History Center, you should first find out what information is already available about your family. Go to a computer in the Family History Center and use the FamilySearch program. Although you may have already used FamilySearch online, the DOS-based version at Family History Centers has different search capabilities. Use FamilySearch to access several databases, including the three databases that we discuss here: the International Genealogical Index, Ancestral File, and the Family History Library Catalog. These and the other databases can give you a good start.

International Genealogical Index

One of the most valuable resources at any Family History Center (and anywhere else for that matter) is the International Genealogical Index. The IGI is a large database indexing more than seven hundred million names primarily from birth, baptism, and marriage records. Deaths and burials are rarely indexed. **The International Genealogical Index is more valuable for Scottish research than it is for research anywhere else in the world.** This is because most baptisms and marriages from Scotland's pre-1855 parish registers (officially known as the Old Parochial Registers) and most births and marriages from the first twenty years (1855–1875) of Scottish civil registration records are indexed on the IGI. See more about parish registers and civil registration records in subsequent chapters.

Research Tip

IGI is available in three versions. Family History Centers have a DOS version in the FamilySearch program on computer. You can get a free four-page printed guide called *Using the Compact Disc Version of the International Genealogical Index* to help you learn to use it. The IGI is also available in Family History Centers on microfiche. Although the microfiche version is out of date, you can still use it for some of your Scottish research. A third choice is to access International Genealogical Index on the Internet at <www.familysearch.org>. We used this version in chapter four. Now let's see the DOS version of the FamilySearch program. Compare the results with the ones we obtained in chapter four.

Using the DOS version of the IGI at Family History Centers

Even without instructions, the IGI is easy to use. Each screen provides instructions, so follow them. Let's use the International Genealogical Index to see if we can find Margaret Kay who was born in 1855 and her sister Christina Kay who was born in 1857. We know that they were born in the County of Perth; we don't know the name of the parish.

At a computer at the Family History Center, use the DOS version of Family-Search and follow the instructions below to see how we located the Kay children. See if you get the same results as those shown in our examples. Then use the same process to find your own ancestors.

Exercise: Finding births

1. From the opening screen of the FamilySearch program, press enter, then select "International Genealogical Index" (Figure 6-1).

Step By Step

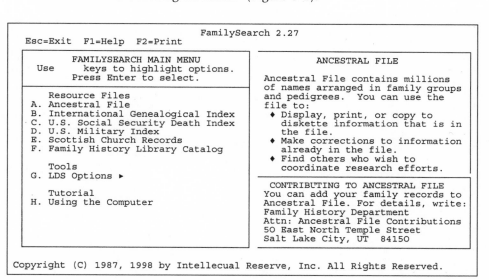

```
                        FamilySearch 2.27
 Esc=Exit  F1=Help  F2=Print

      ┌─────────────────────────────┐ ┌─────────────────────────────┐
      │     FAMILYSEARCH MAIN MENU   │ │        ANCESTRAL FILE        │
      │ Use     keys to highlight options.│ │                          │
      │     Press Enter to select.  │ │ Ancestral File contains millions│
      │                             │ │ of names arranged in family  │
      ├─────────────────────────────┤ │ groups and pedigrees.  You can use the│
      │     Resource Files          │ │ file to:                     │
      │ A. Ancestral File           │ │ ♦ Display, print, or copy to │
      │ B. International Genealogical Index│ │   diskette information that is in│
      │ C. U.S. Social Security Death Index│ │   the file.                │
      │ D. U.S. Military Index       │ │ ♦ Make corrections to information│
      │ E. Scottish Church Records  │ │   already in the file.       │
      │ F. Family History Library Catalog│ │ ♦ Find others who wish to    │
      │                             │ │   coordinate research efforts.│
      │     Tools                   │ ├─────────────────────────────┤
      │ G. LDS Options ▶            │ │ CONTRIBUTING TO ANCESTRAL FILE│
      │                             │ │ You can add your family records to│
      │     Tutorial                │ │ Ancestral File. For details, write:│
      │ H. Using the Computer       │ │ Family History Department    │
      │                             │ │ Attn: Ancestral File Contributions│
      │                             │ │ 50 East North Temple Street  │
      │                             │ │ Salt Lake City, UT  84150    │
      └─────────────────────────────┘ └─────────────────────────────┘

 Copyright (C) 1987, 1998 by Intellecual Reserve, Inc. All Rights Reserved.
```

Figure 6-1
FamilySearch main menu.
Reprinted by permission. © 1987, 1998 by Intellectual Reserve, Inc.

2. From the International Genealogical Index screen, press enter, then select the region you want. Select "British Isles" for all Scottish research.
3. This takes you to the surname search menu (see Figure 6-2). To search for births, select "Individual Search."
4. Enter the name of the person you are seeking. Entering an approximate year helps; otherwise you have to scan through all occurrences of that name for all years. Type in "Margaret Kay," event year "1855." This screen is shown in Figure 6-3. We also need to search two files: the Main File and the Addendum. Almost all of the civil registration indexes are in the Main File, so we use it first. Press the F12 key to start the search.
5. The program produces search results. See Figure 6-4; it shows several Margaret Kays born in 1855, but only one in Perth. The index indicates that her father was James Kay. Press enter on that name to see the details. The details (in Figure 6-5) show that she was born 13 October 1855 and that her parents were James Kay and Isobel Brough.

Figure 6-2
Surname Search Menu. *Reprinted by permission. ©1980, 2000 by Intellectual Reserve, Inc.*

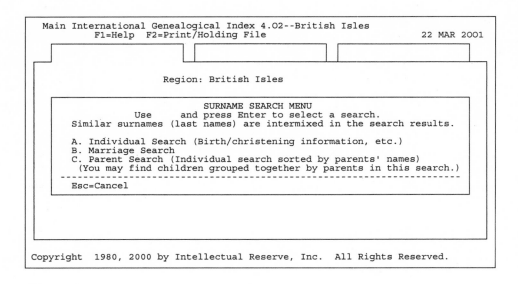

```
Main International Genealogical Index 4.02--British Isles
      F1=Help  F2=Print/Holding File                    22 MAR 2001


                    Region: British Isles

        +-------------------------------------------------------+
        |                SURNAME SEARCH MENU                    |
        |      Use      and press Enter to select a search.     |
        |  Similar surnames (last names) are intermixed in the search results. |
        |                                                       |
        |    A. Individual Search (Birth/christening information, etc.)  |
        |    B. Marriage Search                                 |
        |    C. Parent Search (Individual search sorted by parents' names)  |
        |    (You may find children grouped together by parents in this search.)  |
        |  ---------------------------------------------------  |
        |    Esc=Cancel                                         |
        +-------------------------------------------------------+



Copyright  1980, 2000 by Intellectual Reserve, Inc.  All Rights Reserved.
```

Figure 6-3
Individual Search screen. Enter the name of your ancestor. *Reprinted by permission. ©1980, 2000 by Intellectual Reserve, Inc.*

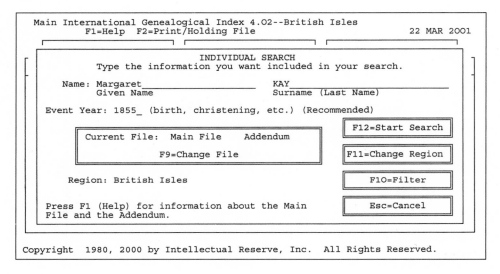

```
Main International Genealogical Index 4.02--British Isles
      F1=Help  F2=Print/Holding File                    22 MAR 2001

     +-----------------------------------------------------------+
     |                   INDIVIDUAL SEARCH                       |
     |      Type the information you want included in your search.  |
     |                                                           |
     |   Name: Margaret_____  KAY_____    |
     |         Given Name                Surname (Last Name)     |
     |                                                           |
     |  Event Year: 1855_ (birth, christening, etc.) (Recommended)  |
     |                                          +-------------+  |
     |   +-------------------------------+      | F12=Start Search |
     |   | Current File: Main File  Addendum |  +-------------+  |
     |   |        F9=Change File          |    +-------------+  |
     |   +-------------------------------+      | F11=Change Region |
     |                                          +-------------+  |
     |   Region: British Isles                  +-------------+  |
     |                                          |  F10=Filter |  |
     |  Press F1 (Help) for information about the Main  +-------------+  |
     |  File and the Addendum.                  |  Esc=Cancel |  |
     |                                          +-------------+  |
     +-----------------------------------------------------------+

Copyright  1980, 2000 by Intellectual Reserve, Inc.  All Rights Reserved.
```

Exercise: Finding other children

6. We can find the names of other children born to these parents by pressing the F8 key—Parent Search. Whenever you find a birth entry, always press F8 to search for others in the family.

7. A screen pops up and asks if we want to do a parent search for James Kay and Isobel Brough or if we want to enter names for a different couple (other parents). Press enter on the first option.

8. The "Parent Search" screen (shown in Figure 6-6) appears and allows you to make changes, enter additional information, filter your search, etc. Simply press the F12 key to begin the search.

9. All children who are indexed on the International Genealogical Index and whose parents were recorded as James Kay (or variations) and Isobel Brough (or variations) now appear in one list. As you can see in Figure 6-7, a Christina Kay is on the list. She was born in 1857, so we have found Christina without conducting a separate search for her. But there are many more children, too.

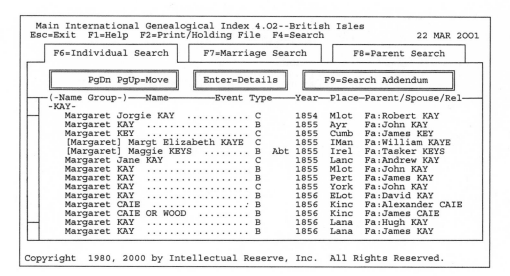

```
Main International Genealogical Index 4.02--British Isles
Esc=Exit  F1=Help  F2=Print/Holding File  F4=Search          22 MAR 2001
  ┌──────────────────┐  ┌──────────────────┐  ┌──────────────────┐
  │ F6=Individual Search │  │ F7=Marriage Search │  │ F8=Parent Search │
  └──────────────────┘  └──────────────────┘  └──────────────────┘
   ┌──────────────────┐  ┌──────────────┐  ┌──────────────────────┐
   │ PgDn PgUp=Move    │  │ Enter=Details │  │ F9=Search Addendum    │
   └──────────────────┘  └──────────────┘  └──────────────────────┘
   (-Name Group-)────Name──────Event Type──Year─Place─Parent/Spouse/Rel──
   -KAY-
      Margaret Jorgie KAY .......... C    1854  Mlot  Fa:Robert KAY
      Margaret KAY ................. B    1855  Ayr   Fa:John KAY
      Margaret KEY ................. C    1855  Cumb  Fa:James KEY
      [Margaret] Margt Elizabeth KAYE C   1855  IMan  Fa:William KAYE
      [Margaret] Maggie KEYS ....... B Abt 1855  Irel  Fa:Tasker KEYS
      Margaret Jane KAY ............ C    1855  Lanc  Fa:Andrew KAY
      Margaret KAY ................. B    1855  Mlot  Fa:John KAY
      Margaret KAY ................. B    1855  Pert  Fa:James KAY
      Margaret KAY ................. C    1855  York  Fa:John KAY
      Margaret KAY ................. B    1856  ELot  Fa:David KAY
      Margaret CAIE ................: B    1856  Kinc  Fa:Alexander CAIE
      Margaret CAIE OR WOOD ........ B    1856  Kinc  Fa:James CAIE
      Margaret KAY ................. B    1856  Lana  Fa:Hugh KAY
      Margaret KAY ................. B    1856  Lana  Fa:James KAY

Copyright 1980, 2000 by Intellectual Reserve, Inc.  All Rights Reserved.
```

Figure 6-4

Individual Search results. *Reprinted by permission. ©1980, 2000 by Intellectual Reserve, Inc.*

```
Main International Genealogical Index 4.02--British Isles
Esc=Exit  F1=Help  F2=Print/Holding File  F4=Search          22 MAR 2001
  ┌──────────────────┐  ┌──────────────────┐  ┌──────────────────┐
  │ F6=Individual Search │  │ F7=Marriage Search │  │ F8=Parent Search │
  └──────────────────┘  └──────────────────┘  └──────────────────┘
   ┌──────────────────┐  ┌─────────────────────────────────────────┐
   │ PgDn PgUp=Move    │  │▌KAY, Margaret                            │
   └──────────────────┘  │                              Sex: F       │
   (-Name Group-)────Name │ Father:   James KAY                      │
   -KAY-                  │ Mother:   Isobel BROUGH                  │
      Margaret Jorgie KAY │                                          │
      Margaret KAY ...... │ Birth                                    │
      Margaret KEY ...... │ 13 Oct 1855                              │
      [Margaret] Margt Eliz│ Crieff, Perth, Scotland                 │
      [Margaret] Maggie KEY│                                         │
      Margaret Jane KAY .. │ Source Batch Number                     │
      Margaret KAY ...... │ C113421                                  │
      Margaret KAY ...... │                                          │
      Margaret KAY ...... │                                          │
      Margaret CAIE ..... │                                          │
      Margaret CAIE OR WOOD│  ┌──────────────────┐  ┌──────────────┐│
      Margaret KAY ...... │  │ Enter=See Full Record │  │ Esc=Cancel ││
      Margaret KAY ...... │  └──────────────────┘  └──────────────┘│
                           └─────────────────────────────────────────┘
Copyright 1980, 2000 by Intellectual Reserve, Inc.  All Rights Reserved.
```

Figure 6-5

Individual Search details. You can press the enter key from this screen to find the Family History Library call number of the original source. *Reprinted by permission. ©1980, 2000 by Intellectual Reserve, Inc.*

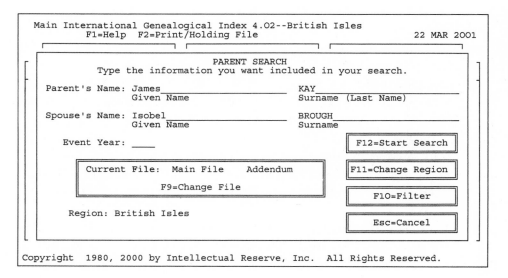

```
Main International Genealogical Index 4.02--British Isles
       F1=Help  F2=Print/Holding File                        22 MAR 2001

                        PARENT SEARCH
          Type the information you want included in your search.

   Parent's Name: James_____   KAY_____
                  Given Name              Surname (Last Name)

   Spouse's Name: Isobel_____    BROUGH_____
                  Given Name              Surname

      Event Year: ____                    ┌──────────────────┐
                                          │ F12=Start Search  │
      ┌──────────────────────────────┐   └──────────────────┘
      │ Current File: Main File  Addendum │┌──────────────────┐
      │                               │   │ F11=Change Region │
      │        F9=Change File         │   └──────────────────┘
      └──────────────────────────────┘   ┌──────────────────┐
                                          │ F10=Filter        │
       Region: British Isles             └──────────────────┘
                                          ┌──────────────────┐
                                          │ Esc=Cancel        │
                                          └──────────────────┘
Copyright 1980, 2000 by Intellectual Reserve, Inc.  All Rights Reserved.
```

Figure 6-6

Parent Search screen. Here you enter or modify the names of the parents. *Reprinted by permission. ©1980, 2000 by Intellectual Reserve, Inc.*

Figure 6-7
Parent Search results. *Reprinted by permission. ©1980, 2000 by Intellectual Reserve, Inc.*

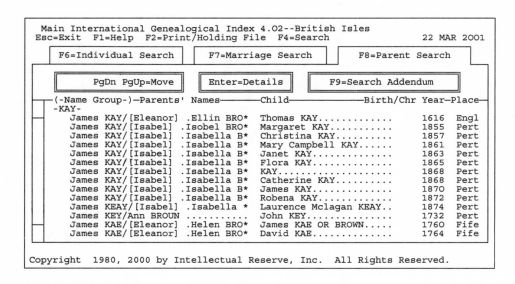

```
 Main International Genealogical Index 4.02--British Isles
 Esc=Exit  F1=Help  F2=Print/Holding File  F4=Search        22 MAR 2001

   ┌ F6=Individual Search ┐  ┌ F7=Marriage Search ┐  ┌ F8=Parent Search ┐

      ┌─── PgDn PgUp=Move ───┐  ┌ Enter=Details ┐  ┌ F9=Search Addendum ┐

 ┌─(-Name Group-)─Parents' Names────────Child─────────Birth/Chr Year─Place─
 │ -KAY-
 │   James KAY/[Eleanor] .Ellin BRO*  Thomas KAY.............  1616  Engl
 │   James KAY/[Isabel]  .Isobel BRO*  Margaret KAY...........  1855  Pert
 │   James KAY/[Isabel]  .Isabella B*  Christina KAY..........  1857  Pert
 │   James KAY/[Isabel]  .Isabella B*  Mary Campbell KAY......  1861  Pert
 │   James KAY/[Isabel]  .Isabella B*  Janet KAY..............  1863  Pert
 │   James KAY/[Isabel]  .Isabella B*  Flora KAY..............  1865  Pert
 │   James KAY/[Isabel]  .Isabella B*  KAY....................  1868  Pert
 │   James KAY/[Isabel]  .Isabella B*  Catherine KAY..........  1868  Pert
 │   James KAY/[Isabel]  .Isabella B*  James KAY..............  1870  Pert
 │   James KAY/[Isabel]  .Isabella B*  Robena KAY.............  1872  Pert
 │   James KEAY/[Isabel] .Isabella *  Laurence Mclagan KEAY..  1874  Pert
 │   James KEY/Ann BROUN  ..........  John KEY...............  1732  Pert
 └   James KAE/[Eleanor] .Helen BRO*  James KAE OR BROWN.....  1760  Fife
     James KAE/[Eleanor] .Helen BRO*  David KAE..............  1764  Fife

 Copyright  1980, 2000 by Intellectual Reserve, Inc.  All Rights Reserved.
```

10. We want to know the exact date and place of birth for all of these children. We can press enter on each person's name and then copy the information, or we can create and print a holding file that will show us all names at once. To create a holding file, press F2—Print/Holding File. Select "Create or add entries to the Holding File."

11. The list of names appears on the screen. Use the arrow keys to move up and down the list. Press enter on each name you want to include in your holding file. Press the F12 key when you are finished; this brings you back to the "Print/Holding File" screen.

12. You can print your list, save it to a diskette, or return to add entries to the file. Select "Print/Holding File." When the next screen appears, make sure an X is next to "Include source information." The source information usually tells you the film number on which to find the microfilm of the original record. Press F12—OK. Our holding file is printed in Figure 6-8. At the next screen, you have options again to save your holding file to a diskette or return to search the index. Press the escape key to return to the listing of children.

Exercise: Finding marriages

13. From the listing of children screen, we can find the parents' marriage information. Press the F7 key. This gives you the option of searching for the marriage of James Kay and Isabella Brough, a child, or a new marriage couple (different parents). Press enter on James Kay and Isabella Brough.

14. At the "Marriage Search" screen, notice that only the name of the man appears. You may want to insert an approximate year of marriage to avoid having to scroll through all marriages of all James Kays for all years. We don't know when the couple was married, so we estimate 1850 and enter that year in "Event Year."

15. A listing of marriages for all men named James Kay who were married in the British Isles in 1850 appears. This shows too many James Kays, so let's filter our search to try to narrow our choices. Press F7 again.

```
International Genealogical Index (R) - Version 4.02

22 MAR 2001                            HOLDING FILE ENTRIES                            Page 1
================================================================================================

                                                                      Batch and Source
Names (Sex)                      Event Date/Place                     Information
------------------------------------------------------------------------------------------------
Margaret KAY (F)...................... B: 13 Oct 1855                 Ba: C113421      +
   Father: James KAY                      Crieff, Perth, Scotland     So: 6035516 REGISTER
   Mother: Isobel BROUGH

Christina KAY (F)..................... B: 11 Jul 1857                 Ba: C113831      +
   Father: James KAY                      Monzievaird And Strowan, Perth,  So: 6035516 REGISTER
   Mother: Isabella BROUGH                Scotland

Mary Campbell KAY (F)................. B: 6 Jul 1861                  Ba: C113781      +
   Father: James KAY                      Madderty, Perth, Scotland   So: 6035516 REGISTER
   Mother: Isabella BROUGH

Janet KAY (F)......................... B: 5 Sep 1863                  Ba: C113831      +
   Father: James KAY                      Monzievaird And Strowan, Perth,  So: 6035516 REGISTER
   Mother: Isabella BROUGH                Scotland

Flora KAY (F)......................... B: 16 Oct 1865                 Ba: C113831      +
   Father: James KAY                      Monzievaird And Strowan, Perth,  So: 6035516 REGISTER
   Mother: Isabella BROUGH                Scotland

KAY (F)............................... B: 29 Jan 1868                 Ba: C113831      +
   Father: James KAY                      Monzievaird And Strowan, Perth,  So: 6035516 REGISTER
   Mother: Isabella BROUGH                Scotland

Catherine KAY (F)..................... B: 29 Jan 1868                 Ba: C113831      +
   Father: James KAY                      Monzievaird And Strowan, Perth,  So: 6035516 REGISTER
   Mother: Isabella BROUGH                Scotland

James KAY (M)......................... B: 16 Jun 1870                 Ba: C113801      +
   Father: James KAY                      Methven, Perth, Scotland    So: 6035516 REGISTER
   Mother: Isabella BROUGH

Robena KAY (F)........................ B: 22 Nov 1872                 Ba: C113421      +
   Father: James KAY                      Crieff, Perth, Scotland     So: 6035516 REGISTER
   Mother: Isabella BROUGH

Laurence Mclagan KEAY (M)............. B: 26 Oct 1874                 Ba: C113801      +
   Father: James KEAY                     Methven, Perth, Scotland    So: 6035516 REGISTER
   Mother: Isabella BROUGH

================================================================================================
        Events:  A=Adult Chr  B=Birth  C=Chr  D=Death  M=Marr  S=Misc  N=Census  W=Will
   Batch/Source: Ba=Batch  So=Source  Pr=Printout  F#=Film Number  P#=Page Number  O#=Ordinance Number
Special Symbols: * Film contains no additional information.  ^ Some information was estimated or altered.
                 @ Names and relationships of others stated in source.  & Parents listed may not be birth parents.
                 > Additional information from Special Services, Temple Dept.  # Additional relatives listed in source.
                 + Additional sources for batch.
================================================================================================
Copyright © 1980, 2000 by Intellectual Reserve, Inc.  All rights reserved.
```

Figure 6-8
Printout of holding file from International Genealogical Index showing children of James Kay and Isobel Brough. *Reprinted by permission. ©1980, 2000 by Intellectual Reserve, Inc.*

16. We now have the option of beginning a new search or modifying our previous one. Select "Modify previous search" and press F10—Filter.

17. We can narrow our search in many ways. We can filter, for example, by the spouse's name, or we can filter to include only people married in a certain location. Let's filter by location. Since all of the children were born in Perthshire, we hope that James Kay and Isabella Brough were married there. Select "Locality" and press F12—Finalize.

18. At the screen containing the names of all counties in the British Isles, use the arrow keys to move to "Scotland," and press enter on "Perth." Press the F12 key once to continue and again to finalize.

19. The results show James Kay and Isabell Brough at the top of the list. We were lucky! Press enter to see the details of the marriage, and press enter again to see the full details of the record. They were married 2 November 1855 in Crieff, Perth. Write down the information, print it, or add the entry to your

holding file and print another page that contains the listing of all children and the parents' marriage.

IGI summary

You can find an individual birth, the births of several children in a family, and the marriages of a child's parents by using the individual search, the parent search, and the marriage search.

Special note: One parent search is not always sufficient. Even if you know the maiden name of the wife, conduct a search without the maiden name because sometimes the original records give the wife's maiden name and sometimes they do not. The parent searches with and without the maiden name produce different results. Remember also that surnames and given names can change among entries. Furthermore, sometimes the name of one parent is incorrectly indexed. These six parent searches usually do the trick:

1. given name and surname of the father; given name and maiden surname of the mother
2. given name and surname of the father; given name of the mother
3. given name of the father; given name and maiden surname of the mother
4. surname of the father; maiden surname of the mother
5. given name and surname of the father only
6. given name and maiden surname of the mother only

Technique

Here's a great example of why you should try all of these parent searches. We will see later in the census records (see chapter eight) that the Kay family had a child named Isabella born about 1860 in the parish of Madderty, Perthshire. We did not find her when we did our first parent search, so she does not appear in our list of holding file entries in Figure 6-8 on page 55. It took several parent searches to find her. We located her when we searched with only the given name and maiden surname of her mother, Isabella Brough. Isabella Kay was born 12 August 1859 in the parish of Madderty. Her parents are listed in the Scottish Church Records index as Isabella Brough and James *Hay*.

You can filter any search to restrict your results by spelling, location, or a range of years. In most cases, you do not want to filter by exact surname spelling because you don't know how the clerk spelled the surname on every record. Remember that if you filter by county and one of the events did not occur in that county, you may not find all of the family births or marriages.

In addition to the other filtering options, you can filter a marriage search by name combination. If we had used this option when searching for the marriage of James Kay and Isabella Brough, the program would have searched for James Kay in combination with his spouse's given name. To enter Isabella's name, select "Name Combination," then enter "Isabella" in the space for spouse's given name. We are not given the option of entering the spouse's surname. The list of results will include all men named James Kay (Key, Keay, etc.) who married a woman named Isabella (Isobel, Isabell, etc.).

If you use the DOS version at a Family History Center, please note that once you have searched the Main File, you should search the Addendum. A search of the Addendum, using the family in our example, did not reveal any additional children for James Kay and Isabella Brough.

Save all printouts from the International Genealogical Index to help you locate the family in the original records. In chapter seven we use the printouts we made from the DOS version.

Explore the International Genealogical Index for each of your Scottish ancestors. If your ancestor's names are included in the IGI, it can help you find dates and places of births, baptisms, and marriages; names of spouses; and names of parents. It is the fastest and most efficient way to begin your research. The IGI is an extremely valuable research tool, but remember that it is only an index. Verify every entry by checking the original source.

Vital Records Index—British Isles

This index contains birth, baptism, and marriage records extracted from records in the British Isles, including records from several nonconformist chapels in Scotland. Many of these are not yet on the International Genealogical Index. **The Vital Records Index—British Isles is available on compact disc.** Many Family History Centers have it. A new edition is planned and may be released by the time this book is published; make sure that the Family History Center has the most recent edition. You can purchase your own copy at <www.familysearch.org> or by contacting the Salt Lake Distribution Center. The Vital Records Index—British Isles contains similar information to that on the IGI, but it has even better search capabilities. For example, when you find your ancestor in a church record, the program can show you all other names that were indexed from that church. Always check the Vital Records Index—British Isles after you check the International Genealogical Index.

CD Source

Ancestral File

Ancestral File contains lineage-linked information on more than twenty million people. With Ancestral File, you can print pedigree charts and family group sheets of families contained in the database. Free published guides on Ancestral File are available in most Family History Centers. Two of these are *Contributing Information to Ancestral File* and *Correcting Information in Ancestral File*. Ancestral File is available in the FamilySearch program at Family History Centers. You can also use it on the Internet at <www.familysearch.org>. Please note that Ancestral File online is different from that at Family History Centers because the online version does not contain the names of living people.

Search Ancestral File for all of your family names. Each screen contains instructions. You may find complete family group records and pedigrees extending many generations. If someone has submitted information about your ancestors, this can save you years of work. However, the information you obtain is only as good as the research of the person(s) who submitted it. The data in this database still has many errors. If you find a name that interests you, record the name and address of the submitters. Contact each of them to find out what documentation they have and whether they have found any new information about the family. You can also

Tip

submit your own research to the database. Because Ancestral File is used all over the world, it is a good way to let others know about your family.

Pedigree Resource File

This resource contains lineage-linked files submitted by individuals over the Internet through the Share My Genealogy option on the FamilySearch Web site. Although most of the families in Pedigree Resource File are American families, the database is continually expanding. You can submit your own pedigree, and it will appear on a future compact disc. Pedigree Resource File contains similar information to that in Ancestral File except that it may contain source information for the names and dates in the pedigrees. Unlike Ancestral File, if two or more people submit pedigrees that contain the same ancestral names, the records are not merged. Each person's records are maintained separately. Again, heed this warning: The family information you find is only as good as the research of the person who submitted it. Verify all sources shown in a record and if the submitter did not include sources, contact him to ask about the source.

Pedigree Resource File is available on several compact discs. It is indexed on the FamilySearch Web site, so search it for the names of all of your ancestors. When you find a reference to your family, see if a Family History Center near you has Pedigree Resource File on compact disc. If not, order any CD you want from the Salt Lake Distribution Center.

Other Family Files

The Family History Library has many other files containing pedigrees submitted by individuals. Soon a new system will combine the best features of Ancestral File and Pedigree Resource File. At the time of this writing, the name of the system has not been announced, but it may be available by the time you read this. See the FamilySearch Web site for details.

Combined Search

In addition to searching each of the above files individually, you can search the International Genealogical Index, Ancestral File, Vital Records Index—British Isles, and Pedigree Resource File all at once. Go to the FamilySearch Web site at <www.familysearch.org> and click on "Search for Ancestors." If you are searching for a common name, the number of search results can overwhelm you. If you are too specific, however, you may obtain no results. Experiment by starting with just the name of your ancestor. Then, one at a time, add details (such as father's name, approximate date of the event, etc.) to narrow your search.

Family History Library Catalog

Mastering the Family History Library Catalog is your key to finding research materials available in the Family History Library. This catalog is available in four formats. You can purchase a copy of the Windows version on compact disc through the Salt Lake Distribution Center. If you will be doing much research, this is highly recommended. A similar Web version of the catalog is online at <www.familysearch.org>. At Family History Centers, the catalog is available in a DOS version on

Important

compact disc, a Windows version on compact disc, on microfiche, and on the Internet (if the Family History Center has an Internet connection). Note that the Windows version and the Web version are periodically updated and revised, so their search capabilities may be different from those described below.

The DOS-based version of the Family History Library Catalog is especially useful when searching through a record (such as civil registration) that has a large number of microfilms or microfiche. When you look at such a record, you can press the F3 key to insert a keyword. For example, if the series of films contains records for all counties, you can go directly to Perth by pressing F3 and typing "Perth." You can also type in a number to go directly to a particular date or microfilm number. The F3 option is not shown on the screen, so you have to remember to use it on your own. The DOS version of the catalog is more convenient than the Windows version when printing, because the DOS version prints the title description and the microform numbers on the same page. It is also the only version where you can search by computer number. Use the Windows version when you want to search by the author or title of a record, for a book by its call number, or to search the entire catalog by keyword. The Web version allows you to search by author but not by title of a record. The biggest advantage to the Windows and Web versions is that they contain recent acquisitions that are not in the DOS-based catalog. Learn to use all of the versions of the Family History Library Catalog.

You can search the catalog in several ways. The DOS, Windows, microfiche, and Web versions of the catalog have different search capabilities, **so not all searches are available in every format.**

Warning

- Surname: The Family History Library has a large number of books containing previous research. Search by your ancestor's surname to find histories and biographies of your family.
- Locality: Items are arranged by locality if the records are from a place or about a place. Search by the name of the place where your ancestor lived to find records pertaining to the locality. On the Web and Windows versions of the catalog, the locality search is called the "place" search. The DOS version of the catalog has two ways to search by locality: "Locality Search" and "Locality Browse." "Locality Browse" is especially useful when you are unsure of the spelling of a place name, because it allows you to browse through an alphabetical list.
- Subject: Records are organized by broad topics such as religions, ethnic groups, occupations, types of records, etc. Search by subject when you want to find general information about a topic.
- Author/Title: If you know the author or title of a book, this may be the quickest way to see if the Family History Library has it. Search by author or title when you want to see if the book you are seeking is available on microfilm or microfiche from the Family History Library.
- Film/Fiche Number: If you know the Family History Library's microfilm or microfiche number for the record you want, you can locate it quickly by searching with the number.
- Call Number: If you know the Family History Library call number for a book or periodical, you can search for the record using this number.

- Keyword: This search is only available in the Windows version of the catalog. With a keyword search, you can often find records that aren't cataloged the way you expect.
- Computer Number: Each record title in the catalog has a computer number. Sometimes the computer number covers an entire collection of records (such as all films of the 1851 census of Scotland). Other times it covers only one record. Searching by computer number in the DOS version of the Family History Library Catalog is the fastest way to bring up a series of records. Computer numbers are still used in all of the Family History Library's Research Outlines. They are not used in this book because computer numbers are not used in the Windows or Web versions of the catalog.

For the DOS version of the catalog, two free four-page guides are available. These are *Using the Compact Disc Version of the Family History Library Catalog* and *Using the Microfiche Version of the Family History Library Catalog*. These are available at most Family History Centers.

Step By Step

Using the Family History Library Catalog

Let's search the Family History Library Catalog. First, use the catalog to look for published family histories or genealogies that have been done by someone else. A distant relative may have already done much of your work for you. Then look for local histories that may contain details about your ancestor or his community. After looking through the many secondary and compiled sources, you are ready to look at original records on microfilm. The majority of the Family History Library's microfilm and microfiche materials are accessible to researchers at Family History Centers for a small fee.

Fiche/Film numbers. Use the catalog to search by fiche/film number for the following resources. These are some of the same references listed in the "Libraries" section of this chapter. If you are using the Family History Library Catalog at a Family History Center, look to see if the FHC has each item in its permanent collection. If not, you may wish to order missing ones so that they will be readily on hand any time you need to refer to them. Please note that one microfiche number may be assigned to a single fiche or to a set of fiche. Before ordering, look to see how many microfiche are covered by the fiche number you want.

Marshall, *The Genealogist's Guide*, FHL film 0496451

Whitmore, *A Genealogical Guide*, FHL fiche 6054492

Barrow, *The Genealogist's Guide*, FHL fiche 6026284

Anderson, *The Scottish Nation, or, The Surnames, Families, Literature, Honours, and Biographical History of the People of Scotland*: Volumes 1–2, FHL fiche 6026306, Volume 3, FHL film 0896898

Lee, *Dictionary of National Biography*, FHL fiche 6051261 (a set of 376 fiche)

Paul, *The Scots Peerage*, FHL films 104157–104161

Some of the most important resources for finding out about Scottish places are the Statistical Accounts of Scotland. To get started you need *The New Statistical*

The New Statistical Account of Scotland			
Vol.	County	FHL Film #	FHL Fiche #
1	Edinburgh		6026383
2	Berwick, East Lothian, West Lothian		6026707
3	Roxburgh, Peebles, Selkirk	990219	
4	Dumfries, Kirkcudbright, Wigtown	990219	
5	Ayr, Bute		6026708
6	Lanark		6026709
7	Renfrew, Argyle		6026710
8	Dumbarton, Stirling, Clackmannan		6026403
9	Fife, Kinross		6026716
10	Perth		6026717
11	Forfar, Kincardine	990223	
12	Aberdeen		6026718
13	Banff, Elgin, Nairn		6026719
14	Inverness; Ross and Cromarty		6026720
15	Sutherland, Caithness, Orkney, Shetland		6026721

Account of Scotland (1845). It is organized by county, and it's available from the Family History Library. Find the county you want in the table above, and order that fiche or film on indefinite loan at your nearest Family History Center so that it will always be available for you to consult. (If an account is available on both microfilm and microfiche, we have listed only the microfiche number. This is because microfiche ordered at a Family History Center automatically becomes part of that FHC's permanent collection; microfilms do not.)

In addition to the sources listed above, consult the following British biographical compilations to see if your family is listed.

British Biographical Archive. This is a collection of biographies that was originally contained in 324 different sources from all of Great Britain. It is easy to use. All of the biographies have been assembled into one alphabetical sequence, so you just need to find the fiche number that contains your ancestor's surname. This series is available on FHL fiche numbers 6029709–735. A second series (FHL fiche numbers 6140789-814) contains even more sources, so be sure to look at both sets.

British and Irish Biographies, 1840–1940. This is a large set of biographies on thousands of microfiche. These biographies were published between 1840 and 1940, so they are about people who lived earlier than that. There is an every-name index on fiche 6342001; however, the fiche no longer circulates to Family History Centers. You can only search the index at the Family History Library in Salt Lake City or at another library that holds this set.

Surname. Now search by surname to find books written about your family. Look for all of your ancestral surnames. **If you find too many listings for an ancestor's surname, you can limit the search in the DOS version of the catalog by pressing the F6 Key—Add Keyword.** Add the name of a location or some other keyword. For example, if we do a surname search for the name Kay, we get fifty-one matches for that spelling and many others for variant spellings. If we press F6 and enter the keyword "Scotland," we get only three matches. As you read each entry, look to see if the family lived in the same area of Scotland and during the same time period

Tip

Subject Headings Used in the Family History Library Catalog	
Almanacs	Manors
Archives and Libraries	Maps
Bibliography	Medical Records
Biography	Merchant Marine
Business and Commerce Records	Migration, Internal
Cemeteries	Military History
Census	Military Records
Chronology	Minorities
Church Directories	Names, Geographical
Church History	Names, Personal
Church Records	Naturalization and Citizenship
Civil Registration	Newspapers
Colonization	Nobility
Correctional Institutions	Obituaries
Court Records	Occupations
Description and Travel	Officials and Employees
Directories	Orphans and Orphanages
Dwellings	Pensions
Emigration and Immigration	Periodicals
Encyclopedias and Dictionaries	Politics and Government
Ethnology	Poorhouses, Poor Law, etc.
Folklore	Population
Gazetteers	Postal and Shipping Guides
Genealogy	Probate Records
Guardianship	Public Records
Handwriting	Religion and Religious Life
Heraldry	Schools
Historical Geography	Social Life and Customs
History	Societies
Inventories, Registers, Catalogues	Statistics
Jewish History	Taxation
Jewish Records	Town Records
Land and Property	Visitations, Heraldic
Language and Languages	Voting Registers
Law and Legislation	Yearbooks

as your ancestors. The catalog also lists related surnames that appear in each book, but please note that the Family History Library Catalog gives only the primary surnames covered in the book.

Locality or Place. This is the most important search feature of the Family History Library Catalog. To use the microfiche version of the catalog, you must know how records are arranged. Locations are arranged from large to small. This means that records for the country are followed by records of each county, and then by the parishes and towns within them. All records pertaining to Scotland are listed first. After the section for Scotland, all counties are listed alphabetically. Records for the individual parishes and towns are at the end of each county's listings. To find records for the Parish of Crieff in Perthshire, look in the catalog under Scotland, Perth, Crieff.

Each locality's records are organized by subject. See the sidebar for subject headings used in the Family History Library Catalog. It is very helpful to be familiar with these headings. For example, notice that there is no "Wills" heading. Part of the reason for this is that in Scotland you would usually look for a "testament" instead of a "will." If you want to find your ancestor's testament, look under the category "Probate Records." All probate records, including testaments and inventories, are included in that category. There is also no "Parish Registers" heading. To find out if the FHL has any parish registers for your ancestor's parish, look under "Church Records." This is because the term *parish registers* applies only to the registers of baptisms, marriages, and burials of the Church of Scotland. It does not include any other records of that church or any nonconformist records. The category "Church Records" includes them all. Parish registers for the Parish of Crieff, Perthshire are cataloged under Scotland, Perth, Crieff, Church Records.

Start by looking for records in your ancestor's town or parish, then look for records of the county. **Don't forget to search for records of Scotland and also of Great Britain.** For example, are there any published indexes to church records of the area? To find out, look under Scotland, [county], [parish], Church Records, Indexes. Then look for Scotland, [county], Church Records, Indexes. Then look under Scotland, Church Records, Indexes.

Reminder

Practice using the locality search feature of the Family History Library Catalog to find records for the places where your ancestors lived. Most Family History Center volunteers should be able to assist you.

Does the Family History Library have materials that are not listed in its catalog?

Yes. The library holds millions of books, periodicals, microfilms, and microfiche covering a wide variety of subjects. The Family History Library Catalog tells you the names and volume numbers of these materials, but it does not give detail about what is in them. For example, the Family History Library Catalog lists the name of a family history society's journal and gives a brief description about it, but the catalog does not tell you the names of the individual articles published in the periodical. Therefore, **many important materials lie buried in the Family History Library's collections.** To assist researchers with finding these resources, Frank Smith and a team of volunteers spent many years going through the books, periodicals, and microforms in the FHL's collections. They produced an inventory called *Smith's Inventory of Genealogical Sources* which contains references to obscure genealogical information found in numerous printed sources and microfilms in the Family History Library.

Important

Smith's Inventory is arranged by place, then by subject. A "General" listing covers subjects that do not apply to a particular place. Each subject listing is followed by a range-of-years listing so that you can find materials for the subject covering a certain time period. The years from 1900 back to 1500 are divided into fifty-year periods. From 1500 to Saxon times (1066), they are divided into hundred-year periods. You, therefore, can search for detailed information such as a pedigree of a family that lived in Monzie, Perthshire, or an article about coal miners in Lanark from 1700 to 1750.

Smith's Inventory of Genealogical Sources: Scotland is available on FHL microfiche 6110528, a set of eighteen fiche. After the sources for Scotland in general, each county is listed in alphabetical order. The counties are labeled at the top of

Smith's Inventory of Genealogical Sources: Scotland	
v. 1, pt. 1 Scotland general (subjects)	v. 18 Kirkcudbright
v. 1, pt. 2 Scotland general (range of years)	v. 19 Lanark
v. 2 Aberdeen	v. 20 Midlothian, Edinburgh
v. 3 Angus	v. 21 Moray
v. 4 Argyll	v. 22 Nairn
v. 5 Ayr	v. 23 Orkney
v. 6 Banff	v. 24 Peebles
v. 7 Berwick	v. 25 Perth
v. 8 Bute	v. 26 Renfrew
v. 9 Caithness	v. 27 Ross & Cromarty
v. 10 Clackmannan	v. 28 Roxburgh
v. 11 Dumbarton	v. 29 Selkirk
v. 12 Dumfries	v. 30 Shetland
v. 13 East Lothian	v. 31 Stirling
v. 14 Fife	v. 32 Sutherland
v. 15 Inverness	v. 33 West Lothian
v. 16 Kincardine	v. 34 Wigton
v. 17 Kinross	

the fiche. For example, the County of Perth is on fiche number 14 of the set. The fiche is labeled "Smith's Inventory of Genealogical Sources: Scotland. From Peebles to Renfrew." On this fiche are 181 pages of sources for Perth. Figure 6-9 is an example of only one of them. The page contains some occupational lists for Perthshire for the years 1851 to 1900. Notice that there is a section about weaving in the Parish of Crieff on pages 173–177 of the book *The History of Criefe From Earlist Times* [*sic*]. If your ancestor had been a weaver, you might want to read this account about weaving, even if he didn't live in Crieff. The Family History Library does not lend books, so search the Family History Library Catalog by title or call number to see if the history is also available on microfiche or microfilm. If not, try to obtain it through a local library. If you can't find the book elsewhere, you can complete a Request for Photocopies form at a Family History Center and have the Family History Library staff photocopy the pages you need. One way or another, you can get it! *Smith's Inventory* can save you many hours of research and enable you to find materials that otherwise would be virtually impossible to locate.

SUMMARY

Step two of the research process is to use resources available in libraries in your area. Become familiar with public, private, and university libraries and get to know the librarians, who can help you further your research. Next, go to a Family History Center. Learn to use the International Genealogical Index, Vital Records Index—British Isles, Ancestral File, Pedigree Resource File, the Family History Library Catalog, and *Smith's Inventory of Genealogical Sources*. With these resources, you can find countless references to your ancestors' lives in Scotland. Then spend the majority of your research time using microfilms of original documents. Most of

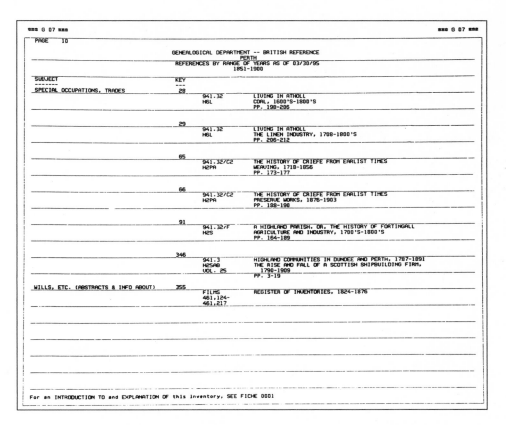

Figure 6-9
Sample page from *Smith's Inventory of Genealogical Sources: Scotland. From Peebles to Renfrew. Reprinted by permission. © 1994 by Intellectual Reserve, Inc.*

these are held only at the Family History Library, but they are accessible to you through any Family History Center.

WHERE DO I GO FROM HERE?

The examples in the rest of this book will give you good practice in reading and analyzing Scottish documents. We follow the paper trail left by a Scottish family through several generations. By reading each chapter, you will learn how to find the fascinating details of your own ancestors' lives.

If you are researching the time period from the mid-1800s to the present, you will want to begin with civil registration and census records. See chapter seven to get started.

If you are researching ancestors who were born before the mid-1800s, you should start your search with the parish registers of the Church of Scotland. However, be sure to read the chapters on civil registration and census because some of your ancestors may have lived long enough to be included in these records. The civil registration and census chapters also give you important background information about Scottish records and how to evaluate them. Furthermore, even if your ancestor left Scotland long before the mid-nineteenth century, he probably left family and friends behind. Learn to use the more recent records to find those people. You can even use these records to find cousins living in Scotland today.

Take this book with you to your nearest Family History Center, and let's find our Scottish ancestors.

SEVEN

Civil Registration

S ince 1 January 1855, births, marriages, and deaths in Scotland have been recorded by governmental authorities. This system of recording is called "civil registration." More than 90 percent of all births since that date have been registered, and the percentages are even higher for marriages and deaths. The system has grown increasingly more effective so that in the twentieth century very few events went unrecorded. Copies of all records are centralized at New Register House, the General Register Office for Scotland in Edinburgh. The officer responsible for the records is the Registrar General. The birth, marriage, and death certificates contain valuable family information that may not be available anywhere else. Best of all, they are indexed for the whole of Scotland. This can help you locate a Scottish ancestor when you don't know exactly where he lived. Civil registration records are an extraordinary resource for family historians.

WHY WERE THE RECORDS CREATED?

The recording of baptisms and marriages in parish registers was introduced in Scotland by the Provisional Council of the Scottish clergy held in Edinburgh in 1551. Errol in the County of Perth has the oldest known surviving parish register—it began in 1553—but many Scottish registers did not start until much later. Death (burial) registers were proposed in 1574, with lists of the deceased to be given to the Court of Sessions annually. This was because the salaries of the Lords of the Session were raised by levies on the estates of those dying. The Lords of the Session used people other than the clergy to obtain the names of the deceased, so the clergy had no incentive or requirement to keep burial registers, and in many parishes they were not actively kept until much later. Over the following century various Acts of the General Assembly of the Church of Scotland and the Privy Council were aimed at the keeping of parish registers. They were obviously not always successful, as many registers in Scotland didn't start until the eighteenth century.

These registers were legal documents that showed relationships and dated events.

This was important because the beneficiaries had to prove relationships to inherit land in Scotland (see more on this in chapter ten). This process often required the use in courts of law of extracts from the parish registers. At the other end of the social spectrum, the registers were needed for proving a person's parish of origin for the administration of the parish poor law.

In the nineteenth and twentieth centuries the Church of Scotland went through a number of schisms. When groups broke away from the Church of Scotland, there was no longer just one place for recording births, baptisms, marriages, deaths, and burials in Scotland.

The Registration of Births, Deaths, and Marriages (Scotland) Act of 1854 introduced civil registration to Scotland. It became effective on 1 January 1855. This moved the recording responsibility from the church to the state. By this time, Scotland had had seventeen years to observe the practice of the English civil registration system. They made modifications to improve on the information sought, thus providing a bonanza for genealogists. In practice, though, the system proved too burdensome, so modifications were made. More on the specifics and the changes appears later in this chapter.

Notes

HOW WERE THE RECORDS CREATED?

From 1 January 1855 a district registrar has been "authorized and required to inform himself carefully of every Birth and Death which shall happen within this Parish or District." His duties besides gathering the facts are to determine if (1) the event occurred within the boundary of his territory, (2) the time allowed has not been exceeded, and (3) the informant is legally qualified to provide the needed information.

In 1855 the system began with 1,027 registration districts. The district registrars kept duplicate sets of registers. The registers were examined for clerical errors and omissions annually by a district examiner who visited the registrars in his district. One set of registers was then forwarded to the Registrar General in Edinburgh. The other set remained with the district registrar, preserved in his custody in a fireproof safe.

The informant and the registrar were required to sign the actual record after checking it for accuracy—meaning, of course, whatever facts the informant provided. These facts are not necessarily the truth. We tend to think of many of our ancestors as having been illiterate, so how could they have read the register to verify that the event was accurately recorded? Actually, the literacy rate at this time was higher in Scotland than in England. For example, in 1855, 88 percent of the men and 77 percent of the women were able to sign their own names at the time of their marriage. This does not necessarily mean that they could read, but it's a good indication that perhaps they could. However, in the civil registration time period, most of your Scottish ancestors could read.

Births

From 1855 to 1965, a birth had to be recorded in the district where the birth occurred. If there were questions about the district boundaries and whether the event should be registered in a particular district, appeals were made to the sheriff of the county.

Births were to be recorded within twenty-one days, otherwise a financial penalty not to exceed forty shillings was levied. The informant had to be someone who had personally attended the birth. The qualified informants were

1. parents (preferred)
2. person in charge of the child
3. "occupier" of house or institution [included guardian, master, governor, keeper, steward, house surgeon, superintendent (of gaol, prison or house of correction, workhouse, hospital, lunatic asylum, or public charitable institution)]
4. nurse present at birth
5. if none of the above were available, then anyone having knowledge of the particulars.

To ensure accuracy, the informants were asked to come to the registrar with the facts of the birth and, if possible, to bring with them an Extract of Marriage for that child's parents, a copy of which would have been given to the parents at the time of their marriage. As a rule, no one under the age of fourteen was to be asked to be an informant.

If a registrar knew of the birth and asked the family to attend to register the birth, personally or in writing, and the family on two occasions did not, then the case was reported to the sheriff. This also applied if the birth was not registered within the prescribed twenty-one days. The sheriff then issued a warrant compelling attendance. Cases of failing to register or giving false information were reported to the Procurator Fiscal. If the parents left the district before registering the birth, the registrar was entitled to request that the informants return to register the event. If they did not return, the sheriff was notified. The sheriff could issue a warrant to compel their return.

In Scotland, personal attendance by the informant in the registrar's office was required. If the district of birth was different from the usual district of residence of the parents, the recording registrar would notify the registrar in the place of usual residence. The notification was done in writing within eight days. The birth was then recorded again in the district of residence. Obviously, this process resulted in the double registration of some births. This can be very useful, for example, in the case of a female domestic servant working outside her home and delivering a child where she worked. In this case, the address of her parents would have been regarded as the woman's usual place of residence. Since 1965 the parents have been able to choose whether to register the birth where it occurred or in their place of usual residence, but not both.

After three months the birth could not be registered without the authority of the sheriff. If anyone tried to register an event after three months without the authority of the sheriff, a higher fine not to exceed five pounds was levied. After three months the registrar expected an additional fee of two shillings to be paid to him for late registration.

Marriages

Under Scots law, a marriage could have been constituted by mutual consent by a male over age fourteen and a female over age twelve. However, marriages between couples this young were rare. In 1929 the minimum age for marriage was raised to sixteen. Scots law has no requirement for parental consent.

Regular marriages

Scotland has two main categories of marriage—regular and irregular. (See examples later in this chapter.) **A "regular" marriage in Scotland is one solemnized by a minister of religion in the presence of two witnesses after the Proclamation of Banns** (or the Publication of Notice, since 1879). Note that "a minister of religion" is required, but the marriage does not have to occur in the Church of Scotland.

\di'fin\ *vb*

Definitions

Between 1854 and 1 January 1879, a regular marriage required the Proclamation of Banns on two consecutive Sundays. This means that on two consecutive Sundays the ministers in the church of the bride and the church of the groom called out the details of the intended marriage. This gave people in both locations the opportunity to object to the marriage due to any legal reason why the marriage should not have occurred. If someone knew, for example, that the groom or bride was already married or that the couple was too closely related to be married, he would make this information known. If the minister knew the couple well, or if others whom he trusted provided information that there were no impediments to the marriage, he could proclaim the banns on only one Sunday, and the certificate to marry could be issued forty-eight hours later. Afterward, the minister performed the ceremony, usually in the church of the bride. The registrar was present at all weddings within his district. He recorded the marriage in the marriage register after he received his fee and payment for travel expenses.

Public opinion frowned upon irregular marriages. Yet not all couples wanted to have banns called in church. Some considered it too embarrassing. This issue was addressed by a Marriage Notices Act allowing one or both parties to obtain a Publication of Notice from the registrar. This means that instead of the ministers publicizing the marriage, the registrar did so. Since 1 January 1879, a regular marriage requires the Proclamation of Banns or Publication of Notice.

To obtain a Publication of Notice, the person intending to marry must state his name, conjugal condition (bachelor, spinster, widow, widower), occupation, age, and residence. The notice states the name of the person giving notice and the name of the person whom he intends to marry. The notice also contains a statement regarding perjury for giving false information. Both parties must have resided in Scotland for at least fifteen days prior to the notice.

When the notice is complete, it is posted in the registrar's office. Anyone has seven days to appear personally and lodge with the registrar a written and signed objection to the marriage. Following the Proclamation of Banns or Publication of Notice, the registrar in the district where the marriage will occur can issue a Marriage Schedule. This is an important legal document that needs to be presented to the presiding minister to be completed with care and accuracy at the time of the ceremony. If there is a legal impediment to the couple's marriage, the Marriage Schedule is not issued. If the objection relates to a statutory requirement (e.g., not residing in the district for fifteen days), then the issuance of the Marriage Schedule is suspended until the problem is resolved with the sheriff or sheriff substitute of the county.

To summarize, before a registrar can issue a Marriage Schedule, the couple has to present

1. a Certificate (or Certificates) of Proclamation of Banns,
2. a Registrar's Certificate (or Registrar's Certificates) applicable to both parties verifying the Publication of Notice by the registrars, or
3. a Certificate of Due Proclamation of Banns from one party and a Registrar's Certificate from the other

At the wedding, the couple, the minister, and two witnesses sign the Marriage Schedule. The married couple must, within three days, either deliver or mail the schedule to the registrar of the parish or district. A fine is assessed if the schedule is not delivered to the registrar.

When the registrar receives the Marriage Schedule, the contents are copied into the two registers. The schedules for each year are numbered consecutively by the registrar. A marriage memo book is used to account for all Marriage Schedules issued. The Marriage Schedules and the duplicate register are transmitted annually by the district examiner to the Registrar General for preservation at the General Register Office in Edinburgh.

The Marriage (Scotland) Act of 1938, which took effect on 1 July 1939, made it possible for a couple to have a civil wedding performed by an authorized registrar instead of a wedding performed by a minister of religion. This act also had a major effect on irregular marriages.

Irregular marriages

Definitions

An "irregular" marriage was any marriage of consent between a couple that was not performed by a minister. Any couple could be married with no notice to anyone else and no waiting period. The only legal requirement for an irregular marriage was that both parties had to consent to the marriage. Nobody had to perform a ceremony for them, and nothing else was necessary. Because no minister or other witness was required, these marriages can be difficult to prove. Over time, irregular marriages became less and less acceptable.

The British Parliament outlawed irregular marriages in 1754 with the introduction of Lord Hardwicke's Marriage Act, but this act did not apply to Scotland. After that time, many English couples eloped to Scotland to obtain a quick and easy marriage. In 1856 the passage of Lord Brougham's Marriage Act required at least one of the marriage partners to reside in Scotland for twenty-one days. This made it more difficult for the English and Irish to elope to Gretna Green and the other Scottish-border marriage sites.

If a Scottish couple had an irregular marriage, how could the parties prove that they were legally married? Evidence of consent was required for the marriage, and the evidence could be written or oral. Documentary evidence was usually a simple written declaration that the couple accepts each other as husband and wife. If the marriage was by declaration (oral), two witnesses were required. The couple could make a joint application to the sheriff or sheriff substitute within three months, and a warrant was issued if the marriage was recognized. The marriage was then recorded by the Registrar upon payment of the appropriate fees. After Lord Brougham's Marriage Act in 1856, this was the usual method of registering an irregular marriage. An irregular marriage could also be registered by obtaining an Extract of Conviction from a Justice of the Peace or other magistrate. Alternatively, an Extract of a Decree of Declarator could be obtained from a court. Either extract could be used to record the marriage with the registrar.

No irregular marriage after the Marriage (Scotland) Act of 1938 (which came into effect on 1 July 1939) is valid, but couples have another alternative for quick marriage. They can get married by a license issued by the sheriff. The license is void if the marriage does not take place within ten days. To obtain the license, both parties have to meet the following requirements:

1. The parties have to apply in person.
2. One party has to have a usual place of residence in Scotland or has to have lived in Scotland for the fifteen days immediately preceding the application.
3. No legal impediment to the marriage exists.
4. The situation is such that Proclamation of Banns or Publication of Notice is not possible prior to the marriage, and some other unusual circumstance (e.g., illness) is in place that keeps the couple from respecting the normal procedures.

Deaths

Deaths had to be registered in the parish or district in which the death occurred, regardless of where the person usually resided. Since 1 January 1966 the death can be registered where the event occurred or at the normal place of residence of the deceased. The preferred informant is a relative who was present at the death or at least visited the deceased during the last illness. If this is not possible, then the occupier of the house or institution is the informant. If all else fails, anyone with knowledge of the particulars can be the informant.

Deaths occurring in a house are to be registered within eight days, with a financial penalty for not doing so. Upon registering the death, the registrar gives the informant a death certificate to be handed to the undertaker so he can complete the burial. The undertaker is required prior to interment to deliver the death certificate to the custodian of the churchyard, cemetery, or crematorium or to the superintendent of interments. If a person is buried without the necessary certificate, the person in charge of the burial place is required to report the event to the registrar within three days.

If registering the death is delayed until the calendar year after the event (e.g., a person drowns and the body is not found until much later), two entries are made in the civil registration indexes—one in the year of death and one in the year of registration. The index for the year of death points you to the actual registration of the death.

Register of Corrected Entries

Under normal circumstances if a clerical error or an error of fact is found on a certificate, the error is neatly crossed out with a single line and the corrected information is inserted. No erasures are to be made. The corrections can be made only with the intervention of the district examiner or the sheriff.

However, a Register of Corrected Entries exists. (See a death extract from this register later in this chapter.) Appropriate records for insertion in this register, again kept in duplicate, are

- Warrant of the sheriff
- Extract of a marriage in the case of legitimation
- Schedule D: minister recording birth; following a baptism
- Schedule E: registering birth of child; parents do not recognize sacrament of baptism
- Schedule F: court ruling on paternity of an illegitimate child
- Result of Precognition
- Circular from the Registrar General regarding a case of bigamy
- Divorce
- Declarator of legitimacy or illegitimacy
- Register of death on a sheriff's warrant, omitted at the time, after a lapse of twelve years (a rare occurrence)

Important

Why Should I Order a Civil Registration Extract?

A certified copy of the content of a register is known as an extract, which is a legal document admissible as evidence. **All extracts contain a lot of genealogically important information.** Using these extracts, you can find your ancestor's name, occupation, and date and place of birth; his parents' names, including his mother's maiden name, and in most time periods the parents' date and place of marriage; information about former marriages; his spouse's name and the date and place of their marriage; the date and place of his death; his cause of death; his residences; and much more.

Ideally, you will obtain birth, marriage, and death extracts for all members of the family because together they can give you a more complete picture of your family. However, this can involve considerable expense, so try to get as many as you can reasonably afford. To locate your family in the census you may need extracts for events that occurred near census years.

To obtain the extracts, use the national indexes to births, marriages, and deaths.

BIRTH, MARRIAGE, AND DEATH INDEXES

Birth, marriage, and death indexes for Scotland are available in more than one index. The most easily accessible index is available on the Scots Origins database, but this index is also the most expensive. (See chapter five.) Most births and marriages from 1855 to 1875 are indexed on the International Genealogical Index (see chapters four and six). For records after 1875, the indexes you probably should use most frequently are the ones available on microfilm. Although the microfilmed indexes give only the name and not the number of the registration district, you can easily find this number. The following descriptions apply to the microfilmed indexes.

Birth Indexes

All indexes are arranged in alphabetical order by surname and given name. Next to the child's name is the name of the parish or district where the birth occurred and the entry number. Surnames beginning with *Mc* or *Mac* are indexed at the end of the letter *M*.

Time Period	Index Changes	Format
1855–1865		Handwritten indexes
1866–1905		Printed indexes
1906–present	1929 and later: mother's maiden name added 1966: registration number of parish or district added	Computer indexes

Warning: The registration districts added after 1966 may be different from earlier years.

Marriage Indexes

Marriage indexes provide the surname and given name, the parish or district of the marriage, and the entry number of the event. If the names of both spouses are known, look up both names in the index. The district and entry number needs to match on both entries, otherwise you don't have the correct individuals.

Time Period	Index Changes	Format
1855–1865 (male)		Handwritten indexes
1855–1863 (female)	Index provides maiden name, with married name(s) recorded in brackets	Handwritten indexes
1864–1865 (female)	Surname of previously married woman not recorded.	Handwritten indexes
1866–1965	Females do not have married surname recorded. 1929 and forward: Surname of spouse added.	Printed indexes
1966–present	Number of parish of registration district added.	Computer indexes

If a woman had been married more than once and she informed the registrar of this, which usually happened, then her marriage is included under all surnames with her other names in brackets.

Death Indexes

All indexes are alphabetical by surname and given name. They provide the district and entry numbers for the event.

What Should I Know Before Using Civil Registration Indexes?

You need to know the name of your ancestor and the approximate year of the event. If your ancestor's name is a common one, you need to know the name of the parish

Time Period	Index Changes	Format
1855–1865 (male)		Handwritten indexes
1855 (female)	Married woman indexed under her married name; maiden name shown beside it.	Handwritten indexes
1856–1858 (female)	No maiden name recorded for married woman.	Handwritten indexes
1859–1865 (female)	Indexed under her married name (with maiden name beside) and under her maiden name (with no indication of married name).	Handwritten indexes
1866–1965	Age at death added. Married women indexed under her maiden and married names. Widows sometimes reverted to the maiden name and may not have been indexed under the married name.	Printed indexes
1966–present	1966 and forward: Registration number of district or parish added. 1974 and forward: Maiden surname of the deceased's mother added.	Computer indexes

or district where the event occurred, so you can distinguish your ancestor from others of the same name. Before using the indexes on microfilm or at the Scots Origins Web site, be sure to have on hand a gazetteer or a list of Scottish parishes and counties. A good parish list is the "Index of Scottish Parishes" on pages 1–31 of the *Register of Births, Marriages and Deaths of Scotland* (FHL fiche 6035516). If you are certain of the county in which the event occurred, you can photocopy a list of parishes for only your county of interest. These county lists are found in the same register. When you find an unfamiliar place in a civil registration index, look up the place to see where it is located. An alternative list can be found online at the Web site of the General Register Office for Scotland in the "Family Records" section. This item, in Adobe Acrobat format, provides a complete list of all parishes and registration districts with counties, appropriate reference numbers, and how they have changed over time. This file is online at <www.gro-scotland.gov.uk/gros web/grosweb.nsf/pages/files/$file/old_opr.pdf>.

Using the Civil Registration Indexes at a Family History Center

Most Scottish births and marriages from 1855 to 1875 are indexed in the International Genealogical Index. Three separate civil registration indexes are also on microfilm: the birth index, the marriage index, and the death index. The names are indexed by year for the entire country. Males and females are indexed separately. The indexes are available on microfilm for 1855–1955 for births and 1855–1956 for marriages and deaths. The film numbers are as follows:

Birth indexes	1855–1949	FHL films 0103244 to 0103341
	1950–1955	FHL films 0203372 to 0203377

Marriage indexes	1855–1950	FHL films 0103539 to 0103584
	1950–1956	FHL films 0203378 to 0203384
Death indexes	1855–1949	FHL films 0103394 to 0103475
	1950–1956	FHL films 0203385 to 0203391

Using the *Register of Births, Marriages and Deaths of Scotland*

The *Register of Births, Marriages and Deaths of Scotland* was compiled by the British Reference staff at the Family History Library. The *Register* is on FHL microfiche 6035516. It lists the microfilm numbers of those civil registration records of births, marriages, and deaths for Scotland that are held by the Family History Library. These microfilms include the indexes mentioned above as well as the actual certificates of birth, marriage, and death for the years 1855–1875, 1881, and 1891.

The *Register* begins with the "Index of Scottish Parishes," an alphabetical listing of all Scottish parishes that shows the county in which they are located and their parish numbers. Next is the section for birth records. It starts with the "General Index of Births," which is a listing of the microfilms for the annual indexes to all births registered in Scotland (see Figure 7-1). After the general index is a listing of microfilm numbers for the birth certificates. This listing is organized by county, then by year and parish number. Similar sections are included for marriages and deaths.

When you use the *Register*, you should consult the "Index of Scottish Parishes" to identify the parishes, as well as their parish numbers, in the area where your ancestor lived. Use the "General Index of Births," the "General Index of Marriages," and the "General Index of Deaths" to get information to order the microfilmed indexes you need.

Birth indexes from 1855 to 1875

To find record of a birth from 1855 to 1875, use the International Genealogical Index first. The IGI is available at no charge on the Internet at <www.familysearch.org> or at Family History Centers as part of the FamilySearch program. You should go to a Family History Center to order the certificate on microfilm once you find the record on IGI. If you don't find the birth during that time period, also try the indexes on microfilm or on the Scots Origins Web site. In most cases, however, it is unnecessary to order microfilmed birth and death indexes or to use Scots Origins for the 1855–1875 time period. You are more likely to get results by verifying that you are searching for the correct names, dates, and places in the IGI.

We found the births of several children in the Kay family when we used the International Genealogical Index on the Internet in chapter four and at a Family History Center in chapter six. Remember that IGI is only an index to the civil registration certificates. Now we want to look at the birth certificates themselves. See the holding file entries in chapter six, Figure 6-8 on page 55. Notice that the source of all of the births is "6035516 REGISTER." This is the *Register of Births, Marriages and Deaths of Scotland* on three microfiche. Whenever you find this reference on IGI, it means that the entry came from a Scottish civil registration certificate of birth or marriage. The next step is to use the *Register* to find the microfilm numbers of the original birth certificates. See "How Do I Order the Certificate?" later in this chapter.

Figure 7-1
General listing of birth indexes for Scotland showing
microfilm numbers.

```
            SCOTLAND CIVIL REGISTRATION

                  GENERAL INDEX

                     BIRTHS

----------------------------------------------------
    YEAR          SEX        SURNAME      MICROFILM
----------------------------------------------------

    1855         Males         A-Z        103,244
    1855         Females       A-Z        103,258

    1856         Males         A-Z        103,245
    1856         Females       A-Z        103,259

    1857         Males         A-Z        103,246
    1857         Females       A-Z        103,260

    1858         Males         A-Z        103,247
    1858         Females       A-Z        103,261

    1859         Males         A-M        103,248
    1859           "           N-Z        103,249
    1859         Females       A-Z        103,262

    1860         Males         A-Z        103,250
    1860         Females       A-Z        103,263

    1861         Males         A-Z        103,251
    1861         Females       A-Z        103,264

    1862         Males         A-Z        103,252
    1862         Females       A-Z        103,265

    1863         Males         A-Z        103,253
    1863         Females       A-Z        103,266

    1864         Males         A-M        103,254
    1864           "           N-Z        103,255
    1864         Females       A-M        103,267
    1864           "           N-Z        103,268

    1865         Males         A-M        103,256
    1865           "           N-Z        103,257
    1865         Females       A-M        103,269
    1865           "           N-Z        103,270

    1866-67      Males &       A-Z        103,271
                 Females
    1868-69        "           A-Z        103,272


                                          Page 32
```

Birth indexes after 1875

When searching for records of births before 1875, we can do a parent search on IGI to find children of the Kay family without even knowing all of the children's names. To find any children born to James Kay and Isabel Brough after 1875, we must know the child's name and approximate date and place of birth. One of the easiest ways to find this information for children born after 1875 is to search for the parents in censuses of 1881 and later. The census lists the name, age, and place of birth for each child present in the home on census night.

To find records of births after 1875, we can use either the civil registration indexes on microfilm or the Scots Origins service on the Internet. These indexes contain almost identical information, but it is much less expensive to order the microfilmed indexes. Let's use the microfilm to search for another child of James Kay and Isabel Brough. His name is David, and he was born in 1877. The Family History Library Catalog and the *Register of Births, Marriages and Deaths of Scotland* both list the film number we need. We have used the *Register* to find the film number for the birth index for males born in 1877. It indicates that male and female births from 1876 to 1877 are indexed on film 0103276.

All of the male births for 1876 are indexed together on this film. All of the female births for 1876 are in a second index. The male index for 1877 births is the third group on the film. Always check the headers at the top of the page to make sure you look at the correct year and to see whether the index covers males or females. See Figure 7-2. The header on the page we want indicates "Male Births-Scotland-1877." It covers surnames whose first three letters are *Joh* to *Kee*; the first surname on the page is Johnstone, and the last surname on the page is Keenan. The surname Kay comes between these two alphabetically. This is a microfilmed copy of an index that was originally in a book. The book, when opened, was not completely flat, so surnames that are close to the binding of the book are sometimes hard to read. David Kay's name is near the binding, so the names in that column are slightly curved. You can see that two David Kays were registered in 1877: one in Methven and one in Kinning Park, Glasgow. Since James Kay had several children born in Methven, we ordered the certificate for the David born there.

To order David's certificate, we needed to record the type of record (birth); the event year, and his name, district, and entry number. (You can see the birth certificate for David on page 93.)

When copying index entries, it is easy to forget to note the type of record (birth, marriage, or death) and the year because they are at the top of the page. When possible, try to make a photocopy that includes the page heading as well as the name you want.

Searching the marriage indexes

Searching the marriage indexes is similar to searching the birth indexes, with one major exception: you look for two names instead of one. **Always search the index for the name of the groom and the maiden name of the bride.**

For marriages from 1855 through 1875, use the International Genealogical Index to find record of the marriage you want. We found the marriage for James Kay and Isabella Brough when we searched the IGI for the children. You can search the

JOH **MALE BIRTHS—SCOTLAND—1877.** KEE

		No.
[illegible], Malcolm	Tarbert Argyll	40
—— [illegible] James	Dunoon, etc.	18
—— Patrick Cowan Penfold	North Leith	392
—— Peter	Kinross	24
—— [illegible]	Kingsbarns	13
—— Robert	Portobello	166
—— Robert	East District Cadder	78
—— Robert	Peebles	18
—— Robert	Gretna	30
—— Robert Hope	Old Machar Aberdeen	585
—— Robert Meldrum	Dumfries	49
—— Robert Macandrew	Johnstone Renfrew	47
—— Robert Thomas	St Andrew Edinburgh	307
—— Robert William	Howmore	31
—— Roderick	Howmore	48
—— Roderick	Middlebie	60
—— Thomas	Castleton	56
—— Thomas	South Leith	959
—— Thomas Fulton White	Dumfries	438
—— Thomas John	Ladhope	58
—— Walter	Drumelzier	7
—— Walter Robert	Moffat	9
—— William	Kirkmichael Dumfries	31
—— William	Morebattle	18
—— William	Kelvin Glasgow	431
—— William	Govan Church	1704
—— William	Kilmaurs	142
—— William	Polmont	74
—— William	Paisley	710
—— William Craig	Bridgeton Glasgow	1470
—— William Evans	Kinning Park Glasgow	636
—— William George	Terregles	8
—— William John Cochrane	Kirkmabreck	25
—— William Makin	Alva Stirling	154
—— William Reid	Auchinleck	188
—— William Scotland	Bo'ness	216
—— ——	Kirkpatrick-Juxta	7
[illegible], James	Bannockburn	150
[illegible], George James	Newington Edinburgh	81
[illegible], Edward Saxby	Mains	63
—— Peter Oswald	Leslie Fife	43
—— William Lorimer	Calton Glasgow	101
[illegible], Richard I——	Kinning Park Glasgow	671
[illegible], Alexander	North Leith	695
—— Archibald	Strathblane	30
—— Charles Davidson	Laurencekirk	32
—— Daniel	Muthill	33
—— Donald Ross	Thurso	83
—— James	St Andrew Dundee	1098
—— James	Stewarton	102
—— John	Brechin	262
Jolly, John	Bridgeton Glasgow	191
—— Joseph Pirie	Fordoun	11
—— William	Strathblane	27
—— William	Farnell	15
—— William Tasker Adam	St Giles Edinburgh	905
Jones, Alexander	Girvan	162
—— Andrew	Hamilton	160
—— Arthur	St George Edinburgh	386
—— Benjamin	Bothwell	106
—— Charles Albert John	Canongate Edinburgh	701
—— Charles Edward	St George Edinburgh	1799
—— Charles Frederick	Blythswood Glasgow	546
—— David	Shettleston	313
—— David	Bothwell	101
—— Francis	Gorbals Glasgow	1095
—— George Robert Walker Grant	West Greenock	442
—— James	Cambusnethan	730
—— James	Ayr	572
—— James John	Hutchesontown Glasgow	396
—— James Lighton Porter	Hutchesontown Glasg.	1124
—— John	Dalziel	382
—— John	Blythswood Glasgow	386
—— John	West Calder	331
—— John	South Leith	186
—— John James	Camlachie Glasgow	999
—— John Park	Annan	54
—— John William	Camlachie Glasgow	359
—— Peter Clark	Newington Edinburgh	1203
—— Phillip George	Kilmallie	53
—— Richard	Riccarton	266
—— Robert	Alloa	316
—— Thomas Alexander Carnochan	Ballantrae	29
—— William	West District Old Monkland	68
—— William	Dennistoun Glasgow	97
—— William	Hutchesontown Glasgow	459
—— William	East District Old Monkland	69
—— William	Govan Church	1790
—— William	Bonhill	209
—— William	Cambusnethan	781
—— William	Dumfries	452
—— William Cowperthwaite	Anderston Glasgow	1311
—— ——	Dailly	29
Jopp, Alexander Youngson	Old Machar Aberdeen	564
—— Peter	Anderston Glasgow	1315
Jordan, David	Milton Glasgow	730
—— Felix	Kelvin Glasgow	1797
—— James	Canongate Edinburgh	407
—— John	Perth	162
—— John	West District Shotts	118
—— John Black	Hutchesontown Glasgow	2138
—— John Laurence Fordyce	Lerwick	75
Jordan, Thomas	North Leith	372
—— William	South Leith	628
—— William Campbell	Irvine	283
Joss, Alexander	Portlethen	29
—— Alexander	Alford	17
—— Alexander	Peterhead	386
—— Alexander	Old Deer	91
—— Arthur	Peterculter	31
—— John	Kinnethmont	21
—— William	Monymusk	39
—— William	Old Machar Aberdeen	861
—— William	Elgin	206
Joyce, Charles	Calton Glasgow	550
—— George	Dunfermline B	508
—— James	East Greenock	315
—— John	Luss	7
—— John	Kinning Park Glasgow	764
—— John	Partick	190
—— Michael	Calton Glasgow	434
—— Michael	East Greenock	657
—— Michael Charles	Calton Glasgow	885
—— Patrick	Hutchesontown Glasgow	1080
—— Peter	Gorbals Glasgow	349
—— Thomas	Cardross	72
—— Thomas	Partick	1452
—— William	Prestonpans	26
Jubert, Karl August Otto	Kelvin Glasgow	1094
Judd, David	Dennistoun Glasgow	1730
Jude, David	Stirling	208
—— Thomas	South Leith	54
Judge, Andrew	Gorbals Glasgow	202
—— Daniel	Canongate Edinburgh	555
—— Hugh	Anderston Glasgow	1380
—— James	Old Cumnock	31
—— John	Auchinleck	109
—— John	Auchinleck	203
—— Martin	Blackfriars Glasgow	188
—— William	Dalry Ayr	137
Juner, Alexander Wylie	Stobhill	38
—— Stevenson	Govan Church	1354
Junner, George Macpherson	Blackfriars Glasgow	1357
—— George Panton	Blackfriars Glasgow	1024
Junor, Alexander Anderson	Rosemarkie	10
—— Donald	Avoch	55
—— James	Old Deer	12
—— James	Avoch	13
—— John	Carluke	237
—— John	Auldearn	24
—— Roderick	Cromarty	62
Jupp, Joseph Hallam	Liff, etc.	14
Justice, William White	St Clement Dundee	518

K.

		No.
[illegible], Alexander	Hutchesontown Glasgow	775
—— Andrew	Hutchesontown Glasgow	776
—— James	St George Edinburgh	1441
—— John	Dumfries	312
—— Robert	West District Cadder	86
—— William John	Lanark	37
—— William John	Shettleston	208
[illegible], James	Kirkpatrick-Durham	27
—— William	Kirkpatrick-Durham	17
[illegible], Andrew	Calton Glasgow	443
—— Bernard	Blackfriars Glasgow	64
—— Dugald	Tradeston Glasgow	232
—— Duncan Archibald	Hamilton	593
—— Edward	Govan Church	1864
—— Henry	St Rollox Glasgow	1624
—— Hugh	Penicuik	146
—— Hugh Alexander	Hutchesontown Glasgow	51
—— James	Mid Greenock	296
—— James	Hamilton	458
—— James	Canongate Edinburgh	1314
—— James Kelly	St Mary Dundee	531
—— John	Kelvin Glasgow	400
—— John	Airdrie	458
—— John	Govan Church	637
—— John Agnew	Mid District Shotts	23
—— Patrick	Irvine	173
—— Robert	Gorbals Glasgow	565
—— William	Fauldhouse	82
—— William George	Milton Glasgow	803
[illegible], Charles Gibson	Bridgeton Glasgow	67
[illegible], Daniel Bonar	West Greenock	255
[illegible], James	Lochee Dundee	417
[illegible], James	Lesmahagow	404
—— Robert	Lesmahagow	403
[illegible], Henry	Renfrew	243
[illegible], William	Prestonkirk	28
[illegible], Frederick Charles	St Andrew Edinburgh	1082
[illegible], James	Beith Ayr	63
[illegible], John	Hawick	14
Kay, Alexander	Dalmellington	56
—— Alexander	St Rollox Glasgow	255
—— Alexander Miller	Ayr	263
—— Andrew	Dysart	92
—— Andrew Temple	St Giles Edinburgh	73
—— Archibald M'Intyre	Anderston Glasgow	1139
—— David	Methven	41
—— David	Kinning Park Glasgow	777
—— Francis	Dalrymple	56
—— Frederick Arthur	St George Edinburgh	830
—— George	St Giles Edinburgh	352
—— George	Rhynd	8
—— George	Hutchesontown Glasgow	521
—— George William	Bothwell	90
—— Henry	Mid District Old Monkland	705
—— Hugh Park	Old Cumnock	108
—— James	Govan Church	918
—— James	Kirkcudbright	87
—— James	Penicuik	27
Kay, James Bertram	Penicuik	121
—— James Hunter	Monifieth	122
—— James Robertson	Kingsbarns	9
—— John	Anderston Glasgow	1013
—— John	Muirkirk	184
—— Joseph	St Rollox Glasgow	725
—— Joseph	Anderston Glasgow	1617
—— Peter	Comrie	19
—— Peter	Blackfriars Glasgow	764
—— Peter	Kelvin Glasgow	885
—— Richard	Dunfermline B	53
—— Robert	Cumbernauld	14
—— Robert	St Andrew Edinburgh	547
—— Robert	Canongate Edinburgh	768
—— Robert	Dunbog	18
—— Robert	Govan Church	1441
—— Robert Govan	Kirkcaldy, etc.	82
—— Thomas Girdwood	Rothesay	190
—— Thomas Murray	Dunfermline L	10
—— Thomas Ramsay	Milton Glasgow	1334
—— Thomas Sands	Gargunnock	9
—— Thomas Seal	South Leith	412
—— William	Bathgate	91
—— William	[illegible]	70
—— William	Kirkcaldy, etc.	432
—— William	Creich Fife	1
—— William Drummond	Rothesay	24
—— ——	Jedburgh	4
Kaye, David Findlay	West District Old Monkland	47
—— Robert	St Nicholas Aberdeen	1592
—— Thomas	South Leith	1400
Kayes, James	Brechin	150
Kays, Albert	Anderston Glasgow	729
Kean, Alexander	Old Machar Aberdeen	1273
—— Alexander Johnstone Edgar	Govan Church	2303
—— Alexander Sim	Cambuslang	219
—— Archibald	Rothesay	178
—— Bernard	Anderston Glasgow	989
—— Charles Kenmure	Anderston Glasgow	1045
—— Francis Blake	Kinning Park Glasgow	769
—— George	St Rollox Glasgow	182
—— George	Blackfriars Glasgow	177
—— Godfrey M'Lean	Mid Greenock	109
—— Henry Laird Harley	St Rollox Glasgow	659
—— James	Eaglesham	33
—— James	Saline Fife	32
—— James	West District Cadder	74
—— James	Monifieth	191
—— James Stewart	Portlethen	16
—— John	Old Kilpatrick	28
—— John	Stoneykirk	44
—— Joseph	St Andrew Dundee	179
—— Michael	West Calder	121
—— Patrick	West Greenock	1027
—— Patrick	Dalziel	148
—— Robert	Canongate Edinburgh	375
—— Robert Wilson	Haggs	17
—— William	Galston	194
Kear, James	Arbroath	77
Kearnan, Peter	Anderston Glasgow	615
Kearney, Bernard	St Giles Edinburgh	1024
—— Edward	Hutchesontown Glasgow	1742
—— Hugh	West Greenock	955
—— William	Port-Glasgow	466
—— William	Paisley	1045
—— William John	Blackfriars Glasgow	8[illegible]9
Kearns, John	St Mary Dundee	151
—— Thomas	Old Machar Aberdeen	354
Keating, Archibald Anderson	Calton Glasgow	1179
—— Denis	Govan Church	2176
Keaveny, Edward	Govan Church	1353
Keay, Alexander Ramsay	St Andrew Dundee	1353
—— David	Glenshee	2
—— Duncan	Logiealmond	5
—— Harry M'Laren	St Andrew Dundee	542
—— John Bell	Lochee Dundee	420
—— Robert Murdoch	Newhills	74
—— William	Errol	58
—— William David	St Mary Dundee	813
Keddie, David Walker	St George Edinburgh	1593
—— George	St Andrew Dundee	359
—— James	Kinross	48
—— James	North Leith	724
—— James Dunn	St George Edinburgh	562
—— James Paterson	Penicuik	141
—— John	Galashiels	283
—— John Robert	Ladhope	86
—— Mitchell John	St Andrew Dundee	1174
—— Robert	Fossoway, etc.	25
—— Samuel	St George Edinburgh	1003
—— William	Forgan	60
—— William Bell	Galashiels	16
—— William James	Newington Edinburgh	115
Keddy, Andrew	Ferry-Port-on-Craig	6
Kedens, Thomas	Auchinleck	311
Kedgley, Alexander	St George Edinburgh	1127
Kee, Joseph	West Greenock	976
Keeffe, Charles	Stranraer	175
Keegan, Charles Barr	St Andrew Edinburgh	1054
—— Francis	South Leith	642
—— John	East District Old Monkland	187
—— Joseph	St Mary Dundee	651
—— Owen	Airdrie	212
Keel, William Edward Henry	Canongate Edinr.	190
Keelen, Joseph	St Andrew Dundee	1236
Keelings, William Craig	Camlachie Glasgow	1365
Keely, James Thompson	Dumbarton	406
Keen, Edward	Canonbie	15
—— Henry John	South Leith	1339
—— Patrick Houston	Portpatrick	20
—— William	St George Edinburgh	1729
Keenan, Charles	South Leith	207
—— David	Slamannan	54
—— David	St Nicholas Aberdeen	361
—— Denis	St Rollox Glasgow	40
—— James	[illegible]	[illegible]

Figure 7-2
Index to Male Births—Scotland for 1877 showing entries for the surname Kay.

IGI for a marriage directly or press the F7 key (in the DOS version) from an individual or parent search.

Starting with 1876 marriages, you can use either the Scots Origins database or the indexes on microfilm to find them. Let's use the microfilm to find the marriage record of Alexander Cameron and Marion Henrietta Stewart. Alexander Cameron is a grandson of James Kay and Isabella Brough, and he was married in 1896. We can use the Family History Library Catalog or the *Register of Births, Marriages and Deaths of Scotland* (FHL microfiche 6035516) to find the film number for the index to 1896 marriages. Both of these sources indicate that the index for males and females for 1896–1898 is on FHL film 0103559, and we can order that film at any Family History Center.

When film 0103559 arrives, remember that three years are indexed on this film, and take care to look in the correct year. In the 1896 index, we find sixteen Alexander Camerons, one Alexander Park Cameron, and one Alexander Wilson Cameron. The best way to determine the correct entry is to search for Marion Henrietta Stewart and find a district and page number that matches those of one of the Alexander Camerons.

Each time you search a marriage index, write down the entries or make a copy of the page that contains the names you are searching for. You need to compare this to the index for the spouse.

Next go to the 1896 female index on the same film. Three Marion Stewarts are in this index, but no Marion Henrietta Stewart. None of the Marions have the same district and page number as an Alexander Cameron. What do we do now? We can assume either that we have the wrong year of marriage or the wrong name for one or both of the spouses. It is also possible that the marriage was never registered, but we won't even consider that until we have exhausted other possibilities.

So, back to the drawing board. We can search for Sandy Camerons because Sandy is a nickname for Alexander. We can try Mary Ann for Marion, and we can try other given name and surname variations. When we do, we find that two women named Marion Henrietta Stuart are in the 1896 index. One of them was married in Kelvin Glasgow, entry number 475. This matches one of the Alexander Camerons. Does this mean we have found the correct couple? Not necessarily, but it is unlikely that two Marion Henrietta Stewarts (or any variation) married men named Alexander Cameron. These are the only matching entries for the years surrounding 1896, so we ordered this certificate.

Searching the death indexes

This is one time when it's a real advantage to be searching for a woman. To see why this is so, let's look for the death of Isabell Brough who married James Kay. She died in 1915.

The death index for 1915 is on FHL film 103441. This film covers only one year, so we don't have to worry about looking at the correct year; we do have to make sure that we look in the female index and not the male index.

If you know the maiden name of a woman, you should start searching for that name first because a woman should be in the index under her maiden name regardless of how many times she married. (The only exception to this is deaths in the years 1856–1858; no maiden names are recorded in that index.) We therefore look

Research Tip

Figure 7-3
Index to Female Deaths—
Scotland for 1915 showing
entries for surname Brough.

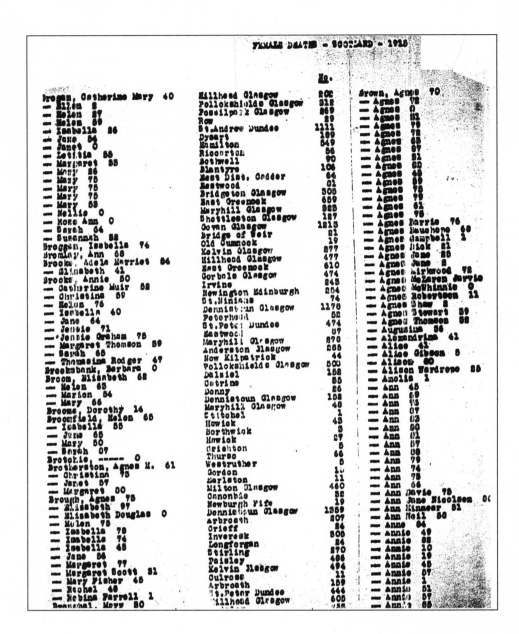

for Isabell Brough. See Figure 7-3. It's a nice, printed index, so we don't have to interpret any handwriting. Remember, though, that somebody else had to, so there's still room for error. You can see that the index has no Isabell Brough, but it has three Isabellas. Ours should have been about seventy-eight years old, and she lived in Crieff. The first one listed could be the one we want. We can make sure by searching for her married name, Isabell Kay.

When we find the 1915 listings for the surname Kay, we again see no Isabell, but we find two Isabella Kays and one Isabella McNaught Kay. The first one is Isabella Kay, age seventy-eight, died in Crieff, entry number 24. This exactly matches the first Isabella Brough, so now we can be pretty confident that we have the correct woman.

If we had been searching for a man, we wouldn't have had this cross-check for a second surname. When looking for a man's entry, therefore, you have to rely on the age and place of death given in the index (although no ages are given for deaths before 1866).

To be able to order the death certificate, record the type of record (death), the event year, the name of the person, the district, and the entry number. See "How Do I Order the Certificate?" later in this chapter.

Why Can't I Find My Ancestor in the Index?

In most cases, if you follow the outlined procedures, you should have little trouble locating your ancestor. However, it is always *your* ancestor's name that somehow fell through the cracks. **Let's look at the usual reasons for not finding an ancestor in the civil registration indexes and see what we can do.**

Notes

Basic facts are incorrect. This is probably the most common reason that you cannot find an ancestor. On what evidence have you based your research? How reliable is that evidence? For example, often we look for a birth of a person based on his age in a census record or on a death certificate, both of which can be unreliable. Information provided by relatives is also often incorrect. Always reexamine the evidence that led you to believe that an event occurred in a particular time and place. Could an error have been made?

Spelling and handwriting. The spelling of names is another common roadblock to finding an entry in the indexes. No standardized spelling of names was used before the late nineteenth century. Names were spelled phonetically, so your ancestor may have spelled his name differently from the way you do. A person who heard his name could have recorded it with a different spelling; the people making the records wrote down what they thought they heard. Think of the kind of accent your ancestor may have had, and remember that some of our ancestors were illiterate. An illiterate person would not have read the entry to see if it was recorded correctly. We have seen forty or more spelling variations to some of our surnames. Be creative with spelling, and if you need help, say the surname to several children and ask them to spell it. We have tried this suggestion many times.

Another potential problem is that an indexer misread the registrar's handwriting and indexed the name under a different spelling. If the indexer misread the first letter of the surname, you can be in for a very long search. This happened with the Kay family. One of the Kay children is missing from the listing of children we made from the International Genealogical Index because the indexer read the surname as Hay instead of Kay. The capital letters *S*, *L*, and *T* look very similar and are commonly misread. Ask yourself which letters of a name could be mistaken for other letters. Here's a suggestion for creative handwriting: Give the surname to several doctors and see how they write it.

Names beginning with *Mc* or *Mac* are indexed separately at the end of the letter *M*, and you need to check both variations. You may also find the name you want by dropping the *Mc* or *Mac*.

Tip

Wrong name. Your ancestor's birth may not have been registered under the name he later used. For example, he may have been given a Gaelic name at birth, and used an English version of the name when he was married. Or your ancestor may have always been known as Patrick, but he is listed as Peter in the birth register.

(Remember that these are variations of the same name.) The best reference for given name variations is Dunkling's *Scottish Christian Names: An A-Z of First Names*. You can also use Withycombe's *Oxford Dictionary of English Christian Names*. Both books give variations and origins of names. Either can help you find nicknames, former name versions that appear in earlier records, and current variations. An inexpensive book that you should have on hand is Bardsley's *First Name Variants*, which gives name variations and nicknames. You may also need to consider surname variations. As we discussed in the sections on surnames in chapter three, your ancestor may have used the surname Wilkinson and been recorded in the birth register as McQuilkin. Consult Black's *Surnames of Scotland*. Less frequently, name variations are not the problem. A child may have been registered with two given names and was always known by the second one (the middle name). A child given one name at registration and a different one at baptism may have used the latter through life.

For women, try searching under the maiden surname if you know it. Using the maiden name is almost always the surest way to search in the indexes, but in the 1856–1858 death indexes, no maiden name is recorded. Remember that a Scottish woman retained her maiden name throughout life. You can find a second or subsequent marriage for a woman by looking in the index under both her maiden name and her former husband's surname. In the death index, a woman usually is listed with her maiden name and the surnames of her husbands. A widow, however, is sometimes listed only by her maiden name and not under the names from her marriage(s). If you know multiple names, check the indexes for all of them. The entries for the maiden name and married name should match. Compare the entries to decide which woman is your ancestor when you find several of the same name.

Wrong place. Your ancestor may not have been born where he said he was born, and the marriage or death may not have occurred where you thought it did. Marriages usually occurred in the parish of the bride, so look for the marriage there. In Scotland a birth certificate gives the date and place of the child's parents' marriage except between 1856 and 1860, but beware that this marriage information may not be accurate. After the marriage, the couple often lived in the parish of the groom, so births of children may have been recorded there. A woman may have gone home to her mother to have the first baby, and prior to 1965 births had to be registered in the district where the event occurred. Therefore, the birth registration of a first child may have been in the district where the maternal grandmother lived. A birth may also have occurred at a hospital in a different district, while the mother was away visiting relatives, or during travel. Your ancestor may not have died at home, but while working or traveling. Deaths often occurred in the homes of relatives. Census records are a good resource to help you find the various places where your ancestor lived.

Perhaps the biggest reason for not recognizing your ancestor in the index is that there are too many names and places. If you don't find an event in the parish where you expect it, look for nearby parishes. Be sure to have a list of parishes on hand so that if you see an unfamiliar place in the index, you can see in which county it is located.

Notes

After 1965 births and burials have been recorded in the place of usual residence or where the event occurred, but not in both.

Wrong sex. Remember that the indexes are divided by sex. If you search for a given name that can be either a male or female name, search the other index for the same time period when you don't find it in the first index.

The event wasn't registered. Never accept this option until you have tried other techniques for finding the certificate you need. A child may not have been named at the time of the registration, so this event appears in the index as a line in place of the child's name and after all the other Christian names for that surname. In this situation you know the sex because the indexes are divided by sex, so check the locality and see if that matches. Sometimes an entry that you think is missing is in the addenda at the end of the male or female section for the year. If you see the notation "Vide Addenda" at the bottom of the page where your ancestor's name should appear, look at the addenda at the end of the surnames. Names that were missing from the index are recorded there.

You usually can rule out the possibility of an unregistered event when you look for a death record; the undertaker and the cemetery custodian had to have a death certificate to proceed with the burial. After 1879 all marriages had to be recorded by the registrar even if a religious ceremony was performed. Between 1855 and 1879 unrecorded irregular marriages were possible, but these became rarer with time. Some births in the early years may have gone unrecorded, but there are no reliable statistics or estimates on how many.

If you cannot find record of a birth, search for a baptism. Baptisms were recorded in church registers and also should have been recorded by the parish or district registrar. See chapter nine for information about using these records.

Illegitimacy. You are almost sure to find illegitimacy in your ancestry. Do not be dismayed about this; **illegitimacy was common in Scotland.** If the person you seek was one of the oldest children in the family, consider this as a possibility. Illegitimate children usually are recorded in the indexes with the mother's maiden surname. This may not be the surname that the child actually used. Examine the birth certificate of one of the younger children; the mother's maiden name appears on that certificate. Depending on the year, the parents' date of marriage is also on the certificate. Next, search the civil registration index for the birth of the older child using the mother's maiden surname. In Scotland, the unmarried father can be named on the birth extract if he goes with the mother to register the birth and sign the birth register. Also note that under Scots law, illegitimate children become legitimate at the later marriage of the parents if the parents could have been married at the time of the birth.

Another problem associated with illegitimacy is that the child may have been born in a different parish than the younger children in the family, so you may search in the wrong registration district.

Adoption. The Adoption of Children (Scotland) Act of 1930 introduced legal adoption to Scotland. Prior to 1930 adoptions were generally arranged on a private basis and more accurately reflect guardianship or fosterage. Since 1930 adoptions normally have been arranged by charitable organizations or local government social work officers. The adoptions are then ratified by the local sheriff courts. The records

Warning

stay with the local courts for twenty-five years, after which the sealed records are transferred to the National Archives of Scotland. The case files can be opened only at the National Archives of Scotland by the adoptee. However, to access these files the adoptee needs to know his birth name, the date of the adoption, and the court that handled the adoption. This information can be obtained from the Registrar General for Scotland through the Adoption Unit at New Register House. An adopted child has two birth certificates. The first is a normal record of the original birth and has "adopted" written in the margin. The second gives the adoptive name, the adoptive parents, and the court that granted the adoption order. A separate set of indexes connects the two sets of birth records. Direct application needs to be made to the Adoption Unit at New Register House, and the unit arranges a counseling session prior to the search for the original certificate. No people born prior to October 1909 are in these registers.

The event was not registered when it occurred. The date of registration is important because this date, not date of the event, determines the year of entry in the indexes. If you do not find a birth, marriage, or death registered in the year you think it occurred, look further. This is especially true if the event occurred near the end of a year; it may not have been registered until the beginning of the following year. A death registration may have been delayed because of an inquest that followed an accident, death under suspicious circumstances, a suicide, or an unexplained death. If a death was not registered within a year of the date of death, then the death only could have been registered with the authority of the registrar general, and this is noted in the column with the date of registration. Another entry should be included in the index for the year in which the death occurred and should point you to the year in which the death was registered.

The event did not occur in Scotland. Even though your ancestor lived in Scotland, his birth, marriage, or death might not have occurred there. If one spouse (especially the bride) had lived outside of Scotland, the couple may have been married in another country. For example, if your ancestor lived near the southern border, he may have married in England. If so, the birth of the first child probably would have also occurred there if the woman went to be with her family at the birth of the child. If you suspect that your ancestor may have lived in England or Ireland, check the civil registration indexes of the appropriate country. It is also a good possibility that the event occurred elsewhere if your ancestor was in the military or had an occupation that required overseas travel. The event still may have been recorded, but not in the regular civil registration indexes. Two sets of alternative indexes need to be checked. Unfortunately the Scottish alternative indexes are not available outside the General Register Office for Scotland; you can search them in person or hire someone to search them on your behalf. The Great Britain alternative indexes are available on microfiche through the FHL. See the sidebars on the Scottish alternative indexes and the Great Britain alternative indexes.

HOW DO I ORDER THE CERTIFICATE?

You have three ways to get Scottish birth, marriage, and death certificates. The certificates are available on microfilm from the Family History Library for the years 1855–

SCOTLAND ALTERNATIVE INDEXES

These indexes are available to search only at the General Register Office for Scotland at New Register House in Edinburgh.

1. Marine register of births and deaths (from 1855): Records of births and deaths on British-registry merchant vessels in any part of the world. One of the child's parents or the deceased usually is a resident of Scotland.

2. Air register (from 1948): Records of births and deaths on British-registry aircraft in any part of the world. One of the child's parents or the deceased usually is a resident of Scotland.

3. Army returns of births, marriages, and deaths abroad (1881–1959) for anyone employed by Her Majesty's Forces.

4. Service Department Registers of births, marriages, and deaths (from 1959) outside the United Kingdom for anyone in or employed by Her Majesty's Forces.

5. Army chaplain registers for marriages outside the United Kingdom (from 1892).

6. War Registers: Deaths of Scottish Soldiers in South Africa War (Boer War) (1899–1902).

7. War Registers: Deaths of Scottish servicemen and women in the First World War (1914–1918). Army, noncommissioned officers and men (no officers); navy, petty officers and men (no officers).

8. War Registers: Deaths of Scottish servicemen and women in the Second World War (1939–1945): Incomplete.

9. Consular returns: Births and deaths from 1914; marriages from 1917.

10. High Commissioners' returns of births and deaths (from 1964).

11. Register of births, deaths, and marriages in foreign countries (1860–1965).

12. Foreign marriages (from 1947).

1875 and for the years 1881 and 1891. For other years, you can order the certificate from the General Register Office, or you can use the Scots Origins Web site.

You may have already used the *Register of Births, Marriages and Deaths of Scotland* to find the microfilm numbers for the civil registration indexes. Now use it to find the microfilm numbers of the actual certificates of birth, marriage, and death. Within each county, the certificates are arranged by year. They are further organized by parish and then by certificate number. To find the certificate you need, consult the appropriate birth, marriage, or death section of the *Register*. Look for the county in which the event occurred. At the beginning of each county is a listing

Step By Step

GREAT BRITAIN ALTERNATIVE INDEXES

All of these indexes except numbers 5 and 23 are available on FHL microfiche numbers 6137109 to 6137491 and may be ordered through a local Family History Center. Locate them in the FHL Catalog under Great Britain-Civil Registration-Indexes.

1. Army chaplains registers of births, marriages, and deaths from 1786–1880

2. Regimental registers of births in the United Kingdom (from 1761) and abroad (from 1790) until 1924, plus indexed regimental registers of marriages

3. Army returns of births, marriages, and deaths abroad (1881–1955) and Royal Air Force returns from 1920

4. Consular records of births, marriages, and deaths for 1849–1965

5. Adopted children's register (from 1927)

6. Marine registers of births (1837–1965) and deaths (1837–1950) on British merchant or naval ships

7. Deaths: Natal and South Africa Forces (Boer War) 1899 to 1902

8. First World War deaths (army) 1914–1921, officers

9. First World War deaths (army) 1914–1921, other ranks

10. First World War deaths (navy) 1914–1921, all ranks

11. Second World War deaths (Royal Air Force) 1939–1948, all ranks

12. Second World War deaths (army) 1939–1948, officers

13. Second World War deaths (army) 1939–1948, other ranks

14. Second World War deaths (navy) 1939–1948

15. Indian Services war deaths 1939–1948

16. U.K. High Commission records of births, marriages, and deaths abroad 1950–1965

17. Army, navy, and Royal Air Force registers of births, deaths, and marriages (abroad), 1956–1965

18. Births and deaths in British civil aircraft from 1947 to 1965

19. Births, marriages, and deaths (military, civil, and chaplains' registers) in the Ionian Isles (1818–1864)

20. Births, marriages, and deaths in Protectorates of Africa and Asia, 1941–1965

21. Miscellaneous foreign registers of births, marriages, and deaths, 1956–1965

22. Registers of births, marriages, and deaths abroad since 1966

23. Registers of stillbirths from 1 July 1927 (available only with consent of the Registrar General)

of parishes or districts for that county. Look up the parish and find its parish number. Then look for the year and parish number to obtain the microfilm number of the certificates.

If you need a certificate that is not available on microfilm from the Family History Library, you can use the Scots Origins Web site to order it, or you can order it at a lower cost from the General Register Office.

If you already have searched the indexes yourself and found the entry you need, you can order the certificate you need by mail, phone, or fax from the General Register Office (GRO) at a cost of eight pounds per certificate (compared with ten pounds when ordering online through Scots Origins). The staff at the GRO will search five years in the indexes for you for an additional five pounds if you provide them sufficient information. You can find more information at the GRO Web site at <www.gro-scotland.gov.uk>. Current prices are listed at <www.gro-scot land.gov.uk/grosweb.nsf/pages/leaflet2#price>.

Mail certificate requests to General Register Office for Scotland, New Register House, Edinburgh EH1 3YT, Scotland U.K.

You can order by telephone by calling the Certificate Ordering Service at [International prefix] + 44 131 314 4411, or fax your order to [International prefix] + 44 131 314 4400. (From the United States the international prefix is 011, but this part of the telephone number depends upon which country you call from. If you call from Scotland or another part of the United Kingdom, the international prefix and the "44" get replaced with "0.") Make payment via Visa, MasterCard, Sterling Check, or British postal order.

Some private parties and businesses will do searches for you. Some of these services are offered over the Internet. One such service is Genfindit Genealogy <www.genfindit.com>. They will send you by e-mail a typed transcript of a certificate. This is much less expensive than the Scots Origins service and comparable to ordering directly from the GRO. The disadvantages of this service, of course, are that you do not get a copy of the original certificate and that someone else has to read and interpret the handwriting. Compare several services and prices and select one that fits your needs.

ANALYZING CIVIL REGISTRATION CERTIFICATES

Your certificate arrives. Let's examine what should be on a birth, marriage, or death certificate. Of course, we know that your certificate will be a little different. Maybe your ancestor or the person recording the information did not follow the rules. Maybe it's just the law of genealogy that dictates that critical information is missing from *your* ancestor's documents. But you'll figure out the facts anyway. Look at each certificate separately and examine each item very carefully. Learn to analyze each piece of information on the certificate and see what you can do when it does not match what you expect. See how you can use the information to lead you to other records. By the time you get through all of these certificates, you'll have had plenty of practice.

Warning

This section is not bedtime reading; it is very detailed. Read it when you have enough time to thoroughly examine each record.

Compare the information on your ancestor's certificate to the birth, marriage, and death certificates in this chapter. Certificates you have found among your family papers are likely to look like the illustrations here. New certificates may look different, but they should contain the same information.

Reading and Analyzing Scottish Birth Certificates
1855 birth record

When you order a certificate on microfilm, you get to see the entire register, not just one record extracted from it. The 1855 birth registers are on microfilm, so the example in Figure 7-4 is a page containing five birth records. Each record contains several columns. Let's look at each section in detail.

Birth register heading. The heading on the page tells you the year, the type of event, the parish and county, and the name of the registrar. This page is 1855 births in the Parish of Crieff in the County of Perth.

Margin. Within the left margin is a notation of how and when the information was received. People had to register births within twenty-one days to avoid a financial penalty. Births could not be registered after three months without a warrant from the sheriff. In Margaret Kay's birth record (last on the page), the margin reads, "On the information of the Father within three months. Time of Birth 13th October 1855 At 9 A.M." The father paid a fine for registering this birth more than twenty-one days after it occurred. All of the other births recorded on this page say that the information was received within twenty-one days of the birth.

Entry number. The entry number appears next. Margaret's record is entry number 95. This means only that hers was the ninety-fifty birth recorded in the Parish of Crieff that year.

Column 1: Name (if given) and whether Informant present or not. Baptismal Name (if different), or Name given without Baptism after Registration; and Date of insertion thereof.

This column contains the name of the child and indicates whether the informant was present at the birth. If the parents had not named the child at the time of registration this column may be blank. For a name given later, with or without baptism, the record shows the date when this information was added.

On our record, the child's name is Margaret Kay. Her father is the informant (see column 8), but he was not present at the birth.

Column 2: Sex

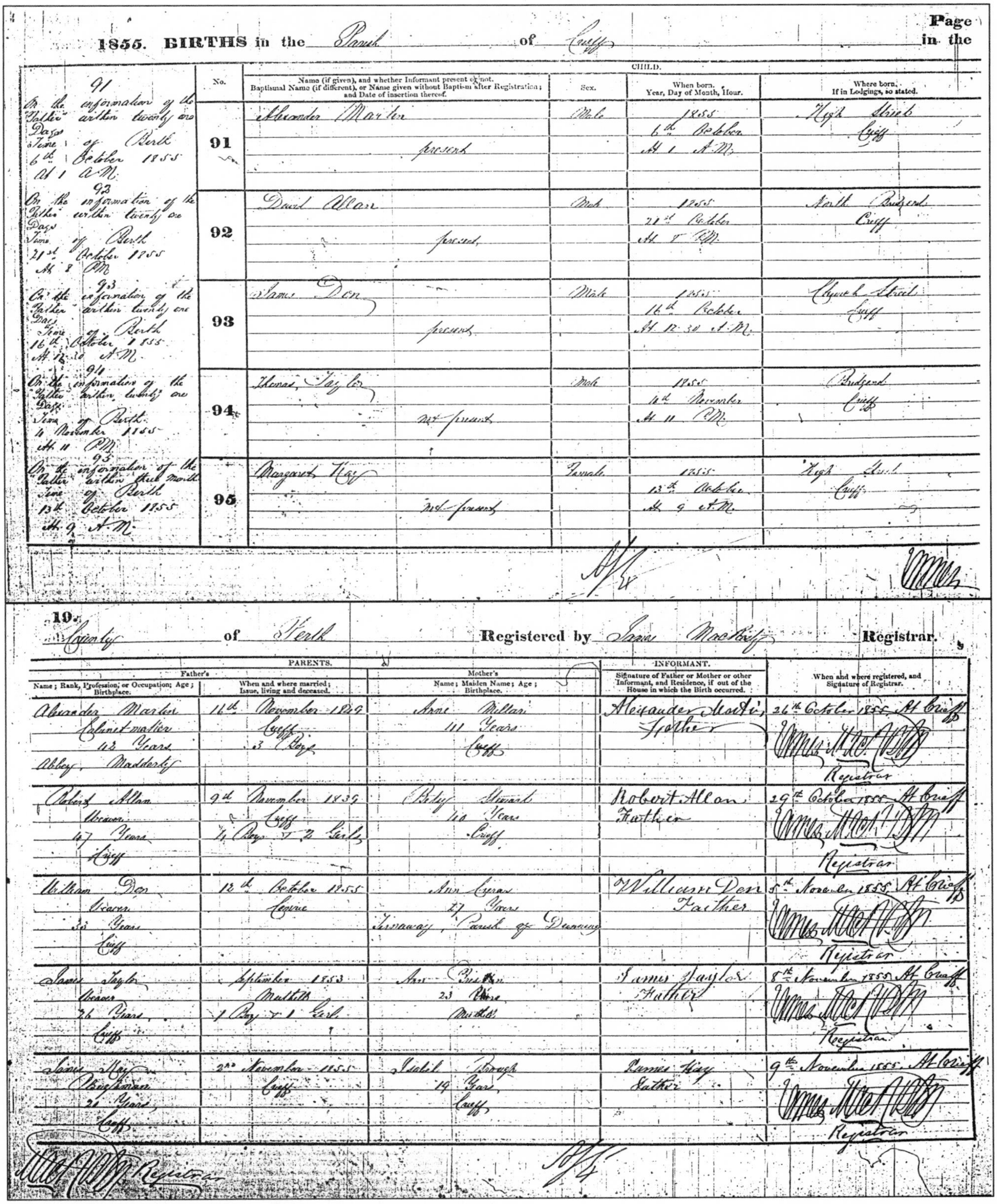

1855. BIRTHS in the Parish of Crieff

Page in the

	No.	Name (if given), and whether Informant present or not. Baptismal Name (if different), or Name given without Baptism after Registration; and Date of insertion thereof.		Sex.	When born. Year, Day of Month, Hour.	Where born. If in Lodgings, so stated.

County of Perth

Registered by James Macbeth

Registrar

PARENTS.				INFORMANT.	
Father's Name; Rank, Profession, or Occupation; Age; Birthplace.	When and where married; Issue, living and deceased.	Mother's Name; Maiden Name; Age; Birthplace.		Signature of Father or Mother or other Informant, and Residence, if out of the House in which the Birth occurred.	When and where registered, and Signature of Registrar.

Figure 7-4

1855 birth register, County of Perth, for Margaret Kay (number 95). This example from microfilm shows five birth records, which are split in half because of the number of columns.

This column reads "male" or "female." One would think that such an obvious characteristic as sex would always be stated correctly, but unfortunately, it is not always that simple. Informants occasionally made mistakes, and the recorders sometimes made incorrect assumptions based on the name of a child. Nobody blew this one; Margaret Kay was a female.

Column 3:   When Born. Year, Day of Month, Hour

This column tells the date and time of your ancestor's birth. It may not match the facts you have from other sources. The information on the birth certificate is usually the most reliable, so this should be the date you note in your records.
Margaret was born 13 October 1855 at 9:00 A.M.

Column 4:   Where born. If in Lodgings, so stated.

Here you find the place of birth. You often can tell if the child was born at the home of her family by comparing this address to the address (if any) in column 8. Margaret was born on High Street in Crieff. The informant (her father) noted in column 8 did not have to state his residence because it was not different from the house in which the birth occurred. We can use this address to look for other records, especially census records, of the family.

Sometimes the place of birth is far from the family's home. For example, the mother may have left the community of residence to have her child. A woman often went to her mother's home to have her first child. In such a case, the address of the birth and that of the informant (perhaps the grandmother, who was present at the birth) may not be what you expect.

"Lodgings" are rooms for rent, and they can be both short- or long-term rentals. They usually are in a private residence, but definitely not in a hotel. Lodgings were very common in the industrial cities. If this was the status of the place where the child was born, then this should be stated on the certificate.

Column 5:   Father's Name; Rank, Profession, or Occupation; Age;
                    Birthplace

This column contains the main facts you need when you look for other records about the father. If no name appears in this column, the child was illegitimate. If the father was deceased at the time of the birth, his name should be followed by the notation "(Deceased)." "Rank, Profession, or Occupation" tells you the father's social status and what he did for a living. The occupation is useful in differentiating him from other men with the same name. His age and birthplace are essential for helping you locate his baptismal record. Margaret's father is James Kay, age twenty at the time of her birth, and he was born in Crieff. His occupation was ploughman.

Column 6:   When and where married; Issue, living and deceased

Column 6 contains information not often found on birth records outside of

Scotland. It gives the date and place of the parents' marriage. Margaret's parents were married 2 November 1855 in Crieff. If this is accurate, we should be able to easily find the marriage record and to trace the family even further. This column also asks for the number of children, both living and dead, born to the couple. This birth record shows that no children were previously born to this couple. Of course, we can't tell if the father told the truth. For example, he could have had another child by a different woman and didn't admit to it. Unless we find other evidence, though, we can assume that Margaret is their first child. Notice on the other birth records on this page that the number of children is divided into number of boys and number of girls.

Column 7:   Mother's Name; Maiden Name; Age; Birthplace

Most important here, the mother should be listed by her maiden name. The informant also reported the mother's age and birthplace. No proof of either was required. On this page, all of the informants were fathers of the children. Was each one certain of the age and birthplace of his wife? James Kay reported that Margaret's mother was Isobel Brough, age nineteen at the time of Margaret's birth, born in Crieff. We should look in Scottish church records for the baptism of an Isobel Brough in the parish of Crieff in about 1836.

Column 8:   Informant: Signature of Father or Mother or other Informant, and Residence, if out of the House in which the Birth occurred.

The name of the informant is essential because it helps you determine the reliability of the information on the birth record. The best informant is the mother; she was certainly present at the birth! Birth information provided by the mother is the most likely to be reliable. The second-best informant is the father. Information provided by others may be less reliable, especially regarding the ages and birthplaces of the parents of the child. When the informant registered the birth, he was asked to sign the register. This column lets you know whether the informant could sign his name. You can also compare the signature to the writing on other documents. On this page, it is obvious that these are the original signatures of the fathers because each name is in a different handwriting style. The column also asks for the residence of the informant if the informant did not live in the house where the birth occurred. James did not have to state his address because he lived in the house on High Street in Crieff.

Column 9:   When and where registered, and Signature of Registrar

The date of registration may not seem interesting, but in this case it is very significant. Compare the date of Margaret's birth to the date of her parents' marriage. She was born 13 October 1855, but her parents weren't married until 2 November 1855. The birth was registered 9 November 1855. In Scotland, illegitimate children were legitimized by the subsequent marriage of the parents. James waited until shortly after the marriage to register the birth of his daughter and was willing to pay a financial penalty to do so. There is no question about legitimacy here; even though Margaret was born before her parents were married, she was legitimate. Her birth record is complete, including the date of her parents' marriage. If James had registered the birth before he married Isobel, this would not have been the case. Compare this birth record to the one in Figure 7-5. Margaret herself had an illegitimate child in 1876. No father's name appears on the certificate, and the child is registered with Margaret's maiden surname. This may not have been the surname he used throughout his life.

EXTRACT OF AN ENTRY IN   **A REGISTER OF BIRTHS**

kept under the Registration of Births, Deaths and Marriages (Scotland) Act 1965

No.	(1) Name and Surname	(2) When and Where Born	(3) Sex	(4) Name, Surname, and Rank or Profession of Father Name, and Maiden Surname of Mother Date and Place of Marriage	(5) Signature and Qualification of Informant, and Residence, if out of the House in which the Birth occurred	(6) When and Where Registered and Signature of Registrar
15	Alexander Jack KAY	1876 March Thirtieth 5h. 0m. P.M. Newro Methven	M	Margaret Kay Domestic Servant	(Signed) Isabella Kay Grandmother Present	1876 April 14th At Methven (Signed) David Murrie Registrar

EXTRACTED from the Register of Births for the..................Parish..................of..................Methven..................

in the..................County..................of..................Perth..................

Given at the General Register Office, New Register House, Edinburgh, under the Seal of the said Office, this..................10th..................day of..................February..................19 72..................

ATTENTION IS DIRECTED TO THE NOTES OVERLEAF

Figure 7-5
1876 birth certificate for Alexander Jack Kay, son of Margaret Kay.

Birth certificates for other years

The birth certificates for 1855 are the only ones that contain the detailed information reviewed above. Let's examine the birth certificate for another child of James Kay and Isobel (Isabella) Brough (see Figure 7-6). This certificate is a birth extract. This means that it is not the birth register; it is information extracted from the register. Notice that although the certificates for Alexander Jack Kay and David Kay contain similar information, Alexander's certificate is typed and David's is photocopied. For certificates among your family papers, the extracts could have been recorded either way. Now you usually receive on your certificate a photocopy of the actual entry.

Only a few columns on David's certificate may need some explanation.

Column 2:   When and Where Born

The time of David's birth was "1 ho. 0 m. A.M." This means he was born at one hour, zero minutes in the morning, or 1:00 A.M. The address was Newro, Balgowan, Methven. We need to look for other records of his family in the parish of Methven.

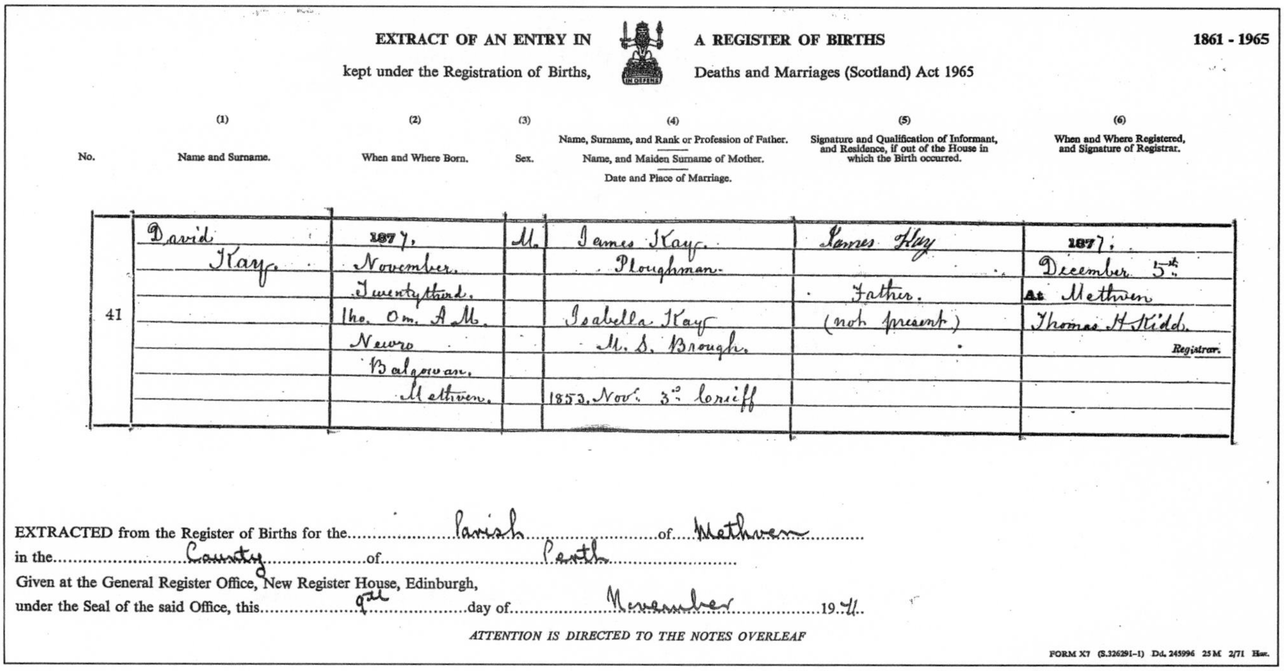

Figure 7-6
1877 birth certificate for David Kay.

Column 4: Name, Surname, and Rank or Profession of Father; Name, and Maiden Surname of Mother. Date and Place of Marriage

This column is genealogically the best column on the certificate. It should contain the names of both parents, the mother's maiden surname, the occupation of the father, and, for births in some years, the date and place of the parents' marriage. If no father's name is listed in this column, the child was illegitimate. If the father was deceased at the time of the birth, his name should be followed by the notation "(Deceased)." "Rank or Profession" tells you what the father did for a living. The occupation of James Kay did not change since 1855. He was still a ploughman. Notice that the mother is listed as "Isabella Kay M. S. Brough." The abbreviation *M. S.* stands for "maiden surname." If your ancestor or one of his siblings was born during the years when the parents' date and place of marriage was recorded, you're in luck. You immediately have all the data you need to find the parents' marriage certificate. However, beware that the date and place of marriage were not verified for the birth registration. The informant gave this information from memory, so you may find an error. Look at the marriage date on this certificate. Even though the children's father, James Kay, was the informant on both Margaret's and David's birth records, the marriage dates do not match. On Margaret's certificate, James said he was married 2 November 1855. On David's, James said he was married 3 November 1853. Both birth records are copies of original records generated by governmental officials. Even official records are only as good as the information provided by the informant.

Column 5:   Signature and Qualification of Informant, and Residence, if out of the House in which the Birth occurred.

The signature on this document is the same signature as the one on Margaret's 1855 birth record. James Kay is the informant, and he was not present at David's birth. He did, however, live at the address where David was born. If he hadn't, a residence would have been recorded for James.

Comparing the certificates

We know from the birth certificates of Margaret and David that James and Isabella lived on High Street in Crieff in 1855 and in Newro, Balgowan, Methven in 1877. Both parents were still alive in 1877, so we should be able to find them in the 1861 and 1871 censuses. See the next chapter for more information about the census. If we never had any later information about the family, we could begin searching the civil registration death indexes for each parent starting in 1877.

Now That I Have Read the Birth Certificate, Where Do I Go Next?

Tip

After you have recorded all of the information about a child's birth, **the next step is usually to use the names of the father and mother to locate their marriage record**. Search the marriage indexes for the parents' names, and order the marriage certificate. Also use the place of birth or the address of the informant to find the family in the census returns. See chapter eight for more about the census.

Reading and Analyzing Scottish Marriage Certificates

Scottish marriage certificates have not changed as much as the birth certificates have. The 1855 certificates are more detailed than later ones, so let's look at an 1855 marriage certificate and one for an 1896 marriage.

1855 marriage certificate

We will analyze the marriage certificate of James Kay and Isabell Brough (see Figure 7-7). An 1855 marriage certificate contains sixteen columns. Let's look at each column individually.

Column 1:   Number

The first column on the certificate contains the entry number in the original marriage record book.

Column 2:   When, where, and how married

This column shows the place and date of the marriage, by whom the couple was married, and the denomination of the church. James and Isabell were married 2 November 1855 in Crieff by a minister of the Free Church. This is important information because it explains why you may not find records of their families in the Church of Scotland. They were married in a nonconformist church, and their

No.	When, where, and how married.	Signatures of the Parties.	Residence.		Age.	Rank or Profession, and Relationship of Parties (if related).	Condition.		Children by each former Marriage.		Birthplace, and when and where registered.	Parents'			If a regular Marriage, Signatures of Officiating Minister and Witnesses.	If irregular, date of Extract Sentence of Conviction, or Decree of Declarator, and in what Court pronounced.	When and where registered, and Signature of Registrar.
			Present.	Usual.			If a Widower or Widow, whether Second or Third Marriage.		Living.	Dead.		Names.	Rank, Profession, or Occupation.				
2	At Crieff On 2nd November 1855 By the Revd. Finlay Macallister Minister of Free Church	(Signed) James Kay (Signed) Isabell Brough	Crieff Crieff	Muthill Muthill	20 19	Ploughman ———	Bachelor Spinster					Crieff Crieff	Robert Kay and Christian Courie ——— ———	Ploughman ———		(Signed) Finlay Macallister Free Church Crieff (Signed) Alexr. Kay Witness James Kerr Witness		5th November 1855 At Crieff (Signed) James MacResty Registrar

TRACTED from the Register of Marriages, for the............Parish............of............Crieff............, in the............County............of............Perth............

this............10th............day of............February............19 72 .

In terms of the 41st section of the Registration of Births, Deaths and Marriages (Scotland) Act 1965, every extract of an entry in a register kept under the provisions of the said Act or any enactment repealed thereby shall be sufficient evidence of the birth, death or marriage to which it relates, provided that it is duly authenticated by the seal of the General Register Office or the signature of the district registrar or assistant registrar.

Any person who falsifies any of the particulars on this extract or knowingly uses, gives or sends as genuine any false extract is liable to prosecution under section 53(1) of the said Act.

Any person who passes as genuine a reproduction of this extract, if such reproduction has not been authenticated by the seal of the General Register Office or by the signature of the district registrar or assistant registrar, is liable to prosecution under section 53(3) of the said Act.

Figure 7-7
1855 marriage certificate for James Kay and Isabell Brough.

families could have attended this church. Because the date of marriage was recorded at the time of the event, it is more accurate than a date you may find elsewhere, so you should record it on your pedigree chart and family group record.

Column 3:   Signatures of the Parties

This is where the names of the groom and bride are recorded. The column also tells you whether they could sign their names. The name of the bride or groom may be very different from the name given at birth. This is quite common. The given name may be a variation or a nickname. For example, you may find the Gaelic version of a given name on a birth record and an English form on the marriage record. A man listed as Donald on his birth record may have signed his name as Daniel on the marriage certificate. **Notice that this is the third spelling variation we've seen for Isabella**; she is Isobel on Margaret's birth record, Isabella on David's birth record, and Isabell on this marriage record. Surnames can vary, too. A person may have the name McKay on one record and Kay on another. Occasionally, the bride or groom adopted a stepfather's surname. People also might have used a mother's maiden name, a clan chief's name, or even a name chosen at random because they didn't like the one they were born with or they wanted to hide their identity. We even found a woman who assumed the surname of the family she was living with when her parents were still alive. Sometimes the names on various records seem to bear no relation to one another. Remember our example from chapter three about the woman named Nancy MacCuaig who is called Ann or Agnes McLeod on other records. Ann, Agnes, and Nancy are all variations of the same given name. MacCuaig is a sept of McLeod, so the family had changed its surname to McLeod. This can get very confusing. Sometimes it helps to look at the parents' names in column 12 to see if the surnames of the bride and groom are the same as their parents'. We can't do that for Isabell Brough because the names of her parents aren't recorded. The law of genealogy strikes again.

Columns 4 and 5:   Residence: Present/Usual

Notes

Column 4 is supposed to tell where the couple lived at the time of the marriage. Column 5 tells where they usually lived. Why were they in Crieff when the usual residence for both parties was Muthill? We don't know yet.

Column 6:   Age

This information is only as accurate as the bride or groom cared to make it. They were not asked for proof of age. The parties were both of legal age to contract the marriage; males had to be at least age fourteen and females had to be at least twelve.

Column 7:   Rank or Profession, and Relationship of Parties (if related)

Rank or profession tells you the social status or occupation of the bride and groom. The occupation can help you differentiate between people with the same name. It is very common for the woman to have been working and for this column to be left blank—remember this is long before the women's rights movement. If the couple were related in any way, this should also be stated on the certificate.

Column 8:   Condition: If a Widower or Widow, whether Second or Third Marriage

The marital status at the time of the marriage should be listed as "bachelor" or "spinster" or "widow" or "widower."

"Bachelor" usually means that a man has not previously been married. However, it is not uncommon for a widower to be listed as "bachelor." A widower is a man whose previous wife has died. A spinster is not an "old maid"; she is a woman who has never been married. A widow is a woman whose previous husband has died. In Scotland, it is also possible for one of the parties to be divorced. A significant item in this column is the indication of a second or third marriage.

Columns 9 and 10:   Condition: Children by each former marriage: Living/ Dead

This column, if filled out, contains great information. It tells the number of children born to the groom and to the bride in former marriages. If there was more than one prior marriage, there should be a separate line for each marriage. The column is divided into the number of children living at the time of the current marriage and the number who were deceased at the time. Later search for these children in church records. Children who were baptized in the Church of Scotland should be indexed and easy to find. However, many children were not baptized in that church, especially after 1843. The numbers given in this column can help you determine whether you have found all of the children.

No numbers appear in this column on our certificate because James was a bachelor and Isabell was a spinster; neither had been married before. Does this mean that they didn't have any children? No, it means that they didn't have any children from a *previous marriage*. They already had a daughter, Margaret, who was born 13 October 1855, a few weeks before this marriage. Therefore, do not assume if the column is blank that no children were born to either party. Illegitimate children may have been born to either or both.

Column 11:   Birthplace, and when and where registered

This column should list the place of birth for each party and also when and where the birth was registered. If a birth occurred before civil registration started in 1855, the column would most likely tell you when the person was baptized. That is fantastic information; however, birth registration dates are missing from our certificate. That is particularly distressing since James's baptism is not recorded in the Church of Scotland. Where was it recorded, if at all? It is possible that neither spouse knew (or wanted to admit) when or if their births were registered.

Columns 12 and 13:   Parents: Names; Rank, Profession, or Occupation

The name of the father and the maiden name of the mother of each party should appear here. The man named in this column should be the natural father of the bride or groom. Notice that we say "should." No parents' names are given for Isabell Brough. Is this because she didn't know her parents' names or because she didn't want to give them? We'll find out a little more about why she didn't name her parents when we examine her death certificate.

If either the bride or groom was illegitimate, no father's name might have been given because they did not know his name. If the father was known, his name may have been stated even if he was not named on the birth or baptismal record. You may also find a stepfather's name or even a fictitious name if the natural father was unknown and they wanted to avoid potential embarrassment.

Column 13 gives the occupations of the parents. In this case, Robert Kay and his son James were both ploughmen. No occupation is recorded for Isabell's father, because he isn't named. Occupations are extremely important because they tell you the social status of your ancestor and, therefore, the most likely records in which to find him. The occupation is sometimes the only way to distinguish your ancestor from others of the same name.

Column 14:   If a regular Marriage, Signatures of Officiating Minister and Witnesses

This column is filled out only if a marriage was a regular marriage. (See the discussion earlier in this chapter about the distinction between regular and irregular marriages.) James Kay and Isabell Brough's marriage was a regular marriage, and the certificate was signed by the minister of the Free Church of Crieff. Again, the indication that the marriage occurred in the Free Church is important. The names of the witnesses are also important. Witnesses were often close relatives. We should find out if or how Alexander Kay and James Kerr were related to the bride and groom. It's quite likely that Alexander Kay is a brother or other close relative of James Kay.

Column 15:	If irregular, date of Extract Sentence of Conviction, or Decree of Declarator, and in what Court pronounced

We'll examine this column further in the next marriage extract. A line was drawn through this column on James and Isabell's record because their marriage was regular.

Column 16:	When and where registered, and Signature of Registrar

Following a marriage ceremony the information on the Marriage Schedule is completed. The couple has three days to return this document by mail or in person to the registrar. A fine is levied if it is not returned within three days. The registrar then registers the marriage, signing and dating the entry.

Marriages after 1855

Let's review the marriage record of Alexander Cameron and Marion Henrietta Stuart (see Figure 7-8) to see how a marriage extract for other years may look. Alexander is the grandson of James and Isabella Kay by their daughter Christina. Notice that this extract is typed; it was obtained from Scotland in 1971. You probably will not get a typed copy now, and you don't want one. The information you receive should be a photocopied extract from the register of marriages. As we saw with the birth records, post-1855 marriage records are far less detailed than the ones for 1855, but they still are more informative than marriage records for many other countries. The certificate contains seven numbered columns. We elaborate on just a few.

Column 1:	When, Where, and How Married

This column contains the date and place of marriage. Our certificate states that the couple was married 16 October 1896 at 173 Shamrock Street in Glasgow. They were married by declaration. (Review the section about irregular marriages earlier in this chapter.) This is an irregular marriage by consent of both parties. In Scotland parental consent for marriage was not needed, and these two were both of legal age to contract a marriage. Imagine how frightening it might be if you knew that your twelve-year-old daughter or fourteen-year-old son could decide to get married, stand and say, "I marry you," and the marriage was valid without your knowledge or consent. Nothing more was required in Scotland at that time for a legal marriage. At this wedding, Alexander and Marion verbally accepted one another as husband and wife, and no minister was present. In this case, two witnesses were required to prove that the marriage had actually occurred. The witnesses were Harry Walker and Mary Ellen Edith Borland or Walker. Mary may have been Harry's wife. Bor-

					1861 - 1921	

EXTRACT OF AN ENTRY IN   **A REGISTER OF MARRIAGES**

kept under the Registration of Births,   Deaths and Marriages (Scotland) Act 1965

No.	(1) When, Where, and How Married	(2) Signatures of Parties — Rank or Profession, whether Single or Widowed, and Relationship (if any)	(3) Age	(4) Usual Residence	(5) Name, Surname, and Rank or Profession of Father — Name, and Maiden Surname of Mother	(6) If a Regular Marriage, Signatures of officiating Minister and Witnesses; If Irregular, Date of Conviction, Decree of Declarator, or Sheriff's Warrant	(7) When and Where Registered and Signature of Registrar
475	1896 on the Sixteenth day of October at 173 Shamrock Street, Glasgow By Declaration in presence of Harry Walker Professor of Music and Mary Ellen Edith Borland or Walker	(Signed) Alexander Cameron Dentist's Assistant (Bachelor) (Signed) Marion Henrietta Stuart (Spinster)	20 20	140 Mains Street Glasgow Viewfield Govan	Hector Cameron Club Proprietor (deceased) and Christina Cameron m.s. Kay John Stuart Building Contractor (deceased) and Agnes Stuart m.s. Henderson	(Signed) Warrant of Sheriff-Substitute of Lanarkshire dated 16th (Signed) October 1896	1896 October 16th At Glasgow (Signed) Wm. L. Campbell Assist Registrar (Initd.) W.B.

EXTRACTED from the Register of Marriages for the .... District .... of .... Kelvin ....

in the .... Burgh .... of .... Glasgow ....

Given at the General Register Office, New Register House, Edinburgh,

under the Seal of the said Office, this .... 3rd .... day of .... June .... 19 71.

ATTENTION IS DIRECTED TO THE NOTES OVERLEAF

Figure 7-8
1896 marriage of Alexander Cameron and Marion Henrietta Stuart.

land is her maiden name. We should find out who they were and whether they were related to the bride or groom. We also need to know more about 173 Shamrock Street. Was this somebody's house? Who lived there? Why did Alexander and Marion choose this place for their marriage?

> Column 5:   If a Regular Marriage, Signatures of officiating Minister and Witnesses; If Irregular, Date of Conviction, Decree of Declarator, or Sheriff's Warrant

Two columns from the 1855 certificate have been combined. Because the couple was not married by a minister, they had to prove to the sheriff substitute of their county that the marriage occurred. It must have been proven to his satisfaction because he issued a sheriff's warrant and the marriage was registered.

Now That I Have Read the Marriage Certificate, Where Do I Go Next?

You should have the ages of the bride and groom and the names of their parents. Although it helps to know the place of birth, you may now be able to easily locate a record of a birth or baptism, especially if it occurred before 1875. If the birth occurred after 1855, see the sections on birth records in this chapter. If the person was born prior to 1855, see chapter nine for information on finding church records of baptism.

You also should know a place of residence which you can use to locate this couple in census returns. The census records can tell you a lot more about your family. See chapter eight to start using the census records.

Reading and Analyzing Scottish Death Certificates

Many genealogists ignore death certificates because they believe that death certificates contain less information than birth and marriage certificates. **But in Scotland,**

Important

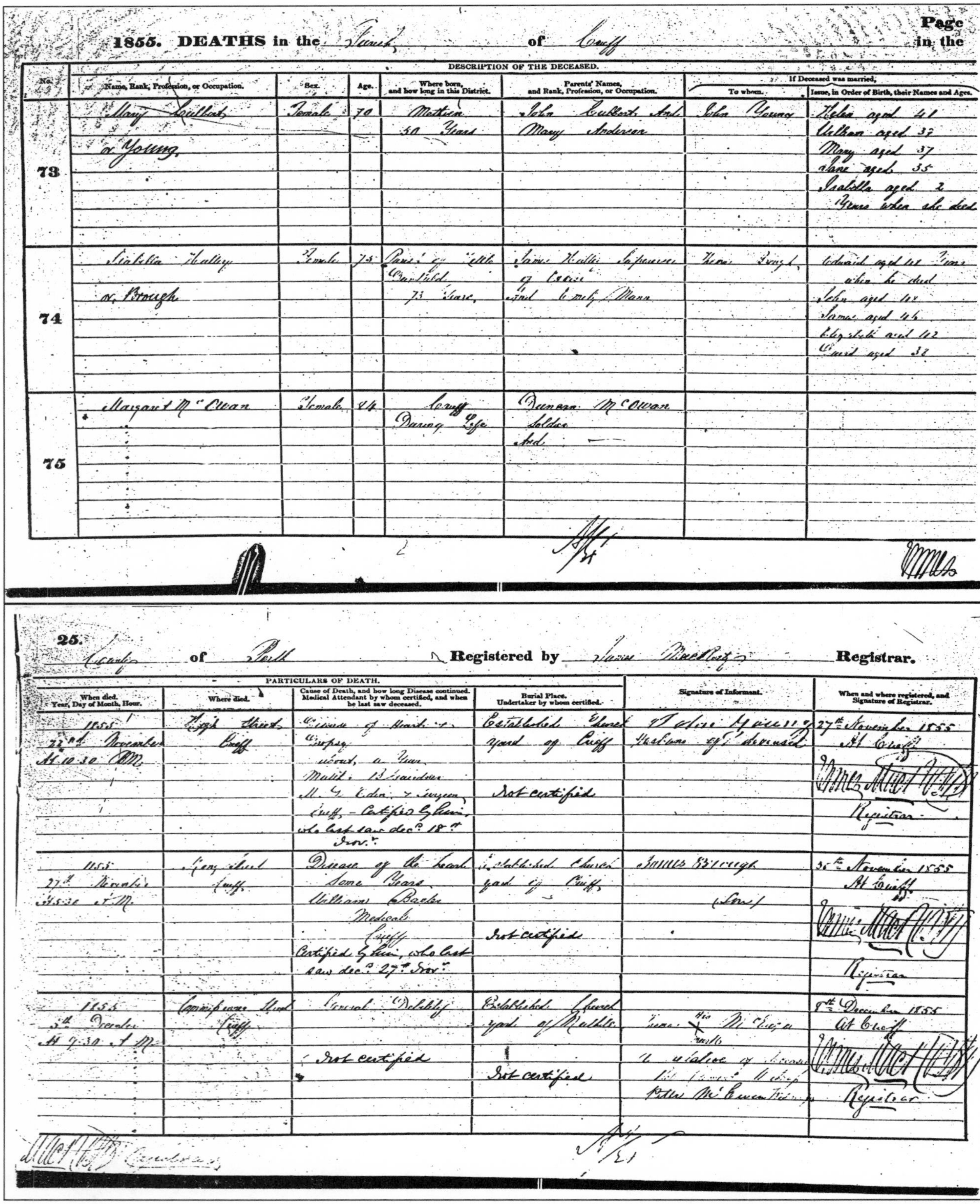

1855. DEATHS in the Parish **of** Crieff — **Page in the**

DESCRIPTION OF THE DECEASED.

No.	Name, Rank, Profession, or Occupation.	Sex.	Age.	Where born, and how long in this District.	Parents' Names, and Rank, Profession, or Occupation.	If Deceased was married, To whom.	Issue, in Order of Birth, their Names and Ages.
73	Mary Cuthbert or Young	Female	70	Methven 50 Years	John Cuthbert And Mary Anderson	John Young	Helen aged 41, William aged 37, Mary aged 37, Jane aged 35, Isabella aged 2 Years when she died
74	Isabella Halley or Brough	Female	75	Parish of Little Dunkeld 73 Years	James Halley Labourer of [illegible] and Emily Mann	Thomas Brough	Edward aged 48 Years when he died, John aged 48, James aged 46, Elizabeth aged 42, David aged 38
75	Margaret McOwan	Female	84	Crieff During Life	Duncan McOwan Soldier And [illegible]		

25. County **of** Perth **Registered by** James MacRosty **Registrar.**

PARTICULARS OF DEATH.

When died. Year, Day of Month, Hour.	Where died.	Cause of Death, and how long Disease continued. Medical Attendant by whom certified, and when he last saw deceased.	Burial Place. Undertaker by whom certified.	Signature of Informant.	When and where registered, and Signature of Registrar.
1855 22nd November At 10.30 PM	High Street Crieff	Disease of Heart & Dropsy about a Year [illegible] M.D. Edin. & Surgeon Crieff, - Certified by him who last saw dec. 18th Nov.	Established Church yard of Crieff. Not certified	John Young Husband of deceased	27th November 1855 At Crieff James MacRosty Registrar
1855 27th November 3.30 AM	[illegible] Street Crieff	Disease of the heart Some Years William Baxter Medical [illegible] Crieff Certified by him, who last saw dec. 27th Nov.	Established Church yard of Crieff. Not certified	James Brough (Son)	30th November 1855 At Crieff James MacRosty Registrar
1855 3rd December At 7.30 AM	Commissioner Street Crieff	General Debility. Not certified	Established Church yard of [illegible]. Not certified	[illegible] his x mark [illegible] relative of deceased [illegible] Peter McEwen [illegible]	9th December 1855 At Crieff James MacRosty Registrar

Figure 7-9
1855 death register for the County of Perth, page 25. The register appears as two pages. Read Isabella Brough's death record (number 74) in the middle of each page above.

death certificates can tell you more than other certificates. In fact, they should be among the first documents you acquire. A Scottish death certificate may give you the deceased's name; occupation; spouse's name and occupation; sex; age; date, time, place, and cause of death; duration of disease; and attending physician's name. It also indicates the name and occupation of the deceased's father; the name and maiden name of the deceased's mother; whether either parent was still alive; and the name, relationship, and residence of the informant. Death certificates are even more informative for people who died in 1855. You can see how Scottish death certificates are essential, especially for tracing someone who was born before 1855. In addition to what they tell you about the deceased, death certificates can help you trace your own medical history; find descendants and other relatives; locate birth, marriage, census, and probate records; and more. You should get the death certificates for all deceased members of your family. There were two Isabella Broughs living in Crieff. They are listed near one another in the 1851 census, which you will see later. One of them died in 1855, and the other died in 1915. We will examine the death records of both, beginning with the 1855 register (Figure 7-9). Since we have already examined the 1855 certificates in detail, we'll take less time with this one.

1855 death register

The 1855 death register in Figure 7-9 on page 100 contains the entry for Isabella Halley or Brough. You will find out more about this woman and her family in subsequent chapters. Read the register from left to right, and we'll point out some important details that you may not get anywhere else. Isabella Halley is the woman's maiden name. She was seventy-five years old at the time of her death, and she was born in the parish of Little Dunkeld in Perthshire. Her parents' names (James Halley and Emily Mann) are listed in the record, as is the occupation of her father. Notice that you have the maiden name of the mother. You may now have enough information to find a record of Isabella's birth. Since you have the names of both parents, you can search for their marriage record. Remember, however, that the birth information and the parents' names listed on a death record may be inaccurate.

The column labeled "If Deceased was married: To whom; Issue, in Order of Birth, their Names and Ages" contains some of the best information on the whole certificate. It tells us that Isabella Halley was married to Thomas Brough. You can search the Scottish Church Records index to find the date and place of marriage (see chapter nine). The next part is fantastic; it lists the name (in order of birth) of every child born to Isabella, indicates whether they were living or not, and gives their ages. This may be the only place where you can verify that all of these children were Isabella's. She had a son named Edward who was forty-eight years old when he died. The next younger son, John, was still living and was forty-eight years old. The other children listed are James, age forty-four, Elizabeth, age forty-two, and David, age thirty-eight. They were born before civil registration started, so you need to look at church records to find records of their births or baptisms. Certainly go to the Scottish Church Records index on CD to do a parent search for Thomas Brough and Isabella Halley to see if you obtain the same list of children from that index. Many times children are listed in an 1855 death certificate but not on the Scottish Church Records index. Notice that Edward was forty-eight when he died and John was forty-eight when his mother died. Since Edward was the first child and no children were born between him and his brother John, you can assume that Edward probably died shortly before his mother did. Try to find a death, burial, and probate record for him.

After the list of children the register shows the date, time, place, and cause of death. The place of burial is listed (Established Churchyard of Crieff), so you can try to find a tombstone transcription. Tombstone inscriptions are called "Monumental Inscriptions" in Scotland. The informant was James Brough, Isabella's son. From the earlier column, we know that he was the third son. The last column on the register shows the date and place of registration and the signature of the registrar.

Scottish 1855 death certificates are some of the best records in genealogy. In this case three generations, including maiden names of the women, all are named on one certificate. Life doesn't get much better than this!

Even if your ancestor didn't die in 1855, look for a death certificate for anybody who possibly could be related who did die that year. For example, we don't know yet if this Isabella Brough is related to our Isabella Brough, but we now have names for the complete family of the older woman. **Order the 1855 death certificate of anybody who could be related to your ancestor!**

Research Tip

Death records for other years

Let's examine a more recent death record in detail. The one in Figure 7-10 is for another Isabella Brough.

Register entry number. To the left of the column is the entry number in the Register of Deaths for the Parish of Crieff. Entry number 24 meants that this is the twenty-fourth death that was registered in that parish that year.

Column 1:   Name and Surname; Rank or Profession, and whether Single, Married, or Widowed

This column contains the name of the deceased, his occupation, and his marital status. The name is the one by which your ancestor was known at the time of his death, and may or may not match the name given at birth. Changing names during life was very common. Obviously, a married woman's surname at death could have been different from her birth surname if her record is under her married name. An illegitimate child, whose father's name may not be on the birth certificate, may nevertheless have used his surname.

This column indicates not only marital status; it usually names the spouse. It should also give a husband's occupation. If a man changed occupations during his lifetime, the occupation given on the death certificate may not match what you find on other records.

Notice that Isabella is listed by her married name, Isabella Kay. We can tell what her maiden name was from the names of her parents. Most married and widowed women were recorded on the death register by their married names, but some widowed women were recorded with their maiden names. No occupation is given for

Figure 7-10
1915 death certificate for another Isabella Brough.

Isabella, which isn't uncommon for a woman. An occupation is given, however, for her deceased husband. Isabella is the widow of James Kay, a ploughman. The indication that Isabella was the widow of James Kay tells us that James died before 1915. If you have no further clues to his date of death, you should start searching the death indexes from 1915 and work backward in time. So far, we know that James died sometime between 1877, when David was born, and 1915, when Isabella died.

Column 2:   When and Where Died

This is the date, time, and place of death. Death certificates were recorded close to the time of death, so record this information on your pedigree chart and family group record.

When a body was found and the precise date of death could not be determined, the certificate may give just the date the body was found. See Alexander Cameron's death record (Figure 7-11 on page 104) for an interesting example. More complete information on the date of death came from the Register of Corrected Entries. The entry was extracted onto the reverse side of the certificate.

The place of death may not be the same as the deceased's place of residence. If you do not recognize the address given in this column, find out what was at that address. It is interesting to know whether it is the address of a relative, a place of employment, or a hospital or other institution. For example, on Alexander Cameron's death record (again, Figure 7-11) his place of death is Aberdeen.

(1)	(2)	(3)	(4)	(5)	(6)	(7)	(8)	
No.	Name and Surname — Rank or Profession, and whether Single, Married or Widowed	When and Where Died	Sex	Age	Name, Surname, and Rank or Profession of Father. Name, and Maiden Surname of Mother	Cause of Death, Duration of Disease, and Medical Attendant by whom certified	Signature and Qualification of Informant, and Residence, if out of the House in which the Death occurred	When and Where Registered and Signature of Registrar	
15	Alexander CAMERON Dental-operator Married to Marian Henrietta Stuart.	1916 Found September Eighth 5h. 0m. A.M. 74 Union Street, Aberdeen.	M	39 years	Hector Cameron Clubmaster (deceased) Christina Cameron m.s. Keay (deceased)	Myocardial degeneration Syncope As cert. by J.C. Bell M.B. Ch.B.	(Signed) Marion H. Cameron Widow (Present)	1916 September 11th At Aberdeen (Signed) James Pratt Registrar	

EXTRACT OF AN ENTRY IN A REGISTER OF DEATHS 1861 - 1965
kept under the Registration of Births, Deaths and Marriages (Scotland) Act 1965

TRACTED from the Register of Deaths for the.................................. District ....of.................. St. Nicholas ....
the.................................. Burgh ..... of.......................... Aberdeen ....
en at the General Register Office, New Register House, Edinburgh,
er the Seal of the said Office, this.................. 18th ....day of.......................... June ....1971... OVER/

ATTENTION IS DIRECTED TO THE NOTES OVERLEAF

Figure 7-11
1916 death certificate for Alexander Cameron with information from the Register of Corrected Entries.

You saw earlier that he was married in Glasgow, and we have found him in Edinburgh in other records.

Isabella Kay's certificate states that she died 17 March 1915 at 5 Addison Terrace in Crieff. Next look for a land and probate record (see chapter ten on how to do this). Also find out more about this address. Was this her home, or was it the home of one of her sons or daughters? Is it an institutional address? If this was a family home, does the place still exist? Can you get a picture of where she lived? Who lives there now? You may want to see the home when you visit Scotland.

Column 3:   Sex

This is shown as "M" for male or "F" for female, although recording mistakes occasionally were made.

Column 4:   Age at Death

Always view skeptically the age at death on the certificate. The deceased did not report her own age, and ages often got more exaggerated as people got older. The informant, therefore, reported what he believed about the age of the deceased. The most reliable age information usually was given by the parents or spouse of the deceased. Information reported by children or others is less reliable.

The age at death of Isabella Kay was reported as seventy-eight years. Because it was reported by her daughter, it is less reliable information than if it had been reported by Isabella's spouse. Children didn't always know how old their parents were. But this indicates at least an approximate date to use to search for Isabella's birth record. According to the death record, her birth should have been around 1837. Compare this to what you found on her marriage record. In 1855 she was nineteen, which dates her birth at about 1836. Since civil registration started in

1855, look for her baptism in church records and use a date range of 1836 to 1837.

Column 5:   Name, Surname, and Rank or Profession of Father;
             Name and Maiden Surname of Mother

This column is one of the most important for tracing the family. It is especially important if your ancestor was born before 1855 and even more so if he was also married before 1855. If the informant knew the names of both parents of the deceased and the occupation of the father he would have given them. Again, do not be surprised if the informant knew the maiden name of the mother. Women were known throughout life by their maiden names. Notice that the column does not ask for the occupation of the mother. If either parent was deceased, that should be indicated here.

On our certificate, Isabella's father was "_____ Brough." He is listed as "Reputed Father." This means that Isabella was illegitimate and the informant did not know the name of her father. Isabella's mother was Margaret Sutherland. The informant believed that both parents were deceased. This is the first time we have seen the name of Isabella's mother. Recall that on the 1855 marriage record, Isabella's parents were not listed. We know now that Isabella may have not named her father on the marriage record because she may have not known it. We still don't know why she didn't name her mother, but we're determined to find out!

Notice that we have seen three generations of children born before the marriage (if any) of the parents. Alexander Jack Kay; his mother, Margaret Kay; and his grandmother Isabella Brough all were born before their parents married. Do not be upset if you find illegitimacy in your lineage. It was not uncommon.

Column 6:   Cause of Death, Duration of Disease, and Medical Attendant by whom certified

This information is important for compiling the health history of your family. However, the cause of death on the certificate can be specific or vague depending upon the informant and the time period. The names given to diseases may be different from the names used today. If you are unfamiliar with the cause of death, use any good genealogical dictionary to learn about it.

Isabella's death certificate indicates that a doctor examined her and determined her cause of death.

Column 7:   Signature and Qualification of Informant, and Residence, if out of the House in which the Death occurred

Column 7 gives the signature and residence of the informant. It also states how the informant was qualified to provide the death information. The informant was often a close relative of the deceased. People who were not related but were present at the death qualified. Data about the informant can help you determine the reliability of the information on the certificate.

The more remote the informant's relationship to the deceased, the less likely it is that the information on the certificate is accurate.

The informant on Isabella Kay's death certificate is Maggie McPheat, who lived on Stirling Street in Blackford. Maggie was qualified to inform about the death because she was Isabella's daughter and she was present at the death. Maggie is a nickname for Margaret. We know of only one daughter named Margaret, so this appears to be the daughter who was born in 1855. We know that Margaret was not married when she had her son Alexander Jack Kay in 1876, but she may have married after that. Search the marriage indexes starting with 1876 for a Margaret Kay whose entry matches someone with the surname of McPheat. Also search any indexed census records to find this couple and search the death indexes for her.

Column 8:   When and Where Registered and Signature of Registrar

Registration is normally very close to the death, sometimes on the day of the death. Eight days are allowed for registering a death. Registration is usually timely because burials cannot take place without a death certificate.

In our illustration, the death was reported on the day after it occurred.

Now That I Have Read the Death Certificate, Where Do I Go Next?

The search for the land and probate records comes next. See chapter ten.

If you have a home address for the deceased or another relative, use this address to locate the family in census returns. See chapter eight.

You have an approximate age to use to locate your ancestor in the microfilmed birth indexes, as described earlier in this chapter. This age combined with the names of the parents should allow you to easily locate a record of birth that occurred between 1855 and 1875. See the sections on International Genealogical Index in chapters four and six. Find a record of baptism for any birth that occurred before 1855. The deceased's age and parents' names can help you locate a baptismal record (see chapter nine). For any time period, however, be aware that you may find more than one child with your ancestor's name who has parents with the same or similar names as that ancestor's parents.

The names of the parents of the deceased may be enough to help you find the parents' marriage record. Remember, though, that you may find more than one couple with the same names as your ancestors.

If you have the name of a surviving spouse or an indication that the spouse had died, use this information to find more about the spouse.

In general, after examining the civil registration certificates, see the census records to look for people who were alive before 1901.

Research Tip

WHERE CAN I FIND OUT MORE?

Bardsley, Alan. *First Name Variants*. 2d ed. Birmingham, England: Federation of Family History Societies, 1996.

Bisset-Smith, G.T. *Vital Registration: A Manual of the Law and Practice Concerning the Registration of Births, Deaths and Marriages.* Edinburgh, Scotland: William Green & Sons, 1902.

Black, George F. *The Surnames of Scotland: Their Origin, Meaning, and History.* New York: New York Public Library, 1946. 11th printing, 1996.

Dunkling, Leslie Alan. *Scottish Christian Names: An A-Z of First Names.* London: Johnson and Bacon, 1978.

Sinclair, Olga. *Gretna Green: Scotland's Gift to Lovers.* Potter Heigham, Norfolk, England: Dove House, 1997. Published in 1989 as *Gretna Green— A Romantic History.*

Withycombe, E.G., comp. *The Oxford Dictionary of English Christian Names.* New York: Oxford University Press, 1945.

EIGHT

Census

CENSUS BACKGROUND

A numerical census was carried out by Rev. Alexander Webster in 1755. He was acting on behalf of the government and was uniquely qualified to apply pressure to ministers for their cooperation. He was the Moderator of the General Assembly of the Church of Scotland, associated with a scheme for the provision of annuities for widows and children of the clergy, and involved the Society for the Propagation of Christian Knowledge with the threat to withdraw charity schools if they did not cooperate. According to this census 1,265,380 people were in Scotland.

The first official national census was taken in Scotland in 1801 to determine the size of the population and the number of men available for the Napoleonic Wars. A census has been taken every ten years since then, except for 1941 because of World War II. The 1801 through 1831 censuses were head counts of the population and did not gather information about individuals. However, some enumerators did record names in order to count the males and females. Some of these listings have survived, and known examples are included in

Gibson, Jeremy and Mervyn Medlycott. *Local Census Listings 1522–1930: Holdings in the British Isles*. 3d ed. Federation of Family History Societies, 1997.

Johnson, Gordon. *Census Records for Scottish Families at Home and Abroad*. 3d ed. Aberdeen & North East Scotland Family History Society, 1997.

Genealogically significant census returns began in Scotland in 1841. The 1841 and subsequent censuses theoretically contain the names of everyone in the country.

How Was the Census Taken, and Why Is It Important?

In Scotland from 1801 through 1851 the schoolmasters were the census takers. In contrast, England and Wales already had a civil registration system in place in 1841 and 1851, so the census taking had been the responsibility of the local registrars. In 1841 and 1851 the local schoolmasters of Scotland were commissioned by the

Registrar General in London through the sheriffs in the counties and the chief magistrates in the royal and parliamentary burghs. Following the establishment of the civil registration system in 1855, the Registrar General for Scotland took responsibility for the census. In 1861 the census data collection was performed by 1,001 registrars and 8,075 enumerators.

Before each census was taken, enumeration districts were determined. The districts were sized so that the enumerator could reasonably be expected to collect census schedules from all the households in one day. For rural districts the number of households may have been small, but the geographic area may have been large. In urban districts the number of households may have been large even within a small geographic area. Each census required a separate act of parliament until the Census Act of 1920 made provision for all future censuses. For the periods 1801 through 1851 and 1901 and later, Scotland was classified in the census acts as part of Great Britain. For the 1861 through 1891 censuses, separate acts of parliament were required in Scotland.

Each census was taken on a specific night and is a snapshot of society on that date. The sidebar shows the census dates for each census.

To record the census, each enumerator received a set of household schedules, an enumerator's book, and an instruction and memorandum book. The enumerator used the memorandum book to keep track of the schedules distributed and collected from each household. During the week prior to census night the enumerator left a household schedule with each householder. The schedule included instructions on how to complete it. The householders were instructed to list only those people who were actually present in the house on the census night.

On the morning after census night, the enumerator collected the schedules. He was supposed to verify that they had been properly completed, and if they had not, he was to ask for the missing details. If a schedule had not been done at all, the enumerator filled in the schedule for that house. After collecting and completing all of the household schedules, the enumerator copied them into his enumerator's book. When he copied the information, the enumerator made a mark (/) at the end of each family in a dwelling. Multiple-family dwellings were common. Two slashes (//) meant the end of the dwelling. The enumerators used common abbreviations when referring to occupations. Some of the most frequently used abbreviations are listed in the sidebar on page 110.

After copying the schedules, the enumerator counted the houses and people and filled in tables with this information. He then turned in the schedules and books to the registrar, who checked them and sent them to the Census Office in London.

At the Census Office, the clerks reviewed the enumerators' books and tabulated various statistics. They often made marks on the pages as they checked the items. You can see many such marks on the microfilmed copies. Sometimes the marks make it appear that your ancestor placed a mark in the "Whether Blind, Deaf, and Dumb" column. Other times these marks make it difficult to read people's ages. The enumerators' books are on microfilm. The original householders' schedules have been destroyed.

Knowledge of the census procedure is crucial to interpreting the census returns. Because the schedule listed only those people actually present on census

Notes

CENSUS DATES

Year	The Night of
1901	31 March/1 April
1891	5/6 April
1881	3/4 April
1871	2/3 April
1861	7/8 April
1851	30/31 March
1841	6/7 June

Important

COMMON OCCUPATIONAL ABBREVIATIONS

Ind.	Person of independent means
F.S.	Female servant
M.S.	Male servant
Ag. Lab.	Agricultural laborer
Rail Lab.	Railway laborer
J.	Journeyman
Ap.	Apprentice
F.W.K.	Framework knitter
N.K.	Not known

night, it is common to find incomplete families on the census. When someone is not listed with the family, do not jump to the conclusion that he or she was deceased. The missing family member may have been enumerated elsewhere because he was living there, temporarily working there, or merely visiting. Sometimes your ancestor may have been listed twice in the census for that same reason. For example, in the 1861 census of St. James Parish, Glasgow, Margaret Quin is listed in two consecutive households: her husband's and her mother's. She must have been in both residences during the evening, so she got listed with both families. If members of the household were working that night (e.g., miners, potters, etc.) but would return in the morning, they were to be included in the household schedule. Those people traveling during the night were to be recorded at the hotel or house at which they stopped or took up residence in the morning.

Different types of errors occurred depending on who reported the information and who completed the census schedule. Some people intentionally lied on the household schedule. A few even evaded the census taker. If your ancestor was illiterate, his schedule could have been filled in by a child in the house, by a neighbor, or by the enumerator. If the enumerator recorded the information, he wrote down what he thought he heard. If someone other than the enumerator completed the schedule, the enumerator interpreted that person's handwriting when he copied the household schedule into the enumerator's book. You have no way to know who actually wrote the original information. So when you read the census, consider both regional accents and handwriting variations. Furthermore, the census return you see is from the enumerator's book and not from the original household schedule. Whenever someone copies information from one record to another, transcription errors are bound to creep in.

What Can the Census Records Tell Me?

If you had ancestors born in Scotland from about 1770 onward, you should search for them or their relatives in the census returns of 1841 and later. The civil registration of births started in 1855, and the census can give you information from even earlier. Census records for 1841 and later give the age and birthplace of everyone recorded and also the names of the parents of children living at home. Scottish census records are genealogical gold mines!

The 1841 census lists each member of the household who was present on census night. It gives the exact age for children under age fifteen and an age rounded down to the nearest five for all others. View the age data with caution. **People often lied or were mistaken about their ages.** Women especially tended to give incorrect ages. Women in their thirties and forties tended to state their ages as younger than the true ages, but older women often said that they were older than they actually were! The rounding of ages in the 1841 census can be very problematic. If a forty-two-year-old woman stated her age as thirty-nine (and who doesn't?), her age in the census appears as thirty-five. The census also lists each person's sex and occupation. The final columns indicate whether the person was born in the county where enumerated ("Y" for yes, "N" for no) or in another country ("I" for Ireland, "E" for England or Wales, "F" for foreign parts).

The 1851 and later censuses include for each member of the household the exact age (as reported to the census taker), the relationship to the head of the household, and marital status. The most exciting part is that the exact place of birth (parish or town and county) was usually provided for those who were not foreign-born. The exact place of birth should have been recorded by the census enumerator or householder, but this was not always done.

The census is one record that reconstructs and documents a family, not just individuals.

Warning

What Census Records Are Available, and Where Are They Located?

In the United Kingdom, the detailed information given on the census is confidential for one hundred years. The 1901 census records became available for public inspection in January 2002 as this book was going to press. For Scotland the 1841 through 1891 census returns are on microfilm. All are available through the Family History Library, which assigns its own film numbers to the records, so you use the FHL film number to locate a census reel. Do a locality search of the Family History Library Catalog at a Family History Center, on CD, or online at <www.familysearch.org>. You can order the film you need at any Family History Center. Remember to note both the census reference and the FHL film number in your census citations.

What Do I Need to Know Before I Search the Census Records?

You need to know how the census is organized and what the census references mean. The census records are at New Register House in Edinburgh, but they are accessible on microfilm at your local Family History Center. They are generally organized by the parish or enumeration district number. The reference number for the census matches the parish or enumeration district number in all census years but 1851. Therefore, when citing the 1851 census, include in the citation the name of the parish.

When you find your family in the census, cite your source so that anyone anywhere who reviews your work can repeat it and ensure its accuracy. Let's look at

Notes

the components of a Scottish census citation. The information you need is contained on the microfilm at the beginning of each census book along with the page where you are finding your family.

The General Register Office census citation format is [parish number]/[enumeration district number]/[entry number]/[census year]. For example, in Figure 8-7 on page 125, the citation 378/2/48/1861 appears in the upper-left corner.

Technically, this citation is correct. However, a modified format can be more helpful to researchers who are not at the GRO. A more informative citation is [parish number]/[enumeration district number]/[entry number]/[census year] at [street address], [name of town or parish], [county name]/[FHL film number].

The modified citation for Figure 8-7 is 378/2/48/1861 at Lochies, Madderty, Perth. Since this figure was actually obtained from the GRO, there is no FHL film number. If this had been taken from an FHL microfilm, you would include the film number. With this format anyone anywhere in the world can look at the citation and go to a Family History Center to view the census. Remember that for the 1851 census the reference number is not the same as the parish number, so it is vital to add the name of the parish to reduce confusion. The better your citations, the easier it is for you to find the record again if necessary and for others to reproduce your work.

SEARCHING THE CENSUS

Technique

Normally you begin with the most recent census available and work backward. Each census gives you clues to help you find the family in a previous census, so you should start with the 1901 census. You can obtain a form to use to record British census information from the FamilySearch Web site.

Unfortunately, British censuses are often more difficult to search than U.S. census records because many places in the British census are not indexed by surname. You need to know the name of the parish where your ancestor lived, and for cities you need a street address. You can find an address from several sources including civil registration certificates of birth, marriage, and death; family letters; probate records; and city directories.

What If I Don't Know Where My Ancestor Lived?

Notes

We have great news: **The 1901, 1891, and 1881 census records of Scotland are indexed for the entire country.** The 1901 and 1891 censuses are indexed on the Scots Origins Web site. You can also use the 1881 census transcription on that site, but you have to pay to use it there. (See chapter five to see how we found Hector Cameron and his wife, Christina Kay, in the 1891 index.) But here's even better news: Not only is the 1881 census indexed, but the entire census has also been transcribed so that you can find all of the significant details right from the index. It's a dream come true for the family historian. Furthermore, it's free! If you do not know enough information about your ancestor to identify him in the 1891 census index, start with the 1881 census index and transcription. The indexed 1881 census transcription is available in two formats: microfiche and CD-ROM. You can order the microfiche edition through any Family History Center. If a Family History

---

1881 BRITISH CENSUS AND NATIONAL INDEX: ENGLAND, SCOTLAND, WALES, CHANNEL ISLANDS, ISLE OF MAN, AND ROYAL NAVY

This set contains twenty-five compact discs:

Family History Resource File Viewer (one CD)

National Index to 1881 British Census (eight CDs)

1881 British Census (sixteen CDs) divided into the following regions:

- East Anglia
- Greater London
- Midlands
- North Central
- Northern Borders and Miscellany
- Southwestern
- Scotland
- Wales and Monmouth

The entire set of twenty-five CDs costs $33 plus sales tax. You can order just the CD for Scotland for $6.50. Order from the Salt Lake Distribution Center at (800) 537-5971.

Center has the CD-ROM version, you can search it there at no charge. You can also purchase your own 1881 census index on CD-ROM and use it at home. See the sidebar above for order information.

Remember, however, that as good as this index is, you must still verify the information by reviewing the census returns on microfilm.

1881 British Census and National Index on CD

Let's look at the CD-ROM version first. You can search one national index that includes the names of everyone in Scotland, England, Wales, the Channel Islands, and the Isle of Man. You can then see a complete transcript of the census returns. If you do not have your own copy of the CD-ROM, see if a nearby Family History Center has this resource. Let's go step-by-step to see what we can find.

The 1881 British Census and National Index comes with a CD called the Family History Resource File Viewer. This program is used to view the census CDs. Load this program onto your computer, then load two discs: National Index to 1881 British Census, disc 1, and 1881 British Census, disc 1.

If you are certain that your ancestor was in Scotland for the 1881 census, you can go directly to the appropriate CD. However, you should usually start with the

CD Source

Figure 8-1
Search results from 1881 census—national index for James Kay born in Perth, or an undefined community in Scotland within four years surrounding. *Reprinted by permission. © 1999 by Intellectual Reserve, Inc.*

Name	Relationship	Year	Birth	Census
KAYE, James	Head	<1834>	Pert	Pert
KEAY, James	Head	<1834>	Pert	Fife
KAY, James	Head	<1836>	Pert	Pert
KAYS, James	Head	<1836>	Pert	Lana
KAY, James	Head Lodg	<1837>	Pert	Lana
KEAY, James	Head	<1839>	Pert	Pert

Warning

Step By Step

National Index in case your ancestor was not at home on census day. Follow along on your copy of the CD as we describe the process.

On the original Scottish CDs many people born in Sutherland have been incorrectly indexed under Sunderland, Durham, England. For example, a birthplace like Clyne, Sunderland, Durham, England appears when in fact it should be Clyne, Sutherland, Scotland. Replacement CDs are available from the Salt Lake Distribution Center.

Exercise: 1881 census

To begin the program, open the Family History Resource File Viewer. Highlight "1881 British Census-National Index" and click "OK." The program begins and a screen pops up that says, "Type Search Information." Here you enter your ancestor's first and last names. Let's look for the family of James Kay. Enter "James" in the field "First Given Name" and "Kay" in the "Last Name" field. Do not enter any other information; you can see how many James Kays lived in Britain in 1881. Click "OK."

Ouch! The search shows that 1,969 James Kays (or variations) are in the 1881 census and lists them in order of the year of birth. One great feature of the CD-ROM version is that it automatically searches for the most common spelling variations and for variants of given names. For example, James and Jas., variants of the same name, are listed together. Lots of spelling variations are shown for Kay, including Kay, Keay, McKay, McCoy, and McCaa. Obviously, you must narrow your search. You should know at least an approximate date of birth. If you know James's county of birth or the county where he lived in 1881, that is even better. If you have civil registration certificates for him, his wife, or some of his children, you may be able to use that information to narrow your search. You can also use information from other censuses. Our James Kay was born about 1836 in Crieff, Perthshire.

Click on the "National Index" tab at the top of the screen to go back to the index and enter a birth year and birthplace. The name is still in the search screen. Type "1836" under "Birth Year." To have the program search for four years before and after this date, select "4" in "Year Range." (Normally you search five years on either side of the birth date, but four is used here just to show that you can choose another number.) Click the arrow under "Birth Place" to select "Perth, Scotland." Now click "OK."

This yields far fewer results: only the James Kays (or variations of that name) who were born in Perth. You may also get those whose birthplace is Scotland with no county listed, but this census has no James Kays born during this time period without a county of birth listed. See Figure 8-1. You can either click on each person individually or narrow the search even further by assuming that James lived in Perth at the time of the 1881 census. Look at the census column, choose any person listed in "Pert" (the abbreviation for Perth), and click in the census column on "Pert." This brings up a list of only the people of that surname listed in that county at the time of the census. (You could do the same with the "birth" column if you had not already limited the search to people born in Perth.) In this case, clicking on "Pert" in the "Census" column leaves only three names.

Decide which census record to examine by looking at the "Relationship" and "Year" columns. The relationship to the head of household is stated in the former. The "Year" column contains the person's approximate year of birth. Since James should have been about forty-five years old, he was old enough to be a head of household, although he could have been listed with someone else on census day. All three of the people in our search results are heads of household, but they were born in different years: James Kaye was born in 1835, James Kay was born in 1836, and James Keay was born in 1839. Let's try the second one because it is the closest to what we believe about our James Kay. Notice that "Pert" is underlined and in color on your computer monitor; this means that it is linked to further information. Double-click on either column across from James Kay's name. This brings up a screen that says, "Insert the following CD: 1881 British Census-Scotland Disc 1. Click OK when completed." Remove the National Index CD from the drive and replace it with the Scotland Region Disc 1. Then click "OK," and James's census record appears.

The screen is split into two sections. The top section repeats the information from the index, but it adds more precise place names. Instead of a birthplace of "Pert," you see that James was born in Crieff. The census place was Methven. If this looks like a good possibility for James (and it does!), view the screen section below that contains extracts from the census. Press the F9 key or click on the "Show Details" icon on the toolbar to see each person's occupation and relationship to the head of the household. With this information you should be able to identify your family. See Figure 8-2 on page 116 for the details. This certainly looks like our James Kay family! The full census reference is listed first. It tells us that James lived at Newro Cottages in Methven, Perth, Scotland. The source is FHL film 0203509 and the GRO reference is volume 380 (the parish number for Methven), enumeration district 5, page 5. Under the reference is James's household information, with the head of household listed in bold lettering. The head of household is James Kay, married, age forty-five, male, born in Crieff, Perth, Scotland. Listed at the same address is Isabella Kay, married, age forty-four. Seven children are also listed. These details are very important.

You can find out even more from this census record. You can see who were the Kays' neighbors. Click on "Neighbors" at the top of the screen. You can now move household by household in the census by using the black arrows on the toolbar. You can also scroll up and down the list to see the many households that were listed before and after the Kays on the census returns. Use the scroll bar to the right of the census information to do this. On the CD you can look at hundreds of households. You can also choose whether to view the families with or without the details

Figure 8-2
1881 census index after selecting "Show Details" icon or pressing F9 reveals more details for James Kay and family living at Newro Cottages, Methven, Perth, Scotland. *Reprinted by permission.* © *1999 by Intellectual Reserve, Inc.*

1881 British Census

Dwelling:	**Newro Cottages**				
Census Place:	**Methven, Perth, Scotland**				
Source:	FHL Film **0203509**	GRO Ref	Volume **380**	EnumDist **5**	Page **5**

		Marr	Age	Sex	Birthplace
James KAY		**M**	**45**	**M**	**Crieff, Perth, Scotland**
	Rel: Head				
	Occ: Ploughman				
Isabella KAY		M	44	F	Crieff, Perth, Scotland
	Rel: Wife				
	Occ: (Ploughmans Wife)				
Flora KAY		U	15	F	Monzievard, Perth, Scotland
	Rel: Daur				
	Occ: Scholar				
James KAY			10	M	Methven, Perth, Scotland
	Rel: Son				
	Occ: Scholar				
Robina KAY			8	F	Crieff, Perth, Scotland
	Rel: Daur				
	Occ: Scholar				
Lawrence KAY			6	M	Methven, Perth, Scotland
	Rel: Son				
	Occ: Scholar				
Hellen KAY			5	F	Methven, Perth, Scotland
	Rel: Daur				
	Occ: Ploughmans Daughter				
David KAY			3	M	Methven, Perth, Scotland
	Rel: Son				
	Occ: Ploughmans Son				
Alexander Jack KAY			5	M	Methven, Perth, Scotland
	Rel: Grandson				
	Occ: (Ploughmans Grandson)				

(occupations and relationships). Always look at neighbors because relatives and close friends may have lived in close proximity to your ancestor.

What should I do with this census information?

Review Figure 8-2. Notice that the children were born in different places. This means that you need to search the records of several different parishes to find more about the family.

James and Isabella had two children who do not appear on our list of children from the International Genealogical Index (see Figure 6-8 on page 55). Helen and David were both born after 1875, and few Scottish births after 1875 are indexed in the IGI. Now that you know about these children, look for them in the civil registration birth indexes. For example, in chapter seven we used David's name and approximate date of birth from this census record to find his birth certificate. We need to do the same for Helen. A grandson also is listed. You can find out about the parents of Alexander Jack Kay from the civil registration certificate of his birth. We did that, too, in chapter seven (see Figure 7-5 on page 92).

You also can use information from this census to help find the family in other censuses. By comparing the census returns, you can see changes in the family which can lead you to even more records.

The 1881 British Census and National Index is a fantastic tool, but remember that it is only a transcription of the census. That means it could have transcription errors. Look at the census return on microfilm. You can order the film you want at any Family History Center. The correct film number is given in the census transcription.

1881 Census Index on Microfiche

You can use the 1881 census index on microfiche at any Family History Center. That census has a national index and an index for each county. Each county has four main sections: the surname, birthplace, and census place indexes and the census as enumerated. The census as enumerated is a transcript of the census. There are also microfiche for miscellaneous notes, a list of vessels and ships, and a list of institutions. A complete listing of microfiche numbers for the 1881 census is available at <www.rootsweb.com/~bifhsusa/sct1881censusix.html>.

In most cases the CD-ROM version is preferable, but if it is not available at your nearest Family History Center, you can order the microfiche for very little cost. Let's find James Kay in the microfiche index and see how the microfiche compares to the CD-ROM version of the 1881 census. James Kay lived in Perth, so start with the surname index for that county. The surname index for Perth is on FHL microfiche 6086646.

The surnames on the microfiche are in strict alphabetical order, so consider spelling and name variations when you search for your ancestor. The header on each page tells the first name that appears on the page. Go through the microfiche until you get to the surname Kay, then go to the page that has James's name. He appears on page 01050 (see Figure 8-3). The index itself gives significant information. The headings are surname, forename, age, sex, relationship to head [of household], marital condition, occupation, name of head [of household], county and parish where born, note, the GRO for Scotland reference, and G.S.U. [FHL] film number. Our James Kay is the third one on the list. It says he is forty-five, male, the head of the household, married, living in Methven, occupation ploughman, born in parish/town of Crieff in the county of Perth, and that his census return can be found in district 380, enumeration district 5, page 5. Use this reference to find the family in the "Census as Enumerated" section or on the microfilm of the census record on FHL film number 1342217. This is great information, so why would you need more than one index?

Suppose that you want to find all of the people with the surname of Kay who were born in Crieff and who lived anywhere in Perthshire in 1881. You can find that information using the birthplace index. Your ancestors may have moved within a city, a county, or across the country. This index and the national birthplace index on FHL microfiche 6086713 can help you find them. The birthplace index is a phenomenal tool for locating ancestors who migrated.

Use the census place index to see all of the Kays who lived in Methven in 1881 and to find where they were born. Use this section to find the birthplaces of missing family members. You may find children that are missing from your family group

					1881 CENSUS–SURNAME INDEX, COUNTY: PERTHSHIRE									

KAY , Isabella   PAGE: 01050

DATA FROM THE 1881 CENSUS OF SCOTLAND © BRITISH CROWN COPYRIGHT 1982.
MICROFICHE EDITION OF THE 1881 CENSUS OF SCOTLAND © COPYRIGHT 1993, BY CORPORATION OF THE PRESIDENT OF THE CHURCH OF JESUS CHRIST OF LATTER-DAY SAINTS.

SURNAME	FORENAME	AGE	SEX	RELATION- SHIP TO HEAD	MARITAL CONDITION	CENSUS PLACE	OCCUPATION	NAME OF HEAD	CO	PARISH	NOTE	VOLUME NUMBER	ENUM. DIST.	PAGE NO	G.S.U. FILM NUMBER
KAY	Isabella	72	F	Sis	U	Comrie	Housekeeper	KAY, James	PER	Methven		341	5	5	0203503
KAY	Isabella	58	F	Head	W	Monzie	---	Self	PER	Monzie		375	3	1	0203508
KAY	Isabella	44	F	Wife	M	Methven	(Ploughmans W+	KAY, James	PER	Crieff		380	5	5	0203509
KAY	Isabella	43	F	Wife	M	Crieff	Milliner	Self	PER	Comrie		342	6	16	0203504
KAY	Isabella	38	F	Sis	M	Fowlis Wester	---	SINCLAIR, Duncan	PER	Logierate		375	1	2	0203508
KAY	Isabella	21	F	Serv	U	Crieff	Housemaid	MAC KENZIE, Dani+	PER	Madderty		342	8	6	0203504
KAY	Isabella	17	F	Daur	-	Perth East Chu+	Dyeworks Assi+	KAY, Mary	PER	Perth		387	3	48	0203511
KAY	James	67	M	Head	U	Comrie	Asst Forrester	Self	PER	Methven		341	5	5	0203503
KAY	James	55	M	Head	M	St Martins	Veterinary Su+	Self	PER	Forgandenny		393-A	3	1	0203514
KAY	James	45	M	Head	M	Methven	Ploughman	Self	PER	Crieff		380	5	5	0203509
KAY	James	41	M	Sldr	U	Perth East Chu+	Private 79 Hi+	I-"THE BARRACKS +	EDN	Edinburgh	*	387	41	7	0203513
KAY	James	32	M	Head	M	Forgandenny	Farm Servant	Self	PER	Gask		353	1	9	0203505
KAY	James	24	M	Son	U	Blackford	Shoemaker	KAY, Margaret	PER	Forteviot		333	2	3	0203502
KAY	James	17	M	Son	-	Perth St Pauls	Plumber	KAY, Mary	PER	Perth		387	33	8	0203513
KAY	James	13	M	GSon	-	Muthill	Scholar	MORRISON, James	PER	Muthill		386-A	5	5	0203510
KAY	James	10	M	Son	-	Methven	Scholar	KAY, James	PER	Methven		380	5	5	0203509
KAY	James	6	M	Vist	-	Auchterarder	Scholar	MC FARLANE, Peter	PER	Crieff		329	9	1	0203501
KAY (KEAY)	James	5	M	Son	U	Perth East Chu+	Scholar	KEAY, John	FIF	Kirkaldy		387	5	25	0203511
KAY	Jane	55	F	Wife	M	Errol	Farmers Wife	COUPAR, William	FOR	Monifieth		351	2	1	0203505
KAY	Jane	48	F	Daur	U	Logie	Chinaware Sho+	KAY, Catherine	PER	Fowlis Wester		374	3	3	0203508
KAY	Jane	39	F	Serv	U	Logie	Housekeeper	ROSS, Alexander	ENG	---		374	3	11	0203508
KAY	Jane	16	F	Daur	-	Comrie	Ser	KAY, Peter	PER	Comrie		341	5	7	0203503
KAY	Janet	8	F	Daur	-	Comrie	Scholar	KAY, Thomas	PER	Comrie		341	3	15	0203503
KAY	Janet L.	52	F	Head	W	Alyth	Domestic Serv+	Self	PER	Alyth		328-A	2	2	0203501
KAY	Jessie	58	F	Vist	W	Comrie	---	MC OWEN, Christi+	PER	Auchterarder		341	2	13	0203503
KAY	Jessie	43	F	Wife	M	Comrie	Farmers Wife	KAY, Duncan	PER	Muthill		341	5	6	0203503
KAY	Jessie	25	F	Daur	U	Alyth	Dressmaker	KAY, Janet L.	FOR	Dundee		328-A	2	2	0203501
KAY	Jessie	22	F	Serv	U	Fowlis Easter	General Serv +	BELL, William	FOR	Murroes		356	1	9	0203506
KAY	Jessie	20	F	Daur	U	Crieff	Dressmaker	KAY, Thomas	PER	Blackford		342	8	10	0203504
KAY	John	77	M	Uncl	O	Muthill	Reture Farmer	KAY, Peter	PER	Monzivail	*	386-A	1	2	0203510
KAY	John	45	M	Head	M	Crieff	Draper	Self	PER	Monzievaird		342	6	16	0203504
KAY	John	37	M	Head	M	Monzievaird & +	Shoemaker	Self	PER	Monzievaird		383	6	1	0203509
KAY	John	28	M	Head	M	Crieff	Shoemaker	Self	PER	Crieff		342	6	21	0203504
KAY	John	23	M	Son	U	Perth Middle C+	Labourer	KAY, --- (Mrs)	PER	Perth		387	26	11	0203512
KAY	John	6	M	Son	-	Comrie	Scholar	KAY, Thomas	PER	Comrie		341	3	15	0203503
KAY	John	3	M	Son	-	Auchterarder	---	KAY, Peter	PER	Auchterarder		329	10	25	0203501
KAY	John L.	13	M	Son	-	Alyth	Scholar	KAY, Janet L.	PER	Alyth		328-A	2	3	0203501
KAY	John S.	23	M	Head(Lodg)	M	Logie	Farmer	Self	FOR	Dundee		374	1	6	0203508
KAY	Lawrence	6	M	Son	-	Methven	Scholar	KAY, James	PER	Methven		380	5	5	0203509
KAY	Maggie	20	F	Serv	U	Ardoch	General Serva+	SHARP, John	LAK	Glasgow		328-B	4	9	0203501
KAY	Maggie S.	22	F	Wife	M	Logie	---	KAY, John S.	---	Glasgow		374	1	6	0203508
KAY	Malles	19	M	Neph	U	Crieff	Mason (Unempl+	KAY, Alexander	EDN	Edinburgh		342	3	8	0203504
KAY	Margaret	53	F	Serv	U	Dunkeld	Head Dairymai+	MUNNICK, Clarice	AYR	Ochiltree		349	1	5	0203505
KAY	Margaret	50	F	Head	W	Blackford	---	Self	PER	Fowlis Wester		333	2	3	0203502
KAY	Margaret	28	F	Wife	M	Blackford	Dykers Wife	KAY, Robert	PER	Blackford		333	5	1	0203502
KAY	Margaret	16	F	DSer	U	Crieff	Dom Serv	HARLEY, James	PER	Blackford		342	8	7	0203504
KAY	Margaret	13	F	Daur	-	Comrie	Sch	KAY, Duncan	STI	Stirling		341	5	6	0203503
KAY	Margret	30	F	Sis	U	Muthill	Housekeeper	KAY, Peter	PER	Muthil		386-A	1	2	0203510
KAY	Marion	26	F	Vist	M	Auchterarder	---	MC FARLANE, Peter	PER	Crieff		329	9	1	0203501
KAY	Martha I.D.	2	F	Daur	-	Comrie	---	KAY, Thomas	PER	Comrie		341	3	15	0203503
KAY	Mary	59	F	Wife	M	St Martins	Wife	KAY, James	PER	St Martins		393-A	3	1	0203514

+ = SEE ORIGINAL CENSUS FOR FULL DATA	m = MONTHS w = WEEKS d = DAYS > = GREATER THAN < = LESS THAN	M = MARRIED U = UNMARRIED W = WIDOW(ER) D = DIVORCED O = OTHER	* = SEE MISCELLANEOUS NOTES

Figure 8-3

1881 microfiche version of the census index showing James Kay. Note that on the microfiche index the entries are in strict alphabetical order. There is no grouping for similar surnames as there is on the CD-ROM version. *Reprinted by permission. © 1993 by Intellectual Reserve, Inc.*

records. It will also give you additional places to search for records of your family.

The fourth major section is the census as enumerated. This is a transcript of the census. Locate the census transcript by referring to the "GRO for Scotland Reference" on the index pages. The same reference appears whether you find the person in the surname index, the birthplace index, or the census place index. James is listed in all three indexes with this GRO for Scotland reference: volume 380 [the parish number for Methven], enumeration district 5, page 5. The Perthshire Census as Enumerated is on FHL microfiche 6086649. The volume numbers (parish numbers) are at the top of each microfiche. Scan the tops of the pages until you come to 380, 5, 5. You can then see all the neatly typed census information. You have no handwriting to worry about! On the microfiche, each column of the census is transcribed in the order that it appeared on the census return. You can easily scan the adjacent households and see them all at once. This is an advantage over the CD-ROM version. However, if there is not enough room in a field, the information in that field is truncated. The truncated field is followed by the symbol " +." **Truncated information is the major drawback to the microfiche version**. To see what was left off, look at the full entry on microfilm or on the 1881 British Census on CD-ROM. But right on this microfiche is everything we need: the name James Kay, his sex, age, marital status, occupation, and birthplace. The names, relationships, marital statuses, ages, sex, and occupations of other members of the household are all listed in full. This is great stuff! Best of all, in the British census, you should find the exact parish of birth. When you find the exact place of birth you can go to the records of that parish to trace the family further. See chapter nine for details.

Because this index is so complete, many people may be tempted to go no further. If you look at the copy of the census schedule on microfilm, you usually see very little difference between it and the transcript. Remember, though, that somebody else interpreted the handwriting of the census enumerator. Even the best indexes and transcripts are no match for the original. *Always* go back to the original source, if possible.

What Indexes Exist for Other Census Years?

No census other than the 1901, 1891, and 1881 censuses currently has a nationwide index. By starting with the 1881 census indexes, you can more easily recognize your ancestors in the 1891 index. You can also use the information you find in the 1881 census to locate your family in the 1871 census and then go from there to other records.

In addition, many individuals and family history societies in Scotland have produced census indexes for their areas. To find out what census indexes exist for your ancestor's place, use Peter Ruthven-Murray's *Scottish Census Indexes: Covering the 1841–1871 Civil Censuses*. You can purchase this at the Web site of the Scottish Association of Family History Societies at <www.safhs.org.uk>. This booklet is arranged by county and lists all known census surname indexes. It tells where the index is located (which may be more than one society or library), the year of the census, and whether the index is available for purchase. This information can save you considerable research time. The book is periodically updated, so be sure that you use the latest edition.

Many family history societies have Web sites on the Internet. A Web site may have a list of the census indexes and how to order them. Because the societies are members of the Scottish Association of Family History Societies, you can obtain a listing of societies for each county at <www.safhs.org.uk>. Each society name is linked to its Web site (if it has one), so you can go immediately to the society's site to see what's available.

Many larger locales have street indexes. **Instead of looking here for your ancestor's name, look for his street**. You can obtain a street address from many sources including civil registration certificates. To find a street index for the place you need, check <www.rootsweb.com/~bifhsusa/ressco.html#census>.

If your ancestor lived in Glasgow, you may be able to locate him in the census using a street address obtained from city directories. Glasgow is the only Scottish city for which you can obtain a long run of city directories on microfiche from the

Family History Library. Glasgow city directories from 1787 to 1886 are on FHL microfiche 6340933–6341018.

If no indexes are available, you have to search page by page through the entire district. Although this may seem tedious, you can do your most effective research when searching every page because you can notice other people with the same surname. You also can notice relatives with different surnames, such as married daughters, whom you might never have found if you had gone directly to your ancestor's entry. For many parishes, it can take less than one hour to go through the entire census page by page. The results pay off handsomely!

Finding the Correct Microfilm Number for Scottish Censuses

Even if you cannot find a census index that contains your ancestor's name, you can still locate him on the census. First, you need to know the name of the parish where your ancestor resided. You can obtain the name of the parish (and sometimes an exact address) from civil registration certificates of birth, marriage, and death. Once you know the parish, use a place search in the Family History Library Catalog to search for the name of the parish. Then select "Census" from the list of topics.

Sources

Another way to find microfilm numbers is to go to a Family History Center and use the *Index to Parishes or Districts in the Census of Scotland for the Years 1841–1891*. Most people just call it the Census Register, and it is on FHL microfiche 6035795. If it is not already available at your nearest Family History Center, you may want to order it. The register is very easy to use. It is organized by county, and all parishes in the county are listed alphabetically with their parish number and the microfilm numbers for each census year. See Figure 8-4.

Now that you know how to find the appropriate microfilm, it's time to see what the census says. Let's trace Isabella Kay (or Brough) through all applicable census years.

1891 Census

For some people, using the 1891 census index on the Scots Origins Web site is the way to go. For others, it is simply not an option. Let's see how we can find our family in the 1891 census if we can't or choose not to use the Scots Origins index.

Step By Step

Let's use information from the 1881 census to find the Kay family. They lived in Methven in 1881, so let's hope they stayed there. Using either the Census Register or the Family History Library Catalog, we find that the 1891 census for the parish of Methven is on FHL film 0208738.

OK, this was too easy. Look at Figure 8-5 on page 122. We'd like to tell you that we used some fancy trick to find them, but we just rolled through the film until we found the family. They were in enumeration district 5, page 6. James and Isabella Kay lived at 26 Packhorse. James was fifty-five, and he was a farm servant (not a ploughman). You can tell that he was employed by someone else because an X is in the "Employed" column. Isabella was his wife, age fifty-four, and she has no occupation listed. They had only two children remaining with them: Helen, age fifteen, and David, age thirteen. Both children were scholars, which means that they attended school. James and Isabella were born in Crieff; Helen and David

```
                    SCOTLAND CENSUS

                         PERTH

PARISH NAME              PARISH NUMBER   YEAR    FILM NUMBER   ENUM DI

Madderty                 378            1841    1042695*
                                                101908
                                        1851    1042247*
                                                103744
                                        1861    103894
                                        1877    104077
                                        1881    203509
                                        1891    208738


Meigle                   379            1841    1042695*
                                                101908
                                        1851    1042247*
                                                103744
                                        1861    103894
                                        1871    104077
                                        1881    203509
                                        1891    208738


Methven                  380            1841    1042696*
                                                101908
                                        1851    1042247*
                                                103744
                                        1861    103894
                                        1871    104077
                                        1881    203509
                                        1891    208738


Moneydie                 381            1841    1042696*
                                                101908
                                        1851    1042247*
                                                103744
                                        1861    103894
                                        1871    104077
                                        1881    203509
                                        1891    208738


Monzie                   382            1841    1042696*
                                                101909
                                        1851    1042247*
                                                103744
                                        1861    103894
                                        1871    104077
                                        1881    203509
                                        1891    208739
```

Figure 8-4
Search results to identify film numbers for census records in the parish of Methven, Perthshire, Scotland using the *Index to Parishes or Districts in the Census of Scotland for the Years 1841–1891,* commonly known as the Census Register. *Reprinted by permission. © 1990 by Intellectual Reserve, Inc.*

were born in Methven. Nobody in the family spoke Gaelic. We have not seen such language information on other records of the family. Nobody in the household was "deaf and dumb," "blind," or "lunatic, imbecile, or idiot." The last column provides the number of rooms they occupied that had one or more windows.

When you obtain a census record, compare it to any others you have to see how the family situation changed. You can do several things with the information you just obtained. For example, in 1881 the Kays had seven children living with them. In 1891 they had only two. Look in the civil registration indexes for the marriages or deaths of the five other children. While you have this census film, go through it to see if any of the older children still lived in Methven. You also have narrowed the time period to search for the death of James Kay. He was alive at the time of

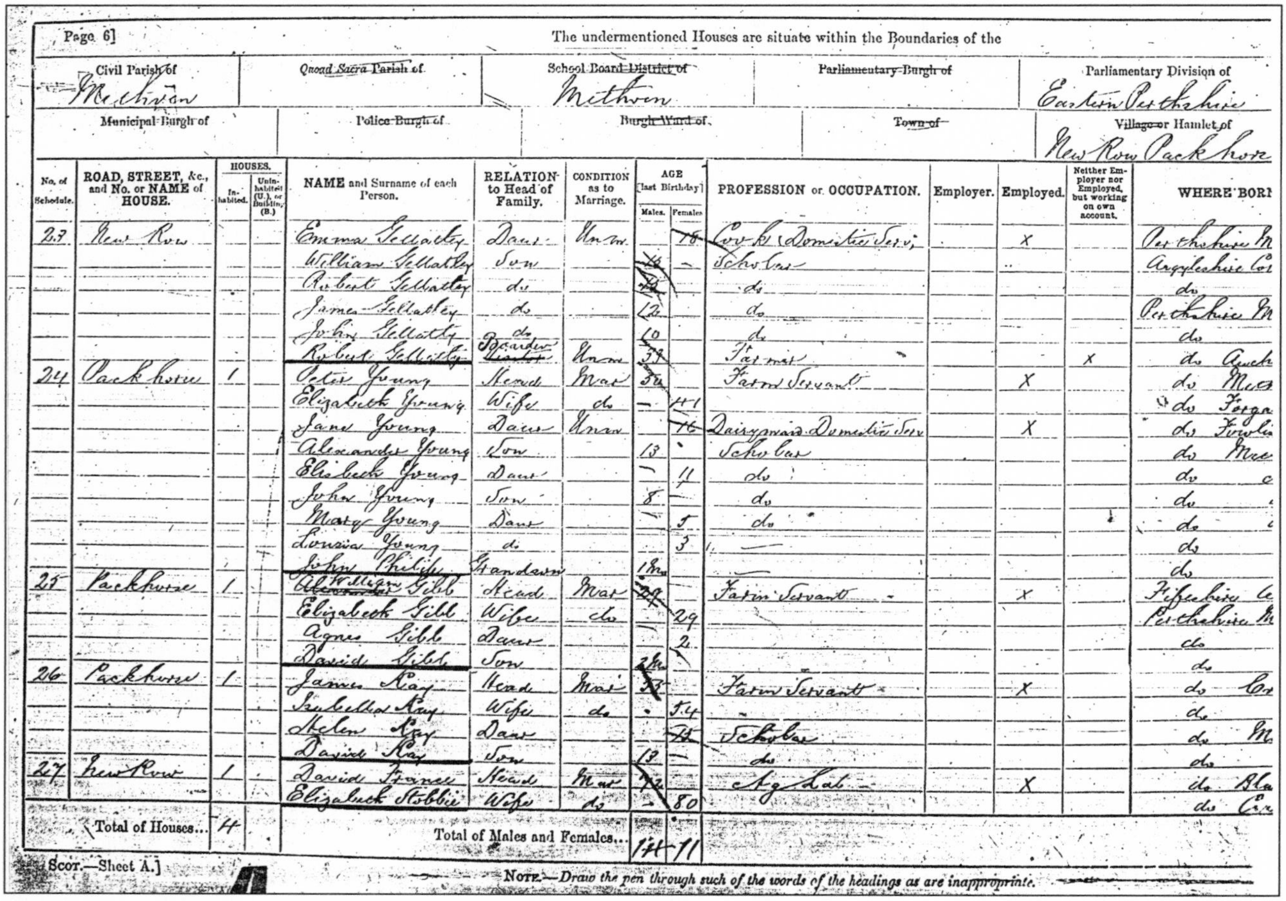
Page 6] The undermentioned Houses are situate within the Boundaries of the

Civil Parish of Methven | Quoad Sacra Parish of | School Board District of Methven | Parliamentary Burgh of | Parliamentary Division of Eastern Perthshire

Municipal Burgh of | Police Burgh of | Burgh Ward of | Town of | Village or Hamlet of New Row Packhorse

No. of Schedule	ROAD, STREET, &c., and No. or NAME of HOUSE	Houses In-habited	Unin-habited (U.), or Building (B.)	NAME and Surname of each Person	RELATION to Head of Family	CONDITION as to Marriage	Age Males	Age Females	PROFESSION or OCCUPATION	Employer	Employed	Neither Employer nor Employed, but working on own account	WHERE BORN
23	New Row			Emma Gellatley	Daur	Unm		18	Cook & Domestic Servt		X		Perthshire M
				William Gellatley	Son		[illegible]		Scholar				Argyleshire Co
				Robert Gellatley	do		[illegible]		do				do
				James Gellatley	do		12		do				Perthshire M
				John Gellatley	do		10		do				do
				Robert Gellatley	Boarder	Unm	3[illegible]		Farmer			X	do Auch
24	Packhorse	1		Peter Young	Head	Mar	5[illegible]		Farm Servant		X		do Meth
				Elizabeth Young	Wife	do		41					do Forga
				Jane Young	Daur	Unm		16	Dairymaid Domestic Serv		X		do Fowlis
				Alexander Young	Son		13		Scholar				do Mve
				Elizabeth Young	Daur			11	do				do
				John Young	Son		8		do				do
				Mary Young	Daur			5	do				do
				Louisa Young	do			5					do
				John Philip	Grandson		1[illegible]						do
25	Packhorse	1		William Gibb	Head	Mar	29		Farm Servant		X		Fifeshire
				Elizabeth Gibb	Wife	do		29					Perthshire M
				Agnes Gibb	Daur			2					do
				David Gibb	Son		[illegible]						do
26	Packhorse	1		James Kay	Head	Mar	[illegible]		Farm Servant		X		do Cr
				Isabella Kay	Wife	do		54					do
				Helen Kay	Daur			15	Scholar				do M
				David Kay	Son		13		do				do
27	New Row	1		David France	Head	Mar	[illegible]		Ag Lab		X		do Bla
				Elizabeth Stobbie	Wife	do		80					do Cr
	Total of Houses	4		Total of Males and Females			14	11					

Scot.—Sheet A.] Note.—Draw the pen through such of the words of the headings as are inappropriate.

Figure 8-5
1891 census entry for the family of James and Isabella Kay living at 26 Packhorse in the Parish of Methven, Perthshire, Scotland.

the 1891 census and deceased at the time of his wife's death in 1915 (see her death certificate in chapter seven).

1871 Census

Let's see what the information from the 1881 census tells us to help find the Kay family in the 1871 census. Look at Figure 8-3 on page 118 and examine the ages of the children. The son James was ten years old, and he was born in Methven. If the Kay family lived in Methven at the time of his birth, we should expect to find the family in the 1871 census in that parish.

The 1871 census for Methven is on FHL film 0104077, and the family is listed in that parish. They were recorded in enumeration district 5, page 12 (see Figure 8-6). This family looks very different from the one we found in the 1881 census.

James and Isabella lived at 46 Newro Cottar House. James was age thirty-five, occupation ploughman, born in Crieff. Isabella was thirty-four and born in Crieff. So far, that corresponds to the 1881 information, but the list of children is very different. Here we have Margaret, age fifteen and born in Crieff; Christina, age thirteen and born in Monzievaird; Isabella, age eleven and born in Madderty; Mary C, age nine and born in Madderty; Janet, age seven, Flora, age five, and Catherine, age three, all born in Monzievaird; and James, age nine months and born in Methven. The first five children do not appear with their parents in the 1881 census. That means they were not at home with their parents on census night that year. They could have been working at or even just visiting another residence. They could have been married and enumerated in their own households, or they may not have been living at all. Look for marriage or death records for them, and go back to the 1881 census index to search for them individually. Furthermore, where was Catherine in 1881? She would have been thirteen that year, but she's not listed with her parents. Was she a domestic servant in another home or married (not likely, but possible) or dead? First look for her name in the civil registration death indexes for 1871 through 1881.

The only two children reported with their parents on this census and again in 1881 are Flora and James. This illustrates why you should look at all census records for a family. The makeup of a family can change quite a bit from one census to the next.

1861 Census

Let's look for the Kays in the 1861 census. Review the 1871 census in Figure 8-6 on page 124 to try to determine where the family might have been ten years earlier.

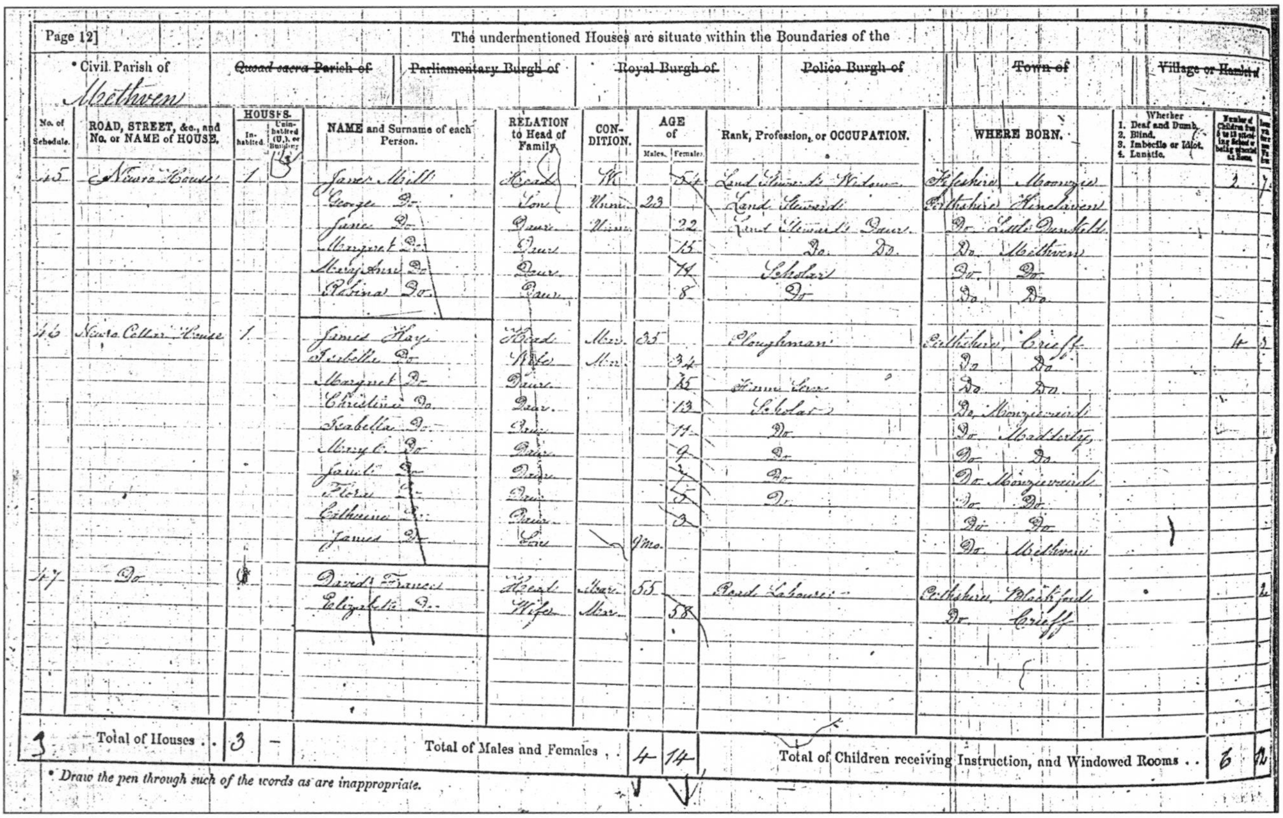

Page 12] The undermentioned Houses are situate within the Boundaries of the

Civil Parish of Methven | Quoad sacra Parish of | Parliamentary Burgh of | Royal Burgh of | Police Burgh of | Town of | Village or Hamlet

No. of Schedule	ROAD, STREET, &c., and No. or NAME of HOUSE	HOUSES In-habited	Uninhabited (U.), or Building (B.)	NAME and Surname of each Person	RELATION to Head of Family	CONDITION	AGE of Males	AGE of Females	Rank, Profession, or OCCUPATION	WHERE BORN	Whether 1. Deaf and Dumb 2. Blind 3. Imbecile or Idiot 4. Lunatic	Number of Children from 5 to 13 attending School	Rooms with one or more Windows
45	Newro House	1		James Mill	Head	W		54	Land Steward's Widow	Fifeshire, Moonzie			
				George Do	Son	Unm	23		Land Steward	Perthshire, Kinclaven			
				Jane Do	Daur	Unm		22	Land Steward's Daur	Do, Little Dunkeld			
				Margaret Do	Daur			15	Do Do	Do, Methven			
				Mary Ann Do	Daur			14	Scholar	Do, Do			
				Rosina Do	Daur			8	Do	Do, Do			
46	Newro Cottar House	1		James Kay	Head	Mar	35		Ploughman	Perthshire, Crieff		4	
				Isabella Do	Wife	Mar		34		Do, Do			
				Margaret Do	Daur			15	Farm Servt	Do, Do			
				Christina Do	Daur			13	Scholar	Do, Monzievaird			
				Isabella Do	Daur			11	Do	Do, Madderty			
				Mary C. Do	Daur			9	Do	Do, Do			
				Janet Do	Daur			7	Do	Do, Monzievaird			
				Flora Do	Daur			5	Do	Do, Do			
				Catherine Do	Daur			3		Do, Do			
				James Do	Son		9 mo.			Do, Methven			
47	Do	1		David Fraser	Head	Mar	55		Road Labourer	Perthshire, Blackford			2
				Elizabeth Do	Wife	Mar		58		Do, Crieff			
3	Total of Houses	3	—		Total of Males and Females		4	14	Total of Children receiving Instruction, and Windowed Rooms			6	12

* Draw the pen through such of the words as are inappropriate.

Figure 8-6
1871 census entry for the family of James and Isabella Kay living at 46 Newro Cottar House in the Parish of Methven, Perthshire, Scotland.

In 1871 daughter Isabella was age eleven and Mary C was age nine. They both were born in the parish of Madderty, so look for the Kay family in the 1861 census for the parish of Madderty (FHL film 0103894).

Madderty is parish number 378. The Kay family appears in enumeration district 2, entry 48 on FHL film 0103894. However, the example shown is an extract received from the GRO (see Figure 8-7). This time the family consists of James, Isabella, and three children. The occupation of James and the ages and birthplaces of all family members correspond to the 1871 census data. No "new" children appear in this record.

Because none of the children was age ten or older in 1861, the children's birth information won't help us find the family in the 1851 census. In fact, in 1851 James would have been fifteen, and Isabella would have been only fourteen. They should not have been married then, so they may be listed in the 1851 census with their parents. Now look for the marriage of James and Isabella Kay. The marriage certificate should show where they lived at the time of the wedding, and it should also give the names of their parents. Since Margaret, the oldest child, was five years old in 1861, we can estimate that the parents were married six years before then (1854–1855). Of course, there is no way to tell by looking at this census record if Margaret was really the first child. A child born earlier could have died before or been away from the parents'

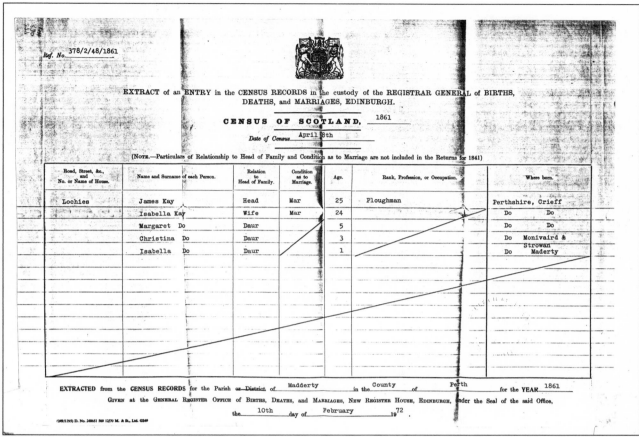

EXTRACT of an ENTRY in the CENSUS RECORDS in the custody of the REGISTRAR GENERAL of BIRTHS, DEATHS, and MARRIAGES, EDINBURGH.

CENSUS OF SCOTLAND, 1861

Date of Census. April 8th

(NOTE.—Particulars of Relationship to Head of Family and Condition as to Marriage are not included in the Returns for 1841)

Road, Street, &c., and No. or Name of House.	Name and Surname of each Person.	Relation to Head of Family.	Condition as to Marriage.	Age.	Rank, Profession, or Occupation.	Where born.	
Lochies	James Kay	Head	Mar	25	Ploughman	Perthshire, Crieff	
	Isabella Kay	Wife	Mar	24		Do	Do
	Margaret Do	Daur		5		Do	Do
	Christina Do	Daur		3		Do	Monivaird & Strowan
	Isabella Do	Daur		1		Do	Maderty

EXTRACTED from the CENSUS RECORDS for the Parish or District of Madderty in the County of Perth for the YEAR 1861

GIVEN at the GENERAL REGISTER OFFICE of BIRTHS, DEATHS, and MARRIAGES, NEW REGISTER HOUSE, EDINBURGH, under the Seal of the said Office,

the 10th day of February 1972.

(249/1395) D. No. 248651 500 12/70 M. & R., Ltd. G249

Figure 8-7
1861 census for family of James and Isabella Kay. This is an extract from the GRO.

home on the census night. Furthermore, **it is certainly not a rule that parents were married one year before the birth of the first child**. Look also at the ages of the parents. When Margaret was born, James would have been twenty years old, and his wife, Isabella, would have been nineteen. Margaret is likely to have been their first child. The best way to find the parents' date of marriage is to use the names and ages of children to order any of their birth certificates. The maiden name of the mother should be on the birth record. Then search the marriage indexes for the names of both parents. If you order the birth certificate of a child born after 1860, your search will be even easier. The mother's maiden name and the parents' date of marriage should be on any birth certificate for 1855 or after 1860.

We examined the marriage record of James Kay and his wife, Isabella Brough, in chapter seven (see Figure 7-7 on page 95). We want to find Isabella Brough in the 1851 census, but her parents are not named on the marriage record. However, her death certificate (see Figure 7-10 on page 103) tells us the maiden name of her mother, Margaret Sutherland; this might help. Isabella was married in 1855 in Crieff. She was born there in about 1836. Search for her in the 1851 census for the parish of Crieff.

Reminder

1851 Census

The 1851 census for the parish of Crieff is on two rolls of microfilm. We didn't know the enumeration district, so we had to search both rolls. To save money, we ordered

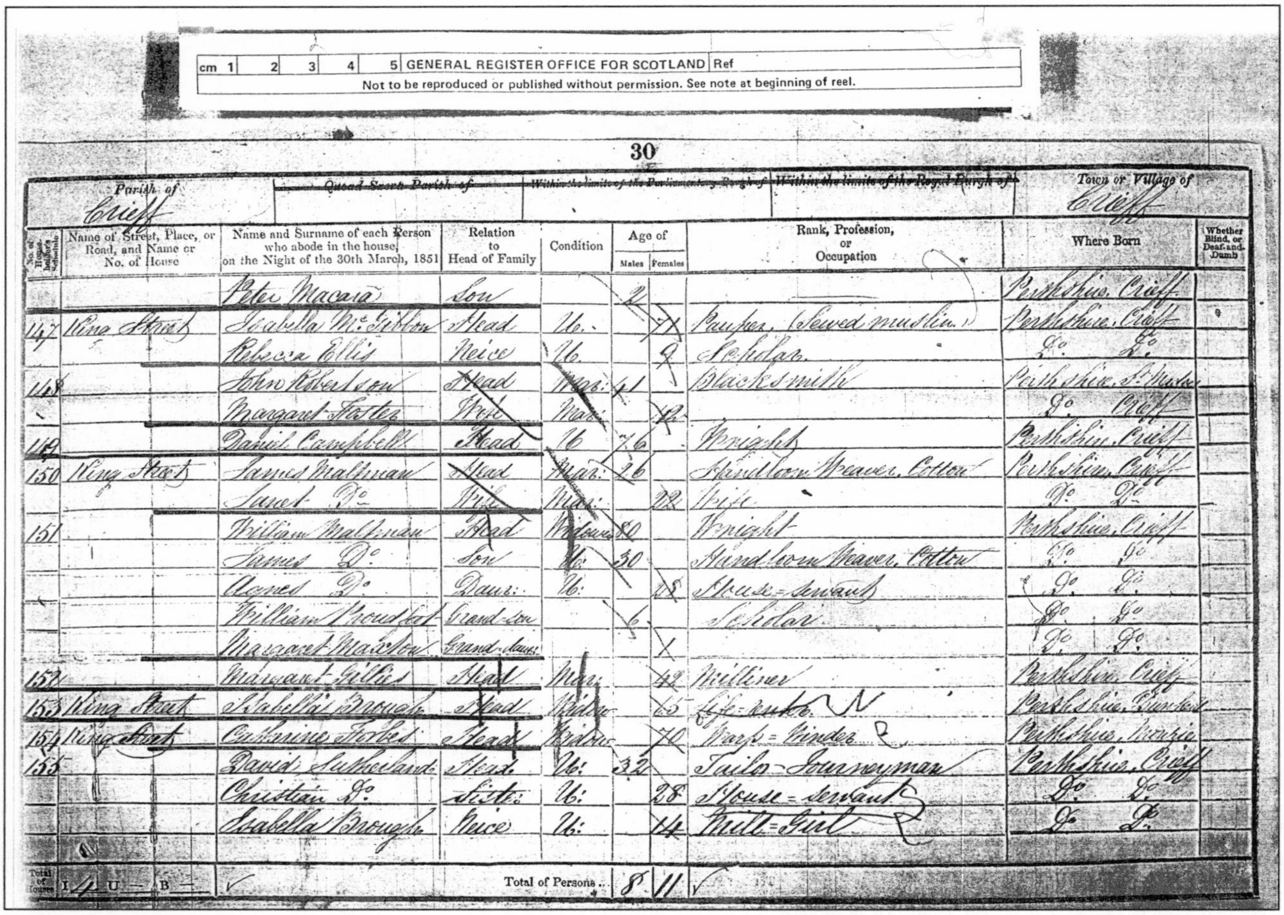

No. of House's Schedule	Name of Street, Place, or Road, and Name or No. of House	Name and Surname of each Person who abode in the house, on the Night of the 30th March, 1851	Relation to Head of Family	Condition	Age of Males	Age of Females	Rank, Profession, or Occupation	Where Born	Whether Blind, or Deaf-and-Dumb
		Peter Macara	Son		2			Perthshire, Crieff	
147	King Street	Isabella McGibbon	Head	U.		71	Pauper (Sewed muslin)	Perthshire, Crieff	
		Rebecca Ellis	Neice	U.		9	Scholar		
148		John Robertson	Head	Mar.	41		Blacksmith	Perthshire, St. Madoes	
		Margaret Stalker	Wife	Mar.		42		Do Crieff	
149		Daniel Campbell	Head	U	76		Wright	Perthshire, Crieff	
150	King Street	James Maltman	Head	Mar.	76		Handloom Weaver, Cotton	Perthshire, Crieff	
		Janet Do	Wife	Mar.		72	Wife	Do Do	
151		William Maltman	Head	Widower	80		Wright	Perthshire, Crieff	
		James Do	Son	U.	30		Handloom Weaver, Cotton	Do Do	
		Agnes Do	Daur.	U.		48	House-servant	Do Do	
		William Broughton	Grand-Son		6		Scholar	Do Do	
		Margaret Malcolm	Grand-daur.			1		Do Do	
152		Margaret Gillies	Head	Mar.		42	Milliner	Perthshire, Crieff	
153	King Street	Isabella Brough	Head	Widow		65	Life-renter	Perthshire, Dunkeld	
154	King Street	Catharine Forbes	Head	Widow		70	Warp-Winder	Perthshire, Monzie	
155		David Sutherland	Head	U.	32		Tailor Journeyman	Perthshire, Crieff	
		Christian Do	Sister	U.		28	House-servant	Do Do	
		Isabella Brough	Niece	U.		14	Mill-Girl	Do Do	
Total of Houses	4 U — B —			Total of Persons	8	11			

Figure 8-8
1851 census entry for Isabella Brough in the parish of Crieff, Perthshire. Note that there are two Isabella Broughs on this census page living in different households.

just one at first and hoped that she was on it. This time we weren't as lucky as we had been in our other census searches: She was not on the first roll. However, she was on the second roll, and it's interesting! Isabella is on page 30 of enumeration district 1 of the parish of Crieff (parish number 342). The census page is cited as "342/1/30/1851 at King Street, Crieff, Perthshire; FHL film 1042262" (see Figure 8-8). We found two Isabella Broughs in the parish of Crieff in 1851, and they are both on this page. Is the younger Isabella Brough named after the older one, or is it only a coincidence that they have the same name? It is easy to jump to the conclusion that one of them is the grandmother of the other, but we can't do that without further evidence. Is the sixty-five-year-old Isabella the same woman whose 1855 death certificate we examined? Review Figure 7-9. The 1855 death certificate says that Isabella Brough died on King Street in Crieff. This corresponds with the census information. But the death certificate says she was born in Little Dunkeld, and the census record states the birthplace as Dunkeld. The woman in this census record should have been seventy in 1855, but the death certificate says she was seventy-five. She is living alone in the census, so we can't match other members of the household to the names on the death certificate. We will try to find this woman in 1841.

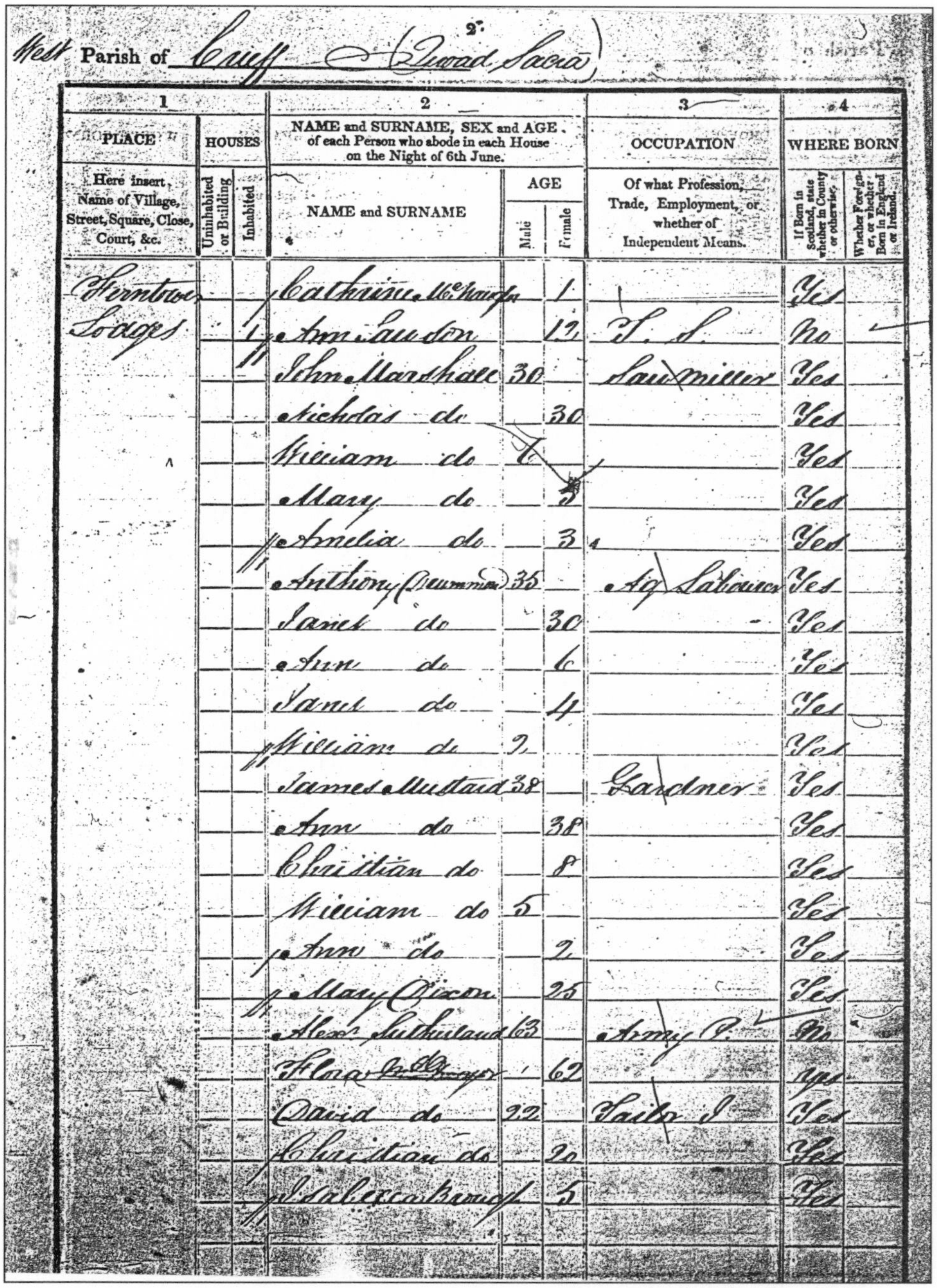

West Parish of Crieff (Quoad Sacra)

1 PLACE — Here insert Name of Village, Street, Square, Close, Court, &c.	HOUSES — Uninhabited or Building	HOUSES — Inhabited	2 NAME and SURNAME, SEX and AGE of each Person who abode in each House on the Night of 6th June. — NAME and SURNAME	AGE — Male	AGE — Female	3 OCCUPATION — Of what Profession, Trade, Employment, or whether of Independent Means.	4 WHERE BORN — If Born in Scotland, state whether in County or otherwise.	Whether Foreigner, or whether Born in England or Ireland.
Ferntower Lodges			Catherine McK[illegible]		1		Yes	
		1	Ann Lawson		12	F. S.	No	
		1	John Marshall	30		Sawmiller	Yes	
			Nicholas do		30		Yes	
			William do	[illegible]			Yes	
			Mary do		[illegible]		Yes	
			Amelia do		3		Yes	
		1	Anthony Drummond	35		Ag Labourer	Yes	
			Janet do		30		Yes	
			Ann do		6		Yes	
			Janet do		4		Yes	
			William do	2			Yes	
		1	James Mustard	38		Gardner	Yes	
			Ann do		38		Yes	
			Christian do		8		Yes	
			William do	5			Yes	
			Ann do		2		Yes	
			Mary Dixon		25		Yes	
		1	Alexr Sutherland	63		Army P.	No	
			Flora McGregor		62		yes	
			David do	22		Tailor J.	Yes	
			Christian do		20		Yes	
		1	Isabella Brough		5		Yes	

Figure 8-9
1841 census entry for the family of Alexander Sutherland, an army pensioner, in the parish of Crieff, Perthshire, Scotland.

The census information for the younger Isabella fits what we know about the girl we were seeking. She is listed at the bottom of the page: Isabella Brough, niece, unmarried, age fourteen, occupation mill girl, born in Crieff. She is listed in the household of David Sutherland and his sister Christian Sutherland. Remember that the mother of our Isabella was Margaret Sutherland. This looks like it's our girl! We scanned up and down the surrounding pages to see if we could find Margaret Sutherland, but if she was there we didn't recognize her. We don't know Isabella's father's name, except that his surname was Brough. We have to find the family of

David and Christian Sutherland to see if they had a sister named Margaret.

We don't know why this fourteen-year-old girl was living with her aunt and uncle. We hope to find Isabella with her parents in the 1841 census. Since she was born in Crieff, try that parish for the 1841 census.

1841 Census

The 1841 census is very different from all the others. For one thing, exact places of birth are not given. Further, for all people age fifteen and older, their ages are supposed to be rounded down to the nearest five. For example, people who stated their ages as twenty-nine are listed as twenty-five. Perhaps worst of all is that no relationships are stated. However, the 1841 census still contains great information.

The 1841 census for the parish of Crieff is on FHL films 1042691 and 1042692. We searched for both Isabella Broughs in this census. There was only one Isabel[la] Brough on King Street. The family included Thomas Brough, age sixty-two, occupation Wright; Isabel, age sixty; and Elisabeth, age twenty-five. All were born in the County of Perth. Although no relationships are stated in the 1841 census, each of these names was mentioned in Isabella Brough's 1855 death certificate. Now look at Figure 8-9 for the family of Alexander Sutherland, who was sixty-three. He was an army pensioner. He lived with a woman named Flora M___ (we can't read her name), age sixty-two; a man named David Sutherland, age twenty-two; a woman named Christian, age twenty; and a child, Isabella Brough, age five. Further research will help determine the relationships of these people, but the age and occupation of David correspond to what we found for David Sutherland in 1851. David, Christian, and Isabella appear to be the same people we found in the 1851 census. If so, David and Christian were siblings, and Isabella was their niece. But who are Alexander and Flora? Their ages indicate that they could have been the parents of David and Christian. If this is true, we may have found Isabella living with her grandparents! (Life doesn't get much better than this.) How will we know? We need to search for this family in church records. See the next chapter for more on this story. It gets good.

Census Search Summary

You can find census records using the following methods:

Technique

1. Use the index to the 1901 and 1891 censuses on the Scots Origins Web site.
2. Use the 1881 British Census and National Index on compact disc. It is available for purchase from the Salt Lake Distribution Center and may also be available at a Family History Center for no charge. It is available for a fee on the Scots Origins Web site.
3. Use the 1881 Census Index on microfiche at a Family History Center. Microfiche numbers are available at <www.rootsweb.com/~bifhusa/sct1881censusix.html>.
4. Use a street index. To find FHL microfilm numbers of street indexes, check <www.rootsweb.com/~bifhusa/ressco.html#census>.
5. Use a surname index. To see what indexes are available, consult Peter Ruthven-Murray's *Scottish Census Indexes: Covering the 1841–1871 Civil Censuses*. You also should consult the Web site of the family history society that covers the area where your ancestor lived.

6. Search without an index. Search the Family History Library Catalog by the name of the parish, then select the topic "Census Records" to get the FHL microfilm numbers for each census year. You can also use the Census Register on FHL fiche 6035795 to find the microfilm numbers.

We started our search with the index to the 1881 census. In theory, all people who lived in Scotland in 1881 should be indexed in that resource. From there, we did not use any indexes to find the family in other census returns. Instead, we used the clues found in each census to lead us to the next one. However, we got lucky. Just because a ten-year-old child was born in a particular parish doesn't mean that his parents lived there. Furthermore, even if the family did live there at the time of the birth, they may have not been there at the time of the census. If no child in the family was born near a census year, use other evidence to help you decide where the family would have been for the census.

We have shown that even if you don't have any indexes, you may still be able to find your family. Finding the Kays would have been much easier if we had used the 1891 census index on the Scots Origins Web site. It would have taken far less time if we had found a surname index for any other census year. But even without indexes we nailed that family! With or without indexes, you can still do it.

After you have read the 1841 census, reexamine your family records to make sure that you have all census records for your family and that you have obtained the necessary civil registration certificates. Once you have these, you should have a basic outline of your family in the nineteenth century. From there, move on to probate records to fill in some details. You also can search for your ancestors further back in time by using the church records of Scotland.

WHY CAN'T I FIND MY ANCESTOR IN THE CENSUS?

You can't find the address in the census. For a rural area this is not a problem: Just search line by line through the district. However, for an urban area this could be a major search. The street name may have changed from one census to the next or from the time of a certificate to the time of the census. The street may not have existed or was under construction at the time of the census. In addition, the houses may have been renumbered; this was especially common in the 1850s. In some urban areas two streets with the same name and numbers may be indexed together. You may find one family at an address and not know that another home has the same street address.

To solve these problems, consult local maps, preferably contemporary, to see what is near the address you are trying to locate. You need to be aware of two sets of maps for major urban areas. The first is *40+ town maps for 1818 through 1825*, originally published by John Wood and reprinted by Caledonian Books, Collieston, Ellon, AB41 8RT, Scotland. These are very detailed and provide names of streets; categories of public buildings; manufacturers and industrial premises; and, where features are numerous, a numerical key. Many of the maps also provide names of property owners. The scale is approximately six inches (15.2cm) to one mile (1.6km). The other set is the Godfrey Ordnance Survey maps, which are gener-

Tip

ally late nineteenth or early twentieth century and are a reduction to sixteen inches (40.6cm) to one mile (1.6km) from the original twenty-five inches (63.5cm) to one mile (1.6km) Ordnance Survey maps. Contact the publisher at Alan Godfrey Maps, Prospect Business Park, Leadgate, Consett, DH8 7PW, England, or at <www.alang odfreymaps.co.uk/>. History books about the community, local archives, or libraries may be able to provide detailed maps for the intervening years. For further ideas see *The Scot and His Maps* by Margaret Wilkes.

Your ancestors may have moved. A great deal of mobility resulted from the Industrial Revolution; people moved from rural areas into the industrial towns. Moving into Glasgow or Edinburgh was particularly common. In urban areas, people commonly moved around within a neighborhood or on the same street to find better accommodations. Moving also was likely around certain stages of life: marriage, childbearing, widowhood, and divorce. You can get a more accurate address from a civil registration certificate for an event that occurred close to the census year. Also look at a city or trade directory that was published one or two years after the census date. Directories took a year or longer to publish, so the addresses they contain were not current at publication.

Your ancestor may not have been present in the household on the census night. The census shows the people who were present in the house on the census night rather than those who normally lived there, although a person who was out working that night and returned home in the morning was to be recorded. Certain occupations such as railroad workers, sailors, and soldiers required working away from home. Fishermen may have been at sea on the census night and were enumerated in the first port where they arrived after the census day. Builders and laborers may have been working in another town. Wealthy people may have been traveling and had their servants with them. Your ancestor may have been absent for some reason other than his occupation. The 1861 census was taken on Easter Sunday, so the family may have gathered somewhere else to celebrate. Your ancestor could have been visiting family or friends or assisting someone who was sick. Children missing from the family listing could indicate possible death, marriage, or apprenticeship. Children also may have been away at boarding school or working as servants in another household. People in institutions (hospitals, jails, workhouses) were enumerated in the schedule of the institution, and women there may be listed by their maiden names. In fact, if your ancestor was away from home for any reason, he should have been enumerated elsewhere. If he was blatantly trying to avoid the enumerator, you may not find him anywhere in the census.

Your ancestor may have been present in the household but is not listed. Especially in the early census, popular belief in some parts of the country was that unbaptized children should not be listed, so many young children were omitted. Young children also may have been omitted to avoid charges of overcrowding.

Your ancestor is not indexed the way you expect. If you are using a surname index, there could be several reasons why you do not find your ancestor. The name spelling on the census return and, therefore, in the index could differ from the spelling you use. An even bigger problem exists if your ancestor is listed under a different surname altogether. **See the discussion on surnames in chapter three.**

Indexers sometimes misinterpreted the handwriting on census returns. If the first

See Also

letter of the name was misread, you can have a very difficult time locating your ancestor in the index. Write out the name and think about what other capital letters look similar to the name's first letter.

Your ancestor could be listed in the index and on the census film under a different name than the one you look for. When a widowed mother remarried, for example, her children may have been recorded with the surname of the stepfather.

Sometimes married women are listed in a census by maiden name, and sometimes they're not. Search any indexes under both the maiden and married names.

Sometimes indexers missed entries altogether. If you are relatively certain that your ancestor should appear in the census of a particular place, proceed as if there were no index: Search every page!

A few of the census returns have been lost or destroyed. This is not common, but for a few places the census has not survived. For example, for the 1841 census no returns for the Fife parishes of Abdie, Auchtermuchty, Balmerino, Ceres, Collessie, Creich, Cults, Cupar, Dairsie, Dunbog, Kinghorn, Kinglassie, Kirkcaldy, Leslie, and Auchinleck (Ayrshire) survived. For 1881 there is no return for Dunscore (Dumfries-shire) or the second half of Dumfries. Use other census returns to locate the family.

Basic information is incorrect. You may rely on incorrect information. For example, you may try to locate a census record of a child using the birthplace given in a later census, but that birthplace may be incorrect. Many people did not know where they were actually born, so they stated the place where they remembered growing up. Some people gave the place of baptism instead of the place of birth. Some stated as the birthplace their current location out of fear of being removed from their new home under the Poor Laws. Always reexamine your evidence and ask yourself how reliable it is.

USING AND INTERPRETING CENSUS INFORMATION

It is important to locate a family in all census years. The information in the census can be unreliable, but conflicting information often comes to light when different year's data are compared. Always question the reliability of the "facts."

Remember:

- Any given piece of information may be incorrect.
- Be suspicious of listed ages.
- Names used by an individual may not be the same as those found in civil registration or church records.
- Names of places and people may have been misspelled or spelled as they sound.
- Individuals missing from a household should be listed elsewhere in the census.

WHERE CAN I FIND OUT MORE?

Family History Library. *Resource Guide: 1881 British Census Indexes* (Item no. 34933).

Gibson, Jeremy and Mervyn Medlycott. *Local Census Listings 1522–1930:*

For More Info

Holdings in the British Isles. 3d ed. Federation of Family History Societies, 1997.

Gibson, Jeremy and Elizabeth Hampson. *Marriage and Census Indexes for Family Historians.* 8th ed. Federation of Family History Societies, 2001.

Guides to Official Sources. No. 2, *Census Reports of Great Britain, 1801–1931.* London: His Majesty's Stationery Office, 1951.

Johnson, Gordon. *Census Records for Scottish Families at Home and Abroad.* 3d ed. Aberdeen & North East Scotland Family History Society, 1997.

Ruthven-Murray, Peter. *Scottish Census Indexes: Covering the 1841–1871 Civil Censuses.* 3d ed. Scottish Association of Family History Societies, 1998.

Sinclair, Cecil. *Jock Tamson's Bairns: A History of the Records of the General Register Office for Scotland.* Edinburgh, Scotland: General Register Office for Scotland, 2000.

Wilkes, Margaret. *The Scot and His Maps.* Motherwell: Scottish Library Association, 1991.

AFTER SEARCHING THE CENSUS, WHAT SHOULD I DO NEXT?

Return to civil registration indexes to obtain the necessary certificates for family members that you have found on the census. Civil registration certificates help you find more census records, and census records help you find more civil registration certificates. Used together, civil registration certificates and census records give you more complete family information. Both indicate ages, addresses, occupational changes, and other important details. See chapter seven on civil registration records.

Look at land and probate records. When someone "disappears" from one census to the next, you can sometimes find the date and place of death, his heirs, and more by searching the national land and probate indexes. See chapter ten on land and probate records.

Begin searching church records. The censuses from 1851 onward give your ancestor's parish of birth. You can search church records in that parish to obtain earlier records of your family. If all you have is a name and a county of birth from the 1841 census, search the International Genealogical Index or Scottish Church Records on compact disc for matching names. See chapter nine for information on how to find your family in church records.

NINE

Church Records

The church records of Scotland are the most important resource for tracing your family tree. Because you will probably spend a lot of time searching church registers, we give you a lot of detail about how to use them and what do to if you can't find an ancestor in them. This is one chapter that you will refer to over and over again.

HISTORICAL BACKGROUND

Your ancestors did not live by a separation of church and state. The government and the church were intimately entwined. Scotland had an official (established) church, and your ancestors were expected to belong to it. However, the religion of the official church did not remain the same. Furthermore, groups broke off from the established church, formed their own churches, and later united with other groups. Eventually, many of them even reunited with the established church. You must know a little about church history in order to find your ancestors in Scottish church records. This section can help you understand why you may not find your ancestors in the records of the Church of Scotland, and it can help you learn what other churches they may have attended.

Scotland is regarded as a Protestant nation with a Protestant established church. Getting there was not a smooth journey. After King Henry VIII of England in 1534 broke from Rome and established himself as the head of the Church of England, he wanted to claim Scotland for Protestantism. He invaded Scotland in 1542, defeating the Scots army of James V at Solway Moss. He invaded again in 1544, and this time he was so brutal that Catholic and Protestant nobles united and sought the assistance of Catholic France.

In the mid-1500s, many believed that the Catholic Church in Scotland needed to be reformed. At this time record keeping was almost nonexistent and certainly not uniform. There were complaints that very few people attended church and that when they did their behavior was not good. There was a shortage of churches in

DEFINITIONS OF SCOTTISH HISTORY TERMS

Catholic: The only church in Scotland prior to the Reformation. It followed the direction of the Pope in Rome.

Covenanters: People who petitioned and fought against arbitrary royal authority and who wanted presbyterianism in the church with the removal of the bishops.

Episcopalian: Protestant church led by bishops who appointed ministers. Broke away at the formation of the Established Church of Scotland to form the Episcopal Church of Scotland.

Established Church of Scotland: Formed in 1690 when the Presbyterian Church and teachings were recognized as the official Church of Scotland.

Jacobite: Originally the supporters of King James VII (1633–1701). The name is derived from Jacobus, the Latin for James. There were major uprisings against the Hanovarian King in 1715 by followers of James Francis Edward Stuart, the "Old Pretender," and in 1745 by followers of his son Charles Edward Stuart, the "Young Pretender."

Patronage: Controversial issue that gave landowners the right to appoint ministers to churches on their land. Was not completely abolished until 1874.

Presbyterian: Protestant church whose ministers were ordained by presbyters (elders). Became the Established Church of Scotland.

Protestant: A protester. Any Christian whose church broke from the Roman Catholic Church.

Reformation: Process officially begun in 1560 when Scotland broke from the Catholic Church of Rome.

Westminster Confession of Faith: Accepted in 1645 as the religious foundation of the Church of Scotland and continues as the basis for the Scottish Presbyterian Church today.

which to worship, especially in the rural areas, and many of those that did exist were in disrepair and staffed by underpaid and poorly educated vicars. The medieval church in Scotland did have money and resources, but they were used for the building and upkeep of the cathedrals, abbeys, monasteries, and universities and for the support of the bishops. Scottish church councils in 1549, 1552, and 1559 passed a number of statutes to change the situation. Unfortunately, they did not provide the money to implement the reforms. One of the reforms from the 1552 council was the requirement that parishes record baptisms and marriages. Of course, we researchers care about this! We wish that every parish had followed this requirement. The parish of Errol in Perthshire has the oldest known parish register, which began in 1553. Only twenty-one parishes have registers that began before 1600, so most parishes did not follow the council requirements. Even by the time of the first national census in 1801, when 885 parishes responded to questions, only ninety-nine had registers that were kept regularly. The rest had only occasional entries or no registers at all. Even with this situation it is amazing how many of us can find our ancestors in the parish registers.

Any reformation in Scotland could only have come as a result of political revolution and in defiance of the Crown. The revolution came from 1559 to 1560 with religious civil war. One important event for today's genealogist was the August 1560 meeting of the Scottish Parliament, which ended the authority of the Pope in Scotland and forbade the celebration of the Roman Catholic Mass. Thus, in 1560 the reformed Church of Scotland was formed.

The new reformed church emphasized service in the parish and required the redistribution of the wealth from the monasteries, abbeys, and collegiate churches. The reformers stressed the preaching of the Word of God and the Sacraments (baptism and marriage, not seven sacraments as in the Roman Catholic Church). The reformers put a strong emphasis on education of the people, replacing Latin with the local language (English, Scots, or Gaelic, depending upon location) and introducing metrical psalms and service books. Over time this led to a well-educated general population who could read and write. The people in the congregations gained more self-control, they were able to elect their own ministers as opposed to having them appointed by bishops, and the kirk session was under the control of lay people (more is said about kirk session records later in this chapter).

Over the next 130 years the reformed Church of Scotland developed and changed to accommodate different forms of religious opinion. There were, in effect, two parties within the one united church: the Presbyterians, who saw the people as equals who could make decisions collectively in councils, and the Episcopalians, who were governed by bishops. Each group led the church in different time periods; during some of these 130 years, all of the churches in Scotland were Presbyterian, and in others they were Episcopalian. So from 1575 to 1690, the party in power alternated: Episcopalian from 1584, Presbyterian from 1592, Episcopalian from 1610, Presbyterian from 1638, Episcopalian from 1661, and Presbyterian from 1690. The reality is that the majority of members in the local church saw very little change, although there were isolated exceptions involving some persecutions.

The period from 1560 through 1690 was a turbulent time in Scottish and English history, with church and politics rarely being separated. This period included Covenanting armies invading England, the English Civil Wars, the defeat and rule of the Scots by Oliver Cromwell, the restoration of Charles II, and then the "Killing Times" where the Covenanters were persecuted. Some of the nonconformist groups (the Independents, Baptists, and Quakers) arrived in Scotland with the English Army, but they had little impact. The details make fascinating reading and certainly can help you put your ancestor in his historical context, but they are beyond the scope of this book. Look to some of the references listed at the end of this chapter for more details.

What is important, though, is that in 1690 the Reformation in Scotland came to an end. The Presbyterian Church was ratified by King William III as the Established

TIME LINE OF SCOTTISH HISTORY

1552	Catholic Church orders registers for baptisms and banns of marriage to be kept.
1560	Catholicism abolished; reformation begins following teachings of Calvin.
1584	Episcopalians gain control of church.
1592	Presbyterians gain control of church.
1610	Episcopalians gain control of church.
1638	Presbyterians gain control of church.
1645	Westminster Confession of Faith accepted as the foundation of the Presbyterian Church.
1661	Episcopalians gain control of church.
1681–1687	The "Killing Time" persecution against the Covenanters.
1690	Presbyterian Church becomes the Established Church of Scotland. Episcopalians break away to form Episcopal Church of Scotland.
1707	Act of Union uniting England and Scotland.
1712	Patronage Act returning to the landowner the right to choose a minister, with no approval from the congregation needed.
1715	Jacobite Rising.
1733	Associate Presbytery formed.
1743	Reformed Presbyterian Church formed.
1745	Jacobite Rising.
1761	Relief Church formed.
1783	Stamp Act requiring three-penny tax to record an event in the parish register.
1793	Catholic Relief Act.
1794	Stamp Act abolished.
1820	Parishes required to keep registers.
1829	Catholic emancipation. (Church records usually begin here.)
1843	Free Church formed.
1847	United Presbyterian Church formed.
1855	Civil registration begins.
1874	Patronage abolished.

Church of Scotland. Not everyone followed along, though, and almost five hundred clergy left their congregations to form the Episcopal Church of Scotland.

Presbyterian Churches

There was not complete unity even within the Established Church of Scotland. The issue of patronage, who had the right to choose the minister of the church, caused many groups to secede from the church.

The Cameronians—followers of Richard Cameron—were the first group to separate. They adhered strictly to the covenants and opposed any king who was not Presbyterian. They refused to take the Oath of Allegiance to the king or to be involved in any civil function. By 1743 they had formed the Reformed Presbyterian Church. This group was strong in the southwest of Scotland. Another small group to break away in about 1730 was the Glassites, who attempted to revert to a primitive Christianity and were against the idea of a structured church or a professional ministry. This group stayed small.

The First Secession came in 1733. This came as a gradual fallout from the Patronage Act of 1712, which gave the right to appoint the minister of the church back to the patron of the church, usually the local laird (lord of the manor). In the early years following the act, the landowners were careful to make their ministerial appointments satisfying to the members of the congregations. With time the situation deteriorated and conflicts occurred. The Seceders, or Associate Presbytery, broke away from the Church of Scotland and gave control over the appointment of ministers back to the people in the local congregation. The Seceder churches started in the Synod of Perth and Stirling but grew rapidly. This group split again over the issue of taking oaths and how it should or should not relate to the state in 1747, 1799, and 1806, resulting in the Old Light Burghers, New Light Burghers, Old Light Anti-Burghers and New Light Anti-Burghers.

In 1761, the Relief Presbyterian Church arose directly over issues of patronage. The adherents believed that the presbytery should not force any minister on the people and that members of the local congregation should have complete control over choosing a minister. They also accepted anyone into communion who acknowledged himself as a Protestant Christian, and they quarreled with no one. The church grew as a result of this attitude.

In 1843, a large break called the Disruption occurred. This dispute was again over patronage and whether the state (in this case the lairds) could appoint ministers. Trouble had been brewing since the General Assembly of the Church passed the Veto Act of 1834. This act was tested in the courts all the way to the House of Lords and eventually declared unconstitutional. The Disruption came when 395 minsters left because they felt that the people in the church should have the final say in who their minister should be. About 39 percent of the ministers and about a third of the people left the Church of Scotland to form the Free Church of Scotland.

The Disruption was the opposite of the nineteenth-century trend where Presbyterian groups began to merge. Look at Splits and Reunions of the Church of Scotland 1560–1929 at <www.btinternet.com/~stnicholas.buccleuch/chart.htm> for a good visual of this history.

Non-Presbyterian Churches

The Episcopal Church of Scotland formed in 1690 when the Presbyterian Church became the established Church of Scotland. A split occurred in 1712 with the Act of Toleration. A group of ministers and other people accepted the parliamentary settlement of succession. They were given protection and allowed to follow the liturgy of the Church of England. These became known as the English congregations, and they were serviced by ministers from England. They grew especially in Lowland Scotland in the second half of the eighteenth century.

The remaining section of the Episcopal Church of Scotland consisted of supporters of the Jacobite cause. This created problems for the church after the rebellions in 1715 and 1745. After 1715 it became illegal for the ministers to serve congregations with more than eight members. After 1745 many Episcopal chapels were burned down, service attendance was reduced from eight to four members, and penalties were imposed on the laity. The government tried to destroy the church, but it did not succeed. The congregations survived especially in the northeast and the western Highlands. After the death of Charles Edward Stuart in 1788, the church chose to accept the English monarch, and the two branches of the Episcopal Church moved toward unity. The Episcopal Church was strong with the landed gentry and the upper middle classes. It was unwilling or unable to accept the lower classes and thus did not grow in the urban industrial areas of Scotland as many of the other churches did. The Episcopal Church of Scotland has strong connections with the Episcopal Church in post-Revolutionary America. For more information on the Episcopal Church see Frederick Goldie's *Short History of the Episcopal Church in Scotland From the Restoration to the Present Time.*

The Roman Catholic Church became almost extinct for a while in Scotland after the beginning of the Reformation in 1560. Pockets of support (generally among the landed families who had private chaplains) existed in the Highlands, the western islands, and Kirkcudbrightshire. Catholicism was especially linked to certain clans: Chisholm, Fraser, Gordon, Maxwell, Macdonald, Macdonnell, and MacNeill. The Catholics were intensely persecuted at different times, especially because of their association with the Jacobite cause. Persecutions continued into the late eighteenth century and ended in 1793 with the Catholic Relief Act for Scotland. The church was relatively small, with twenty thousand to thirty thousand members, from 1680 until the early nineteenth century. The big increase came in the nineteenth century with the large number of Irish immigrants and the insistence of the church that the children of mixed-religion marriages be raised Catholic. Information on Roman Catholic records is in Michael Gandy's publications listed in the bibliography.

The Congregational Union of Scotland is the next largest group and was formed in 1896 by the merger of the Independents and the Evangelical Union. The Independent tradition emerged from Scottish Presbyterianism between 1730 and 1770 among groups in society open to the economic opportunities in commerce and industry. These groups included the Glassites, Old Scots Independents, Scotch Baptists, and Bereans. They were strong in the parishes along the River Tay and on the Fife and Kincardineshire coasts, with some members in Glasgow and Paisley. In 1808 the Baptists split from the group. The Evangelical Union was started in the 1840s with a breakaway from the United Secession Church. Records of this group can be hard to find, but check McNaughton's *Scottish Congregational Ministry, 1794–1993* for information about the congregations and the ministers.

Baptist views came to Scotland with the soldiers of the English Army. The first Baptist Church was formed in 1652, but the numbers declined and it eventually disappeared after the English Army left in 1659. The Baptist views were revived in Scotland in 1751 by the Macleanist or Scotch Baptists, but this movement died out in Scotland in the mid 1800s. The first modern Baptist churches began as a split from the Macleanists and grew rapidly in the early 1800s especially in the High-lands, the western islands, and among the fishing communities of the east coast. In 1835 the Scotch Baptist Association formed, and its name changed in 1842 to the Baptist Union of Scotland. For more information see Bebbington's *Baptists in Scotland*.

Methodist preaching was introduced to Scotland in 1741. The first society was organized in 1751, and the first chapel was built in 1764. The peak of Methodism in Scotland was in 1819—3,786 members—and it declined through the rest of the nineteenth century. In the twentieth century the church has grown partly due to the English in Scotland. For more information see Swift's *Methodism in Scotland*.

Over time other religious groups may have gained a local presence, but none became major groups throughout Scotland.

If you research any of these denominations, search the FHL Catalog under Scot-land, Church History. Many of the books listed have not been microfilmed, but once you know of the existence of a resource you can generally obtain it through interlibrary loan at your local public library.

Effect of this History on Your Research

One major effect of this turbulent church history is that many Scottish families at some time or another have had connections with nonconformist groups. This means that not all family baptisms may appear within one church register. A register may show gaps as some children were baptized elsewhere. Marriage records may not be where you expect to find them. Nonconformist burials may not have been recorded at all.

Important

The effects of the breakaways from the Established Church of Scotland vary by locality within Scotland. For example, by the 1790s more than 70 percent of the adult population of Jedburgh belonged to one or another of the dissenting groups. The dissenting groups accounted for about one-third of the population in Glasgow, very few people in the southwest Lowlands, but about one-quarter of the rest of the country.

The number of dissenters belonging to the other Presbyterian groups grew rap-idly in the early 1800s, especially in the cities. With the Disruption and the forma-tion of the Free Church of Scotland in 1843 the numbers involved in the dissenting churches increased markedly. By the time of the 1851 religious census, we find the following:

	Number of Churches
Established Church of Scotland	1,183
Free Church (Presbyterian)	889
United Presbyterian	465
Independent (became Congregational)	192
Episcopal	134
Baptist	119
Roman Catholic	117
Wesleyan Methodist	82
Reformed Presbyterian	39

Original Secession (Presbyterian)	36
Evangelical Union (became Congregational)	28
Church of Jesus Christ of Latter-day Saints (Mormon)	20
Others (less than sixteen each)	91

The number of nonconformists is even more dramatic if we look at attendance in church. The Established Church had 19.7 percent of all worship attenders at the time, while the Free Church had 19.2 percent and the United Presbyterians had another 11.2 percent. In spite of the inaccuracies claimed because of underreporting in worship attendance, these figures indicate a good chance that not all of your ancestors appear in the Established Church of Scotland records. Your chances of finding your ancestors vary depending upon time period and location. By 1929 when many of the major Presbyterian groups had merged, the Church of Scotland accounted for more than 90 percent of Scottish Protestants.

In addition to nonconformity, governmental taxation policies also might have affected the recording of your ancestors' activities. In 1783 the Stamp Act was passed and required three pence to be paid to record any event (baptism, marriage, or burial) in the parish register. This caused the underregistration of events in the parish registers. The act was repealed in 1794. So if you can't find your ancestors in the 1783–1794 time period, this tax may be the reason.

Now let's put this history to use. We first look at the Church of Scotland records to see how they are organized, what they contain, and how to use them. Then we address what to do if your ancestors were nonconformists.

PARISH REGISTERS OF THE RECORDS OF THE CHURCH OF SCOTLAND
How Are the Parish Registers Organized?

As we discussed in chapter three, one of the unique characteristics of Scottish research is that every parish has its own identification number. This numbering occurred when all the registers were gathered in one place following the 1854 Civil Registration Act. **You need to know the parish number of your ancestor's parish.** You can find it in several sources, including Bloxham's *Key to the Parochial Registers of Scotland*. The parish number is also listed along with the parish name in the Family History Library Catalog.

Important

What Do the Parish Registers Contain?
Baptismal registers

The amount of detail found in the registers can vary greatly. An entry might be as simple as the date of baptism, name of the child, and name of the father. However, an entry may provide the date of baptism (and sometimes the date of birth); name of the child; name of the child's father and often name of the child's mother, including her maiden name; occupation of the father; where the family lived; and names of the witnesses.

Proclamation and marriage registers

In many parishes recording the proclamation of the forthcoming marriage was more common than recording the marriage itself. (Proclamations are called banns in most other countries.) In theory the upcoming marriage was to be proclaimed on the successive Sundays prior to the marriage. However, this requirement could be waived on payment of a fee, and all three proclamations were made at the same time.

What was actually recorded in the registers varies greatly. The information may include the dates of proclamations (often noted as one entry even if they took place on three Sundays); the date of the marriage; the names, the parishes, and sometimes the places of residence of the bride and groom; occupation of the man; occasionally the name of the bride's father; rarely the name of the groom's father; and the name of the minister. Occasionally you can find the names of the cautioners, usually relatives, who gave pledges at the time of the proclamation for the good behavior for the bride and groom (with the pledge being redeemed at the time of the wedding) and the names of the witnesses. If the bride and groom lived in different parishes, the proclamation was made in both. However, the dates in those registers do not match if the proclamations occurred on different days. Additionally, one register might show the proclamation, and the other might show the marriage.

Burial and mortcloth dues registers

In many parishes burials were not recorded until relatively modern times. Recording was difficult due to the custom in some areas of carrying the deceased to his native parish. Some parishes had up to eight different burial places. In some parishes the registers show age at death, cause of death, residence, and occupation. Occasionally very complete details are included about the circumstances of the death.

For many parishes the only burial record is that of dues paid for the rental of the mortcloth (funeral pall), which is the cloth draped over a coffin prior to burial. The problem for researchers is that dues were not paid by the poor or by the landed families who donated the mortcloth. A mortcloth may not have been used for children under ten years of age. In some parishes privately owned mortcloths could be rented at a cheaper rate than those belonging to the parish. Such rentals were not recorded in the parish register.

What Do I Need to Know Before Searching This Record?

You need to have some background on the history of your parish. Despite your urge to dive right into the parish registers, do not do so. Knowing the environment in which your ancestor lived—the villages within the parish, the local geography, the types of agriculture and industry in the area, health issues, religious forces, etc.—is very helpful.

To find out more about the geography, locate the parish on a map and look in several gazetteers to find out more about the parish. You should know the names of nearby places and the routes your ancestor would have traveled to get to these places. You can determine possible migration routes by looking at the rivers, canals, roads, and railroads in the area. You also need to know who had jurisdiction over

Notes

\di'fin\ *vb*

Definitions

the local records. You can find this information in sources such as Humphrey-Smith's *Phillimore Atlas and Index of Parish Registers* (available in some Family History Centers and some public libraries), Lewis's *Topographical Dictionary of Scotland* (available in many public libraries), and Groome's *Ordnance Gazetteer of Scotland* (available on microfiche from the Family History Library).

A knowledge of local history is essential. For example, the parish history may tell you how your ancestor lived, what he likely did for a living, where he likely would have moved to obtain work, what the predominant religions were and when large numbers of people converted, when emigration agents were active in the area, when diseases were rampant, etc. You can waste a lot of time searching in surrounding areas when a parish history may provide the answers you need. It is impossible to do effective family history without knowing what was happening in the area where your ancestors lived.

Look for a history of your parish or county. In Scotland the first places to check are the excellent locality descriptions from the 1791–1799 and 1837–1845 Statistical Accounts of Scotland. All of the pages of these multivolume publications are online at <http://edina.ac.uk/cgi/StatAcc/StatAcc.cgi>. At the time of this writing The Third Statistical Account of Scotland series was not online. The first account was carried out under the guidance of Sir John Sinclair, who requested from each minister information about local occupations, trades, industries, prices, major landowners, local monuments, agricultural improvements, the church and nonconformist groups, and anything else that took the minister's fancy. The Statistical Accounts give a fascinating history of your ancestor's parish that will certainly help you bring your family history to life. Some of these reports are very detailed, and you never know what you will find. In addition, if you read both the first and second accounts, you can see changes over time in the community.

A second place to look is the GENUKI site on the Internet. Go to "United Kingdom and Ireland" then "Scotland" then the county and look under the "History" heading. After you have read some county history, look under the name of the parish. If nothing is listed yet for your parish, check the histories of surrounding parishes or towns.

How Do I Find Out What Parish Registers Exist?

Once you know the location of your ancestor's parish and some local history, you are ready to find out what parish registers exist for the areas where your ancestors lived. **You can obtain a listing of all parish registers for the Church of Scotland in V. Ben Bloxham's *Key to the Parochial Registers of Scotland*.** This book tells which registers exist for each parish. One version of this book is organized by county, then alphabetically by parish; the other version is organized by parish. It doesn't matter which one you use. If your local library doesn't have a hard copy, you can use it on microfiche (FHL fiche 6036348) at any Family History Center. It is important to use this resource rather than other sources that list only the beginning and ending dates of the registers; this book lists the years covered for each record and notes any missing records or gaps in the registers. It also indicates when records of one type are interspersed with records of another type, which is helpful to know in advance of searching the microfilm. The book tells the condition of the original

Printed Source

```
        CRIEFF (342)

Genealogical Society Holdings          Original Registers-Edinburgh

BIRTHS: (102704) 1692-1854.            BIRTHS: (1) 1692-1819; (2) 1820-54.

MARRIAGES: (102704) 1692-1854.         MARRIAGES: (1) 1692-1819; (2) 1820-54.

DEATHS: No entries.                    DEATHS: No entries.


Condition of Original Registers:

BIRTHS: Mothers' names are not recorded until 1752, and sometimes they are omitted during the subsequent
ten years. Families occasionally recorded in groups.

MARRIAGES: Recorded for 1692-1713 intermixed with the baptisms for same period. No entries Mar
1713-Nov 1748. The pages previous to 1784 are headed "Proclamations;" after that date "Proclamations
and Marriages," but the form of entry is the same throughout, generally consisting of only the names of
the parties. The words "not married," are added to one or two of the entries.
```

Figure 9-1
Crieff entry from the *Key to the Parochial Registers of Scotland* by V. Ben Bloxham.

records. It also gives FHL microfilm numbers of the registers, but they are the numbers of the first filming. Use the microfilm number in *Key to the Parochial Registers of Scotland* to search the FHL Catalog by film/fiche number and get a list of film numbers for both the first and second filmings. In most cases, you should order the second filming.

The Parish of Crieff is in the Perthshire section of the book (see Figure 9-1). It tells us that the parish register contains births (baptisms) and marriages, available on microfilm for 1692 through 1854, but no death (burial) entries. It also gives other information that is helpful to know before searching the parish register, such as that no marriages for 1713 through 1748 are recorded. This helps to explain why we can't find an ancestor's marriage record in the Scottish Church Records index (see next section).

Another valuable source is Turnbull's *Scottish Parochial Registers: Memoranda of the State of the Parochial Registers of Scotland, Whereby Is Clearly Shown the Imperative Necessity for a National System of Regular Registration,* available on FHL film number 0496422, item 3. This was written to show why parish registers were an inadequate means of preserving Scotland's vital records and that a system of civil registration was needed (one had been instituted in England and Wales in 1837). The parish records are listed by county and then by the name of the parish. Compare Turnbull's account (pages 120–121) for the parish registers of Crieff to the one in Bloxham's book:

> CRIEFF.—The registers of Crieff do not extend far back, and they are very incomplete. The earliest entry is 20th November 1692; and from that date to the present (August 1837) the register of proclamations of banns is complete, with the exception of one blank between the 1st of March 1713, and the 6th of November 1748. The register of births and baptisms extends from the 27th December 1692, to the present time, with the exception of a blank between the 8th of June and the 16th of November 1746. The records of discipline are very defective. They begin 3d October 1699; and from that date to the present time there are no fewer than four blanks, viz., 15th of February 1713, to 16th September 1723; 14th October

1739 to 1st November 1746; 26th October 1760, to 12th July 1761; and 6th December 1772, to 11th April 1833. The accounts of the poor's funds commence 19th June 1700; and from that to the present time, the following blanks occur, viz., 18th March 1713 to 25th October 1747, and 19th November 1790 to 24th May 1807. The whole is comprised in eleven volumes of different sizes. The deaths have never been recorded.

As you can see, both books have advantages. Bloxham's book tells what parish registers are held by the Family History Library (Genealogical Society of Utah) and the General Register Office, Scotland (Edinburgh). It also gives different information about the parish registers. Turnbull's account gives information, for example, of the state of records other than just the parish registers. You should look at both sources.

Notes

Once you know what parish registers exist, you should find out which ones are indexed. The amazing news is that **baptisms and marriages from all parish registers of the Church of Scotland have been indexed,** and the indexes are all on the Scottish Church Records CD. However, remember the religious history above. There have been numerous breakaways from the Church of Scotland, and the registers from those churches are generally not included in the index.

INDEXES TO SCOTTISH CHURCH RECORDS
The Scottish Church Records Index on Compact Disc

The Scottish Church Records index includes almost all pre-1855 baptisms and marriages from parish registers of the Church of Scotland. It also indexes some nonconformist records. At the time of this writing the Scottish Church Records CD was available only in the DOS version of the FamilySearch program at Family History Centers; it was not available on the FamilySearch Web site. However, most of the names from the Scottish Church Records CD are also in the International Genealogical Index, available at Family History Centers and on the FamilySearch Web site. You can search the Scottish Church Records index at no charge. You can search the same information online on the Scots Origins Web site for a fee, but no good Scot wants to spend money unnecessarily.

Searching the Scottish Church Records index for baptisms, marriages, and family groups

The Scottish Church Records index is similar in format to the International Genealogical Index, so you can do individual, marriage, and parent searches.

Step By Step

Let's use the Scottish Church Records CD to look for the baptism of Isabella Brough. We know from civil registration and census records that she was born about 1837 in the parish of Crieff. All parish registers from the Church of Scotland are indexed, so if she was baptized in that Church, we should have no trouble finding her.

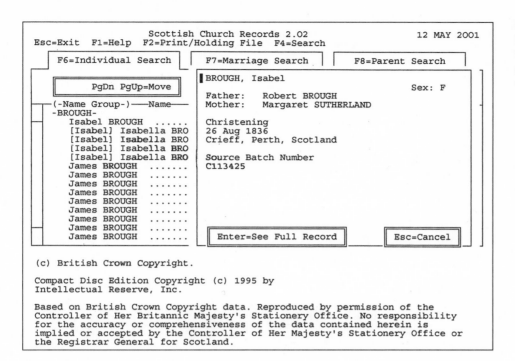

Individual search for baptisms

At any Family History Center, use the Scottish Church Records index, and follow these instructions. From the Scottish Church Records opening screen, press the enter or F4 key to begin the search.

Next is the "Surname Search" menu. To find a birth or baptism, select "Individual Search."

The "Individual Search" screen appears. Here you can enter a name and date and even filter your search to include only names from a certain locality. In this case, type "Isabella" in the "Given Name" field, "Brough" in the "Surname" field, and "1836" in the "Event Year" field. Do not filter your search. Press the F12 key.

The search results appear and include only one Isabella Brough born in 1836. Furthermore, she was born in Perthshire. Press the enter key to see abbreviated details.

The detail screen appears on top of the list of names. Refer to Figure 9-2. Here you can see that the parents of Isabella Brough were Robert Brough and Margaret Sutherland. Isabella was baptized 26 August 1836 in the parish of Crieff. Notice that the Scottish Church Records index uses the term *christening* for all baptisms.

Get the source of this information; press the enter key to see the full record, which shows the complete details including the source (see Figure 9-3). The "Source Information" section shows a number for "Source" and a number for "Printout." The source is microfilm 1040076. If you search the Family History Library Catalog by film number, you find that film 1040076 is the microfilmed copy (second filming) of the original parish register of Crieff, Perthshire. Isabella's baptism is on that film. The printout is on microfiche 6900657. This is a computerized listing of people born and baptized (christened) in the parish. Always order the original register and the computer printout. (We explain these later in the chapter.) However,

Figure 9-3
Complete details and source information for a search for Isabella Brough, born in 1836 in Perthshire from the Scottish Church Records index. *Reprinted by permission. © 1995 by Intellectual Reserve, Inc.*

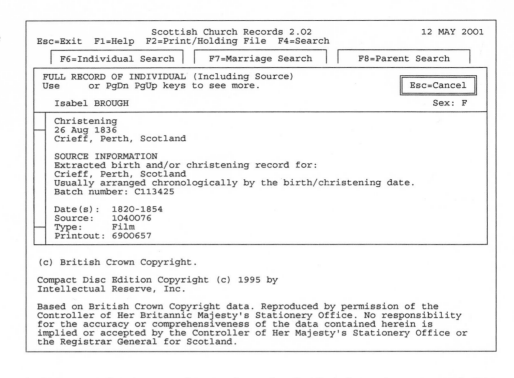

```
                    Scottish Church Records 2.02              12 MAY 2001
     Esc=Exit  F1=Help  F2=Print/Holding File  F4=Search

       F6=Individual Search  |  F7=Marriage Search  |  F8=Parent Search

     FULL RECORD OF INDIVIDUAL (Including Source)
     Use      or PgDn PgUp keys to see more.              | Esc=Cancel |

       Isabel BROUGH                                          Sex: F

           Christening
           26 Aug 1836
           Crieff, Perth, Scotland

           SOURCE INFORMATION
           Extracted birth and/or christening record for:
           Crieff, Perth, Scotland
           Usually arranged chronologically by the birth/christening date.
           Batch number: C113425

           Date(s):   1820-1854
           Source:    1040076
           Type:      Film
           Printout:  6900657


     (c) British Crown Copyright.

     Compact Disc Edition Copyright (c) 1995 by
     Intellectual Reserve, Inc.

     Based on British Crown Copyright data. Reproduced by permission of the
     Controller of Her Britannic Majesty's Stationery Office. No responsibility
     for the accuracy or comprehensiveness of the data contained herein is
     implied or accepted by the Controller of Her Majesty's Stationery Office or
     the Registrar General for Scotland.
```

before you order any records, see what other family information you can find in the index. **Get all you can for free!**

Money Saver

Parent search for baptisms of other children in the family

We searched for a marriage record of Robert Brough and Margaret Sutherland to show you, but it is not in the Scottish Church Records index. We also did a parent search to find other children born to this couple. The parent search showed only one child—Isabella. However, we are not yet at a dead end in finding Isabella's family. We found in the 1851 census an Isabella Brough who lived with her uncle David Sutherland and aunt Christian Sutherland. In the 1841 census, these people appear to be in the family of Alexander and Flora Sutherland. (See chapter eight to review those census records.) Were David and Christian the brother and sister of Isabella's mother, Margaret? Let's see if we can find the family of David Sutherland to see if he had a sister named Margaret. The 1851 census indicated that he was born in about 1817 in the parish of Crieff, Perthshire.

When we do an individual search for David Sutherland, event year 1817, we find David was the son of Alexander Sutherland and Flora McGregor. Find Alexander and Flora's other children to see if this couple had daughters named Christian and Margaret. To do this, press the F8 key to do a parent search on Alexander Sutherland and Flora McGregor. The program searches for variant spellings of these names, such as McGregor and MacGregor. It then produces a list of children. See Figure 9-4 for the details of the children from this search.

All of these people appear to be in the same family, but we can't be certain without other evidence. To find such evidence, order the microfilmed parish register and the computer printout for each child. These children were born in various areas of Scotland, so perhaps more than one Alexander Sutherland married a Flora

```
Scottish Church Records - Version 2.02

18 JUL 2001                          HOLDING FILE ENTRIES                          Page 1
====================================================================================
                                                          Additional      Batch and Source
Names (Sex)                     Event Date/Place          Information      Information
------------------------------------------------------------------------------------
William SUTHERLAND (M)............... C: 20 Feb 1808                        Ba: C110912
    Father: Alexr. SUTHERLAND          Ardersier, Inverness, Scotland   FR287   So: 990663
    Mother: Flora MC GREGOR                                                 Pr: 6902546

Margaret SUTHERLAND (F)............. C: 18 Dec 1809                         Ba: C110472
    Father: Alexander SUTHERLAND       Dornoch, Sutherland, Scotland    FR 226  So: 990561
    Mother: Flora MACGREGOR                                                Pr: 6902466

Cathrine SUTHERLAND (F)............. C: 30 Jan 1811                         Ba: C110472
    Father: Alex. SUTHERLAND           Dornoch, Sutherland, Scotland    FR 233  So: 990561
    Mother: Flora MC GRIGOR                                                Pr: 6902466

Flora SUTHERLAND (F)................ C: 24 Apr 1815                         Ba: C113424
    Father: Alexander SUTHERLAND       Crieff, Perth, Scotland          FR164   So: 1040076
    Mother: Flora MCGREGOR                                                 Pr: 6900657

David SUTHERLAND (M)................ C: 18 May 1817                         Ba: C113424
    Father: Alexander SUTHERLAND       Crieff, Perth, Scotland          FR170   So: 1040076
    Mother: Flora MCGREGOR                                                 Pr: 6900657

====================================================================================
       Events:   B=Birth  C=Christening  M=Marriage  S=Miscellaneous
    Batch/Source:  Ba=Batch  So=Source  Pr=Printout
Special Symbols:  * Film contains no additional information.   �度 Some information was estimated or altered.
                  @ Names and relationships of others stated in source.   # Additional relatives listed in source.
                  + Additional sources for batch.
====================================================================================
(c) British Crown Copyright. Compact Disc Edition Copyright (c) 1995 by Intellectual Reserve, Inc.
Based on British Crown Copyright data. Reproduced by permission of the Controller of Her Britannic Majesty's Stationery
Office. No responsibility for the accuracy or comprehensiveness of the data contained herein is implied or accepted by
the Controller of Her Majesty's Stationery Office or the Registrar General for Scotland.
```

Figure 9-4

Printout of holding file from a Parent Search to find all the children born to Alexander Sutherland and Flora McGregor in Scottish Church Records index. Notice the differences in the birth places of the children. This could mean that the parents moved or we have more than one Alexander Sutherland and Flora McGregor having children. *Reprinted by permission. © 1995 by Intellectual Reserve, Inc.*

MacGregor. That would be a good possibility if the names were more common. However, in this case it is more likely that the family moved several times. Perhaps the father had an occupation that required travel. If all the children were from the same family, notice that David Sutherland did, indeed, have a sister named Margaret. She was baptized in 1809. This should be Isabella's mother! But why isn't his sister Christian Sutherland on this list?

We mentioned that one parent search in the International Genealogical Index isn't enough. The same is true with the Scottish Church Records index. Always repeat the parent search without the mother's maiden name. A search for Alexander Sutherland and wife Flora [no maiden name] yields a different list of children, but not the one we expect. This search produced only one child.

We had hoped to find a daughter named Christian. Instead the search results show Margaret Sutherland, baptized in 1812. Her parents are Alexander Sutherland and Flora Macgregor (see Figure 9-5). This is surprising for three reasons:

1. This is the second child named Margaret born to this family, which probably means that the Margaret who was born in 1809 died as an infant. This shows one of the dangers of assuming without corroborating evidence that someone is your ancestor. Margaret Sutherland (born in 1809) looked like the target ancestor, but if she died as an infant she couldn't be Isabella's mother. Just because the names match doesn't mean you're done!

2. This Margaret didn't appear in the first parent search with the other children. Her mother's maiden name is recorded, so why did we only find this entry when we searched without the maiden name? You have to be really paying attention to find the reason for this one. Notice that Alexander Sutherland's surname appears

Figure 9-5
Results of a Parent Search to find children born to Alexander Sutherland and Flora [no name inserted] in Scottish Church Records index. One additional child was found, and not the one we expected to find. *Reprinted by permission.* © *1995 by Intellectual Reserve, Inc.*

```
                         INDIVIDUAL RECORD
18 MAY 2001                                                 Page 1
==================================================================
NAME: SUTHERLAND, Margaret
------------------------------------------------------------------
SEX:  F

EVENT: Christening
       6 Dec 1812
       Forres, Moray, Scotland
FATHER: Alexander SUTHERLAND
MOTHER: Flora Macgregor

==================================================================
SOURCE INFORMATION
==================================================================

Extracted birth and/or christening record for:
  Forres, Moray, Scotland
Usually arranged chronologically by the birth/christening date.
------------------------------------------------------------------
Batch          | Dates     Source Call No.  Type | Printout Call No. Type
-------------- | ------------------------------- | ---------------------
C111372        | 1675-1819 990803          Film | 6901961        Fiche
               | 1820-1855 990804          Film |
==================================================================
```

in all capital letters. Flora's does not. Because the name MacGregor was not typed into the database in all capital letters, the computer doesn't recognize it as Flora's maiden name; it appears as her middle name. One parent search isn't enough!

3. Christian's name didn't appear when we did this search. She may have been baptized in a nonconformist church that isn't indexed in the Scottish Church Records index, or she may have never been baptized at all. Perhaps the census was incorrect when it listed her as the sister of David Sutherland. It is also possible that she was baptized and indexed in the Scottish Church Records index, but we haven't located her yet.

To find other children, you can conduct a parent search with Alexander Sutherland's name and no wife's name at all. However, this produces too many possibilities. You would have to look at the details of each of the entries, and even if you did, without a mother's name you would have difficulty distinguishing this Alexander Sutherland from the many others. Therefore, try to find additional children via other methods.

Technique

Summary: using parent search to reconstruct family groups in the Scottish Church Records index

1. The Scottish Church Records index on compact disc does not index all baptisms because most nonconformist churches are not indexed. Even if the entries are indexed, you may have to try more than one technique to find all members of a family.

2. You should do a parent search in the Scottish Church Records index. Although the parent search feature can be very useful for locating the children of a couple, the result of a parent search is only a list of children who had parents of the name(s) in the search. Therefore, the children in the search results are not guaranteed to be the children of your ancestors. This can be a significant problem if your ancestors had common names. You must check the source—the microfilmed church registers—for each child to verify that children belong to the same family.

3. The parent search results may not include all children of a family. For example, it may not show any children baptized in a nonconformist church. It does not show children who were not baptized in any church. It does not index children born or baptized after 1854.

4. The names and baptism dates of children may not be what you expect. Sometimes more than one child in a family has a particular given name. This usually happened when the first child with that name died, but not always. If, for example, the parents used the traditional Scottish naming pattern and both of their fathers were named John, they could have named two of their children John. A child may also have been baptized long after birth. Sometimes the family baptized several children on the same day. Two or more children of the same parents baptized on the same day does not necessarily indicate that they were twins, triplets, etc.

5. Do more than one parent search for a couple. Some baptismal records include only the father's name. Others include the mother's given name but not her maiden name, and still others include the mother's maiden name. A baptismal record may include only the name of the mother. Furthermore, sometimes a parent is listed by her first name and other times by a middle name. Also consider nicknames. Do not try only one parent search and think that you have found all of the children. Try at least the following searches:

    a. father's given name and surname, mother's given name and maiden surname

    b. father's given name and surname, mother's given name

    c. father's given name and surname, no mother's name

    d. mother's given name and maiden surname, no father's name

Marriage Search

Now let's see if we can find the marriage of Alexander Sutherland and Flora McGregor. From the search screen of the Scottish Church Records index on compact disc, select "Marriage Search." You can enter the name of one of the spouses. As we saw when we did an IGI search, this can produce a long list of names. This time, let's filter our search. By selecting F10-Filter, "Name Combination" is among the options (see Figure 9-6). Filtering by name combination directs the program to search for two names, so enter Alexander Sutherland's name and his spouse's given name—Flora. By adding that given name, the search results include only two marriages. Alexander Sutherland's marriage to Flora McGrigor (another variant spelling for MacGregor) is on the list. The details of the marriage are shown in Figure 9-7. Alexander and Flora were married in Edinburgh. This couple did get around! Of course, we need to verify that this is our couple and not some other couple with the same names. Once you find the marriage in the index, order the computer printout on microfiche and the parish register on microfilm. If you don't find the marriage, try searching for it using the other spouse's name, if known.

Step By Step

Register of Neglected Entries

This register could have been included under Civil Registration because of when it was created, but it also fits here because of the time period in which the events fall. The Register of Neglected Entries was created by the Second Amending Act of 1860

Figure 9-6
Marriage Search screen on the Scottish Church Records index showing the use of the "Name Combination" filter used in searching for the marriage of Alexander Sutherland and Flora. *Reprinted by permission. © 1995 by Intellectual Reserve, Inc.*

```
                        Scottish Church Records 2.02              18 MAY 2001
            F1=Help  F2=Print/Holding File
┌─────────────────────────┐     ┌──────────┐   ┌───────────────────────────┐
│                           MARRIAGE SEARCH                                 │
│          Type the information you want included in your search.           │
│                                                                           │
│          Name: Alexander_____    SUTHERLAND_____ │
│                Given Name                     Surname (Last Name)         │
│                                                                           │
│     Event Year: _____   (Recommended)                                    │
│                          ┌──────────────────────────┐   ┌───────────────┐ │
│                          │   MARRIAGE FILTER OPTIONS │   │F12=Start Search│ │
│                          │ Use     and press Enter to│   └───────────────┘ │
│  If you want to in       │ mark/unmark desired options.                    │
│  F10 to select the       │                          │   ┌───────────────┐ │
│                          │ [ ] Exact Surname Spelling│   │  F10=Filter   │ │
│  Filtering is opti       │ [ ] Locality             │   └───────────────┘ │
│  your search.  Pre       │ [ ] Event Year Range     │                     │
│                          │ [ ] Name Combination     │   ┌───────────────┐ │
│  NOTE: Filtering m       │ ┌──────────┐ ┌──────────┐│   │  Esc=Cancel   │ │
│                          │ │F12=Finalize│ │Esc=Cancel││   └───────────────┘ │
│                          │ └──────────┘ └──────────┘│                     │
└──────────────────────────┴──────────────────────────┘─────────────────────┘

(c) British Crown Copyright.

Compact Disc Edition Copyright (c) 1995 by
Intellectual Reserve, Inc.

Based on British Crown Copyright data. Reproduced by permission of the
Controller of Her Britannic Majesty's Stationery Office. No responsibility
for the accuracy or comprehensiveness of the data contained herein is
implied or accepted by the Controller of Her Majesty's Stationery Office or
the Registrar General for Scotland.
```

Figure 9-7
Details and source information for marriage of Alexander Sutherland to Flora Mc-Grigor. *Reprinted by permission. © 1995 by Intellectual Reserve, Inc.*

```
                                INDIVIDUAL RECORD

18 MAY 2001                                                          Page 1
==========================================================================
NAME: SUTHERLAND, Alexander
--------------------------------------------------------------------------
SEX:  M

EVENT: Marriage
       30 Mar 1803
       Edinburgh Parish, Edinburgh, Midlothian, Scotland
SPOUSE: Flora MCGRIGOR
(no parents listed)
--------------------------------------------------------------------------
ADDITIONAL INFORMATION

     FR2374

==========================================================================
SOURCE INFORMATION
==========================================================================

Extracted marriage record for:
  Edinburgh, Edinburgh, Midlothian, Scotland
Usually arranged chronologically by the marriage date.

Batch         Dates       Source Call No.  Type   Printout Call No. Type
---------------------------------------------------------------------------
M119833       1800-1811  1066690,  103048 Film    6900815          Fiche

==========================================================================
```

for the Registration of Births, Deaths, and Marriages in Scotland. This section of the act meant that anyone could appear before the sheriff with proof, pay a fee and have recorded any previously unrecorded birth, marriage, or death that occurred between 31 December 1800 and 1 January 1855.

First let's examine the process of registering an event. To register, a person(s) petitioned for a warrant by appearing with proof of an event before the sheriff of the county. Since the event was unlikely to have documentary proof, the evidence was often in the form of witness statements. The sheriff could make inquiries as to the validity of the claim. If satisfied, the Sheriff would issue a warrant. He would then send the warrant and all the proof, along with a five-shilling fee, to the Registrar General for recording.

The event was then recorded in the Register of Neglected Entries. From 1855 through 1885 the Old Parochial Registers for 1820 through 1854 were still in local custody, so a copy of the entry from the Register of Neglected Entries was sent to the parish where the event was supposed to have occurred for recording there. These entries can be in a separate register or at the back of the local register.

Luckily for us, almost all entries in the Register of Neglected Entries that we sought were recorded in the original parish. The neglected entries for the parish were microfilmed with all the other registers and then subsequently indexed. The original two volumes of the Register of Neglected Entries for all of Scotland have also been microfilmed (FHL film 0103538) and provide you with another document source.

So how do you know if your ancestor is in this register? There may be an indication in the Scottish Church Records CD. If a copy was recorded in the parish, two entries could be in the Scottish Church Records index. The frame number in the "additional information" column can help you find the event in the parish register. If there is an additional entry from the Register of Neglected Entries, the frame number in the "additional information" column can look like FR RNE 3323. Remember, after you find an entry in any index you have to look at the original source. This is especially true for these entries. In this case you have the entry from the Register of Neglected Entries and in the parish records if it was recorded there.

If you are lucky enough to have an ancestor in this register, then you have hit a gold mine. Let's look at the wealth of information in a typical entry from the Register of Neglected Entries. The typical and standard format entry for William Ross reads:

> William Ross, Seaman, residing at Number 35 Page Street, New Hendon, Sunderland, son of William Ross, Plasterer's Labourer, Aberdeen, and Isabella Ingram, or Ross, his wife (both now deceased) was born on the Twentyfifth day of December 1838, in St. Andrews Street, in the Parish of St. Nicholas, and County of Aberdeen.
>
> Registered this 8th day of October, 1889 on the authority of a relative Warrant by William Alexander Brown, Esquire, Advocate, Sheriff Substitute of Aberdeen, Kincardine, and Banff, dated 21 September 1889.

Besides all the details about an individual event, other events relating to the same family are often in the Register of Neglected Entries. Generally a significant event, usually a death, triggered the recording of these events. For the Ross family, the register has records of the parents' marriage and the birth of four children, of which William was the only one still alive. These entries provide lots of valuable names, dates, places, and relationships.

Reminder

The vast majority of births and marriages in the Register of Neglected Entries are also in the Scottish Church Records index. The deaths are not in that index.

The last event recorded in the register in April 1930 is the birth of Anne Cowan

Thomson in June 1838 in the Parish of Shettleston. This was recorded almost a hundred years afer the birth!

Why can't I find my ancestor in the Scottish Church Records index?

You're looking for the wrong name. Remember that Scottish given names and surnames can vary in the records. Review the section on surnames and given names in chapter three, then repeat your search in the Scottish Church Records index. You can try searching through your ancestor's county in the microfiche index to the Old Parochial Registers. (See the "Index to the Old Parochial Registers on Microfiche" section in this chapter.) Search the given name index and the surname index to christenings or marriages in the county where you believe the event occurred.

Too many people had the same name. You may have seen your ancestor's name several times in the index, but you couldn't be sure which was the right person. This problem is not unusual. Some common surnames are found all over Scotland, and many given names have been very popular. Even uncommon names multiplied rapidly when Scottish families followed the traditional naming pattern, naming children for their parents and grandparents. Within a couple of generations, lots of people with the same names may have lived in an area. Some, but not all, may have been related to your ancestor. You may need to reconstruct the community, extracting the records of everyone with the surname you are looking for plus any of the families allied with yours, such as the in-laws. This may be the only way to determine who belongs to whom.

You are looking in the wrong place. If you do not locate an event in the Scottish Church Records index in the county where you expect it, you may need to look at other areas. For example, your search may produce a long list of people with the same name as your ancestor, but the events may have all occurred in one particular county. On the other hand, a search filtered by county generates no results if the event occurred in a different county. **The event you are seeking could have occurred in the neighboring parish, a neighboring county, or even out of the country.** You may not recognize a baptism if the mother of the child went to her parent's parish to have the child baptized. If your ancestor was in the military, his children may have been born where he was stationed. A couple may have married in the big city away from the country home. Therefore, you may have to learn more about the family. You can obtain other clues to your ancestor's whereabouts by tracing his siblings. Be creative about why your ancestor was not in the place you expect. Check the local histories again for clues. Repeat your search in the Scottish Church Records index and look at other locations.

The event occurred between 1783 and 1794. The 1783 Stamp Act imposed a tax of three pence to record an event in the parish register. This was a very unpopular tax in Scotland; when it came to burials it was regarded as a tax upon the misfortunes of the community. The penalty for not paying was omission of the entry from the register. Many parishes and sometimes whole counties stopped registering events. The tax was abolished in 1794. Check in *Key to the Parochial Registers of Scotland* by Bloxham to see if registers exist for this time period.

Your search criteria was too narrow. Sometimes you won't get useful results if you restrict your search too much. For example, both the younger Margaret Suther-

Reminder

land and her sister Christian are in the Scottish Church Records index (you'll see how we found Christian's record later in this chapter), but we did not find them in our first search because we included the mother's maiden name in our search criteria. You may need to perform several searches with and without surnames, dates, and filtering. If you still don't find your ancestor, use the suggestions in the rest of this chapter.

The marriage was not recorded in the parish registers. Marriages did not have to be performed in any church or by any official. A couple could even marry themselves with no witnesses present. These marriages were perfectly legal. A marriage that was not recorded in a church register is not in the Scottish Church Records index. Many irregular marriages, however, are recorded in kirk session minutes. Search for the marriage around the time of the birth of the first known child. See the section "Other Records of the Church of Scotland" to find them.

Your ancestors were nonconformists. Depending upon the time period and the county, nonconformity had a big impact on records, especially after 1843. The Scottish Church Records CD indexes the parish registers of the Church of Scotland and some registers of nonconformist churches, but your ancestor may have attended a church that is not indexed. See the section "Records of Nonconformist Churches."

The event was missed during indexing or wasn't recorded at all. Either of these is certainly possible, but don't even consider giving up until you have exhausted all other possibilities. Mistakes were made during indexing, and people did fall through the cracks (especially the ancestor we really want to find!), but more often our ancestors are in the records somewhere and we just haven't recognized them. One of the biggest mistakes we make when we can't find a record is to assume that the event wasn't recorded. Search the original parish register on microfilm to make sure that your ancestor's entry wasn't misread or left out of the index altogether. If you do not find the record, remember that sometimes an event was not recorded in the parish register but may have been recorded in other records of the church. For example, a baptism of an illegitimate child may not have been recorded in the parish register, but a reference to the birth usually can found in kirk session minutes. See the section "Other Records of the Church of Scotland" to find out more. Then try the other techniques in this chapter.

Now That I've Found My Ancestor in the Index, What Do I Do Next?

See what other family members lived in your ancestor's parish and in the surrounding parishes. Two amazing indexes give lists of names and dates to assist you with searching the original parish registers: the computer printouts and the old parish register (OPR) indexes on microfiche.

Computer Printouts

After the parish registers of Scotland were extracted, a computerized printout was made for each parish. Each computer printout (sometimes called a parish register printout) is an alphabetically arranged list of extractions for the parish from the beginning of the parish register to the year 1854. All parishes have two types of

Figure 9-8
Computer printout for the parish of Crieff, Perthshire showing several Brough entries. *Reprinted by permission. © 1995 by Intellectual Reserve, Inc.*

SURNAME	DATES	GIVEN	REL	PARENTS AND OTHER DATA	BATCH #	SER NUMBER
BRUGH	CHR 17 JUN 1739	HELEN	D*	EDWARD BRUGH	C11342-2	01636-4
BRUGH	CHR 13 DEC 1741	EDWARD	S*	EDWARD BRUGH	C11342-2	01759-9
BRUGH	CHR 13 MAY 1753	ANN	D	WILLIAM BRUGH AND CATH. DRUMMON OTHER INFO FR43	C11342-4	00395-6
BROUGH	CHR 30 NOV 1755	WILLIAM	S	WILLIAM BROUGH OTHER INFO FR46	C11342-4	00510-2
BROUGH	CHR 23 APR 1758	CATHARINE	D	WILLIAM BROUGH AND CATHA. DRUMMOND OTHER INFO FR49	C11342-4	00635-0
BROUGH	CHR 19 AUG 1770	JOHN	S	EDWARD BROUGH AND ISABELL BROUG OTHER INFO FR68	C11342-4	01245-3
BROUGH	CHR 9 AUG 1772	ISABEL	D	EDWARD BROUGH AND ISABEL BROUGH OTHER INFO FR71	C11342-4	01368-8
BRUGH	CHR 1 NOV 1776	THOMAS	S*	EDWD. BRUGH AND ISOBEL BRUGH OTHER INFO FR79	C11342-4	01650-1
BRUGH	CHR 2 JAN 1780	EDWARD	S*	EDW. BRUGH AND ISOBEL BRUGH OTHER INFO FR86	C11342-4	01858-3
BRUGH	CHR 14 AUG 1795	JANET	D	THOMAS BRUGH AND JANET THOMSON OTHER INFO FR115	C11342-4	02944-1
BROUGH	CHR 6 JAN 1805	EDWARD	S	THOMAS BROUGH AND ISABEL HALLEY OTHER INFO FR133	C11342-4	03621-4
BROUGH	CHR 19 NOV 1805	CHRISTIAN	D	THOMAS BROUGH AND ANN CRERAR	C11342-4	03704-8
BROUGH	CHR 5 OCT 1806	JOHN	S	THOMAS BROUGH AND ISABEL HALLEY	C11342-4	03786-3
BROUGH	CHR 31 JAN 1808	JAMES	S	THOMAS BROUGH AND ISABEL HALLEY	C11342-4	03906-9
BROUGH	CHR 5 JUN 1808	ANN	D	THOMAS BROUGH AND ANN CRERAR	C11342-4	03938-0
BROUGH	CHR 28 MAY 1810	ELIZABETH	D	THOMAS BROUGH AND ISABEL HALLEY OTHER INFO FR148	C11342-4	04122-2
BROUGH	CHR 17 JUN 1810	ANN	D	THOMAS BROUGH AND ANN CRERAR OTHER INFO FR148	C11342-4	04128-3
BROUGH	CHR 19 DEC 1812	ROBERT	S	THOMAS BROUGH AND ANN CRERAR OTHER INFO FR157	C11342-4	04380-2
BROUGH	CHR 1 APR 1815	DAVID	S	THOMAS BROUGH AND ISABEL HALLEY OTHER INFO FR164	C11342-4	04592-6

(Table header: BIRTHS OR CHRISTENINGS — PAGE 46)

Important

printouts: birth/christening and marriage. Let's see how to find the microfiche number for a computer printout and then see what the printout contains.

When you find an ancestor's christening or marriage record in the Scottish Church Records index, look at the source information for the record. Refer again to Figure 9-3 to see the source for Isabel Brough's baptism (christening). **The column labeled "Printout" gives us the microfiche number of the computer printout.** We ordered FHL microfiche number 6900657 to see the printout that contains Isabel's baptism.

The computer printout on FHL fiche 6900657 contains all extracted baptisms and births for the parish of Crieff. Most often, the entries are arranged by surname, then by the date of the event. Consult the first few pages of the printout to see how the names are listed. One of the pages containing the surname Brough is shown in Figure 9-8. On this page and the surrounding ones, we can see everyone with that surname whose birth or baptism was recorded in the parish of Crieff. The entries are sorted by surname, then by date. Baptisms are called christenings and are abbreviated CHR. We look at page 46 because it shows a lot of people with the surname Brugh/Brough. Isabel Brough's baptism is at the top of page 47 of the printout (not shown). The printout tells us that Isabel was christened 26 August 1836, and that she is the daughter (D) of Robert Brough and Margaret Sutherland. The title on that page is "Crieff, Perth, Scot[land] 1692 to 1854." However, entries made after 1854 are on the page! This is rare—the printout for Crieff contains all extracted names from the parish register *and* from the first twenty years (1855–1875) of civil registration certificates.

The computer printouts are available on microfiche. Perhaps best of all, the cost of renting microfiche from the Family History Library is currently fifteen cents apiece. You can see everyone born or baptized in a parish from the date the parish register begins to the year 1854 for as little as fifteen cents! This is one of the most incredible deals in genealogy. If you order the birth/christening printout and the marriage printout, you have lists of people in the parish who had your ancestor's surname. You also have lists of all other surnames in that parish. Because the printouts are sorted by surname then by date, you can find other families with your ancestor's surname who were in the parish in the same time period. From the information given, you may be able to quickly assemble entire family groups. When you search the microfilm of the original parish register, refer to the computer printout. The printout gives the exact dates you need to find family members in the register, and you have a checklist to make sure you don't miss anyone. The computer printouts are invaluable!

Always order the computer printout for your ancestor's parish.

Important

Index to the Old Parochial Registers on Microfiche

Rare is the family where all events for several generations occurred in the same parish. To illustrate, your ancestor or one of his family members may have been baptized in one parish and married in another. You can get a list of all baptisms and marriages for an entire county by consulting the Old Parochial Registers (OPRs) on microfiche.

The counties are in alphabetical order on FHL fiche 6025611–6025742. Within each county are four indexes (and sometimes more):
1. given name index to christenings
2. surname index to christenings
3. given name index to marriages
4. surname index to marriages

Notes

The OPRs contain the same information as the computer printouts but in a different format. For example, the given name index to christenings lists everyone with the given name of Isabel who was baptized (christened) in the county of Perth. The names are arranged alphabetically by given name, then by date. This is useful, especially when you need to search areas where the patronymic system was used. It may also be helpful if you look for a woman whose maiden name you don't know. The index can narrow down the possibilities. We can use the surname index to christenings to look for Christian Sutherland. We did not find her in the Scottish Church Records index on compact disc, but she is in the OPR index on microfiche. She is listed as Christian Sutherland, christened 18 June 1820 in the parish of Crieff. Only one parent is listed—Alexr. Sutherland. We didn't find Christian when we searched the Scottish Church Records CD because we didn't want to go through all the listings for Alexander Sutherland, but she is in the CD index as well as in the microfiche index!

A frame number is in the miscellaneous column for some entries. This usually means that the entry was not in chronological order in the parish register. Therefore, you may not find your ancestor in the register if you look by date; you need to use the frame numbers at the top of every page (at the edge of the microfilm).

The OPRs on microfiche differ from the parish computer printouts in several ways:

- You can search by given name. This is the most important reason for using the OPRs on microfiche. The ability to search by given name is especially critical in areas where patronymics were used. Searching by given name is also useful if you don't know a woman's maiden name. In fact, you should use the given name index anytime you can't find your ancestor. Your ancestor's surname may have changed, or you may not have considered the spelling that was used on your ancestor's baptism or marriage record. When you scan the given name listing, you may recognize your ancestor.
- The names are arranged in strict alphabetical order. This means you have to consider all possible spelling variants. If you search for the surname Brough, you also have to look for Brugh, Burgh, and others.
- The OPRs on microfiche contain entries only for the Church of Scotland. No printouts are arranged by county for nonconformist churches.
- The OPRs on microfiche contain addenda indexes. The addenda contain some entries after 1854, but mostly entries that were missed in the original series. The addenda are on FHL fiche 6025610.

Because the OPRs on microfiche cover an entire county, you may want to use them with parish boundary maps so you can see each parish's proximity to other parishes in the county. You may want to check more than one county, especially if your ancestor's parish is near the county boundary.

Some Scottish cities have their own OPRs on microfiche. This information is included in the county OPRs, which most Family History Centers have as part of the permanent collection. If you are certain that your ancestors' christenings and marriages occurred within a city, then these sets may reduce the number of people you must investigate. You can find out if your city has its own OPR index by searching the Family History Library Catalog under Scotland, [County], [City], Church Records, Indexes.

MICROFILMED PARISH REGISTERS OF THE CHURCH OF SCOTLAND

For Scotland, you are more likely to find a record of baptism than you are to find a marriage record or a burial record. Once you have ordered the computer printout for your ancestor's parish, you're ready to consult the parish register itself.

Finding Baptism Records

Let's look for the baptism of Isabel Brough. We already have much of the information extracted from the parish register. From the Scottish Church Records index on CD, the computer printout, or the OPRs on microfiche, we have the name Isabel Brough, the names of her parents, and the date and place of her baptism. What

Microfilm Source

more could we get from the microfilmed copy of the original record? You never know until you look.

The baptism record of Isabel Brough is on FHL film 1040076, the parish register of Crieff, Perthshire. The index told us that she was baptized 26 August 1836 in that parish. Since the entries in parish registers are usually arranged chronologically, search for 1836, then for the month of August, then for the date. Isabel's record says "Isabel N. d to Robert Brough and Margt. Sutherland." In this register the letter *D* is the abbreviation for *Daughter*, and the letter *N* is the abbreviation for the word *Natural*. The entry says that Isabel was the natural daughter of Robert Brough and Margaret Sutherland and indicates that Isabel was illegitimate. This important clue tells us that we should not look for a marriage of Robert Brough and Margaret Sutherland before the date of this baptism.

We believe that we found our Isabella with her grandparents in the 1841 census. She was only five years old, but she was not listed with her parents. When we searched the Scottish Church Records index, we did not find a marriage record for them, nor did we find any other children born to them. We suspect that Margaret Sutherland and Robert Brough were never married. We have to find out if our assumptions are correct. What happened to Isabella's mother? Did Margaret Sutherland marry, die, or leave the parish? What happened to Isabella's father? Was Robert Brough required to make payments to support his child? The parish register doesn't give any of those details.

Other than the significant letter *N*, the original record gives no new information. Does that mean the records have new information only if the child's parents weren't married? Let's look at Margaret Sutherland's 1812 baptism record to see if it has any surprises.

Margaret Sutherland's baptism is recorded in the parish of Forres, Moray, on FHL film 0990803. It says, "Margaret Lawful Daughter to Alexander Sutherland Serjeant in the 42d Regiment of Foot, and Flora Macgregor his Spouse, was born 28th November and baptized 6th December 1812, Witnesses James Cameron, Shoemaker, Mary Lile in Forres." This is fantastic information!

The term *lawful* means that Margaret's parents were married at the time of her baptism. But there is a lot more here. We see Margaret's date of birth as well as her date of baptism. Sponsors or godparents were often witnesses in the parish registers, and their names are listed in this one. Witnesses were often family members, so we should look for further information about James Cameron and Mary Lile. Perhaps the most exciting information is that Alexander Sutherland was a serjeant in the 42nd Regiment of Foot. We can search for military records for him.

In summary, even though the Scottish Church Records index contains great information, you may be able to find even more in an original entry of baptism. **Always search the microfilmed copy of the original parish register!**

Finding Marriage Records

We know the date and place of the marriage of Alexander Sutherland and Flora McGrigor from the Scottish Church Records index. The source of the marriage information is FHL film 1066690, listed in the "Source" column in Figure 9-7 on page 150. A search of the Family History Library Catalog by film/fiche number

Important

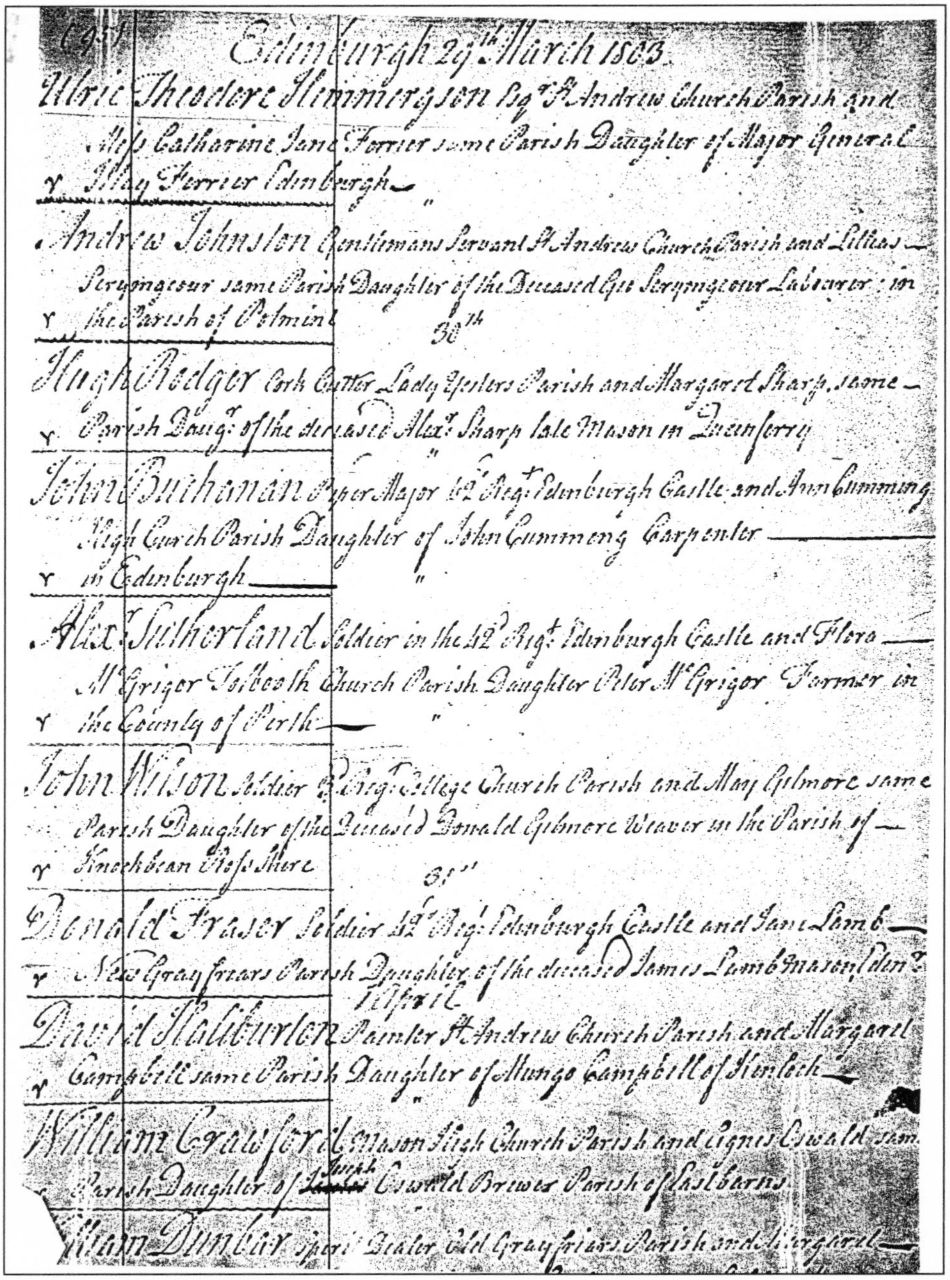

Figure 9-9
Marriage entry in Edinburgh parish register for Alexander Sutherland and his wife, Flora McGrigor, showing all the additional information that is often available in the original record that is not in the index. You have to find the original record to see what additional information may be present.

shows that this record is a microfilmed copy of marriages from 1787 through 1821 from the parish registers of Edinburgh. Again you may wonder why you should bother to search the parish register on microfilm. Order FHL microfilm 1066690 and find out.

Wow! This one is a winner! See Figure 9-9. The entry says, "Alex^r Sutherland Soldier in the 42d Reg^t Edinburgh Castle and Flora McGrigor Tolbooth Church Parish Daughter Peter McGrigor Farmer in the County of Perth." The lack of punctuation makes it somewhat difficult to decipher. It means that Alexander Sutherland was a soldier in the Forty-second Regiment at Edinburgh Castle; Flora McGrigor was from Tolbooth Church parish; and Flora was the daughter of Peter McGrigor, who was a farmer in the County of Perth. The header of the page and the subsequent date "30th" (after the second marriage entry) tell us that they were married in Edinburgh on 30 March 1803. The Scottish Church Records index gave us the names of the groom and bride and the date and place of their marriage, but now we know much more!

The marriage record told us more about Flora. She was in the Tolbooth Church parish of Edinburgh at the time she married, but her father, Peter McGrigor, was a farmer in the County of Perth. We should find out why Flora was in Edinburgh. We also learned that Alexander was a soldier in 1803. He was in the same regiment that he served at the time of his daughter Margaret's 1812 baptism, and the 1841 census tells us that he was an army pensioner. We will certainly look for his military records; they can be a gold mine of information.

This marriage record explains why the couple's children were born in so many different places in Scotland. We can research Alexander's regiment to find out all the places where it was stationed, and we may be able to find more children by looking in the parish registers of those towns. If he was ever stationed outside of Scotland, we may even find children born in foreign countries. Had he left the army when he moved to Crieff? If so, why did he and Flora decide to live there? The 1841 census states that Flora was born in the County of Perth, but Alexander was not. Was Crieff where Flora's father lived? This marriage record gives us many clues and also raises many questions.

We can't stress this enough: Always search the microfilm of the original parish register. You never know what you might find.

Finding Burial Records

Death (burial) registers were proposed in 1574, with lists of the deceased to be given to the Court of Sessions annually. This was because the salaries of the Lords of the Session were raised by levies on the estates of those who died. Since the Lords of the Session used people other than the clergy to obtain the names of the deceased, the clergy had no incentive or requirement to keep burial registers, and in many parishes they were not actively kept until much later.

Burial records can be very difficult to find because they are not indexed in the Scottish Church Records index, the Old Parochial Registers on microfiche, the International Genealogical Index, or the Vital Records Index—British Isles. Furthermore, some parish registers contain burial records for some time periods but not for others. Many parish registers do not include any burials at all. You can find out what burial records exist in the Old Parochial Registers by consulting Bloxham's *Key to the Parochial Registers of Scotland* or Turnbull's *Scottish Parochial Registers*.

Some parishes only have record of the payment for the mortcloth rental. As discussed earlier, not all families are included in the mortcloth rental records.

The good news is that family history societies in Scotland are indexing all known burial records to create a national burial index. That will be a terrific resource. Until then, the best way to find an index of burials is to contact the family history society in the area where your ancestor lived. For example, the pre-1855 burials

Warning

for the County of Fife are all available on compact disc. The CD includes burial records from parish registers and also death information from monumental inscriptions, testaments, newspapers, and the like. You can purchase the *Pre-1855 Fife Deaths Index* CD-ROM from the Fife Family History Society.

What should you do if there's no index? Because you work backward in time, you often get from other documents a general idea of when your ancestor died. But sometimes, you have to resort to searching the registers page by page. Although burial records usually contain scanty information, you always should search for them because the records generated at an ancestor's death and afterward often tell more about him than documents generated in his lifetime do. Burial records are a good place to start, and they can lead you to probate records which can be the most genealogically valuable records of all.

Bloxham's *Key to the Parochial Registers of Scotland* tells us that there are no burial records for the Parish of Crieff. However, Crieff has some mortcloth records that were not part of the Old Parochial Registers. They are included at the end of the microfilm that contains the Old Parochial Registers (FHL film 1040076). The section "Other Records of the Church of Scotland" in this chapter explains how we found out about these additional records. Look at Figure 9-10 for an example of mortcloth rental records. This page lists payments made in 1762–1763 to rent mortcloths. On 26 December 1762, the family of John Brugh paid 2-0-0 (two pounds) to rent the best mortcloth (abbreviated "M.C."). We don't know if John Brugh was related to our Brough family, and we can't tell his age or if he was married. We do know from this record his approximate date of death. The best mortcloth in Crieff carried a higher rental fee than the "second" mortcloth, which was rented for Catrin Crerer on 24 April 1763. The family paid 1-4-0 for that one. The little mortcloth could be used for children and was even less expensive. It was rented for "Donald Gilberts Cherld [child]" on 6 March 1763 at the cost of 1-0-0. The mortcloth rental records are useful because they give an approximate date of death and can indicate your ancestor's financial status.

MONUMENTAL INSCRIPTIONS (MIs)

Tip

\di'fin\ *vb*

Definitions

Monumental inscriptions include inscriptions on tombstones and other monuments to the deceased. They usually were paid for and erected by immediate family members, and sometimes by descendants. Although monumental inscriptions are not records of the Church of Scotland, we discuss them here because they can be good substitutes for missing burial records. In fact, the information on a monumental inscription is often better than what you would find in a burial record.

Many monumental inscriptions have been published, often by the local county family history society. If you don't find any in the Family History Library Catalog under the name of the parish, look under the name of the county. The category is Scotland, [County], Cemeteries. As a last resort, try searching under Scotland, Cemeteries.

We found a listing for "Pre-1855 Monumental Inscriptions in South Perthshire" on FHL film 0962930. The inscriptions for the Parish of Crieff were transcribed in this resource, which has maps of the cemeteries. Our Isabella Brough (who mar-

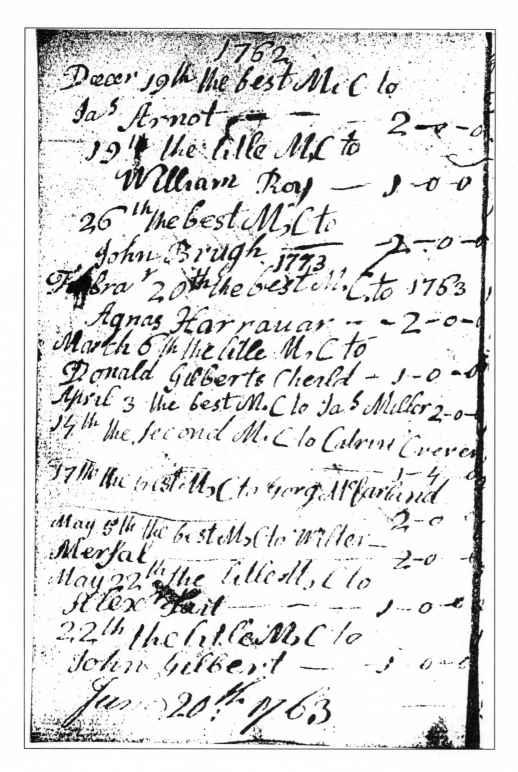

ried James Kay) is not on this film because she died long after 1855. However, earlier family members may be recorded here. One entry records the tombstone of Edward Brough, wright [his occupation], who died 26 November 1797 at age fifty-six. His wife, Isabella, died 24 February 1802 at age sixty-two. The stone was erected by their son Thomas. Are these people related to Robert Brough (the father of our Isabella)? This is a page to keep for future reference.

You may find monumental inscriptions in a parish for people who aren't buried there. For example, entry number 60 in the Crieff Churchyard (not shown) records the inscription for James Wilson, late merchant in Charlestown [Charleston], South Carolina. This does not necessarily mean that James was buried in Crieff; it means only that someone erected a monument to him in Crieff.

You may even find inscriptions recording several generations of a family. Entry number 56 in the Crieff Churchyard is the tombstone erected by Alexander Campbell. It names his father, John; his mother, Margaret McEwan; his brothers Peter and John; his sister Elizabeth; his grandfather John Campbell; his grandmother Catherine Taylor; and Margaret Campbell, whose relationship is not stated. The dates of and ages at death for all of these people are recorded on the tombstone.

Some monumental inscriptions even contain biographical information. One inscription in Crieff tells about the Reverend George Barlas, Minister of the Associate Congregation of Dundee, who came to Crieff for recovery of his health. Although he may not be your ancestor, this may give you a clue regarding a nonconformist congregation in the area.

Monumental inscriptions really can help you trace your family. Even if you find your ancestor in a burial register, look also for monumental inscriptions.

After 1855, of course, you should use the civil registration index to find death certificates instead of (or in addition to) burial records. The death certificates are usually far more informative than the burial registers, and they may be better sources than monumental inscriptions. See chapter seven for more information about civil registration certificates.

OTHER RECORDS OF THE CHURCH OF SCOTLAND

\di'fin\ *vb*

Definitions

After you look at the parish register, check the Family History Library Catalog to see if any other records are filmed for the parish. Then look for other records of the Church of Scotland in the inventory to Church of Scotland synod, presbytery, and kirk session records. **The kirk sessions are the records of the local parish court.** Some kirk session records began in the late 1550s, but the majority were established in the early seventeenth century under the direction of local bishops. These courts addressed cases dealing with marriage, divorce, fornication, adultery, and slander. They also dealt with the parish administrative issues of education and poor relief. Therefore, because Isabel Brough's birth was illegitimate, we expect to find in kirk session records information about the circumstances surrounding this event. Her parents, Margaret Sutherland and Robert Brough, were probably required to perform some kind of penance, and the details should have been recorded. We may find out in the records of the kirk sessions whether Robert Brough was required to make payments to support his daughter.

Kirk session records are held by the National Archives of Scotland and organized as class CH 2 under the method of cataloging their collection. An inventory of CH 2 records is on FHL microfiche 6084820, and the index is on FHL fiche 6084821. Let's use the inventory to see what records are held for the Parish of Crieff.

CH 2 INVENTORY ON FHL MICROFICHE 6084820

Fiche number	Classes covered
1 of 26	CH 2/1–CH 2/64
2 of 26	CH 2/65–CH 2/122
3 of 26	CH 2/122–CH 2/171
4 of 26	CH 2/171–CH 2/216
5 of 26	CH 2/216–CH 2/280
6 of 26	CH 2/281–CH 2/337
7 of 26	CH 2/337–CH 2/400
8 of 26	CH 2/401–CH 2/446
9 of 26	CH 2/447–CH 2/501
10 of 26	CH 2/502–CH 2/542
11 of 26	CH 2/543–CH 2/593
12 of 26	CH 2/594–CH 2/631
13 of 26	CH 2/632–CH 2/694
14 of 26	CH 2/695–CH 2/720
15 of 26	CH 2/721–CH 2/781
16 of 26	CH 2/782–CH 2/833
17 of 26	CH 2/833–CH 2/890
18 of 26	CH 2/891–CH 2/950
19 of 26	CH 2/951–CH 2/1008
20 of 26	CH 2/1009–CH 2/1062
21 of 26	CH 2/1063–CH 2/1116
22 of 26	CH 2/1117–CH 2/1174
23 of 26	CH 2/1175–CH 2/1223
24 of 26	CH 2/1225–CH 2/1281
25 of 26	CH 2/1282–CH 2/1337
26 of 26	CH 2/1338–CH 2/1390

1. Look up the name of the parish in the index on fiche 6084821. This is a set of three fiche, and Crieff is on the first one. The inventory indicates that there are kirk session records for three churches in Crieff: St. Michael's CH 2/545; West Q.S. CH 2/758; South CH 3/698. Let's look at the reference for St. Michael's kirk session records, CH 2/545.

2. Find the reference(s) in FHL fiche 6084820, a set of twenty-six fiche. Unfortunately, each fiche has the same title, so you cannot tell what is covered on an individual fiche. We have compiled the table in the sidebar to allow you to quickly locate the records you need.

The reference CH 2/545 is on fiche number 11 (see Figure 9-11). It has two pages of references to records of Crieff. There's a lot of information, most of which is not on microfilm! A very important item in the CH 2 inventory for the Parish of Crieff is the listing of pre-1855 birth, marriage, and death entries. The inventory

Figure 9-11
Kirk session records for parish of Crieff held by the National Archives of Scotland, organized as class CH 2 and listed on FHL microfiche 6084820.

CH2	545. CRIEFF Kirk Session.
1.	Minutes 1699-1713 Poors' money 1700-13
2.	Minutes 1723-39 1761-72 1817 1820 Accounts 1825
3.	Minutes 1746-60 Accounts 1747-71 1825-30
4.	Minutes 1833-48
5.	1847-9
6.	1848-76
7-12.	Scroll minutes 1849-79
13.	Accounts (poors' money) 1756-69
14.	1807-25
15.	1830-5
16.	1846-74

17.	1874-95
18.	Baptisms 1754-68 Proclamations 1755-64 Mortcloths 1762-93
19.	Baptisms 1792-1818
20.	Proclamations 1783-1814
21.	1880-1
22-4.	Communion rolls 1867-75
25.	Deacons' court minutes 1876-9
26.	Supplementary stipend fund committee minutes 1875-7
27.	Scheme of division of seats 1829
28.	Seats in new church (pew-register) n.d.
29,30.	Revenue of church 1835-46
31.	Petition of town and parish of Crieff to parliament, protesting against proposed education bill. Signed by many inhabitants. n.d
32.	Misc. accounts and papers [2 boxes]
33.	Marriage register 1895-1938
34.	Certificates for proclamation 1896-1909

tells us that for Crieff records of baptisms are available for 1754–1768 and 1792–1818, proclamations are available for 1755–1764 and 1783–1814, and mortcloth rentals are available for 1762–1793. Bloxham's *Key to the Parochial Registers of Scotland* states that the Old Parochial Registers of Crieff have births from 1692 to 1854, marriages from 1692 to 1854, and no death records, but the records mentioned in the CH 2 inventory are from an additional book! Here's the good news: When the Old Parochial Registers for Crieff were microfilmed, the book from CH 2/545 was included at the end of the film. We saw a page from this book in the section above on burial records.

A separate listing of these parishes is available online at the General Register Office for Scotland Web site at <www.gro-scotland.gov.uk>. This Adobe Acrobat file is accessible at the page entitled "List of Parishes/RDs."

When you find something interesting in the CH 2 inventory, you can hire a researcher in Scotland to look at the records. You can save yourself a lot of money by giving the researcher the specific record class you want him to search. For example, notice the petition to Parliament signed by many inhabitants of the parish in item 31 of Figure 9-11. (The notation "n.d." means that no date is on the document.) To see this document, reference it as CH 2/545/31 and order it from the National Archives of Scotland or ask a researcher to look at it.

RECORDS OF NONCONFORMIST CHURCHES

If you do not find your ancestor in the Scottish Church Records index or in the kirk session records for your ancestor's parish, he may have been a nonconformist. **Most nonconformist churches are not indexed in the Scottish Church Records index**. Check the following resources in order:

Reminder

1. **International Genealogical Index.** Some entries on the International Genealogical Index are not on the Scottish Church Records index. Information about your ancestor may have been submitted to the IGI by a member of The Church of Jesus Christ of Latter-day Saints. See chapters four and six for two different ways of searching the International Genealogical Index.

2. **Vital Records Index—British Isles.** This contains a list of entries that have been extracted from original records but may not yet be on the IGI. Some Scottish nonconformist churches are indexed in this resource. See chapter six.

3. **Statistical Accounts and Gazetteers.** Use these to see what other churches existed in the area. *The Statistical Accounts* name the nonconformist churches in your ancestor's parish. *The Statistical Account of Scotland* tells what nonconformist churches existed in your ancestor's parish in the 1790s, and *The New Statistical Account of Scotland* tells what churches existed in the late 1830s or early 1840s. As mentioned in chapter six, *The Statistical Accounts* are available on the Internet at <http://edina.ac.uk/cgi/StatAcc/StatAcc.cgi>.

Good gazetteers also list nonconformist churches. Groome's *Ordnance Gazetteer of Scotland: A Survey of Scottish Topography, Statistical, Biographical, and Historical* is probably the best gazetteer of Scotland. All Scottish places in the Family History Library Catalog are cataloged according to the listings in this gazetteer. In addition to other information about a parish, you can find the names of the nonconformist churches that existed in the 1880s. The gazetteer is available on FHL microfiche 6020391–6020411. The Family History Library Catalog and the headings on the microfiche do not tell you the places covered on each fiche, so consult the table at <www.rootsweb.com/~bifhsusa/ressco.html#groome>.

To find nonconformist chapels in Crieff, we consulted the first two Statistical Accounts and Groome's gazetteer. The following accounts show how important it is to consult each source.

The first statistical account (1790s) gave a history of nonconformity in Crieff and said that from 1699 to 1755 "none separated from the church who had been previously of the establishment but a number still adhered to the Episcopacy whose forefather's had . . . embraced [it]." This means that there were no nonconformists from 1699 to 1755 except Episcopalians. *The Statistical Account* then tells us that in about 1763 the Anti-Burghers formed a congregation, and later the Bereans formed one. The Bereans, Episcopals, and "Papists" (Roman Catholics) had no clergyman in Crieff at the time of the first statistical account, but the Relief sect (formed in 1785) and the Anti-Burghers did.

The New Statistical Account for the Parish of Crieff, written in 1837, reports that there were "three Dissenting or Seceding chapels in the parish exclusive of a Popish one, viz. the United Secession, the Relief, and the Original Seceders. . . . The Original Seceders have no stated minister; and the Priest who died lately has hitherto had no successor." Some in Crieff belonged to other denominations, but they had neither a place of worship nor a minister. The most useful part of the account is a table for Crieff showing the number of adherents belonging to each denomination in 1835: Establishment, 3,427; Relief, 370; United Secession, 357; Original Secession, 36; Scottish Episcopalians, 43; Independents, 10; Papists, 36; Bereans, 8; Quakers, 1; and "not known to belong to any denomination," 24. Remember that a long delay may have occurred between the time an account was written and the time it was published. For example, the second statistical account for the parish of Crieff was written in 1837 but published in *The New Statistical Account of Scotland* in 1845. This is why we find no mention of the Free Church in the second statistical account for the parish. The Free Church, however, had a significant impact in the parish, and you can find out about it by consulting the Third Statistical Account or a parish history.

Groome's *Ordnance Gazetteer of Scotland* tells us that in the 1880s Crieff had two church buildings for the Church of Scotland. There were also Free Church, United Presbyterian, Roman Catholic, Episcopal, Baptist, and Independent chapels.

If your family remained in a parish for many years, and even for several generations, you may need to consult all three Statistical Accounts of Scotland and at least one gazetteer. A good history of the parish can also help you find which nonconformist churches existed at various times.

4. **National Index of Parish Registers, volume 12.** Now that you know what nonconformist churches existed in your ancestor's parish, you may want to read a brief explanation of the religions and their records in the *National Index of Parish Registers* (NIPR), a multivolume set published by the Society of Genealogists, London. Volume 12, devoted to Scotland, describes various sources for Scottish research, and it is particularly strong on nonconformist churches. The large section

on nonconformity includes a general church history as well as a description of each denomination.

For example, a group called the Bereans was in Crieff. NIPR tells us that the sect was formed in 1773 by a man named John Barclay who was an assistant minister for the Church of Scotland in Fettercairn. He was rejected as minister there, so he formed his own church. He and his followers took the name Bereans because "the disciples at Berea mentioned in the Acts of the Apostles 'searched the Scriptures daily.' " By the time Barclay died in 1798, Berean churches had been founded at Marykirk, Edinburgh, Glasgow, Stirling, Crieff, Dundee, and Arbroath. The book further states that in 1843 "there were only four Berean ministers—at Edinburgh, Glasgow, Laurencekirk, and Dundee. Soon after the denomination died out altogether." You can see how useful this information is for finding ancestors in the Parish of Crieff. *The New Statistical Account of Scotland* states that in 1835 there were only eight Bereans (with no minister) in Crieff. The *National Index of Parish Registers* lets us know that this was not a temporary situation; the sect was dying out. We need not bother to look for records of this church in Crieff in the 1840s.

NIPR volume 12 also has two appendices relating to nonconformity: Appendix I is a list of pre-1855 registers of seceding Presbyterian churches in the Scottish Record Office (now the National Archives of Scotland), and Appendix II is a list of registers of the Scottish Episcopal Church. These lists are out of date. You should instead consult the National Archives of Scotland's CH inventories (see page 169).

5. **Parish and Vital Records List.** We know that all baptisms and marriages from the parish registers of the Church of Scotland have been indexed. The names appear in the Scottish Church Records index, and most of them are also in the International Genealogical Index. But which nonconformist records have been indexed in these resources? You can find out by consulting the Parish and Vital Records List (PVRL).

The PVRL contains a list of parishes showing what records have been extracted by the Genealogical Society of Utah. It tells us what we can expect to find in the Scottish Church Records index, the International Genealogical Index, and the Vital Records Index—British Isles.

The Parish and Vital Records List is available on microfiche at every Family History Center. It has not been assigned a microfiche number by the Family History Library, so you need to have the Family History Center staff show you where it is filed in their center. Search the PVRL the same way you search the Family History Library Catalog. Look for the name of the country first, then the county, then the name of the parish. To find what records have been extracted for Crieff, look under Scotland, Perthshire, Crieff. Our example is from the July 1998 edition of the Parish and Vital Records List. At the time of this writing, that is the most recent microfiche edition.

Now look at Figure 9-12. There are several entries for the parish of Crieff. The first two columns tell us the name of the county and parish. If only the name of the parish is mentioned, the records are for the Parish Church (the Church of Scotland) or for the civil registration records in that parish. Otherwise, the name of the nonconformist church appears. In our example several lines describe the extracted entries for Crieff; the last one (Crieff, Relief United Presbyterian) is a nonconformist register. Columns 3 and 4 tell what kind of record was extracted (birth, christening,

SCOTLAND   PARISH AND VITAL RECORDS LIST   OCT 1998   PAGE 3,584

1. 2. COUNTY – TOWN AND/OR PARISH	3. PERIOD FROM – TO	4. RECD TYPE	5. PRINTOUT CALL NO.	NUM FCH	6. PROJECT	7. SOURCE CALL NO.
PERTH CLUNIE	1794-1819	MAR	# 6903059	1	M11339-4	1040074, 0102701
PERTH CLUNIE	1820-1854	MAR	# 6903059	1	M11339-5	1040074
PERTH CLUNIE	1855-1875	MAR	NONE		M11339-1	6035516 REGISTER
PERTH COLLACE	1855-1875	BIR	NONE		C11340-1	6035516 REGISTER
PERTH COLLACE	1713-1786	CHR	# 6903060	1	C11340-2	1040074
PERTH COLLACE	1786-1854	CHR	# 6903060	1	C11340-4	1040356
PERTH COLLACE	1720-1855	MAR	# 6903061	1	M11340-4	1040356, 0102702
PERTH COLLACE	-1806	MAR	# 6903061	1	M11340-2 **	1040356, 0102702
PERTH COLLACE	1855-1875	MAR	NONE		M11340-1	6035516 REGISTER
PERTH COMRIE	1855-1875	BIR	NONE		C11341-1	6035516 REGISTER
PERTH COMRIE	1693-1737	CHR	# 6900656	3	C11341-2	1040075
PERTH COMRIE	1738-1820	CHR	# 6900656	3	C11341-4	1040075
PERTH COMRIE	1820-1855	CHR	# 6900656	3	C11341-5	1040075
PERTH COMRIE	1700-1710	MAR	# 6901891	1	M11341-2	1040075
PERTH COMRIE	1747-1820	MAR	# 6901891	1	M11341-4	1040075
PERTH COMRIE	-1771	MAR	# 6901891	1	M11341-6 **	1041175
PERTH COMRIE	1820-1855	MAR	# 6901891	1	M11341-5	1040075
PERTH COMRIE	1855-1875	MAR	NONE		M11341-1	6035516 REGISTER
PERTH CRIEFF	1855-1875	BIR	NONE		C11342-1	6035516 REGISTER
PERTH ~ CRIEFF	1692-1746	CHR	# 6900657	3	C11342-2	1040076
PERTH CRIEFF	1746-1820	CHR	# 6900657	2	J11342-4 **	1040076
PERTH CRIEFF	1746-1820	CHR	# 6900657	2	K11342-4 **	1040076
PERTH CRIEFF	1820-1854	CHR	# 6900657	3	C11342-5	1040076
PERTH CRIEFF	1692-1713	MAR	# 6900658	2	M11342-2	1040076
PERTH CRIEFF	1748-1819	MAR	# 6900658	2	M11342-4	1040076
PERTH CRIEFF	1819-1856	MAR	# 6900658	2	M11342-5	1040076
PERTH CRIEFF	1855-1875	MAR	NONE		M11342-1	6035516 REGISTER
PERTH CRIEFF, RELIEF UNITED PRESBYTERIAN	1825-1854	CHR	# 6902028	1	C19134-1 **	1068235
PERTH CULROSS	1855-1875	BIR	NONE		C11343-1	6035516 REGISTER
PERTH CULROSS	1641-1687	CHR	# 6903062	3	C11343-2	1040076
PERTH CULROSS .	1687-1820	CHR	# 6903062	3	C11343-4	1040077
PERTH CULROSS	1820-1854	CHR	# 6903062	3	C11343-5	1040077
PERTH CULROSS	1640-1687	MAR	# 6903063	1	M11343-2	1040076
PERTH CULROSS	1687-1818	MAR	# 6903063	1	M11343-4	1040077
PERTH CULROSS	1820-1854	MAR	# 6903063	1	M11343-5	1040077
PERTH CULROSS	1855-1875	MAR	NONE		M11343-1	6035516 REGISTER
PERTH DOUNE, BRIDE OF TEITH ASSOCIATE CONGREGATION	1758-1764	CHR	NONE		C19004-1 **	0304670, 0889474
PERTH DOUNE, BRIDE OF TEITH ASSOCIATE CONGREGATION	1759-1766	MAR	NONE		M19004-1 **	0304670, 0889474
PERTH DOUNE, DEANSTON BURGHER AND FREE	1802-1871	CHR	NONE		C19153-1 **	1484191
PERTH DOUNE, DEANSTON BURGHER AND FREE	1802-1871	MAR	NONE		M19153-1 **	1484191
PERTH DOWALLY	1855-1875	BIR	NONE		C11344-1	6035516 REGISTER
PERTH DOWALLY	1705-1820	CHR	# 6903064	1	C11344-2	1040078, 0102707
PERTH DOWALLY	1820-1854	CHR	# 6903064	1	C11344-4	1040078
PERTH DOWALLY	1746-1820	MAR	# 6903065	1	M11344-2	1040078, 0102707
PERTH DOWALLY	1820-1856	MAR	# 6903065	1	M11344-4	1040078
PERTH DOWALLY	1855-1875	MAR	NONE		M11344-1	6035516 REGISTER
PERTH DRON	1855-1875	BIR	NONE		C11345-1	6035516 REGISTER
PERTH DRON	1682-1749	CHR	# 6903066	1	C11345-2	1040078
PERTH DRON	1748-1819	CHR	# 6903066	1	C11345-4	1040079

     * THE PRINTOUT IS ON MICROFILM ONLY   ** RECORDS IN THIS BATCH AND PERIOD ARE NOT IN THE 1988 EDITION OF THE IGI
     # THE PRINTOUT IS ON MICROFICHE ONLY

Figure 9-12
The entry for Crieff listed under Scotland, Perthshire, Crieff in the Parish and Vital Records List showing what records have been extracted. *Reprinted by permission. © 1995 by Intellectual Reserve, Inc.*

or marriage) and the time period covered. Column 5 of the PVRL tells us if a computer printout was made of the extracted entries. If there is one, order the referenced microfiche number. The printout can be very valuable because it contains alphabetically arranged extracts of the church registers. See the "Computer Printouts" section above. Column 7 gives the call number of the original source. The extracted Church of Scotland christenings and marriages for Crieff were taken from FHL film 1040076.

The PVRL states that births for the Parish of Crieff have been extracted from 1855 to 1875, but there is no printout. Even though these civil registration entries don't have a separate printout, the post-1854 records are included in the computer printout for christenings for the Church of Scotland in Crieff (FHL fiche 6900657). The extracted marriages from 1855 to 1875 are included in the computer printout of marriages from the Church of Scotland (FHL fiche 6900658). This is not true for all Scottish parishes; in fact, it is very rare. **Order the computer printout for your ancestor's parish to see if any post-1854 entries are included.**

We found that the 1825–1854 christenings have been extracted for the Crieff

Tip

Relief United Presbyterian Congregation. This means that they are indexed, so we should have already found any of our family names from this extraction in the Scottish Church Records index, the International Genealogical Index, or the Vital Records Index—British Isles. Order the computer printout for this church to verify that none of your family names is among the extractions. If you look for baptisms 1825–1854 and find no family names in the printout, concentrate on the records of other nonconformist churches in the area. Remember, however, that it is possible other records (marriages or burials) in the register were not extracted.

When you find records in the Parish and Vital Records List, see if the dates coincide with when your ancestor or his family lived in the parish. If they do, order the computer printout(s) for any nonconformist churches to ensure you didn't miss anyone when you searched the indexes. If any family names appear in the printout or if it is possible that your ancestor attended that church, order the microfilm of the original register to see if it contains additional information.

6. **Family History Library Catalog.** Now check the Family History Library Catalog to see if any other nonconformist registers are on microfilm. Order the microfilmed registers of any churches that were not listed in the Parish and Vital Records List.

For example, the FHL Catalog contains records for three churches in Crieff: Church of Scotland, Parish Church of Crieff (1692–1854); Crieff Relief United Presbyterian. Congregation (1825–1854); and Crieff Second United Presbyterian Church (1853–1863). We have already searched the records of the Church of Scotland, and we should have checked the Relief United Presbyterian Congregation when we found it listed in the Parish and Vital Records List. The Crieff Second United Presbyterian Church was not listed in the Parish and Vital Records List; therefore, its records are not in the indexes we have consulted. We need to search through the microfilm of the original register for this church.

7. **Inventories of Records in the National Archives of Scotland.** Most records of nonconformist churches are not available on microfilm through the Family History Library. Many of them, however, are housed at the National Archives of Scotland (NAS). Inventories of church records at the NAS are available on microfiche from the FHL. An inventory of Roman Catholic Records is available on microfilm.

Church	NAS Inventory Number	FHL Film/Fiche Number
Free Church records	CH 3	6084809
Religious Society of Friends	CH 10	6084816
Methodist records	CH 11	6084817
Episcopal Church of Scotland	CH 12	6084818
Miscellaneous smaller churches	CH 13–17	6084819
Roman Catholic records	RH 21	1368203

The inventories are organized in the same fashion as the Church of Scotland inventory (CH 2). Some have an index to parishes, but some do not. For example, the inventory to the Episcopal Church of Scotland is on FHL microfiche 6084818, a set of nine fiche. The index of parishes is on the first fiche of the set, pages 2–3. The index of Roman Catholic parishes is on pages 5 and 6 of the RH 21 inventory.

CH 3 INVENTORY ON FHL MICROFICHE 6084809

Fiche Number	Classes Covered
1 of 30	CH 3/1–CH 3/67
2 of 30	CH 3/68–CH 3/132
3 of 30	CH 3/133–CH 3/197
4 of 30	CH 3/198–CH 3/200
5 of 30	CH 3/201–CH 3/267
6 of 30	CH 3/268–CH 3/321
7 of 30	CH 3/322–CH 3/380
8 of 30	CH 3/381–CH 3/400
9 of 30	CH 3/401–CH 3/462
10 of 30	CH 3/463–CH 3/512
11 of 30	CH 3/513–CH 3/568
12 of 30	CH 3/568–CH 3/600
13 of 30	CH 3/601–CH 3/661
14 of 30	CH 3/662–CH 3/721
15 of 30	CH 3/721–CH 3/777
16 of 30	CH 3/778–CH 3/800
17 of 30	CH 3/801–CH 3/861
18 of 30	CH 3/862–CH 3/929
19 of 30	CH 3/930–CH 3/980
20 of 30	CH 3/980–CH 3/1043
21 of 30	CH 3/1044–CH 3/1060
22 of 30	CH 3/1061–CH 3/1128
23 of 30	CH 3/1129–CH 3/1189
24 of 30	CH 3/1190–CH 3/1247
25 of 30	CH 3/1248–CH 3/1300
26 of 30	CH 3/1300–CH 3/1341
27 of 30	CH 3/1342–CH 3/1375
28 of 30	Index: Aberdeen—Glasgow
29 of 30	Index: Glasgow—Wishaw
30 of 30	Index: Yell—Yetholm

The largest inventory is the one for the Free Church. It is on a set of thirty fiche. Again, the titles on the fiche do not tell what is on each one, so it is cumbersome to use without the CH 3 table in the sidebar.

The index to the CH 3 inventory has records for four churches in the parish of Crieff. They are listed with the following descriptions: Anti-Burgher, First U. P., North; Second U. P. Church, South; Free Church, South U. F.; Free Church. First look at the inventory for each church, then hire a researcher to examine at the National Archives of Scotland the ones you need. Another inventory of nonconformist records is in Diane Baptie's *Registers of the Secession Churches in Scotland.*

8. **Local Custody.** Not all records of nonconformist churches have been transferred

to the National Archives of Scotland; some are still in local custody. A list of the locations of registers of the Episcopal Church of Scotland is in D.J. Steel's *National Index of Parish Registers,* volume 12. The bibliography in that book may also be useful. For Roman Catholics, see Michael Gandy's *Catholic Missions and Registers* (volume 6, *Scotland*). For other nonconformist registers that are not at the National Archives of Scotland, check the archives of the church head office and the local church and the local archives or library. Perhaps the easiest way to find them is to ask someone in the family history society for the county where your ancestor lived.

Technique

CHECKLIST FOR FINDING SCOTTISH CHURCH RECORDS

- Scottish Church Records index. This source indexes all pre-1855 baptisms and marriages from the parish registers of the Church of Scotland. It also indexes baptisms and marriages from some nonconformist registers. The Scottish Church Records index is available for use at no charge at Family History Centers in a DOS version on compact disc as part of the FamilySearch program. You can also search this database for a fee on the Scots Origins Web site.
- Old Parochial Registers on microfiche; indexes are arranged by county.
- The International Genealogical Index.
- Vital Records Index—British Isles.
- National Burial Register of Scotland. At the time of this writing, this resource is in progress. In the meantime, to find burial indexes contact the family history society in the area where your ancestor lived.
- Computer (parish register) printouts.
- Microfilm of original parish registers of the Church of Scotland. Learn what records exist by consulting Bloxham's *Key to the Parochial Registers of Scotland.* This book lists FHL film numbers, but they are for the first filming (old films) of the registers. Search the FHL Catalog to find the new film numbers for a parish. To use the catalog, either search by film number using the old film numbers, or search by place using the parish name.
- Look for other records of the Church of Scotland in the kirk session records inventory (CH 2) on FHL microfiche 6084820. To find the parish you want, use the index on FHL fiche 6084821.
- If you do not find your ancestor in the records of the Church of Scotland, use *The Statistical Accounts of Scotland* online at <http://edina.ac.uk/cgi/StatAcc/ StatAcc.cgi> or Groome's *Ordnance Gazetteer of Scotland* (FHL fiche numbers 6020391–6020411) to find the denominations of other area churches.
- Consult the Parish and Vital Records List to see which nonconformist churches are extracted and indexed. Order parish register printouts.
- Search the Family History Library Catalog to see if other nonconformist records are available on microfilm. Order microfilmed records.
- Check the inventory of nonconformist records held at the National Archives of Scotland to see what else is available. The inventories are on FHL microfiche numbers 6084809 and 6084816–6084819. The inventory of Roman Catholic Records (RH 21) is on FHL microfilm 1368303.

- If the records for the church you want are not at the Family History Library or among the holdings of the National Archives of Scotland, see if the records are still in local custody.

For More Info

WHERE DO I FIND OUT MORE ABOUT THIS TOPIC?
Genealogical Information

Baptie, Diane. *Registers of the Secession Churches in Scotland*. The Scottish Association of Family History Societies, 2000.

Bloxham, V. Ben. *Key to the Parochial Registers of Scotland: From Earliest Times Through 1854*. 2d ed. Reprint, Provo, Utah: Stevenson's Genealogical Center, 1979.

Gandy, Michael. *Catholic Family History: A Bibliography for Scotland*. London: the author, 1996.

———. *Catholic Missions and Registers*. Vol. 6, *Scotland*. 1993.

———. *Catholic Parishes in England, Wales and Scotland: An Atlas*. 1993.

Humphrey-Smith, Cecil R. *The Phillimore Atlas and Index of Parish Registers*. 2d ed. Chichester, England: Phillimore & Co., Ltd., 1995.

Lewis, Samuel. *A Topographical Dictionary of Scotland*. 2 vols. Reprint, Baltimore, Md.: Genealogical Publishing Co., Inc., 1989.

McNaughton, William D. *The Scottish Congregational Ministry, 1794–1993*. Glasgow, Scotland: The Congregational Union of Scotland, 1993.

Steel, D.J. *National Index of Parish Registers*. Vol. 12, *Sources for Scottish Genealogy and Family History*. Chichester, England: Phillimore & Co., Ltd., 1970.

Turnbull, William B. *Scottish Parochial Registers: Memoranda of the State of the Parochial Registers of Scotland, Whereby is Clearly Shown the Imperative Necessity for a National System of Regular Registration*. Edinburgh, Scotland: Thomas George Stevenson, 1849.

Willsher, Betty. *Epitaphs and Images From Scottish Graveyards*. Edinburgh, Scotland: Canongate Books, 1996.

———. *Understanding Scottish Graveyards: An Interpretative Approach*. 1995.

Scottish Church History

Bebbington, D.W. *The Baptists in Scotland*. Glasgow, Scotland: Baptist Union of Scotland, 1988.

Black, C. Stewart. *The Scottish Church: A Short Study in Ecclesiastical History*. Glasgow, Scotland: William Maclellan, 1952.

Brown, Callum G. *Religion and Society in Scotland Since 1707*. Edinburgh, Scotland: Edinburgh University Press, 1997.

Burleigh, J.H.S. *A Church History of Scotland*. London: Oxford University Press, 1960.

Donaldson, Gordon. *Scotland: Church and Nation Through Sixteen Centuries*. Naperville, Ill.: SCM Book Club, 1960.

———. *Scottish Church History*. Edinburgh, Scotland: Scottish Academic Press, 1985.

Goldie, Frederick. *A Short History of the Episcopal Church in Scotland From the Restoration to the Present Time*. London: SPCK, 1951.

Swift, Wesley F. *Methodism in Scotland*. London: Epworth Press, 1947.

Scottish History

Brown, P. Hume. *Scotland: A Concise History*. Glasgow, Scotland: Lang Syne Publishers, 1908. Revised by Rennie Owen, 1990.

Cowan, Edward J. and Richard Finlay. *Scotland Since 1688: Struggle for a Nation*. New York: Barnes & Noble, 2000.

Daiches, David, ed. *The New Companion to Scottish Culture*. Edinburgh, Scotland: Polygon, 1993.

Devine, T.M. *The Scottish Nation: A History, 1700–2000*. New York: Viking Penguin, 1999.

Donaldson, Gordon. *Scottish Kings*. 1967. Reprint, New York: Barnes & Noble Books, 1992.

Donaldson, Gordon and Robert S. Morpeth. *A Dictionary of Scottish History*. 1977. Reprint, Edinburgh, Scotland: John Donald Publishers, 1999.

Donnachie, Ian and George Hewitt. *A Companion to Scottish History: From the Reformation to the Present*. New York: Facts on File, 1989.

Fisher, Andrew. *A Traveler's History of Scotland*. 4th ed. New York: Interlink Books, 2000.

Fry, Peter and Fiona Somerset Fry. *The History of Scotland*. London: Routledge, 1982. Reprint, 1996.

Gardiner, Juliet and Neil Wenborn, eds. *The History Today Companion to British History*. London: Collins & Brown, 1995.

Mackie, J.D. *A History of Scotland*. 2d ed. 1978. Reprint, New York: Penguin, 1991.

McGregor, Iona. *Getting Married in Scotland*. Edinburgh, Scotland: NMS Publishing, 2000.

Mitchison, Rosalind. *A History of Scotland*. London: Methuen & Co., 1970.

Smout, T.C. *A Century of the Scottish People, 1830–1950*. London: Collins, 1986.

————. *A History of the Scottish People, 1560–1830*. London: Collins, 1969.

AFTER SEARCHING CHURCH RECORDS, WHAT SHOULD I DO NEXT?

Because the parish registers and other church records are so important and cover such a large time span, you will use them, check other sources, and come back again. If your ancestor was alive after 1840, find him in the census (see chapter eight). If he was married or died after 1854, search the civil registration indexes (see chapter seven). Census and civil registration records contain clues that can help you trace your family further in the church records. Also see if your ancestor's name appears in Scottish probate or land records (see chapter ten). Again, additional clues you gain from probate and land records can lead you back to church records.

If you have used the basic sources from this book and can't find anything more about your ancestor, see chapter eleven, "What's Next?"

TEN

Scottish Land and Probate Records

Research Tip

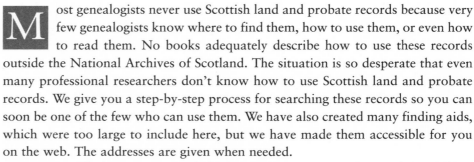ost genealogists never use Scottish land and probate records because very few genealogists know where to find them, how to use them, or even how to read them. No books adequately describe how to use these records outside the National Archives of Scotland. The situation is so desperate that even many professional researchers don't know how to use Scottish land and probate records. We give you a step-by-step process for searching these records so you can soon be one of the few who can use them. We have also created many finding aids, which were too large to include here, but we have made them accessible for you on the web. The addresses are given when needed.

Many people don't use Scottish land and probate records because they believe that their ancestor are unlikely to be in them. This is true; many of your ancestors never had any land and didn't have enough personal property to consider writing a testament. Furthermore, some families just divided the property without going through any legal process. However, **you should always check the indexes to Scottish land and probate records because even ancestors from quite humble circumstances are in these records**. Furthermore, even if your ancestor didn't have much property, he may be listed in the documents of someone who did.

If you have done much genealogy, you have looked for your ancestor's American land records, his will, or the administration of his estate if he died without a will. However, in Scotland you may not find anything called land records, probate records, wills, or administrations. Scotland has three major types of land and probate records, and they have names that may be unrecognizable elsewhere. The Scottish names for land and probate records are sasines, Services of Heirs, and testaments. Scottish land records are called sasines. Scottish probate records are divided into two types: testaments and Services of Heirs. Even though the names sound intimidating, they're really not too bad once you understand the process. In fact, it can be much easier to locate your ancestor's Scottish land and probate records than it is to locate his American ones. This is because most of the Scottish records are in one place, indexed, and available on microfilm.

SCOTTISH PROBATE RECORDS

Testaments

Let's start by defining the difference between a will and a testament. In legal terms, a last will and testament involves two types of transactions. The will is used to designate how a person wants his real property (land and buildings) to be distributed after his death. A testament is used to describe who gets his personal (moveable) property. Under Scottish law, until 1868 your ancestor had no choice about who would get his land. Real property automatically went to his nearest legal heir. Therefore, your ancestor could not write a will before that date. He could only decide who would get his personal property, and he recorded his wishes in a testament.

\di'fin\ *vb*

Definitions

The two types of testaments are a *testament testamentar*, written by the person before his death, and a *testament dative*, created by the court when a person died without leaving a written testament. When a widow and children survived, the moveable estate was divided into thirds. The widow received one-third, the children received one-third, and the deceased left the remaining one-third to whomever he wished. The testator could leave the widow and children more than one-third each of the personal estate, but not less. If there was no surviving spouse, the children received one-half of the personal property, and one-half went to whomever was designated by the deceased. Testaments are valuable documents that can indicate family relationships, financial status, and lifestyle.

When a person died, the relatives first petitioned the commissary clerk for an Edict of Executry to be issued. This edict was placed on the church door in the parish of the deceased so that creditors who had claims could come forward. The edict named the next of kin and the executor selected by the deceased in his *testament testamentar* or by the commissary clerk in the case of no testament. Sometimes this is all the family did to determine debtors, and they did not complete the whole process. Therefore, some entries in the Edicts of Executry are not in the testament indexes because the processes were not completed. Unfortunately, these records have not been microfilmed, and not all records have survived for all courts. After 1823 the notice to creditors had to be inserted in the *Edinburgh Gazette*. After 1858 the notice no longer had to be posted on the church door, but it was posted on the door of the commissary courthouse or in some other conspicuous place in the courthouse or office of the commissary clerk.

If the deceased had written a testament, the executor presented it to the court. Each court kept a Register of Testaments into which the clerk copied the original record. Some originals are still in the custody of the court. These originals are called warrants. The executor also gave to the court an inventory of the estate. For events before 1804, you can find testaments and inventories in the same register.

Testaments to 1823

Until 1823 testaments were proved in the local commissary court. Each commissary court handled the testaments within its own area, called a commissariot. The Commissary Court of Edinburgh could confirm testaments for the whole of Scotland and for people who had died outside of Scotland.

Microfilm Source

The registers of testaments to 1823 are housed at the National Archives of Scotland. **They are available on microfilm from the Family History Library.** The registers have been indexed, and these indexes are also on microfilm and microfiche. The registers of testaments are cataloged in the Family History Library Catalog under the name of the commissary court. The Commissary Courts of Scotland were Aberdeen, Argyll, Brechin, Caithness, Dumfries, Dunblane, Dunkeld, Edinburgh, Glasgow, Hamilton & Campsie, Inverness, The Isles, Kirkcudbright, Lanark, Lauder, Moray, Orkney & Shetland, Peebles, Ross, St. Andrews, Stirling, and Wigtown.

Note that although the registers of testaments are on microfilm for all courts, the warrants (original testaments), if they exist, have usually not been filmed.

Searching the indexes

The Scottish Record Society has published printed indexes to testaments covering the years 1514 to 1800. The records indexed are usually the Registers of Testaments, although warrants, minute books, and other records are indexed to cover gaps in the registers. The indexes are arranged by commissary court and are available on FHL microfiche 6068611–6068631. The courts are in alphabetical order on the fiche. You can find the appropriate commissariot and the microfiche number of its index by looking up your ancestor's parish at <www.rootsweb.com/~bifhsusa/sct-test-pre1801.html>. If you want to see how close your ancestor lived to the commissariot border, look at maps of the courts in Cecil Humphery-Smith's *The Phillimore Atlas and Index of Parish Registers*. The maps show all of the parishes and the commissariots to which they belonged. Be aware, however, that these maps have a few errors. Maps of jurisdictions and a list of Family History Library film holdings are on FHL fiche 6054479.

The indexes to testaments from 1514 to 1800 are also available on the Internet as part of a paid subscription to Ancestry's UK and Ireland Collection <www.ancestry.com>. Using this service, you can search through all commissary courts at one time. This can be a great time-saver. However, at the time of writing, the commissary court indexes were not cataloged with all of their corresponding counties. Therefore, your ancestor's testament may be listed in a county where he never lived.

The indexes to the year 1800 give the name and designation of the deceased and the date of confirmation. Married women are listed under their maiden names and cross-referenced at the husband's entry. Therefore, you can find a woman if you know either her maiden name or her married name. For example, here are two entries from the Argyll index:

> **Cors**, Jean, Spouse to John Whyte, shoemaker in Campbeltoun, par. of Kilkearen. 27 Apr. 1676.
> **Whyte**, John, shoemaker in Campbeltoun. *See* Cors, Jean.

The post-1800 indexes are slightly different from the earlier ones and are on FHL film 0231259. The post-1800 indexes give the name and designation of the deceased, the date of confirmation, the commissariot, and the volume and folio numbers or warrant numbers of the testament. Note that the film does not include indexes for the commissariot of Peebles or the commissariot of Orkney & Shetland.

If you do not find your ancestor in the court nearest to his place of residence, then check the Edinburgh court, which covered all of Scotland. The Commissary Court of Edinburgh had the power to prove any testament more than £50 Scots from anywhere in Scotland.

Remember that all members of a family did not necessarily live and die in the same parish. Search the indexes of all courts that covered your ancestor's county as well as the courts of adjacent counties. You can use the table on pages 178 and 179 to locate the appropriate county, its courts, and the FHL microform numbers. This table also gives you the years for which testaments exist for each court.

Reminder

Step By Step

Now let's use the testament indexes to look for the Brough family in Crieff. It doesn't matter whether we find our ancestor's name. We should look at all testaments for anybody with his surname. Crieff is in the commissariot of Dunkeld. The index for 1682–1800 is on FHL fiche 6068617. When you search the index, remember to consider variant spellings for the surname. Brugh and Burgh are variant spellings for Brough. There are three testaments for the surname Burgh in Crieff.

See Figure 10-1 on page 180 for an example of the testament indexes. The Register of Testaments contains court copies of the original testaments. However, the Register of Testaments of the Commissary Court of Dunkeld has gaps. The missing records are from 1696 to 1712 and from 1776 to 1804. The existing warrants were used to fill in the gaps. In the index, the letter *T* next to the date means that the record is a warrant. The Register of Testaments for the Commissary Court of Dunkeld (CC 7/6) is on microfilm at the Family History Library; the Warrants of Testaments (CC 7/7) are not. Note in the index that the earliest Burgh testament was for Edward Burgh, carrier in Crieff, in 1742. You can order it on microfilm from the Family History Library. The testament for Edward Burgh and Janet Burgh in 1781 is a warrant. You have to order that one from the National Archives of Scotland.

Always read the introduction to the testament index for your court to see what records are indexed. If your ancestor's testament came from a minute book, warrant, or other record, see if the record is on microfilm at the Family History Library. If not, you can order a copy from the National Archives of Scotland. Use the repertory to commissary court records on FHL fiche 6068610 to find the appropriate NAS reference.

Be sure to order testaments for everybody with your ancestor's surname who lived in his parish. Depending upon how common the surname was, you may be able to widen this search to include the surrounding parishes.

Finding the testament
After you locate your ancestor in the index, you can usually order from the Family History Library a microfilmed copy of his testament. To find the testament of Edward Burgh, carrier in Crieff, use the table at <www.rootsweb.com/~bifhsusa/sct-testaments.html> to locate the Commissariot of Dunkeld. The table shows the class reference numbers for the National Archives of Scotland followed by the name of the commissariot, the years covered, and the FHL film numbers. Once you find the name of the appropriate commissariot, use the Family History Library Catalog

Microfilm Source

Indexes to Scottish Testaments to 1823

County	Commissariot	Years Indexed	Fiche Number	Index: Years 1801–1823
Aberdeen	Aberdeen	1715–1800	6068611	0231259, Item 4
	Moray	1684–1800	6068625	0231259, Item 4
Angus (Forfar)	Brechin	1576–1800	6068613	0231259, Item 4
	Dunkeld	1682–1800	6068617	0231259, Item 4
	St. Andrews	1549–1800	6068629	0231259, Item 2
Argyll	Argyll	1674–1800	6068612	0231259, Item 4
	The Isles	1661–1800	6068622	0231259, Item 4
Ayr	Glasgow	1547–1800	6068619	0231259, Item 1
Banff	Aberdeen	1715–1800	6068611	0231259, Item 4
	Moray	1684–1800	6068625	0231259, Item 4
Berwick	Lauder	1561–1800	6068626	0231259, Item 4
Bute	The Isles	1661–1800	6068622	0231259, Item 4
Caithness	Caithness	1661–1664	6068614	0231259, Item 4
Clackmannan	Dunblane	1539–1800	6068616	0231259, Item 4
	Stirling	1607–1800	6068630	0231259, Item 4
Dumbarton	Glasgow	1547–1800	6068619	0231259, Item 1
	Hamilton & Campsie	1564–1800	6068620	0231259, Item 4
Dumfries	Dumfries	1624–1800	6068615	0231259, Item 4
East Lothian (Haddington)	Edinburgh	1514–1800	6068618	0231259, Item 3*
	Dunkeld	1682–1800	6068617	0231259, Item 4
Fife	Dunkeld	1682–1800	6068617	0231259, Item 4
	St. Andrews	1549–1800	6068629	0231259, Item 2
	Stirling	1607–1800	6068630	0231259, Item 4
Inverness	Argyll	1674–1800	6068612	0231259, Item 4
	Inverness	1630–1800	6068621	0231259, Item 4
	Moray	1684–1800	6068625	0231259, Item 4
	The Isles	1661–1800	6068622	0231259, Item 4
Kincardine	Brechin	1576–1800	6068613	0231259, Item 4
	St. Andrews	1549–1800	6068629	0231259, Item 2
Kinross	Dunblane	1539–1800	6068616	0231259, Item 4
	Dunkeld	1682–1800	6068617	0231259, Item 4
	St. Andrews	1549–1800	6068629	0231259, Item 2
Kirkcudbright	Dumfries	1624–1800	6068615	0231259, Item 4
	Kirkcudbright	1663–1800	6068623	0231259, Item 4
	Wigtown	1700–1800	6068631	0231259, Item 4
Lanark	Glasgow	1547–1800	6068619	0231259, Item 1
	Hamilton & Campsie	1564–1800	6068620	0231259, Item 4
	Lanark	1595–1800	6068624	0231259, Item 4
Midlothian (Edinburgh)	Edinburgh	1514–1800	6068618	0231259, Item 3*
Moray (Elgin)	Moray	1684–1800	6068625	0231259, Item 4
Nairn	Moray	1684–1800	6068625	0231259, Item 4
Orkney	Orkney & Shetland	1611–1684	6068627	

County	Commissariot	Years Indexed	Fiche Number	Index: Years 1801–1823
Peebles	Peebles	1681–1699	6068628	**
Perth	Dunkeld	1682–1800	6068617	0231259, Item 4
	Dunblane	1539–1800	6068616	0231259, Item 4
	St. Andrews	1549–1800	6068629	0231259, Item 2
Renfrew	Glasgow	1547–1800	6068619	0231259, Item 1
	Hamilton & Campsie	1564–1800	6068620	0231259, Item 4
Ross & Cromarty	Inverness	1630–1800	6068621	0231249, Item 4***
	The Isles	1661–1800	6068622	0231259, Item 4
Roxburgh	Peebles	1681–1699	6068628	
Selkirk	Peebles	1681–1699	6068628	
Shetland (Zetland)	Orkney & Shetland	1611–1684	6068627	
Stirling	Stirling	1607–1800	6068630	0231259, Item 4
	Glasgow	1547–1800	6068619	0231259, Item 1
	Hamilton & Campsie	1564–1800	6068620	0231259, Item 4
Sutherland	Caithness	1661–1664	6068614	0231259, Item 4
West Lothian (Linlithgow)	Edinburgh	1514–1800	6068618	0231259, Item 3*
	Dunkeld	1682–1800	6068617	0231259, Item 4
Wigtown	Wigtown	1700–1800	6068631	0231259, Item 4

* The index for Edinburgh covers 1801–1829.
** Some may be indexed in Edinburgh for 1801–1829, FHL film 0231259, Item 3.
*** Commissariot of Ross (formed in 1802).

to find the film number that covers the time period you need. Searching by film/ fiche number in the catalog, insert the first film number for your court to bring up a list of all film numbers for that court.

Finding a testament on these films can be difficult because the indexes do not give you a page number. You have to search through the film until you find the appropriate year and then page by page until you find the testament. **Although finding the date may sound easy, it can be confusing.** For example, the year 1742 is recorded in Edward Burgh's testament in the unique Scottish way: "Jajvijc forty two." You can see it in Figure 10-2 on page 181 in the paragraph "Summa Inventory" where it says, "This Testament was Conformed att Dunkeld the third day of August Jajviic forty two." The letter *c* has a tail called a suspension mark on it indicating that it is an abbreviation. *Jajvijc* is the year 1700. The year 1800 is *Jajviijc*.

Let's interpret how these numbers are generated. *Jaj* is the sign for one thousand. It is a corruption of 'im' (1,000), which was originally written as four strokes, and you might actually see it written as *Jm*. You are more likely to find the corruption with the first and the last strokes elongated to form *j*s and the middle strokes modified into an *a*. Then the rest of the number is the century number, again with

Warning

Figure 10-1
Testament index for Commissariot of Dunkeld showing entries for Edward Burgh, carrier in Crieff in 1742, and Edward Burgh and Janet Burgh in 1781. The letter *T* next to the date means that the record is an original testament (warrant).

1682-1800.] *Commissariot of Dunkeld.*	**5**

Brown, George, in the Green of Innermay   21 July 1715
  „   James, in Balindoch   T. 5 Aug. 1697
  „   James, in Lamerkin   T. 22 Aug. 1701
  „   Mr. James, late tacksman of Milns of Kethick
       30 Jan. 1718 and 11 Aug. 1719
  „   James, in Croft-town of Ballbrougie   29 Sept. 1724
  „   James, sometime at the Walkmiln of Huntingtour   19 Sept. 1740
  „   John, in Wester Cultmalindie, and Marjorie Burt, his relict   25 Mar. 1725
  „   John, in Airntully, and Barbara B., his spouse   29 Oct. 1741
  „   Robert, in Over Olney   20 Mar. 1733
  „   Thomas, wright in Aberdour Wester, and Elizabeth Young,
       his spouse   1 Aug. 1751
  „   Walter, late in Woodend, in par. of Cargill   19 Feb. 1760
  „   William, wright in Sheills, and Helen Crawfurd, his spouse,
       par. of Beath   18 June 1690
Bruce, Agnes, lawful daughter to umquhile Andrew B., sometime
       in Westertown of Ashintully   30 Dec. 1712
  „   Donald, in Spittall of Gleanshie, and Marion Spalding, his spouse
       10 Feb. 1691
  „   Donald, of the Milltoun of Pitcarmick   T. 15 July 1697
  „   Donald, in Rochbeg   22 Jan. 1741
  „   Donald, in Parretry   30 Nov. 1775
  „   Donald, in Wester Pitcarmick.   *See* **Doulich**, Grizell.
  „   George, portioner of Couper-Angus   18 Aug. 1748
  „   John, in Easter Pitcarmick   T. 7 Sept. 1703
  „   John, in Inveredrie in Glenshee, and Margaret M'Intosh,
       spouses   13 Dec. 1750
  „   John, younger, of Milntoun of Pitcarmick   17 Dec. 1765 and 11 Mar. 1766
  „   John, at Milntoun of Pitcarmick, residing in Mains of
       Easter Pitcarmick   31 Jan. 1769
  „   John, in Black-Lounans.   *See* **Mair**, Elspeth.
  „   Robert, in Ballnagaird   28 Nov. 1732
  „   Robert, of Dalnabreck   15 Mar. 1739
  „   Thomas, brother-german to the deceased John B., portioner
       of Easter Pitcarmack   5 Aug. 1725
  „   Thomas, in Coupar of Angus   3 Dec. 1728
  „   William, in Dunhead of Cairnbaddy   16 Jan. 1759
Brugh, James, in Wester Dullarie   1 Feb. 1688
  „   John, in Galpvelmore   17 May 1688
Brydie, Annas, spouse to Andrew Hagart, in Little-hour, par. of Capeth
       16 Aug. 1688
  „   Elizabeth, relict of Donald M'Gildonich, in Dalguss   T. 9 Jan. 1701
  „   Isobel, spouse to Patrick Strachan, weaver in Abernyttie
       T. 24 Mar. 1701
  „   James, in Gourdie   3 Jan. 1689
  „   James, in Wester Gourdie   T. 23 Nov. 1697
  „   James, only lawful son of the deceased James B., sometime in Fordie
       T. 7 Dec. 1705
Buchannan, Agnes, relict of Alexander M'Cowslan, of Caldonach   19 Oct. 1721
Burgh, Edward, carrier in Crieff   5 Aug. 1742
  „   Edward, in Crieff   T. 1 May 1781
  „   Janet, in Crieff   T. 1 May 1781
  „   Margaret, spouse to the deceased Donald Craw, in
       Bellycloan, sometime in Chaplehill of Cowgask   8 Aug. 1728
Burn, Patrick, in Airntullie   14 and 14 Apr. 1690
       See also **Sanders**, Elspet.
  „   Robert, in Drume of Muckarsie, par. of Kinclevine   23 Feb. 1688
Burnman, John, in Coupar-Angus   T. 21 July 1781
Burns, John, tenant in Whitefield.   *See* **Kelt**, Janet.
Burt, Agnes, relict of Patrick Robertson, Procurator-Fiscal to
       the Commissariot of Dunkeld   9 Nov. 1721

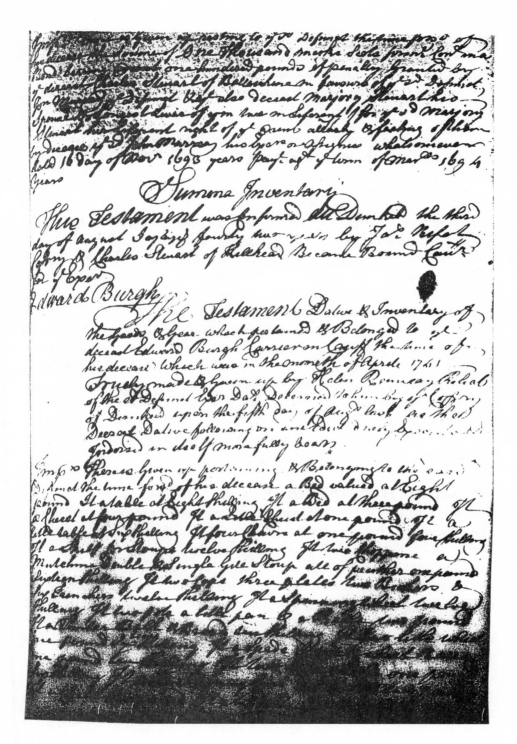

Figure 10-2
First page of Edward Burgh's testament, 1742. (CC 7/6/4)

the last stroke elongated into a *j*. Therefore, six is *vj*, seven is *vij*, and eight is *viij*. A final *c* signifies "hundreds." Then the year within the century is written out. Yes, it is different, but with a little bit of practice you can master it.

Now let's look at Edward Burgh's testament. It is found in CC 7/6/4 at the National Archives of Scotland or on FHL microfilm 0231028. The first page from the microfilm is shown in Figure 10-2. Believe it or not, this is much clearer than the second page! Sometimes the testament records (and other records in this chapter) are almost unreadable on the microfilm. You can try to see the original at the National Archives of Scotland in case it is any better, although in many cases the records are so old that the originals aren't easier to read. Edward's testament starts about halfway down the page:

> The Testament Dative & Inventory of the Goods & Gear which pertained & Belonged to ye deceased Edward Burgh Carrier in Crieff the time of his decease which was in the moneth of Aprile 1741 Truely made & Given up by Helen Ramsay Relict of the sd Defunct Exor Dat. . . .

Following the introductory paragraph is an inventory of the estate. It includes a bed valued at eight pounds, a table at eight shillings, a bed at three pounds, etc.

So what is important about that record? First it tells us that Edward Burgh did not write a testament because his record is a *testament dative*. But perhaps more important, we get the name of the deceased, his occupation, his residence, his date of death, and the name of his wife (the word *relict* means "widow"). The name of the wife is important because no marriage record for this couple is in the Scottish Church Records index. This may be because they were married during the years 1713–1748 when no marriages at all were recorded in the parish register of Crieff. This testament may be the only place where we can find the name of the wife, and it is even her maiden name! Furthermore, we have a list of every item owned by the deceased along with the estimated value of each one. This is extremely important for finding out about how your ancestor actually lived. It puts flesh on the bare bones of genealogy.

Testaments From 1823 to 1875

From 1823 to 1875, the sheriff's courts were responsible for recording testaments. Sheriff's courts did not use a standard format; each had its own way of organizing its records. For the 1824–1875 time period, an index that covers all courts for the years 1846–1867 is available on microfilm from the Family History Library. The index is called *Index to the Inventories of the Personal Estates of Defuncts*. The courts for other years are being indexed. Consult the Web site of the National Archives of Scotland to see what is currently available.

The testaments for 1824–1876 are not available on microfilm from the Family History Library except those for the counties of Argyll, East Lothian, Fife, Midlothian, Perth, Renfrew, Ross & Cromarty, Stirling, West Lothian, and Wigtown. However, most of the testaments are at the National Archives of Scotland. To find the applicable sheriff's court, the FHL film number of the index, and the reference number of the testaments in the National Archives of Scotland, see the table on pages 183 and 184.

Step By Step

Using the index to the inventories of the personal estates of defuncts

The indexes for the county of Perth are item 1 on FHL film 1368216. An example from this index is in Figure 10-3. Again, look for any entries pertaining to the Brough family. The letters and numbers at the left will not help to locate the testa-

Scottish Testaments After 1823			
County	Sheriff's Court	FHL Film Number for Index 1846–1867	NAS Ref. #
Aberdeen	Aberdeen	1386216, Item 2	SC 1
Angus (Forfar)	Dundee (from 1832)	1368216, Item 1	SC 45
	Forfar	1368216, Item 1	SC 47
Argyll	Dunoon	1368215, Item 3	SC 51
Ayr	Ayr	1368217	SC 6
Banff	Banff	1386216, Item 2	SC 2
Berwick	Duns	1368217	SC 60
Bute	Rothesay	1368215, Item 3	SC 8
Caithness	Wick	1386216, Item 2	SC 14
Clackmannan	Alloa	1368216, Item 1	SC 64
Dumfries	Dumfries	1368217	SC 15
Dunbarton	Dunbarton	1368215, Item 3	SC 65
East Lothian (Haddington)	Haddington (from 1830)	1368215, Items 1–2	SC 40
Edinburgh City	Edinburgh	1368215, Items 1–2	SC 70
Fife	Cupar	1368216, Item 1	SC 20
Glasgow City	Glasgow	1368215, Item 3	SC 36
Inverness	Inverness	1386216, Item 2	SC 29
Kincardine	Stonehaven	1386216, Item 2	SC 5
Kinross	Alloa (until 1847)		SC 64
	Kinross (from 1847)	1368216, Item 1	SC 22
Kirkcudbright	Kirkcudbright	1368217	SC 16
Lanark	Glasgow	1368215, Item 3	SC 36
Midlothian (Edinburgh)	Edinburgh	1368215, Item 3	SC 70
Moray (Elgin)	Elgin	1386216, Item 2	SC 26
Nairn	Elgin (to 1838)		SC 26
	Nairn (from 1839)	1386216, Item 2	SC 31
Orkney	Kirkwall	1386216, Item 2	(in Kirkwall)
Peebles	Peebles	1368217	SC 42
Perth	Dunblane	1368216, Item 1	SC 44
	Perth	1368216, Item 1	SC 49
Renfrew	Paisley	1368215, Item 3	SC 58
Ross & Cromarty	Dingwall	1386216, Item 2	SC 25
	Stornoway (to 1850)	1386216, Item 2	SC 33
Roxburgh	Jedburgh	1368217	SC 62
Selkirk	Selkirk	1368217	SC 63
Shetland	Lerwick	1386216, Item 2	(in Lerwick)

County	Sheriff's Court	FHL Film Number for Index 1846–1867	NAS Ref. #
Stirling	Stirling	1368216, Item 1	SC 67
Sutherland	Dornoch	1386216, Item 2	SC 9
West Lothian (Linlithgow)	Linlithgow (from 1830)	1368215, Items 1–2	SC 41
Wigtown	Wigtown	1,368,217	SC 19

ment; you need the court and the date. Notice that there is a man named Edward Brough, china merchant in Crieff. His inventory was recorded as

F 713 Brough, Edward, china-merchant, Crieff. 54. P. 11.2.54.

The letter to the far left of his name tells whether the estate is testate (*testament testamentar*) or intestate (*testament dative*). The letters *D*, *F*, and *H* indicate intestate estates; the letters *C*, *E*, and *G*, testate estates. The letters *A* and *B* make no such indication. The number following the letter is the number of the inventory in the Stamp Office Register; you do not need this number. Next comes the name and designation (in this case, occupation and residence) of the deceased. The number after the designation refers to the year in which the inventory was recorded. Next is the first letter of the commissariot. The final numbers are the day, month, and year of death.

In this example, Edward Brough's estate was intestate (indicated by the letter *F*), so we know that he did not write a testament. The inventory was recorded in 1854 ("54") in the County of Perth ("P"). Edward died 11 February 1854.

Finding the testament

Let's order Edward Brough's testament and see what it tells us. Find the film number using a place search of the Family History Library Catalog under Scotland, [County], Probate Records. If the records are not at the Family History Library, you must order the inventory from the National Archives of Scotland.

Edward Brough's record should be in SC 49/31/57 at the National Archives of Scotland and on FHL film 0461130. (We ordered the microfilm.) Edward's testament is another *testament dative*, which means that he did not leave a written testament. It goes on for nine pages, and the first page is shown in Figure 10-4 on page 186. You can see a transcription of the entire document at <www.rootsweb.com/~bifhsusa/brough.html>.

It is different from the 1742 inventory we saw for Edward Burgh. First, this has no item-by-item description of his personal property. Edward Brough's property (beds, tools, etc.) was listed on a separate document. However, lots of names are in the inventory! For example, the inventory tells us who rented Edward Brough's properties in 1853 and how much they paid. Several other significant items are in this record. One of the more important items is the date of death. Edward died in 1854, a year before civil registration started. There are no burial records in the Parish of Crieff for that time, so this may be the only place where we can find

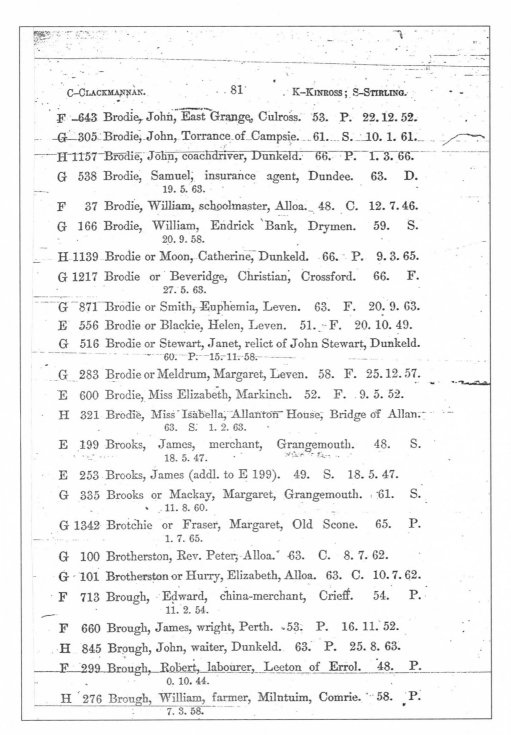

C—CLACKMANNAN. · 81 · K—KINROSS; S—STIRLING.

F 643 Brodie, John, East Grange, Culross. 53. P. 22. 12. 52.

G 305 Brodie, John, Torrance of Campsie. 61. S. 10. 1. 61.

H 1157 Brodie, John, coachdriver, Dunkeld. 66. P. 1. 3. 66.

G 538 Brodie, Samuel, insurance agent, Dundee. 63. D. 19. 5. 63.

F 37 Brodie, William, schoolmaster, Alloa. 48. C. 12. 7. 46.

G 166 Brodie, William, Endrick Bank, Drymen. 59. S. 20. 9. 58.

H 1139 Brodie or Moon, Catherine, Dunkeld. 66. P. 9. 3. 65.

G 1217 Brodie or Beveridge, Christian, Crossford. 66. F. 27. 5. 63.

G 871 Brodie or Smith, Euphemia, Leven. 63. F. 20. 9. 63.

E 556 Brodie or Blackie, Helen, Leven. 51. F. 20. 10. 49.

G 516 Brodie or Stewart, Janet, relict of John Stewart, Dunkeld. 60. P. 15. 11. 58.

G 283 Brodie or Meldrum, Margaret, Leven. 58. F. 25. 12. 57.

E 600 Brodie, Miss Elizabeth, Markinch. 52. F. 9. 5. 52.

H 321 Brodie, Miss Isabella, Allanton House, Bridge of Allan. 63. S. 1. 2. 63.

E 199 Brooks, James, merchant, Grangemouth. 48. S. 18. 5. 47.

E 253 Brooks, James (addl. to E 199). 49. S. 18. 5. 47.

G 335 Brooks or Mackay, Margaret, Grangemouth. 61. S. 11. 8. 60.

G 1342 Brotchie or Fraser, Margaret, Old Scone. 65. P. 1. 7. 65.

G 100 Brotherston, Rev. Peter, Alloa. 63. C. 8. 7. 62.

G 101 Brotherston or Hurry, Elizabeth, Alloa. 63. C. 10. 7. 62.

F 713 Brough, Edward, china-merchant, Crieff. 54. P. 11. 2. 54.

F 660 Brough, James, wright, Perth. 53. P. 16. 11. 52.

H 845 Brough, John, waiter, Dunkeld. 63. P. 25. 8. 63.

F 299 Brough, Robert, labourer, Leeton of Errol. 48. P. 0. 10. 44.

H 276 Brough, William, farmer, Milntuim, Comrie. 58. P. 7. 3. 58.

Figure 10-3
Page from the Index to the Inventories of the Personal Estates of Defuncts for the county of Perth. Notice entry for Edward Brough, china-merchant in Crieff.

Edward's date of death. The testament also tells us quite a bit about Edward's financial status. Only one person with the surname of Brough was mentioned: James Brough, brother of Edward, lived in Crieff and was a mason. As next of kin he was the executor. The inventory also raises a lot of questions. For example, why was his brother next of kin? We should find out if Edward ever had any children. If not, he can't be the ancestor of our Isabella Brough.

Figure 10-4
First page of the *testament dative* for Edward Brough, 1854. (SC 49/31/57)

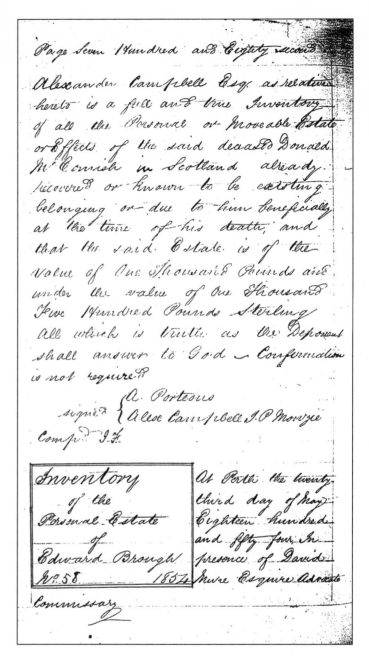

The confirmation was usually obtained within three months, but this was not always the case. The confirmation date can help you estimate the date of death when it is not provided. In our example, Edward Brough died 11 February 1854, and the confirmation was granted on 19/20 May 1854, just three months after the death.

Testaments or Wills After 1876

Remember that after 1868 your ancestor could have made a will, so unlike previous records land may be mentioned. For records after 1876, you don't have to worry about looking in the correct court index; indexes for 1876 to 1936 are on microfiche and cover testaments for all of Scotland. The index is called the Calendar of Confirmations and Inventories and is arranged by year, then alphabetically by surname. Each entry gives the name and designation (usually occupation or place of residence) of the deceased, the date and place of death, whether testate (*testament testamentar*) or intestate (*testament dative*), the name of court where confirmation was granted, the date of confirmation, the names and designations of the executors, and the value of the estate. If the deceased was testate, the date of the will is given as well as when and where it was recorded. Testaments (wills) after 1876 have not been microfilmed, but the Calendar of Confirmations and Inventories is available on microfiche:

1876–1922: FHL fiche 6068884–6068930
1923–1927: FHL fiche 6069735–6069738
1928–1936: FHL fiche 6070135–6070143

Let's use that index to see if we can find anything for Isabella Brough who married James Kay. We found her death record in 1915, so we looked to see if she was listed on the Calendar of Confirmations for the year 1915 (on FHL fiche number 6068923). This is what we found:

Step By Step

> Kay Isabella, 5 Addison Terrace, Crieff, died 30 Dec 1914 at Crieff, Testate. Confirmation granted at Perth 23 Jan to Flora Kay, 5 Addison Terrace aforesaid, executrix nominated in Will or Deed, dated 16 April 1904, and recorded in Court Books of Commissariot of Perth, 19 Jan 1915. Value of Estate, £97, 9s, 9d. Eik granted, 19 February to above Executrix. Value of Additional Estate, £10, 2s, 8d.

You may not expect to be able to find a woman, but lots of them are in the indexes. We know from other records we have examined in this book that our Isabella Kay lived at 5 Addison Terrace and that she had a daughter named Flora. We don't know yet why Isabella's date of death is different on this index than the one on her death certificate; we have to obtain the record to find out. Since the wills after 1876 are not on microfilm, her record must be obtained from the National Archives of Scotland.

We ordered the record and waited for it to arrive from Scotland. The will we received from the NAS was a typed copy of the original, and we have extracted part of it here with the same spelling errors and lack of punctuation. For example, in the transcription the word *niece* is spelled "miice." We don't know if Isabella really spelled it that way or if that is how the clerk interpreted her handwriting. The will (SC 49/32/18, pages 36–38) and the inventory (SC 49/31/223, pages 69–72) are transcribed on the next page. Was this worth the money and wait? Judge for yourself.

What did we learn from the will and inventory of Isabella Kay? First, we expected to find a probate record for Isabella Kay in 1915, and we did find one. But this is *not* the record of Isabella Brough who married James Kay. This is the will and inventory of her daughter! Next, the record tells us that Isabella was living with her mother (Isabella Brough Kay), and that her sister Flora lived there, too. Further, Isabella mentions the married names of two of her sisters, and she tells us how she felt about Alexander Jack Kay (her nephew). Many other clues to further family research are in this record. But perhaps the most important lesson (again!) is that somebody is not necessarily your ancestor just because he or she has the same name as your ancestor. This Isabella Kay had the same name, address, and probate record

Will and Inventory of Isabella Kay, 1915

Recorded 9th January 1915

Holograph Will by Isabella Kay [Written on Envelope] My Will To be opened at my death by Miss Flora Kay. April 16th 1904. 18 Duke Street Edinburgh, April 16th 1904.

I Isabella Kay being in sound mind and good health do will my money and one or too other thing which I now mame that my sister Flora Kay if unmarried at my death shall receive £60 Sixty Pounds St that my sister Catherine Kay if unmarried at my death shall receive £40 fourty Pounds that my sister Jessie Kay or Ritchie shall receive £10 ten pounds that my sisters Flora Kay and Catherine Kay shall pay to my mother too Pounds each a year as long as the mony now left shall last that if eather of them marry the money goes to the one unmarried if Boath shall marrie before my death the said money to be divided pennys about betuine my sisters Flora Kay Catherine Kay Jessie Kay or Ritchie Robina Kay or Robertson that my neice Bella Robertson shall receive my Gold Watch that my sister Flora Kay shall divide my things as she shall see fit but that my Brothers and Sisters shall each get a small remembrance that Alexander Jack Kay shall rank as my brother as such I have always felt for him as a Brother I leave my sister Flora Kay to see these my last wishes carried out if there is anny money over after paying funaril expences and paying the above named somes I disire it to be given to eather at my Brother's or Sister's or to be kept by my sister Flora Kay as she may think fit that my miice Bella Ritchie shall receive my Gold Brotch that my nephew James Kay shall receive this granfathers watch which is now in my posssion. (Signed) sinded. Isabella Kay.

Inventory of the Personal Estate of Isabella Kay Deceased.

At Perth, the Nineteenth day of January Nineteen Hundred and fifteen the following Inventory of the Personal Estate of the late Isabella Kay was presented for registration in this register, along with relative writ conform to law by Flora Kay residing at Five Addison Terrace Crieff. Inventory of the Moveable or Personal Estate and Effects, wheresoever situated, of the late Isabella Kay late of 5 Addison Terrace Crieff who died at Crieff on the 30th day of December 1914.

I. Scotland	£	S.	D.
Cash in House	Nil		
Personal Belongings	1–		
Deceased lived with her mother & had no furniture	——		
Sum in Bank with interest to date of death, viz: In the Edinburgh Savings Bank conform to Pass Book No. 342133	96	9	9
[Total]	97	9	9

(signed) Flora Kay John Dickson S. C. D.

year as we expected for the other Isabella Kay, but she was not the woman we expected to find. Always review the original documents, if possible.

Why Can't I Find My Ancestor's Testament or Will?

There is no testament for your ancestor. This is the most common reason for not finding a testament. Most of our ancestors did not have enough personal property to be concerned about leaving a testament. However, you should always look just in case. Even if you don't find a testament for your ancestor, the testaments of other people in his parish may provide clues about your ancestor or his family.

You are looking for the wrong name. Remember to look for variations of the surname and given name. For example, for the name M'Ewen, "son of Ewen," you would only find one woman in the register of testaments for Argyll. The other women are listed under N'Ewen, meaning "daughter of Ewen." Other patronymic listings are at the end of the Argyll index, such as *Mary nein Ewin V'Laughlan* and *Duncan M'Donald V'Gavich*.

The name was spelled differently than you expect. The indexes are alphabetical, and they do not group similar names together as in the IGI. Therefore, think of different spelling and pronunciation variations for the names you are researching.

You are looking in the wrong court. This is especially common when the name of the county matches the name of a court. For example, if your ancestor was in Lanarkshire, you might be tempted to check only the Lanark Commissary Court. However, you also need to check two other local commissary courts: Glasgow plus Hamilton & Campsie. Make sure you haven't missed any courts appropriate for your ancestor's county. Also, be sure to look in the Commissary Court of Edinburgh. Furthermore, your ancestor may have held property in more than one country. If he held land in Scotland and England, for example, you need to check the probate records (after 1707) of the Prerogative Court of Canterbury.

Indexing errors were made. We rely heavily on the existing indexes in our search for Scottish testament records. Errors and omissions are known to exist. When these errors and omissions are discovered, the data gets added to an index at the National Archives of Scotland. Check the index at the NAS to be thorough.

Testament registers are missing and have gaps. The indexes of the commissary court registers to the year 1800, published by the Scottish Record Society, are usually indexes to the Registers of Testaments. Carefully read the introduction of the index you search and find out what records were indexed, whether the records have any gaps, and whether there are any appendices to the index. Also consult the Commissary Court Repertory (CC) on FHL microfiche 6068610 to find out what other records are at the National Archives of Scotland in addition to the Register of Testaments.

Your ancestor's testament is in family papers. Some testaments were never recorded, so the testament may have remained with the family papers. The papers of some families have been given to the National Archives of Scotland. If your ancestor's family papers have been deposited, they are among the gifts and deposits (GD).

Your ancestor's testament was recorded in the registers of deeds. Your ancestor could record any legal document in the registers of deeds, so his testament may be recorded there. See the section "Registers of Deeds" on page 209 for more information.

SCOTTISH LAND RECORDS

Most of our ancestors never held any land, but even people in quite humble circumstances are named in the land records of Scotland. We usually don't know whether our ancestors held heritable land that they could pass on at death or if they leased the land. If they held heritable land, they can be found in the land records. If they leased the land, you need to find the name of the person with the heritable right, for often the tenants are named in some of that person's records. If your ancestor inherited land or passed land to his heirs, look for the record of inheritance in the Services of Heirs. Also look for a copy of the land transaction in the sasine records. If your ancestor had other kinds of land transactions (e.g., he used the land as security for a loan), you can find those recorded in the sasines. The rest of this chapter takes you step-by-step through the process of checking the indexes and interpreting the actual records. The genealogical information you can obtain about your family is well worth the effort of the search.

Scottish Services of Heirs

The Services of Heirs, also known as retours, record the transmission of inheritance of landed property in Scotland. They are part of the Chancery records in the National Archives of Scotland. Services of Heirs are some of the most genealogically valuable records for Scottish research. The records are well indexed, and the indexes and Services of Heirs are available on microfilm through the Family History Library.

\di'fin\ *vb*

Definitions

Before 1868 land descended according to the law of primogeniture: The eldest son inherited the land subject to the widow's retention of one-third of the estate for her lifetime. This was called her "liferent." You saw this term in the 1851 census of Crieff (see Figure 8-8), where Isabella Brough is a widow and her "Rank, Profession, or Occupation" was listed as "liferant." If the deceased had no living sons, the land was divided equally among the daughters after the same one-third widow's retention. Because each daughter received an equal portion, she was known as an heir portioner.

When a landowner died, an inquest was held to determine the lands held and the legal heir. Heritable property did not pass automatically from the ancestor to the heir. The heir had to prove his right to inherit, and his claim had to be formally recognized by a Brieve of Succession. The Court of Chancery issued a brieve to the judge, usually sheriff, where the land was located. The judge was instructed to assemble a jury who would ascertain the truth of the claimant's asserted right as heir. The jury was selected as the people who would best know the truth of the claim, so these people were often relatives and family friends. The verdict of the jury was returned ("retoured") to Chancery answering the brieve. The document sent to Chancery was called a retour. The proceedings of the court were kept by the clerk of the court where the inquest was held, and some of these survive in the records of those courts. Before 1821 only the verdict was sent to Chancery, so you can find only the brieve and the retour in the Chancery records. Between 1821 and 1847, certain classes of services were required to have the entire proceedings returned to Chancery. After 1847, the entire proceedings of all services were transmitted to Chancery.

In theory, the Service of Heirs registers should be complete. In practice they are not, because not all verdicts from the courts were retoured to Chancery. In addition the regality and stewartry courts (areas in which the lord had been granted exemption from the authority of the other royal courts) were exempt. Regalities and stewartries were abolished in 1747.

The five main types of retours were: Special and General Services of Heirs and retours of tutory, curatory, and extent. By far the most numerous and useful to family historians are the Services of Heirs. A Special Service of Heir relates to claims of inheritance to particular lands held by the ancestor. A General Service was not a claim to any specific lands but was a general claim of heirship to the ancestor. Therefore Special Services of Heirs name lands, and General Services of Heirs do not. A Service of an Heir lists the name of the heir, the relationship of the heir to the deceased, the name of the deceased, and sometimes the date of death. Some records list several generations of descent.

Services of Heirs were documented in Latin until 1847. Now before you throw up your hands and say, "But I can't read Latin!" rest assured that you really don't need to know much. The Services of Heirs were recorded in a standard format, and all you need to know is where to find the information about your ancestor.

Warning

We show you how to do this in the Format of General Retour on page 192 and Format of Special Retour on page 193. For complete examples see Peter Gouldesbrough's *Formulary of Old Scots Legal Documents* (The Stair Society, 1985).

For assistance with Latin personal names mentioned in these documents, consult volume 3 of *Genealogical Research in England and Wales* by Gardner and Smith. Even though the volume is about England and Wales, the list includes ancient and unusual names found in records of Scotland. Refer to chapter three for more resources regarding Latin vocabulary.

Index and abstracts of retours, 1547 to 1699

The retours from 1547 through 1699 are all abstracted and indexed. The indexes and abstracts (abridgements) are in three printed volumes called *Inquisitionum ad Capellam Domini Regis retornatarum Abbreviatio*. The abstracts are in Latin, but don't let that intimidate you; they aren't difficult to read. The most important Latin words are those that describe the relationship of the deceased to the heir. The vocabulary list in the "Relationships in Latin" sidebar gives translations of these critical words (see page 196). The indexes and abstracts are on FHL film 0908847. There are abstracts of Special and General Services of Heirs with supplements.

In the Special Service, the jury was required to determine the lands and annual rents that the ancestor held within the jurisdiction of the court, the annual value of the lands, the name of the feudal superior who held the lands and by what kind of tenure, in whose possession the lands currently were, and if the claimant was the nearest lawful heir and of lawful age. The abstract gives the date of service, the name and designation of the heir, the type of heir (heir, heir portioner, etc.), the name and designation of the ancestor, the relationship of the ancestor to the heir, a description of the lands and annual rents, the value according to two valuations called the Old Extent (A.E.) and the New Extent (N.E.), and the volume and folio number of the record. Here is a sample record:

FORMAT OF GENERAL RETOUR

Court: The general retour usually begins with the words *Haec inquisition facta fuit in [Curia Vicecomitatus de Perth tenta in burgo de Perth]* ("This inquisition was made in [the court of the sheriffdom of Perth held in the burgh of Perth]"). Substitute the name of the appropriate court in the brackets.

Date: Immediately after the name of the court is usually the date, written out in full. For example, *decimo tertio die mensis Martii anno Domini millesimo octingentesimo trigesimo quinto* ("thirteenth day of the month of March year of our Lord one thousand eight hundred thirty-five").

Names of court officials (macers) and jurors: Immediately following the date, you should find words similar to *coram honorabilibus et discretis viris* ("in the presence of honorable and discreet men"). The names and offices of the macers are then listed. Then look for words like *per hos probos et fideles homines patriae subscriptos vizt* ("by these worthy and faithful men of the country underwritten, namely"). The names of the jurors follow. Pay attention to these; they may have been related to your ancestor.

Name of the deceased, relationship to heir, and name of heir: Next comes the part you really need. Find the words *QUI JURATI DICUNT*. Often these words are in larger letters than the rest of the text. The complete phrase is usually something like *Qui jurati dicunt magno sacramento interveniente quod quondam [Edwardus Brough aliquando feudifirmarius in Crieff avus] [Thomae Brough residens in Crieff], latoris praesentium, obiit ad fidem et pacem S.D.N. regis Et quod dictus [Thomas Brough] est propinquior et legitimus haeres apud legem in generali dicti quondam [Edwardi Brough sui avi] Et quod est legitimae aetatis* ("Who being sworn say after administration of a great oath that the former [Edward Brough, sometime tenant in feu ferme (fee farm) in Crieff, grandfather] [of Thomas Brough resident tenant in Crieff], bearer of these presents, died at the faith and peace of our sovereign lord the king and that the said [Thomas Brough] is nearest and lawful heir at law in general of the said former [Edward Brough, his grandfather] and that he is of lawful age"). This means that the above jurors had been sworn, and they said that Thomas Brough was the legal heir of Edward Brough, his grandfather. The reason that he was the heir sometimes follows. For example, it may name Thomas Brough's father and state that he was deceased and that Thomas was the oldest living son. The name of your ancestor and his heir appear in place of the names in the brackets. The abbreviation "S.D.N." stands for *Supremi Domini Nostri* (our sovereign Lord).

Witness and enclosures: This section begins with the words *In Cujus Rei Testimonium* ("In witness whereof"). It gives the name of the witness (usually described as *scribae* ["writer"] or *scribae signeti regii* ["writer to the royal signet"]) and lists the documents being returned.

FORMAT OF SPECIAL RETOUR

The name of court, the date, and the names of the macers and jurors are in the first part of the retour. The names and details of your ancestor follow the words *Qui Jurati Dicunt*:

QUI JURATI DICUNT Quod quondam [Joannes Brugh, aliquando feudifermarius in Crieff, pater] [Edwardi Brugh residens in Crieff] latoris praesentium, obiit ultimo vestita et sasita ut de feodo ad fidem et pacem S.D.N. regis de totis et integris terris de [name of land] *cum manerie, domibus, edificiis, hortis, molendino ejusdem cum omnibus et singulis partibus, pendicullis et pertinentiis, iacentibus infra vicecomitatum de* [name of sherrifdom]. *Et quod dictus [Edwardus Brugh] est legitimus et propinquior haeres ejusdem quondam [Joannis Brugh], sui [patris] in totis et integris praedictis terris, molendino aliisque antedictis cum pertientiis Et quod est legitime aetatis Et quod dicte terre de* [name of land] *cum manerie, domibus, hortis, molendino ejusdem et pertinentiis antedictis nunc valent per annum* [amount] *libris moneste regni Scotiae.*

This translates as follows:

> WHO BEING SWORN SAY that the former [John Brugh, sometime tenant in feu ferme in Crieff, father] [of Edward Brugh resident tenant in Crieff] bearer of these presents, died last vest and seised as of fee at the faith and peace of our sovereign Lord king of all and whole the lands of [name of land] with manor, houses, buildings, yards, mill of the same place, with all and sundry parts, pendicles, and appurtenances, lying in the sherrifdom of [name of sherrifdom]. And that the said [Edward Brugh] is lawful and nearest heir of the same former [John Brugh] his [father] in all and whole the aforesaid lands, mill, and others aforesaid with appurtenances And that he is of lawful age And that the said lands of [name of land] with manor, houses, yards, mill of the same, and appurtenances aforesaid are now worth per year [amount] pounds money of the realm of Scotland.

(59) Nov. 29, 1591. GEORGIUS BANERMAN, *haeres* Alexandri Banerman de Watertoun, *patris*, in terris de Watertoun, Eister Elloun, Crecheid--A. E. 40s. N. E. 8l.--I. 98.

This says that George Banerman is heir to Alexander Banerman of Watertown, his father, in the lands of Watertown, Eister Elloun, Crecheid. The annual value of the land follows that information.

The General Service does not name land, but it gives date of service, name and designation of the heir, type of heir, name and designation of the ancestor, relationship, and volume and folio number. Its format is as follows:

(1594) Mar. 27, 1630. JOANNES SOMERVELL, de Cambusnethen, *haeres* Joannis Somervell de Cambusnethen, *avi*. xi. 232.

INDEXES ON CD-ROM

Retours of Services of Heirs: Inquisitionum ad capellam domini regis retornataram abbreviatio 1544–1699, Vols. I–III (£32) and *Decennial Indexes to the Services of Heirs in Scotland 1700–1859*, Vols. I–IV (£37). Published 1999 by The Scottish Genealogy Society, 15 Victoria Terrace, Edinburgh, EH1 2JL, Scotland.

The value and content of these indexes are described in the accompanying text. The two CD-ROMs contain scanned images of all the printed volumes.

The *Retours of Services of Heirs* disc contains three volumes. Volumes one and two provide Latin summaries of the retours. Special retours are arranged by county and within the county by name and place. Volume three contains bookmark indexes to the printed abstracts. The indexes reference abstract entry numbers (not page numbers) in the earlier volumes. The CD contains the same information as FHL microfilm 0908847.

The four volumes of *Decennial Indexes for the Services of Heirs in Scotland* cover the time period 1700 to 1859. The CD is the same as FHL microfilm 0990340. Each volume contains multiple sets of indexes. For each ten-year time period, there is an index plus a supplemental index, making a total of thirty-two bookmark indexes to check for the occurrence of your family names. You cannot go directly to any particular name on the disc; you have to scroll through each complete ten-year listing. There is no quick way to get to the correct letter in the alphabet let alone the individual entry. When printing, use "Shrink to Fit" to get the entire page.

No enhanced search capabilities are on the compact discs to make them easier to use than the microfilm, and they are considerably more expensive than ordering the microfilm on indefinite loan at a Family History Center. The advantage to the compact discs, however, is that you can own a complete set of these major indexes.

This record says that John Somervell of Cambusnethen is heir to John Somervell of Cambusnethen, his grandfather.

The General and Special Services of Heirs are the retours having the most genealogical value, but three other types of retours are in these volumes. You will rarely use the following, but you won't know if your ancestor is there unless you check the indexes:

Reminder

1. The tutory retour is one in which a person was appointed as "tutor" to administer the affairs of a minor "pupil" under the age of puberty (age fourteen for a boy, age twelve for a girl). The tutor was usually the nearest agnate (male relative of the father) of at least age twenty-five. The curatory retour appointed an administrator of the affairs of an heir of mental incapacity. Tutory and curatory retours are combined in the *Inquisitionum de Tutela*.

2. The inquisition of the extent, or estimated value of the whole of the lands of

a county or other district, is called *Inquisitiones Valorum*.

3. There were also inquisitions pursuant to an Act of the Parliament of Scotland in 1584 to determine the real estates forfeited for treason of which the person was in possession for five years preceding the date of forfeiture (*Inquisitiones de Possessione Quinquennali*).

There are so few of the last two types of records that they are printed in their entirety rather than being abridged.

Each of the different types of retours has a separate index. The names of the heir, ancestor, tutor, and pupil are all in the indexes. In the name and place indexes, the number referenced is the running number of the abstract, not the page number. Remember, though, that the most important records are the Services of Heirs. The order on FHL film 0908847 is as follows:

Volume 3: *Indices nominum et locorum* (name and place indexes)
    Indexes to Special Services: name and place index arranged by county in which the land was situated
    Index to General Services
    Index to Inquisitions of Tutors
    Index to Inquisitions of Value of Extent
    Index to Inquisitions of Forfeiture for Treason
Volume 1: Abridgements of Special Services: Aberdeen to Orkney and Shetland
Volume 2: Abridgements of Special Services: Peebles to Wigtown
    Abridgements of Special Services: Supplement
    Abridgements of General Services
    Abridgements of General Services: Supplement
    Abridgements of Inquisitions of Tutors
    Abridgements of Inquisitions of Tutors: Supplement
    Inquisitions of Value of Extent (in entirety)
    Inquisitions of Forfeiture for Treason (in entirety)

Look up your ancestor's name in each index, then find the abridgement number in the appropriate section. For example, if you find your ancestor's name in the indexes to Special Services, be sure that you look in the appropriate county of the Special Services for the abridgement. It is easy to get the sections confused, and if you're in the wrong section the number you find won't contain any information about your ancestor.

Indexes to Services of Heirs, 1700–1859

For records after the year 1700, the procedure is much easier. **Decennial (ten-year) indexes to Services of Heirs for 1700–1859, in English, are on FHL film 0990340.** They are indexed by name of the person who inherited—that is, the heir or person served—not by the name of his deceased ancestor. The index gives the name of the heir, the heir's designation, his relationship to the ancestor, the name and designation of the ancestor, the type of heir, the lands, the date of service, the date of recording, and the monthly number.

Microfilm Source

RELATIONSHIPS IN LATIN

The relationships in the abstracts of Services of Heirs, 1544–1699, are stated in the genitive case. The most common relationships in the abstracts are *patris* (father) and *fratris* (brother). Also frequently occurring are the following:

abavi	great-great-grandfather
amitae	aunt (father's sister)
atavi	great-great-great-grandfather
avi	grandfather
aviae	grandmother
avunculi	uncle (mother's brother)
filii	son
fratris germani	brother-german (full brother)
matris	mother
patrui	uncle (father's brother)
patrui magni	great-uncle on father's side
proavi	great-grandfather
sororis	sister
tritavi	great-great-great-great-grandfather

ABBREVIATIONS USED IN SERVICES OF HEIRS INDEX ENTRIES

Conq. or Conqt.	Conquest
Daur.	Daughter
Genl. or Gl.	General
Gdfather.	Grandfather
Gt-gdfather.	Great-grandfather
Hr.	Heir
Port. or Portr.	Portioner
Prov. or Provn.	Provision
Spl.	Special
Tail.	Tailzie
Wid.	Widow

At the end of each ten-year period is a supplement which lists the names of ancestors (persons served to) whose heirs did not have the same surname. No details of the service are given, but the name of the heir is referenced. Refer to the heir in the principal index to get the particulars of the service. The most common occurrence of different surnames is in the case of a son inheriting from his mother. Because women are listed by the maiden name, a large number of women is in the supplements.

Let's use this index to see if we can find any Services of Heirs for the Brough

Step By Step

1830–1839.

BRA—BRO.

Name of the Person served.	Distinguishing Particulars.	Date of Recording.	Monthly No.	Dated before 1830, viz. in.
Brander—Jean—(or *Mellis*) .	Pennsylvania, to her Mother Jean Muterer or Brander there, once at Cloves, Elginshire—Co-heir of Provision Special, in an Annualrent of £500, over Lingieston, Parish of Forres-Elginshire—dated 7th May 1838	1838, June 11	21	
Brander—John Muterer .	Pennsylvania, to his Uncle John Muterer of Lingieston, Elginshire, who died 6th November 1838—Heir of Provision Special, in Part of Calfward, in the Burgh of Forres-Elginshire—dated 7th September 1839	1839, Oct. 3	4	
Brander—John Muterer .	above designed, to his Mother Jean Muterer or Brander, Pennsylvania, once at Cloves, Elginshire—Co-heir of Provision Special, in an Annualrent of £500, over Lingieston, Parish of Forres-Elginshire—dated 7th May 1838	1838, June 11	21	
Brander—Margaret .	to her Mother Jean Muterer or Brander, Pennsylvania, once at Cloves, Elginshire—Co-heir of Provision Special, in an Annualrent of £500 Sterling, over Lingieston, Parish of Forres-Elginshire—dated 7th May 1838	1838, June 11	21	
Brander—Robert .	to his Mother Jean Muterer or Brander, Pennsylvania, once at Cloves, Elginshire—Co-heir of Provision Special, in an Annualrent of £500 Sterling, over Lingieston, Parish of Forres-Elginshire—dated 7th May 1838	1838, June 11	21	
Brander—Robina .	to her Mother Jean Muterer or Brander, Pennsylvania, once at Cloves, Elginshire—Co-heir of Provision Special, in an Annualrent of £500 Sterling, over Lingieston, Parish of Forres-Elginshire—dated 7th May 1838	1838, June 11	21	
Brander—William .	to his Mother Jean Muterer or Brander, Pennsylvania, once at Cloves, Elginshire—Co-heir of Provision Special, in an Annualrent of £500, over Lingieston, Parish of Forres-Elginshire—dated 7th May 1838	1838, June 11	21	
Brands—Charles .	Peterhead, to his Sister Mary Brands, Wife of Wm. Matthew, Ship Carpenter there—Hr. of Conqt. Gl.—16th Mar. 1839	1839, Mar. 23	32	
Brash—Alexander .	Grocer, Leith, to his Father Alexander Brash, Grocer there—Heir in General—dated 24th June 1839	1839, June 28	59	
Brash—Isabella .	at Chirnside, to her Grandfather Robert Brash, Portioner of Mudiesburn—Heir in General—dated 7th September 1831	1831, Sept. 20	40	
Brash—James .	Bookseller, Glasgow, to his Uncle James Brash, Bookseller there—Heir of Line and Conqt. General—8th Sept. 1837	1837, Sept. 15	29	
Brash—John Gourlay .	Clerk, Edinburgh, to his Father John Brash, Sec., N.B. Insurance Company there—Hr. Gl., *c. b. Invent.*—25th Mar. 1839	1839, April 3	6	
Brasnell—William .	in London, to his Father The Hon. William Brasnell, Tobago—Heir of Line and Conqt. General—8th August 1833	1833, Aug. 15	36	
Bray—Mary—(or *Mackenzie*) .	London, to her Uncle Murdoch Mackenzie of Groundwater, Capt., R.N., who died 27th January 1829—Co-heir of Provision Special, in Groundwater, Troup, Holland, etc., of Orkney—dated 2d September 1833	1833, Oct. 4	2	
Breakenridge—John .	Campbelltown, to his Brother Thomas Breakenridge, Merchant, Jamaica—Heir General—dated 11th May 1839	1839, June 14	22	
Brebner—Elizabeth—(or *Kilgour*) .	Aberdeen, to her Father William Kilgour, Chaise Hirer there—Heir General—dated 23d January 1833	1833, Feb. 19	31	
Brechin—Elizabeth—(or *Sime*) .	in Dundee, to her Brother John Sime, Merchant there—Heir of Line and Conquest General—3d December 1834	1834, Dec. 4	7	
Brechin—Janet—(or *Park*) .	in Cambuslang, to her Father James Brechin, Farmer and Miller, Clydesmill there—Heir General—28th June 1837	1837, July 17	31	
Brechin—Walter .	Surgeon, Glasgow, to his Wife Mary Charity or Brechin—Heir of Provision General—dated 24th December 1834	1835, Jan. 5	7	
Bremner—Christian—(or *Mullikin*) .	in Wick, to her Brother Robert Mullikin there—Heir General—dated 21st June 1834	1834, June 25	43	
Bremner—James .	Merchant, Forres, to his Father James Bremner, Gardener, Forres, once in Windyhills—Heir General—3d May 1831	1831, May 13	20	
Bremner—James .	Yarn Dresser, Glasgow, to his Father William Bremner, Weaver, Kilbarchan—Heir General—dated 24th April 1838	1838, May 7	11	
Bridges—Margaret King—(or *Grant*) .	Widow of Major J. G. King, in Nairn, to her Uncle Lieut. James Dunbar, Edinburgh-Hr. Port. Genl.—18th Apr. 1836	1836, April 22	46	
Bridie—William—(or *Brodie*) .	Tailor in Elie, to his Grandfather Colin Bridie, Farm Servant, Arncroach—Heir General—10th December 1832	1832, Dec. 13	18	
Brisbane—John .	Tailor, Rutherglen, to his Uncle James Brisbane, Weaver there—Heir General—dated 31st October 1835	1836, April 1	3	
Brisbane—Thomas, Dr .	in Largs, to his Uncle Fergusson Cunninghame of Monkredding—Heir Port. of Line and Prov. Genl.—7th June 1830	1830, June 15	24	
Brisbane—Thomas Makdougall, Sir .	of Makerstoun and Brisbane, K.C.B., to his Father Thos. Brisbane of Brisbane-Hr. of Tail. & Prov. Gl.—14th Apr. 1834	1834, April 18	31	
Brock—John .	Weaver, Glasgow, to his Grandfather John Brock, Weaver there—Co-Heir of Provision General—2d March 1831	1831, April 4	6	
Brock—Robert .	Travelling Merchant, now in Edinburgh, to his Sister Agnes Brock, Glasgow—Heir of Conqt. Genl.—14th April 1837	1837, May 24	54	
Brock—William .	Weaver, Glasgow, to his Grandfather John Brock, Weaver there—Co-heir of Provision General—2d March 1831	1831, April 4	6	
Brock—William .	Farmer at Spittal, to his Father Peter Brock, Farmer there—Heir General—dated 1st September 1838	1838, Sept. 13	20	
Brockie—Jean—(or *Henderson*) .	Selkirk, to her Mother Margaret Henderson, Wife of Walter Henderson, Flesher there—Hr. Port. Gl.—23d June 1830	1830, June 30	57	
Brodie—Alexander .	Tenant in Stronafyne, to his Brother John Brodie, Tenant there—Heir General—dated 16th August 1837	1837, Aug. 23	31	
Brodie—Ann—(or *Hay*) .	Bogrotten, Banffshire, to her Cousin James Hay, Mason, Glasgow—Heir of Conquest General—6th November 1832	1832, Nov. 22	34	
Brodie—Bridget—(or *Logan*) .	Dumfries, to her Aunt Agnes M'Millan there—Heir General—dated 1st July 1839	1839, July 10	17	
Brodie—Isabella—(or *Grant*) .	Mains of Bogrotten, to her Mother Ann Hay, Wife of William Brodie, Farmer there—Heir General—6th Feb. 1833	1833, Feb. 9	17	
Brodie—James Campbell .	to his Cousin Mrs Sophia Dunbar Brodie of Lethen, who died—September 1829—Heir of Tailzie and Provision Special, in the Barony of Lethen, Kilboghaugh, Nether Ruives, etc.-Nairn, Elgin, and Forres—26th May 1830	1830, Oct. 30	39	
Brodie—John .	Tacksman of Rumblingwell Tollbar, to his Father John Brodie, Crossford—Heir General—dated 22d December 1830	1831, Jan. 10	15	
Brodie—John .	Tutor, Drumblair, to his Father Francis Brodie, Tailor, Aberdeen—Heir in General—2d December 1833	1833, Dec. 5	9	
Brodie—William—(or *Bridie*) .	Tailor in Elie, to his Grandfather Colin Bridie, Farm Servant, Arncroach—Heir General—10th December 1832	1832, Dec. 13	18	
Brook—Elizabeth—(or *Stiven*) .	in Gask of Cruden, to her Father John Stiven in Teuchan—Heir Portioner General—dated 16th September 1837	1837, Sept. 28	47	
Brough—Thomas .	Crieff, to his Grandfather Edward Brough, Feuar there—Heir General—dated 13th March 1835	1835, Mar. 27	47	
Broun—Archibald .	to his Brother Thomas Hamilton Broun of Johnstonburn, who died 14th August 1830—Heir Special, in Nether Plewlands, Johnstoneburn, etc.-Edinburgh and Haddingtonshires—dated 7th March 1831	1831, Mar. 10	17	
Brown—Agnes—(or *Fairweather*) .	Dundee, to her Sister Isabella, Daughter of Robert Fairweather, Weaver there—Co-hr. of Prov. Gl.—17th Aug. 1831	1831, Aug. 27	27	
Brown—Agnes—(or *Lyall*) .	in St Andrews, to her Mother Agnes Colin, Widow of George Brown, Farm Servant there—Hr. Port. Gl.—16th April 1833	1833, April 22	33	
Brown—Agnes—(or *Smith*) .	Carnwath, to her Uncle Alexander Hamilton, Stone Hewer, Edinburgh—Heir in General—dated 13th J......			

Figure 10-5
Decennial index to Services of Heirs.

family in Crieff, Perthshire. An example from the 1830–1839 index is shown in Figure 10-5. A General Service of Thomas Brough to his grandfather Edward Brough is on that page.

In the decennial index for the years 1850–1859, we found three Services of Heirs for one man in Crieff. They read as follows:

Brough—John	Joiner, Glasgow, to his Brother Edward Brough, China Merchant, Crieff—Heir General—dated 10th March 1854. Recorded 1854, Mar. 20. Monthly No. 42.
Brough—John	above designed, to his Father Thomas Brough, Crieff, who died in May 1842—Heir Special, in a House and Yard in

Crieff-Perthshire dated 21st June 1854. Recorded 1854, June 26, Monthly No. 61.

Brough—John   above designed, to his Brother Edward Brough, China Merchant, Crieff, who died 11th February 1854—Heir Special in a Piece of the Lands of Gavelmore in the Parish of Crieff-Perthshire—dated 21st June 1854. Recorded 1854, June 26, Monthly No. 62.

You can tell a lot from the index entries. The John Brough above is the brother of Edward Brough, whose testament we discussed earlier in this chapter. In that testament, only a brother, James Brough, was mentioned. We now know that their father is Thomas Brough, who died in 1842. Remember that this is only the index. To get more details, order the microfilm that contains the record you want to see. We look at two of these services later in this chapter.

Indexes to Services of Heirs, 1860–1929

Annual Indexes to Services of Heirs, 1860–1929, in English, are on FHL fiche 6068606 (a set of 102 fiche). The format is similar to that of the decennial indexes. The following are examples of the kind of details you may find:

> Adam, Mary Ann (or *M'Kellar*)--Wife of A. M'Kellar at Whiteinch Glasgow, to her Uncle James Wright Seaman in America once in Paisley--Heir Genl.--1860, 8th Nov--21
>
> Alexander, Robert--Engineer in Bristol, to his Grandmother Martha Taylor or Alexander in Glasgow--Co-heir of Provision Special in a Flat in the Lawnmarket High Street Edinburgh-1860, 11th Jany--28

The indexes are organized by year and then alphabetically by surname of the heir. The supplements list the names of the deceased (person served to) if the heir had a different surname. The fiche in the set are numbered 1 to 102, but unfortunately the titles on each fiche do not show the years or surnames covered. Use the table at <www.rootsweb.com/~bifhsusa/servheirs.html> to locate the appropriate fiche number within the set.

Services of Heirs, 1547–1900

When you find the entry you want in any of the above indexes, you can order the complete record on microfilm from the Family History Library. The Services of Heirs, 1547–1900, are on FHL films 0231260–0231566. Search the Family History Library Catalog by film/fiche number to see the entire list, or search by locality under Scotland, Land and Property. Note that if your ancestor lived in a royal burgh, his record may be found in the burgh registers of Services of Heirs. Some of these are available from the Family History Library. For example, burgh registers of Services of Heirs for Edinburgh from 1606 to 1792 are on FHL films 0298494–0298497.

Let's locate the Special Service of John Brough to his father, Thomas Brough. Again, here is the index entry:

Brough—John [Joiner, Glasgow], to his Father Thomas Brough, Crieff, who died in May 1842—Heir Special, in a House and Yard in Crieff-Perthshire dated 21st June 1854. Recorded 1854, June 26, Monthly No. 61.

Search the Family History Library Catalog to find the film number that contains the date 26 June 1854. Here's what we found in the catalog:

Record of services, v. 24–25, 1853–1854 FHL film number 0231432
Record of services, v. 26–27, 1854   FHL film number 0231433
Record of services, v. 28–29, 1854–1855 FHL film number 0231434

For most years, it is obvious which film you need to order, but for 1854 it isn't. The index to the Services of Heirs gives a date, but not a volume number, so we don't know which of the three films contains the date 26 June 1854. Consult the Repertory of Chancery Records on FHL fiche 6029998. For dates up to 15 November 1847, see C 22 in the repertory. For dates after that, see C 28. There you can find the volume numbers and the dates they cover. The Repertory of Chancery Records tells us in C 28 that volume 26 covers the dates 23 May 1854–15 August 1854, so we should order FHL film number 0231433.

Here is the Special Service we found in June 1854, monthly number 61:

No. 61. Special Service John Brough at Perth the twenty first day of June in the year Eighteen hundred and fifty four Sitting in Judgment Hugh Barclay Esquire Sheriff Substitute of Perthshire in the Petition of John Brough Joiner and Cabinet Maker in Glasgow. Found and hereby finds that the late Thomas Brough residing in Crieff died on or about the [blank space] Day of May Eighteen-hundred and forty two last vest and seized as of fee in All and Whole that part of piece of land of the lands of Galvelmore lying on the South side of the Town of Crieff consisting of thirty falls as the same was measured off, and is bounded meithed and marched in terms of the original feu Charter of the same in manner following vizt.: on the North by the houses and yard disponed by the deceased James Drummond of Perth to Alexander Gentle Wright in Crieff. On the East by the yard disponed by the said James Drummond to John Taylor Merchant there. On the South by a rough stone dyke and that Croft of land sometime possessed by David Thomson Writer in Crieff and on the West by the Kings highway with the houses and yards built on said lands by Edward Brugh or Brough Merchant in Crieff deceased lying within the Parish of Crieff, Stewartry of Strathearn and Shire of Perth, and which subjects are now bounded and described as following, Vizt.: On the North by a feu the property of William Fenwich, On the East by a feu the property of John McEwen, on the South by the march between the said deceased Edward Brugh or Broughs feu and the property of James Dewar and William Maltman, and on the West by Kings Street, but always with and under the provisions and declarations contained in a Feu Charter of the said subjects granted by the said deceased James Drummond in favor of the said deceased Edward Brugh or Brough dated the third day of March Seventeen hundred and thirty nine Conform to Precept of Clare Constat made and granted by John Dundas Clerk to the Signet Cimmissioner nominated and appointed by the Right Honorable Clementina Sarah Drummond of Perth Lady Willoughby De Eresby Spouse of the Right Honorable Peter Robert Drummond Lord Willoughby De Eresby with consent of her said husband and him for his interest to and in favor of the said Thomas Brough dated the seventeenth day of June Eighteen hundred and thirty five, and to Instrument of Sasine in his favor following thereon dated the ninth and recorded in the New Particular Register of Sasines Reversions &c kept at Perth for Perthshire the thirteenth day of April, Eighteen hundred and forty two. That Edward Brough China Merchant in Crieff was the eldest Son of the said deceased Thomas Brough but he died without lawful issue. And the said John Brough, who was the immediate younger Brother german of the said Edward Brough is now the eldest Son surviving of the said deceased Thomas Brough and therefore nearest and lawful heir in Special of his Father the said deceased Thomas Brough in the lands and others foresaid—And the said Sheriff grants warrant to any Notary Public to whom this Decree may be presented to infeft seize the said John Brough in the said lands . . .

What did we find out from the original service? Aside from a description of the land, we found some good family information. We know that John Brough was a joiner and cabinetmaker in Glasgow. He inherited the lands of his father, Thomas Brough. Why did John inherit in 1854 the land of his father who died in 1842? The service tells us that Edward Brough, china merchant in Crieff, was the eldest son of Thomas Brough of Crieff who died May 1842. The eldest son inherited the lands of the father, but Edward has now died without children (lawful issue). As the second son of Thomas Brough, John Brough was the next to inherit these lands.

The index also indicates a service of John Brough to his brother Edward Brough in monthly number 62, which is next on the film. We found even more details on that record! From these two records, we know that Edward Brough, merchant in Crieff, received the land from James Drummond in 1739. Edward's grandson, Thomas Brough, wright in Crieff, inherited it. Thomas Brough gave the land in 1835 to his son Edward. Thomas died in 1842. Edward Brough died in 1854 without children. His immediate younger brother, John Brough, became the legal heir. We can see the descent of this land for over one hundred years! Because these are special services that record the inheritance of land, there is also a sasine record for them. We examine sasine records in the next section.

The index also listed a General Service of John Brough to Edward Brough. We may find more details if we examinine this record. Furthermore, we certainly want to look at the 1835 service of Thomas Brough to his grandfather.

After 1900

If you need Services of Heirs dated after the year 1900, you can order an abstract on microfilm (Abstracts of Services, 1855–1955, on FHL films 1441082–1441099). These are in English and neatly typed. Remember, also, in the case of a Special Service (which names lands) to look for a sasine record.

VOCABULARY USED IN SERVICES OF HEIRS

Brieve—a warrant from Chancery authorizing an inquest by a jury.

Retour—a return of a decision sent to Chancery by the jury or inquest.

Types of Heirs
Heir or **Heir of Line**—the heir at law.

Heir Portioner—one of several females or their issue succeeding jointly.

Heir of Provision and **Co-Heir of Provision**—an heir who succeeds by express provisions as in a marriage settlement.

Heir Male of the Body and of Provision—an heir succeeding to land which has been restricted to male descendants and prohibits inheritance by females or their issue.

Heir Male and of Provision—an heir who inherits lands restricted to male descendants, collaterals, or ascendants.

Heir of Entail, Taillie, or Tailzie—an heir succeeding under an entail.

Heir of Conquest—one inheriting lands that the ancestor acquired by means other than inheritance, usually property obtained by purchase. For example, the inherited property of a childless man who died intestate goes to his immediate younger brother, but his conquest goes to his immediate elder brother (or his issue).

Heir *cum beneficio Inventarii*—an heir who gives an inventory of the ancestor's real property to obtain an exemption from liability beyond the value of the property.

Sasines

Sasines record the transfer of land, and the registers of sasines are land registers. The word *sasine* is the Scottish form of the English word *seizin*. When land was transferred in Scotland, the transaction was recorded in a Register of Sasines. Different sasine registers cover different time periods and locations.

\di'fin\ *vb*

Definitions

Prior to 1599 sasines were recorded by Notaries Public in their own books. Those registers are called Notarial Protocol Books, and not all these records have survived. To find what's available on microfilm, search the Family History Library Center under Scotland, [County], Notarial Records. You can also do a keyword search in the Windows version of the Family History Library Catalog under "Notarial Protocol." To find Notarial Protocol Books held at the National Archives of Scotland, consult the inventory on FHL fiche 6091660.

From 1599 to 1609 the registers were kept by the Secretary of State. Most of the secretary's registers did not survive. From 1617 to 1868 a General Register of Sasines was used for property anywhere in Scotland, and particular registers of sasine were used for the lands belonging to each district. From 1681, royal burghs were required to maintain their own sasine registers.

No one could complete a valid title to land by succession, purchase, or any other method without record in an appropriate Register of Sasines. The document, called an Instrument of Sasine, was a deed executed by a notary public stating that formal possession had been given and taken upon a certain warrant and before specified witnesses.

Sasines to 1780

Check the particular registers first because you are most likely to find your ancestor's sasine record there. Indexes to the particular registers of sasines are listed in the table on page 203.

A typical entry from the index to the particular registers for Lanark (FHL film 0896606) reads:

> WOOD, Agnes, daughter of Gavin W. in Corsbalt, and spouse of John Holmes, younger, of Blakburnemilne, (RS 40) IIB.271

Important

The actual sasine records have not been microfilmed, so use the document number shown to order the record from the National Archives of Scotland. The introduction to the Lanark index shows that RS 40 IIB corresponds with the dates 14 March 1622–12 January 1627. Even before you get the full record from the NAS, you can find additional information from the minute books if they are available on microfilm for the time period you need. The minute books contain a summary of the sasine record. The minute books of particular registers are on FHL film numbers 216980 to 217025. The entries are in chronological order, and the information from the index narrows down the time period to be searched.

Notice that the County of Perth has no index for particular registers after 1609. If there is no index for a county, order the minute books for that county. The minute book entries are abstracts of the sasines arranged in chronological order on the microfilm. It helps to know an approximate date, but if you don't have one, you can still benefit from searching page by page. Search the Family History Library Catalog by fiche/film number and enter film number 216980 to see the entire list of minute books.

The minute books for the particular registers of Perth are on four rolls of microfilm. Let's see the transfer of land from James Drummond to Edward Brugh in 1739. We know the date because it is in the special service of James Brough to his brother Edward Brough. We ordered FHL film number 217012 which covers the years 1724–1756. Here is the summary recorded in the minute books:

> BRUGH from PERTH; Garvellmore: Instrument of Sasine in favour of Edward Brugh mer[chan]t in Crieff of all and haill that part or piece of land of the lands of Galvellmore lyeing on the South side of the town of Crieff consisting of thirty falls as the same is measured & bounded as therein men[tioned] lyeing within the parish of Crieff stewartry of Strathearn and Shire of Perth dated the twelfth of March last. Proceeding upon a Charter of Feu Ferm granted to him by James Drummond of Perth . . .

In most cases, the minute books give all the genealogically valuable information from the sasine record. Notice in our example that the name of the land is spelled

Indexes to Particular Registers of Sasines

County, Bailiary, or Stewartry	Years Indexed	FHL Film Number
Aberdeen until 1660 (RS 4–5)	1599–1609; 1617–1629	0896586, Item 1
	1630–1660	0896590, Item 1
Kincardine until 1657 (RS 6–7)	1600–1608; 1617–1657	0896590, Item 2
Aberdeen and Kincardine from 1661 (RS 8)	None	None
Argyle, Dunbarton, Bute, Arran and Tarbet (RS 9–10)	1617–1780	0896587
Ayr, Kyle, Carrick, and Cunningham (RS 11–14)	1599–1609	0896593, Item 1
	1617–1634	0896595, Item 2
	1635–1660	0896596, Item 1
Banff (RS 15–17)	1600–1609; 1617–1780	0896591, Item 1
Berwick and Lauderdale (RS 18–19)	1617–1780 A-H	0896588, Item 3
	1617–1780 I-Z	0896589, Item 1
Caithness from 1646 (RS 20–21, see also Inverness, etc.)	1646–1780	0896596, Item 3
Dumfries, Kirkcudbright, and Annandale (RS 22–23)	1617–1671	0896592, Item 2
	1672–1702	0896593, Item 3
	1703–1732	0896594, Item 2
	1733–1760	0896603, Item 2
	1761–1780	0896603, Item 4
Edinburgh, Haddington, Linlithgow, and Bathgate (RS 24–27)	1599–1609	0896602, Item 3
	1617–1623	0896598, Item 1
	1624–1630	0896599, Item 1
	1631–1636	0896600, Item 1
	1637–1643	0896601, Item 1
	1644–1653	0896601, Item 3
	1654–1660	0896602, Item 2
Elgin, Forres, and Nairn (RS 28–29)	1617–1700	0896604, Item 1
	1701–1780	0990068, Item 3
Fife and Kinross until 1685 (RS 30–31)	1603–1609	0896604, Item 3
	1617–1660 A-K	0896604, Item 5
	1617–1660 L-Y	0896605, Item 1
Fife from 1685 (RS 32)	None	None
Kinross from 1688 (RS 39)	None	None
Forfar (RS 33–35)	1620–1700	0896605, Item 3
	1701–1780	None
Inverness, Ross, Cromarty, and Sutherland (RS 36–38)	1606–1608; 1617–1660	0896606, Item 1
	1661–1720	0896606, Item 3
	1721–1780	0896606, Item 4
Lanark (RS 40–42)	1618–1720; 1721–1780	0896606, Item 6
Midlothian and East Lothian (See also Edinburgh, etc.)	1741–1780	0217006
Orkney and Shetland (RS 43–47)	1617–1660	None
Perth (RS 48–52, see also Stirling and Clackmannan)	1601–1609	0217010
Renfrew and Glasgow (RS 53–54)	None	None
Roxburgh, Selkirk, and Peebles (RS 55–57)	None	None
Stirling and Clackmannan (RS 58–59)	None	None
West Lothian (See also Edinburgh, etc.)	1701–1760	0217023
Wigtown (RS 60–61)	None	None

Notes

INDEXES TO THE GENERAL REGISTER OF SASINES

Date	FHL Film #
1617–1630	216970
1631–1640	216971
1641–1652	216972
1652–1660	216973
1660–1670	216974
1671–1690	216975
1691–1700	216976
1701–1720	874420

Research Tip

two different ways in the same document: "Garvellmore" and "Galvellmore." Several other spellings of this land were in various records. Remember to try variant spellings for everything!

After you examine the appropriate particular register, also check the General Register in case more land transactions for your ancestor are recorded there. The microfilm numbers of the indexes to the General Register of Sasines are in the sidebar.

There is no index to the General Register of Sasines from 1720 to 1781, so the minute books must be used. Minute books to the General Register of Sasines for the years 1717–1782 are on FHL films 216977 to 216979. Again, they are in chronological order and contain abstracts of the sasines. If your ancestor lived in a royal burgh, also check the burgh registers of sasines. The Family History Library has some burgh records. They are discussed in the section on burgh records of sasines in this chapter. The inventory (repertory) of burgh records in the National Archives of Scotland is on FHL fiche 6029991.

Sasines 1781 to the present

For records from 1781 to 1868 the process is much easier. Printed Abridgements of Sasines are in one series that combines the Particular Registers and the General Register. The abridgements include all of the significant information found on the original sasine records. The Abridgements of Sasines 1781–1868 are on FHL films 217088–217141. The Index of Persons to Abridgements of Sasines 1781–1868, arranged by county, is on FHL microfilms 217026–217074. If your ancestor had a common surname, you can be overwhelmed looking for him in that index. Within each county, the index is broken into smaller time periods, so you may have to search several sections of the index to find all references to your family. An example from the 1851–1855 index of Perth is shown in Figure 10-6. **Make a note of the dates covered by the index pages as well as the running numbers of the abridgements.** If you know the name of your ancestor's piece of land, you can use the Place Name Index to Abridgements of Sasines 1781–1830 on FHL films 217075–217087 (see Figure 10-7 on page 207). Notice that the place names are not the parish names; they are the names of the lands on which your ancestor lived. We cannot, for example, look up the parish of Crieff. We have to know that the name of the land on which the Brugh family lived was Galvellmore.

The Abridgements of Sasines are typed and easy to read. They are organized by county, and then by the running number at the left of the abridgement (see Figure 10-8 on page 208). There are several abridgements for the Brough family. An abridgement for Thomas Brough is found in Perth, 1842, number 486. It reads:

> (486)   Apr 13, 1842
>
> THOMAS BROUGH residing in Crieff, as heir to Edward Brugh or Brough, Merchant there, his grandfather, *Seised*, Apr. 9, 1842,—in 30 Falls of the lands of GALVILMORE with the Houses and Yards thereon, on the east side of King Street, CRIEFF, par. Crieff;—on Pr. Cl. Con. by the Commissioner for Clementina Sarah Drummond of Perth, Lady Willoughby de Eresby, and Peter Robert Drummond, Lord Willoughby de Eresby, her husband, Jan. 17, 1835;—and ISABELLA

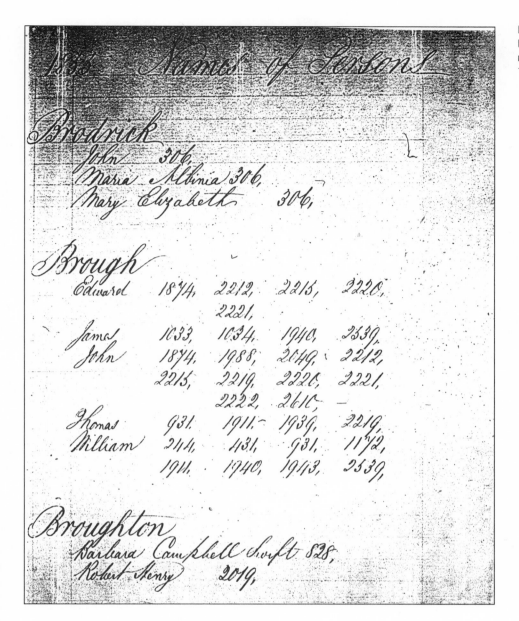

Figure 10-6
Index of Persons to Abridgements of Sasines, 1851–1855, Perthshire.

HALLEY, his spouse, *Seised*, *eod. die*, in liferent of said subjects, *propriis manibus* of the said Thomas Brough.

P.R. 230. 216.

The wife of Thomas Brough was Isabella Halley. We saw Isabella's death record in chapter six. It names her husband, Thomas, and lists the names and ages of her children: Edward (48 when he died), John, James, Elizabeth, and David. We also found Isabella in the 1851 and 1841 censuses (see chapter seven). We found a lot more about this family in the land and probate records we have examined in this chapter!

Once you find your ancestor in the Abridgements of Sasines, you will know the name of the land on which he lived. Always go back to the place indexes if they are available for the time period you need. Remember, however, that the place name indexes are only available for the years 1781–1830, but they are well worth using! We looked up Gavelmore in the place name indexes for Perth. This place has been spelled so many ways it could make your head spin: Galvellmore, Galvelmoir, Galvelmore, Galvillmore, Galvilmore, Garvillmore, Garvelmoir, Gavillmore, Gavellmore, Gavelmoir, and the list goes on. All of the variants are listed in the index with the notation "vide Galvelmore"; this is a reference to the spelling "Galvelmore," under which all of the entries are indexed. Under that spelling, as shown in Figure 10-7, the index has more than fifty references to sasine records. Here is one of the most interesting ones:

> 5681 Nov. 24. 1804   JOHN HALLY, late Farmer, Crofthead near Langtown, England, afterwards at Sarkfoot, and now at Skails, *gets. Ren.* Nov. 24. 1804, by James Bruce, formerly Accountant, now Accountant General of Excise, Edinburgh,—of a Tenement & portion of the lands of GAVILMORE on the West side of CRIEFF, and others;—and of £200, in Bond, Sept. 1. 1791. (*Vide* No. 2687). G. R. 712. 244.

Who is John Hally? Could he be related to Isabella Halley, spouse of Thomas Brough? We certainly have some places where we can look to find more about him! We may never have known that he had lived in England had we not seen these land records. These abridgements show how important it is to use the place name indexes. You may find many additional family members.

Burgh registers of sasines

From 1681, royal burghs were required to maintain their own sasine registers. **If your ancestor lived in a royal burgh, his sasine records are in these registers.** A table listing all of the burgh sasine records at the Family History Library is online at <www.rootsweb.com/~bifhsusa/burghsasines.html>.

Reminder

Why Can't I Find My Ancestor in Scottish Land Records?

You are looking in the wrong place. From 1617 a sasine could be recorded in the general register or in a particular register. Your ancestor could have chosen either one. You need to do more research to see if and where your ancestor may have had properties, and then check the particular registers for all areas and the General Register. Remember, also, that burghs had their own registers.

You stopped looking too soon in time. Most heirs took legal possession within a year of the death. However, many did not record the process until much later, if at all. You may not find the recording of the event until the next generation needed to prove possession. Keep looking into later years.

Your ancestor is not in the index. The indexing is incomplete. The indexed sasine records have gaps, and some counties have no indexes at all. At this point you need to search through the minute books for the county.

Your ancestor lived in a royal burgh. The burghs kept their own burgh registers of sasines. Many of the minute books have been microfilmed by the Family History Library. Consult the table of burgh registers at <www.rootsweb.com/~bifhsusa/

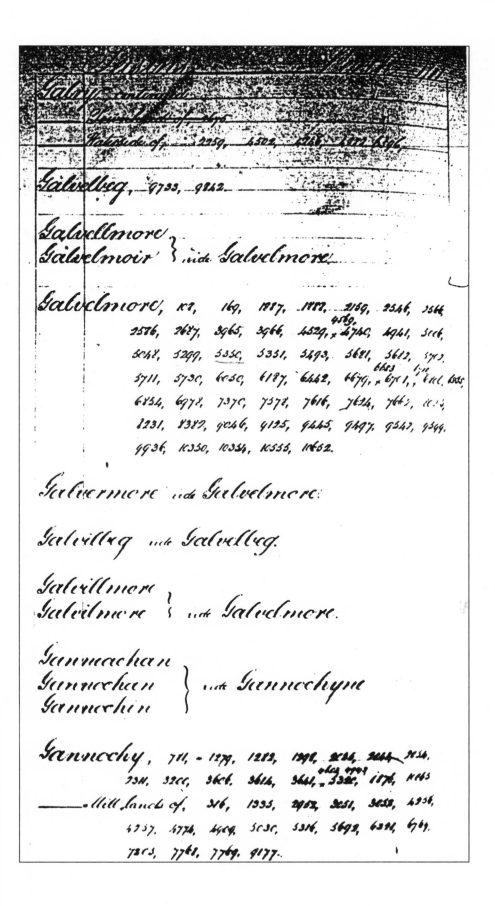

Figure 10-7
Index of Places to Abridgements of Sasines, Perth.

Writer, Edinburgh, now in America, or elsewhere abroad, and the Factor for John Erskine, sometime Tin and Coppersmith, Crieff, now in Montreal, North America, or elsewhere abroad, to the said Edward Brough, Jul. 18.—Aug. 14. 1850; and Decr. Gen. Serv., Mar. 10. 1854. P. R. 276. 55.

(2216) Oct. 18. 1854.
The Trustees of the Quoad sacra CHURCH AND PARISH OF LOGIEALMOND AT CHAPELHILL IN CONNECTION WITH THE CHURCH OF SCOTLAND, Seised,—in an annual sum or rent of £90, and an annual sum of £2. 5s. 6d.,—upliftable forth of the lands of BANKHEAD and FOSTENS PARK, being part of the lands and Estate of LOGIEAL-MOND, par. Monzie;—on Bond by William David, Earl of Mansfield, Sept. 19. 1854. G. R. 2700. 239.

(2217) Oct. 18. 1854.
The Trustees of the Quoad sacra CHURCH AND PARISH OF LOGIEALMOND AT CHAPELHILL IN CONNECTION WITH THE CHURCH OF SCOTLAND, Seised,—in 40 Poles of the lands and Estate of LOGIEALMOND with the Church and other Buildings thereon, par. Logiealmond;—on Feu Ch. by William David, Earl of Mansfield, Sept. 19. 1854.
G. R. 2700. 216.

(2218) Oct. 19. 1854.
AGNES ANNE BELFRAGE, presently residing at Newcastle-upon-Tyne, with consent of her Curators, grants Disch., Oct. 2.—12. 1854;—of Bond Corrob. and Disp. for £1212. 19s. 7d., by John Henry Belfrage (of Colliston), with consent of his Curators, Jul. 8. 1852, (Vide No. 942),—and declares the lands of COLLINSTAIN or COLLISTON and STRENTON, bar. Cuthill Gourdie,—disburdened thereof. (Vide KINROSS). G. R. 2700. 275.

(2219) Oct. 20. 1854.
JOHN BROUGH, Joiner and Cabinetmaker, Glasgow, as heir to Thomas Brough residing in Crieff, his father, Seised,—in 30 Falls of the lands of GALVELMORE, with the Houses and Yards thereon, on the east side of King Street, CRIEFF, par. Crieff;—on Decr. Sp. Serv., Jun. 21. 1854.
P. R. 276. 59.

(2220) Oct. 20. 1854.
JOHN BROUGH, Joiner and Cabinetmaker, Glasgow, as heir to Edward Brough, sometime Wright, thereafter China Merchant, Crieff, his brother, Seised,—in 600 Ells of ground on the south side of Commissioners Street, (CRIEFF), par. Crieff;—on Ch. Novod. by the Commissioner for Clementina Sarah Drummond of Perth, Lady Willoughby D'Eresby, spouse of Peter Robert Drummond, Lord Willoughby D'Eresby, to the said Edward Brough, Aug. 9. 1843; and Decr. Gen. Serv., Mar. 10. 1854. P. R. 276. 61.

(2221) Oct. 20. 1854.
JOHN BROUGH, Joiner and Cabinetmaker, Glasgow, as heir to Edward Brough, Wright, and thereafter China Merchant, Crieff, his brother, Seised,—in a new House with the Yard at the back thereof on the east side of King Street, CRIEFF, par. Crieff;—on Decr. Sp. Serv., Jun. 21. 1854.
P. R. 276. 63.

(2222) Oct. 20. 1854.
WILLIAM ROY, Veterinary Surgeon, Crieff, gets Bond and Disp. for £100, by John Brough, Joiner and Cabinetmaker, Glasgow, Oct. 17. 1854,—over 2 Shops with the Flat and Garrets above the same now demolished and a new House erected on the Site thereof in the High Street of CRIEFF, Piece of Garden ground consisting of 170 square Yards on the west side of John Millars Yard, and a small Patch of ground in the Village of Crieff, par. Crieff. P. R. 276. 65.

(2223) Oct. 20. 1854.

Seised,—in 45 Falls of ground in the Village of NEW SCONE, par. Scone;—on Feu Disp. by Andrew Murray of Murrays-hall, Advocate, with consent of David Chisholm, Wright, New Scone, to the said Walter Crawford, Apr. 7. 11. 1845; and Disp. and Settl. and Assig. by him, Jun. 24. 1846.
P. R. 276. 74.

(2225) Oct. 20. 1854.
GEORGE AUGUSTUS GREGOR residing in Methven, gets Bond and Disp. for £50, by David Martin, Smith, New Scone, Oct. 20. 1854,—over 24 Falls of ground with the Houses thereon at NEW SCONE, par. Scone.
P. R. 276. 82.

(2226) Oct. 21. 1854.
The Trustees of THOMAS DRUMMOND of Easter Newton, get Disp. and Convey., Aug. 12. 1854, by the Commissioners of H.M. Woods and Forests,—to the TEINDS of the north half of the Town and lands of EASTER NEWTON, par. Longforgan. P. R. 276. 84.

(2227) Oct. 23. 1854.
The Trustees of JOHN, late MARQUESS of BREADAL-BANE, get Assig., Sept. 23. 1854, by John, now Marquess of Breadalbane,—to Bond and Disp. for an annuity of £28. 12s. during the life of Robert Campbell of Dalserf, and the sum of £1177. 11s. 11d., by the said Robert Campbell, to John Campbell, W.S., Feb. 6. 1815,—secured over parts of the Lands and Barony of MUCKHART, viz., the lands of EASTER BALLELISK, and others. (Vide No. 2132).
G. R. 2701. 79.

(2228) Oct. 25. 1854.
FRANCES BRUCE DUNDAS, and MARGARET ELPHINSTONE DUNDAS, both residing at Blair Castle, and Jane Dundas residing in Edinburgh, relict of St. John Henry Gallwey, M.D., of Anbar, Co. Cork, Ireland, as heirs portioners to Lieut.-Col. Richard Leslie Dundas of Blair Castle, their brother, Seised,—in the lands of BLAIR; Pottisfollis otherwise Poffils, Salt Pan of Culross and ground whereon it is built with 5 Particates or Parcels of land belonging thereto; 1 Particate of land called Windmillcross; Town and lands of Langside; Meadow called Bruce Meadow; 1 Acre of land called Breadies Acre; lands of Bordie; lands of Birkenhead; Piece of ground with the Dwelling House thereon consisting of 32 Roods within the little Park called Tom Tod's Park on the north side of the High Road from Culross to Alloa; Dwelling House in Blairburn; and part of the Forest lands of Culross, viz., Birkenshaw ground containing 5½ Acres, and Teinds, par. Culross;—on Decr. Sp. Serv., Oct. 4. 1854. G. R. 2701. 134.

(2229) Oct. 25. 1854.
HALDANE WYLIE, Shipowner, Kincardine, grants Disch., Oct. 21. 1854,—of 2 Bonds and Disp. for £150, and £50, by Thomas Scotland, Shipping Agent, Glasgow, with consent of James Scotland, Commission Agent there, and Agnes Drysdale, his spouse, Apr. 6. 1852, and Apr. 22. 1853,—declaring 8 Falls of ground and Houses thereon, on the north side of John Street, KINCARDINE, par. Tulliallan,—disburdened thereof,—and restricting the security for a balance of £100, to other subjects. (Vide No. 697, and 1304). P. R. 276. 86.

(2230) Oct. 25. 1854.
JOHN BUCHANAN, Shipmaster, Kincardine, and Catherine Rae, his spouse, and longest liver of them, Seised,—in 8 Falls of ground and Houses thereon, on the north side of John Street, KINCARDINE, (under reservation), par. Tulliallan;—on Disp. by Thomas Scotland, Shipping Agent, Glasgow, with consent of Agnes Drysdale, and James Scotland, Commission Agent, Glasgow, her husband, Oct. 10. 17. 1854. P. R. 276. 87.

Figure 10-8
Abridgements of Sasines for the county of Perth.

burghsasines.html> to find the appropriate FHL microfilm numbers. To find other sasine records, check the Repertory of Burgh Records at the National Archives of Scotland; it is available on FHL microfiche 6029991. Note, however, that not all have been centrally deposited. For example, the Glasgow burgh registers have been at the Strathclyde Regional Archives, the Aberdeen registers at the Aberdeen City Archives, and the Dundee registers at the Dundee District Archives. There are also burgh registers of Services of Heirs. Some are on microfilm at the Family History Library. To find Services of Heirs in burgh records deposited at the National Archives of Scotland, check the repertory of burgh records mentioned above.

Your ancestor lived in a regality or stewartry. Regalities and stewartries were areas where a lord had judicial powers. They were exempt from the jurisdiction of the sheriff's court, the Courts of Justiciary, and the Courts of Session. They had the power to register deeds and services of heirs. Regalities and stewartries were abolished in 1747. If the records have been deposited at the National Archives of Scotland, they are listed in the Local Court Repertory RH 11. If the court records you are seeking are not at the NAS, they may be in the National Library of Scotland, a county record office, or among personal papers.

The particular registers of sasines are sometimes incomplete. For most counties the registers from 1617 to the present are complete. However, some registers have gaps, especially in the border counties. Read the introductions to the indexes to see if there are any gaps and if another source has been used to complete the index.

AMERICANS IN SCOTTISH PROBATE AND LAND RECORDS

You may notice that a lot of Americans are mentioned in the indexes, and even more are mentioned in the actual Services of Heirs. American heirs have been extracted and indexed from Services of Heirs in David Dobson's *Scottish-American Heirs, 1683–1883* (Genealogical Publishing Co., 1990). Many Americans had their estates recorded in the Commissariat Court of Edinburgh. The American references in testaments and inventories have been extracted and made available by David Dobson in *Scottish-American Wills, 1650–1900* (Genealogical Publishing Co., 1991).

REGISTERS OF DEEDS

Deed registers are where most Americans expect to find land records, but as we have shown, your ancestor's land records have been recorded in the registers of sasines. So what is recorded in the registers of deeds? **A deed can be any document that someone wants recorded for preservation.** Many deeds are contracts. These include marriage contracts and apprenticeships. Testamentary settlements are also very common. The registers of deeds may also contain the dispositions that we read about in the sasine records. Settlements and dispositions were used to get around the rule that heritable property could not be bequeathed until 1868. Family letters can even be recorded in the registers of deeds. This definition of *deed* has confused many genealogists who have found marriage contracts and other documents in the deed registers of Colonial America. Deeds were not just records of land transac-

\di'fin\ *vb*

Definitions

tions! Because they can contain rich genealogical information, the registers of deeds are valuable resources for finding details about the lives of your ancestors.

Most courts of law had a register of deeds, and before 1809 any court in Scotland could register deeds. After that time, only sheriff's courts, burgh courts, and the Court of Session could do so. The Court of Session recorded deeds in the Books of Council and Sessions, sometimes known as simply The Register of Deeds. The actual registers of this court are not available through the Family History Library, but it does have indexes and minute books. From 1542 to 1659, there are five series of registers, each named for the office that compiled the record: Scott, Gibson, Hay, Dounie, and Brown. When the dates overlap, you must check each register. For 1596 through 1660 there are no indexes, so you must use the minute books. Minute books are arranged chronologically by the date the deed was registered, and they are on FHL film numbers 231791–231798.

From 1661 to 1770, there are three concurrent series, again named for the offices which compiled the registers: Dalrymple, Duries, and Mackenzie. A deed could be recorded in any of them, so you must search them all. The minute books are on FHL film numbers 231799–231806. Sometimes the minute books are almost useless, especially when you are looking for a common name—some of the minute books list only the surnames. However, printed indexes are available from 1661 to 1696. They combine all three series in one index. Unlike the minute books, these indexes are wonderful. You can easily identify your ancestor in them because they give your ancestor's full name and designation. The indexes are on FHL films 896584–896586 and 896588–896606. Search the Family History Library Catalog by film/fiche number and enter film number 896584 to see the complete listing of films and the years covered by each.

For 1770–1851 manuscript indexes are on microfilm (FHL films 231807–231817).

The deeds themselves are available only at the National Archives of Scotland. To order a deed from the National Archives of Scotland, use the indexes or minute books, then consult the Repertory to the Register of Deeds on FHL film 231790 to find the call number of the record you want.

Remember, however, that other courts recorded deeds. Most deeds were recorded in the sheriff courts, but royal burghs, commissary courts, and, up to 1747, the courts of regality also registered deeds.

For More Info

WHERE CAN I FIND MORE INFORMATION?

For more examples of the records in this chapter, see the discussions *In Search of Scottish Ancestry*, chapters six, "Testaments"; seven, "The Sasine Register"; eight, "Service of Heirs"; and nine, "Registers of Deeds." The other sources listed below can help you understand the legal process and give assistance with unfamiliar words, expressions, and dates. The books listed that were published before 1940 are available on microform from the Family History Library.

Brown, James Cowie. *Index to An Introductory Survey of the Sources and Literature of Scots Law*. Edinburgh, Scotland: Neill & Co., Ltd., 1939.

Burness, Lawrence R. *A Scottish Historian's Glossary*. Scottish Association of Family History Societies, 1997.

Cheney, C.R., ed. (Revision by Michael Jones). *A Handbook of Dates*. New ed. Royal Historical Society Guides and Handbooks 4. Cambridge, England: Cambridge University Press, 2000.

Craigie, John. *Digest of the Scottish Law of Conveyancing: Moveable Rights*. Edinburgh, Scotland: Bell and Bradfute, 1888.

———. *Scottish Law of Conveyancing*. Edinburgh, Scotland: Bell and Bradfute, 1899.

Craigie, Sir William A. *A Dictionary of the Older Scottish Tongue: From the Twelfth Century to the End of the Seventeenth*. Chicago, Ill.: University of Chicago Press, 1937.

Gibb, Andrew Dewar. *Students' Glossary of Scottish Legal Terms*. Edinburgh, Scotland: W. Green & Sons, 1946.

Hamilton-Edwards, Gerald. *In Search of Scottish Ancestry*. 2d ed. Chichester, England: Phillimore & Co., Ltd., 1983.

An Introduction to Scottish Legal History. Vol. 20. The Stair Society, Edinburgh, Scotland: Robert Cunningham & Sons, Ltd., for The Stair Society, 1958.

An Introductory Survey of the Sources and Literature of Scots Law. Vol. 1. The Stair Society, Edinburgh, Scotland: Robert Maclehose & Co., Ltd., for The Stair Society, 1936.

The Legal System of Scotland. 2d ed. Edinburgh, Scotland: Her Majesty's Stationery Office, 1977.

Scottish Record Office. *Guide to the National Archives of Scotland*. Edinburgh, Scotland: The Stationery Office, Ltd., 1996.

AFTER SEARCHING PROBATE AND LAND RECORDS, WHAT SHOULD I DO NEXT?

You have no doubt found the names of new family members. Return to the other records discussed in this book to find more about them. Then consult the following sources to find even more Scottish records:

Cox, Michael, ed. *Exploring Scottish History*. 2d ed. Edinburgh, Scotland: Scottish Library Association, 1999.

Moody, David. *Scottish Local History: An Introductory Guide*. London: Batsford, 1986.

Sinclair, Cecil. *Tracing Your Scottish Ancestors: A Guide to Ancestry Research in the Scottish Record Office*. Edinburgh, Scotland. Her Majesty's Stationery Office, 1990.

———*Tracing Scottish Local History: A Guide to Local History Research in the Scottish Record Office*. Edinburgh, Scotland. Her Majesty's Stationery Office, 1994.

When you find interesting records in any of these books, check the Family History Library Catalog to see if the records have been microfilmed. If they have not been microfilmed, you can hire a researcher in Scotland, ask the depository to copy the relevant records for you, or go to Scotland to look at them yourself. You do want an excuse to do some research in Scotland, don't you?

ELEVEN

What's Next?

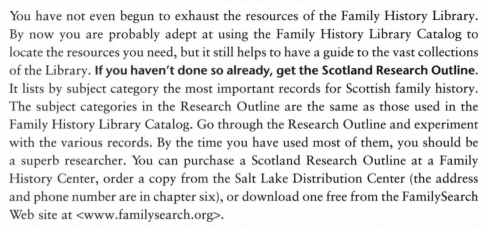

T
he stories of our families are never finished. There are always more mysteries to solve and more clues to follow. The story of the family in this book
isn't finished either. We have intentionally left some cliff-hangers because
the unanswered questions about our families are the ones that fascinate us. For
example, did Robert Brough and Margaret Sutherland ever marry? What happened
to them? Who were Robert's parents? Were the Isabella Broughs who died in 1855
and 1915 related? These mysteries are often what motivates other family members
to get involved. Your family history is the same. There are questions that you still
haven't answered. You have now successfully gathered lots of information about
your ancestors, and you're ready to find out what else exists. Civil registration,
census, church, probate, and land records are the basic resources for Scottish family
history, but there is more! Sources for Scottish family history are seemingly endless.

THE FAMILY HISTORY LIBRARY HAS MORE

You have not even begun to exhaust the resources of the Family History Library.
By now you are probably adept at using the Family History Library Catalog to
locate the resources you need, but it still helps to have a guide to the vast collections
of the Library. **If you haven't done so already, get the Scotland Research Outline.**
It lists by subject category the most important records for Scottish family history.
The subject categories in the Research Outline are the same as those used in the
Family History Library Catalog. Go through the Research Outline and experiment
with the various records. By the time you have used most of them, you should be
a superb researcher. You can purchase a Scotland Research Outline at a Family
History Center, order a copy from the Salt Lake Distribution Center (the address
and phone number are in chapter six), or download one free from the FamilySearch
Web site at <www.familysearch.org>.

The Scotland Research Outline describes so many resources that you may wish
to visit the Family History Library in Salt Lake City to immerse yourself in them.

Important

The majority of the records described in the Research Outline are instantly accessible in the Family History Library. Most genealogists agree that a week in the Family History Library is equivalent to a year or more of research anywhere else. Many genealogical societies conduct annual research tours to Salt Lake City, and you may be more comfortable going with a group the first time. However, even on your first trip, you will quickly learn to get around the library all by yourself. Consultants are always available to assist you. The Family History Library is located at 35 North West Temple Street, Salt Lake City, Utah 84150.

Also keep in mind that the Scottish collection at the Family History Library is constantly growing. The library is currently working on accumulating copies of poor law records, workhouse registers, and kirk session minutes. All these records help us trace our more humble ancestors. So check the catalog on a regular basis to identify recently acquired materials that might assist you.

THE NATIONAL ARCHIVES OF SCOTLAND

Even though the Family History Library has a huge collection, many more records can help you trace your family. The largest repository of original Scottish documents is the National Archives of Scotland located in Edinburgh, Scotland, and formerly known as the Scottish Record Office. To find out about the genealogically useful records held there, read Cecil Sinclair's *Tracing Scottish Family History: A Guide to Family History Research in the Scottish Record Office*. A similar book with many additional resources is Sinclair's *Tracing Scottish Local History: A Guide to Local History Research in the Scottish Record Office*. The most comprehensive guide to the records at the National Archives of Scotland is *Guide to the National Archives of Scotland* by the Scottish Record Office. This book took over twenty years to compile, and it contains descriptions of genealogically valuable records as well as many not normally used by genealogists. Visit the NAS Web site at <www.nas.gov.uk>.

THE PUBLIC RECORD OFFICE

The Public Record Office (PRO) is located in Kew, Surrey, England. It holds many British records that may contain references to your Scottish families. Some of its records are also available on microfilm from the Family History Library. Do not ignore British records located in England! To find out about these records, read Amanda Bevan's *Tracing Your Ancestors in the Public Record Office*. Visit the PRO Web site at <www.pro.gov.uk>. The Public Record Office helps researchers with more than a hundred information leaflets on various subjects, which can be found at <www.pro/gov.uk/leaflets/riindex.asp>. The Research Information Leaflets discuss the many records at the PRO including British military records, apprenticeship books, and more.

When *Tracing Your Ancestors in the Public Record Office* or a Research Information Leaflet refers you to a specific record class, you can find the exact reference you need in the catalog of the Public Record Office. The catalog is online at <www.pro.gov.uk/finding/catalogue/>.

Notes

Before you have a chance to ignore our suggestion to check records in England, check out this example of only one record we found there that helped us find more information about the family in this book.

We decided to look up Alexander Sutherland's army pension papers. He was the father of Margaret Sutherland and the grandfather of Isabella Brough. British military records are held in the Public Record Office in England. Some of them are also available on microfilm through the Family History Library. They are not, however, in Scotland. Alexander Sutherland's military records were gold mines. One of the more interesting parts was a physical description of him [height 5′5″ (1.65m), fair hair, grey eyes, fresh complexion, by trade a labourer]. Even more fascinating were the names of places where he had served and the length of time he was there. For example, Alexander Sutherland had been in Madeira Bay and several places in England, France, Ireland, and Scotland. He served one year and 304 days in India. Perhaps the best part was the heading of one of the documents: "Serjeant Alexander Sutherland in Capt. Maxwell's Co in the 2d Batt of the Regiment aforesaid, born in the Parish of Croy in or near the Town of Inverness in the County of Inverness, was enlisted at the age of twenty-two Years and hath served in the said Regiment for the space of Twenty Two Years and Two hundred twenty Days, as well as in other Corps, after the age of Eighteen, according to the following Statement, but in consequence of wounds is rendered unfit for further Service and is hereby discharged; having first received all just Demands of Pay, Clothing, &c. from his entry into the said Regiment to the Date of this Discharge, as appears by the Receipt on the back hereof." He was in the 42nd (Royal Highland) Regiment of Foot from 9 February 1793 to 24 September 1814.

Many other records that will help you trace your Scottish ancestors are in England. Don't forget to look for them.

Library/Archive Source

OTHER ARCHIVES AND LIBRARIES

Original documents for Scottish counties are often found in district archives, other archives, or in libraries. A list of all Scottish counties with links to information about each is available on the GENUKI Web site. (See chapter four for more information about this Web site.) Click on the county of interest to find information and addresses of the important record offices for the county.

Don't forget repositories in England. For example, the largest collection of nineteenth-century Scottish newspapers is not in Scotland, but in the British Library Newspaper Library at Colindale, London.

Sometimes you can access the catalog of a library or archive without traveling there. Some of them are online, and many of them have been published by Chadwyck-Healey in a microfiche series called the *National Inventory of Documentary Sources in the United Kingdom* (NIDS). NIDS may be available at large public or university libraries. The Family History Library also has it, so you can order from a Family History Center the microfiche that pertains to your area of interest. A listing of repositories included in NIDS with Family History Library Catalog computer numbers is on the Internet at <www.rootsweb.com/~bifhsusa/nids/nids.html>.

FAMILY HISTORY SOCIETIES

When you know where your Scottish ancestors lived, you should join the family history societies in the area. We talked about this in chapter two, but it is even more vital now that you want to go beyond the basics into more advanced research. You need to know who is doing what, as well as what records and indexes are available in your ancestor's locality. The local family history society is the best way to stay on top of the advances in local research. See the GENUKI Web site to find the names of family history societies for the area where your ancestor lived.

Most genealogical societies in Great Britain are called family history societies, and most in America are called genealogical societies. Don't forget to consider joining a society in the area where you live. It can also be helpful to join a society in North America that specializes in helping its members find their British ancestry. The biggest is the British Isles Family History Society-U.S.A. This society publishes a journal and newsletters; sells books to members at discounts; conducts research tours to England, Ireland, Scotland, and Wales; holds annual seminars with internationally renowned speakers; and more. Find out more about the society from its Web site at <www.rootsweb.com/~bifhsusa> or by writing to the society (British Isles Family History Society-U.S.A., 2531 Sawtelle Boulevard, PMB 134, Los Angeles, California 90064-3124).

You might also join a regional society such as the British Interest Group of Wisconsin and Illinois (BIGWILL, P.O. Box 192, Richmond, Illinois 60071), the British Isles Family History Society of Greater Ottawa (BIFHSGO, P.O. Box 38026, Ottawa, Ontario K2C 3Y7), or the British Isles Genealogical Research Association (BIGRA, P.O. Box 19775, San Diego, California 92159-0775). These and other societies hold monthly meetings, conduct annual conferences, and offer many other services that can help you further your research. See if your local genealogical society has a Scottish or British Special Interest Group, and if not, maybe you can start one. You can find online lists of most British, Scottish, and general genealogical societies at Cyndi's List (see chapter four for more information). Your local librarian can help you find genealogical societies in your area. The most important aspect about joining a genealogical society is that you regularly get together with others who share your passion for family history.

Consider joining the International Society for British Genealogy and Family History. The society publishes a quarterly newsletter that can keep you up-to-date on the latest developments in Scottish research and alert you to recent acquisitions in the Family History Library. Contact the International Society for British Genealogy and Family History by mail at P.O. Box 3115, Salt Lake City, Utah 84110-3115.

Notes

GOOD REFERENCE BOOKS

Several books can help you find more Scottish records. One of our favorites is Gerald Hamilton-Edwards's *In Search of Scottish Ancestry*. This book is full of information and examples of a wide variety of records, and it's an easy and entertaining read. A more comprehensive book is David Moody's *Scottish Local History: An Introductory Guide*. Moody has another one called *Scottish Family History*,

Printed Source

but the one on local history contains many more records. It is not necessarily an easy read, but it discusses records that are not mentioned elsewhere. A third one we like is Kathleen B. Cory's *Tracing Your Scottish Ancestry*. Cory researches on a regular basis in Edinburgh and knows the records well. The book has a nice case study. Another book, written for North Americans, that may give you ideas on other avenues to explore is Sherry Irvine's *Your Scottish Ancestry: A Guide for North Americans*. When these recommended books do not tell you whether the records are held by the Family History Library and are, therefore, available to you outside of Scotland, check the Family History Library Catalog for any record that interests you. For a list of more books, see our compiled bibliography for this book with updates at <www.rootsweb.com/~bifhsusa/sct-biblio.html>.

For More Info

WHERE DO I GET MORE INFORMATION?

Cory, Kathleen B. *Tracing Your Scottish Ancestry*. Baltimore, Md.: Genealogical Publishing Co., Inc., 1993.

Hamilton-Edwards, Gerald. *In Search of Scottish Ancestry*. 2d ed. Chichester, England: Phillimore & Co., Ltd., 1983.

Hatcher, Patricia Law. *Producing a Quality Family History*. Salt Lake City, Utah: Ancestry, Inc., 1996.

Irvine, Sherry. *Your Scottish Ancestry: A Guide for North Americans*. Salt Lake City, Utah: Ancestry, Inc., 1997.

Scottish Record Office. *Guide to the National Archives of Scotland*. Edinburgh, Scotland: The Stationery Office, Ltd., 1996.

Sinclair, Cecil. *Tracing Your Scottish Ancestors: A Guide to Ancestry Research in the Scottish Record Office*. Rev. ed. Edinburgh, Scotland: The Stationery Office, Ltd., 1997.

WHERE DO I GO FROM HERE?
A Trip to Scotland

The information you gather in your many hours of research leads to a wonderful benefit for you. Having found the town or village of your ancestors, you are ready to walk in your ancestors' footsteps. You accomplished a marvelous feat in finding your ancestral homeland, and you richly deserve a treat. The fourth step of the research process is a trip to Scotland.

Scotland is a wonderful place to visit. Although the Scots speak English, you may have a difficult time understanding it in some areas. Accents may be local and indicative of the way your ancestors spoke. In addition, the customs sometimes vary greatly. Many of these are the customs your ancestors followed centuries ago. For example, consider attending a Church of Scotland service. You may sit in the same seat that your ancestor once did. Include a visit to the cemetery and spend a few quiet moments there.

For many, taking a tour is the way to go on the first visit. These are not designed for you to spend time in the particular locations you need, but they're good for a general introduction to Scotland. For your best experience, though, get off the tour bus that shows you the lovely, historic places of Glasgow. Walk the streets in the old, crowded area of Glasgow where your ancestor once lived. Some of the same streets and perhaps even your ancestor's original house or place of business may still be there. Walk across the bridge over the river Clyde. You will feel as if you've stepped back in time. Experience Glasgow on foot!

Your ancestor, however, probably lived somewhere else earlier. If, for example, you take a train to see his former home in Sanquhar, you'll be amazed at the beauty of the countryside and all the trees on the way. You may wonder, "How could he have left here to move to Glasgow?" In fact, during your entire trip, you may wonder how your emigrant ancestor could have left Scotland at all. Remember, though, that our ancestors rarely left Scotland by choice; they emigrated because of economic or other necessity.

Even without a tour, Scotland is a country that's easy for most Americans to access. Some wonderful systems are in place that can make your trip delightful. One is Book a Bed Ahead (BBA). Simply speaking, you book your first two nights and your last two nights from your home. Once in Scotland, you can avail yourself of the BBA and book your rooms one day in advance for wherever you wish to go. This allows you great flexibility. In terms of getting around, you have the option of renting a car or using public transportation. With a rental car you have lots of flexibility to go anywhere at any time. However, remember that driving on the "wrong" side of the road can make you (and your passenger!) nervous. Think about how comfortable you will be with narrow lanes and different traffic laws. Consider traveling by train; you will enjoy it and meet lots of locals in the process. Purchase a BritRail Pass before you leave for Scotland. They must be purchased outside of Scotland. A BritRail Pass allows you unlimited train access not only to Scotland, but to England and Wales as well. Scotland also has a very good bus system. Even if you take a train, you may often take a bus into the village of your ancestors. If no bus goes there, consider asking a local taxi driver how much it would cost to have him take you there, wait for you, and bring you back. Some of the drivers are accommodating and will show you the village and tell you much more about the area than you would learn in two or more days on your own. Be sure to tell the driver that you will pay for waiting time, and get a price before you go. Schedule a trip to your ancestors' hometowns at the beginning of your vacation, not at the end. That way if you find a wealth of information in the village, you can plan an extra day or two there and skip some of the other sightseeing. With Book a Bed Ahead and your car or BritRail Pass, you make your own arrangements to suit your fancy.

To make your trip more enjoyable, take very little luggage with you, and bring comfortable walking shoes. The Scottish countryside can be breathtaking; be prepared to walk around and enjoy it.

Write Your Family History

You may have been doing a lot of this research for the pure joy of it, but why keep it to yourself? Submit your genealogy to the Pedigree Resource File or other equivalent and to various sites on the Internet. Create a Web site about your family.

Important

Write your family history. Don't just publish a list of names and dates; nobody will read that. Tell how your ancestors lived in Scotland. Illustrate with documents that you have found about your family. Include pictures from your trip to Scotland that show some of the original buildings and the beautiful scenery. Talk about how your ancestors worked, played, loved, and suffered. Relate the experiences of your immigrant ancestor. You don't have to know the answers to all your family questions. In fact, it's best if you leave some unanswered questions for others to pursue. Solving the puzzle is part of the fun. As the British family historian Michael Gandy says, "You don't want to give your children a crossword puzzle book with all the answers filled in!" For advice on how to write a good family history, read Patricia Law Hatcher's *Producing a Quality Family History*.

Tracing your Scottish ancestry can be exciting, challenging, and fun. Share this joy with your family, and get together with others who enjoy your passion. But most of all, be sure to preserve the stories of your ancestors so that their lives, and your heritage, will not be forgotten. You, your family members, and researchers for many generations to come will be glad you did.

Descendants of Peter MacGregor

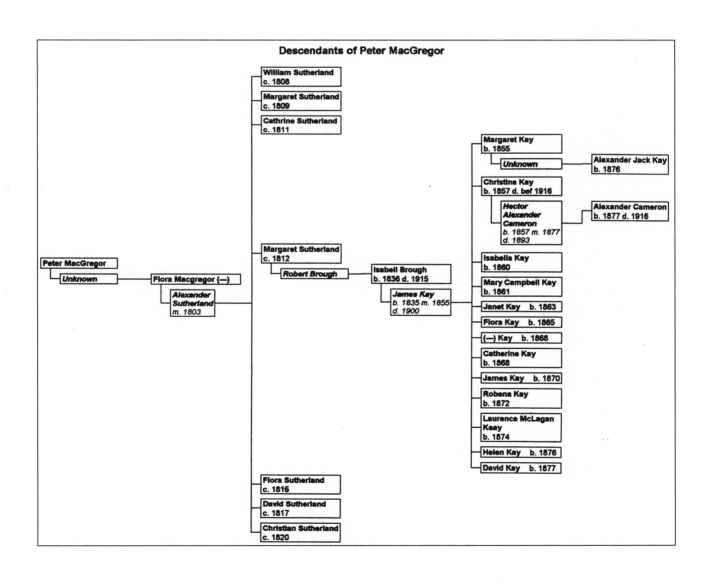

Descendants of Peter MacGregor

Peter MacGregor
— Unknown

Flora Macgregor (—)
— Alexander Sutherland
m. 1803

- William Sutherland
  c. 1808
- Margaret Sutherland
  c. 1809
- Cathrine Sutherland
  c. 1811
- Margaret Sutherland
  c. 1812
  — Robert Brough
  - Isabell Brough
    b. 1836 d. 1915
    — James Kay
    b. 1835 m. 1855
    d. 1900
    - Margaret Kay
      b. 1855
      — Unknown
      - Alexander Jack Kay
        b. 1876
    - Christina Kay
      b. 1857 d. bef 1916
      — Hector Alexander Cameron
      b. 1857 m. 1877
      d. 1893
      - Alexander Cameron
        b. 1877 d. 1916
    - Isabella Kay
      b. 1860
    - Mary Campbell Kay
      b. 1861
    - Janet Kay   b. 1863
    - Flora Kay   b. 1865
    - (—) Kay   b. 1868
    - Catherine Kay
      b. 1868
    - James Kay   b. 1870
    - Robena Kay
      b. 1872
    - Laurence McLagan Keay
      b. 1874
    - Helen Kay   b. 1876
    - David Kay   b. 1877
- Flora Sutherland
  c. 1815
- David Sutherland
  c. 1817
- Christian Sutherland
  c. 1820

Index

*Get all the tools you need to fill
in the family tree—more problem-solving,
timesaving titles from Betterway Books.*

The Weekend Genealogist—Maximize your family research efficiency! With this guide, you can focus your efforts on searching for family documents while still gaining the best results. Organization and research techniques are presented in a clear, easy-to-follow format perfect for advanced researchers and beginners. You'll learn how to work more efficiently using family history facilities, the Internet—even the postal service!
ISBN 1-55870-546-5, paperback, 144 pages, #70496-K

The Genealogist's Computer Companion—Master the basics of online research, and turn your computer into an efficient, versatile research tool. Respected genealogist Rhonda R. McClure shows you how, providing guidelines and advice that enable you to find new information, verify existing research, and save valuable time. She also provides an invaluable glossary of genealogical and technical terms.
ISBN 1-55870-591-0, paperback, 208 pages, #70529-K

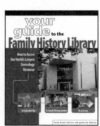

Your Guide to the Family History Library—The Family History Library in Salt Lake City is the largest collection of genealogy and family history materials in the world. No other repository compares for both quantity and quality of research materials. Written for beginning and intermediate genealogists, *Your Guide to the Family History Library* will help you use the library's resources effectively, both on site and online.
ISBN 1-55870-578-3, paperback, 272 pages, #70513-K

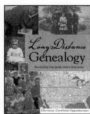

Long-Distance Genealogy—Gathering information from sources that can't be visited is a challenge for all genealogists. This book will teach you the basics of long-distance research. You'll learn what types of records and publications can be accessed from a distance, problems associated with the process, how to network, how to use computer resources, and special "last resort" options.
ISBN 1-55870-535-X, paperback, 272 pages, #70495-K

Your Guide to the Federal Census—This one-of-a-kind book examines the "nuts and bolts" of census records. You'll find out where to view the census and how to use it to find ancestors quickly and easily. Easy-to-follow instructions and case studies detail dozens of scenarios for tracing family histories through census records. You'll also find invaluable appendices, a glossary of census terms, and extraction forms.
ISBN 1-55870-588-0, paperback, 288 pages, #70525-K

These books and other fine Betterway titles are available from your local bookstore or online supplier, or by calling (800) 448-0915.